On the Wrong Line

Christian Wolmar is a writer and broadcaster special-
ising in transport and other social policy issues. He has
written regularly for various newspapers including the
Independent, The Observer and the *Evening Standard,* and
magazines such as the *New Statesman, Public Finance*
and *Rail.* He also appears frequently on television and
radio as a commentator on rail and other transport
matters, and speaks at conferences and after-dinner
events.

His recent books include *Down the Tube* (also
published by Aurum) and *The Subterranean Railway,* a
history of the London Underground published by
Atlantic in 2004. He can be contacted through his
website at www.christianwolmar.co.uk. He has three
children and lives in North London. Cycling is his main
form of transport and he plays cricket for the Beamers.

On the Wrong Line

HOW IDEOLOGY AND INCOMPETENCE
WRECKED BRITAIN'S RAILWAYS

CHRISTIAN WOLMAR

First published 2005 by
Aurum Press Limited, 25 Bedford Avenue, London WC1B 3AT
www.aurumpress.co.uk

This is a revised and updated edition of *Broken Rails*
by Christian Wolmar, first published by Aurum Press in 2001.

A catalogue record for this book is available from the British Library.

ISBN 1 85410 998 7

1 3 5 7 9 10 8 6 4 2
2005 2007 2009 2008 2006

Text design by Geoff Green Book Design

Typeset by SX Composing DTP, Rayleigh, Essex

Printed and bound in Great Britain by
MPG Books Ltd, Bodmin, Cornwall

Contents

This book is dedicated to my friend Roger Ford, who knows far more about the railways than I ever will and who keeps me sane through our regular conversations about the madnesses of the privatised railway.

Introduction

The first half of this book is for the most part an updated version of *Broken Rails*, which was initially published in late 2001 and then revised and republished in early 2002 in the immediate aftermath of Railtrack's demise. The rest of the book, including virtually everything from Chapter 9 onwards, is new, including the conclusion. I have also rewritten Chapter 1, with help and advice from the railway historian Adrian Vaughan. The other material from *Broken Rails* has been thoroughly revised, edited and updated. Some passages which may sound slightly dated in the light of subsequent events have been retained in their original form; *Broken Rails* was, in part, an almost contemporaneous account of the privatisation of the railways and I wanted to ensure some of that story remained available as it is an important piece of history. It is just too easy to write everything with the benefit of hindsight. The early days of Railtrack, for example, may not seem relevant now that we find ourselves in a different world in which the railway's infrastructure is run by what is effectively a public-sector company, but the fact remains that Railtrack's actions in its first few years had a profound and long-term effect on the history of the railway, as well as providing the world with an object lesson in how not to privatise an industry.

The accounts of the accidents remain largely in their original form, apart from a few corrections and some additional material, especially on Hatfield. Of course, it has been necessary to provide a new chapter on the Potters Bar accident, which occurred after the publication of the second edition of *Broken Rails*. The account of Hatfield in the early editions has proved to be very accurate, and re-reading it for this new book highlighted the awful sequence of events and demonstrated the way in which the accident, which led to the deaths of four men, was so clearly the result of callous political decisions. In fact, the story actually appears more shocking now in the cold light of hindsight than when I wrote about it so soon after the disaster. There really is blood on the hands of those who created the privatisation fiasco and I have left in the detail of the accident as a painful reminder of this terrible calamity. Fortunately, as the book outlines, the whole system of maintenance on the railway has been changed as a result of that disaster.

There have also been two other major accidents in the period since privatisation but both Great Heck in February 2001 and Ufton Nervet in November 2004 were caused by cars on the track and are therefore of little relevance to the issues discussed in this book.

Chapters 9, 10 and 11 cover events that occurred after January 2002, when the second edition of *Broken Rails* went to press, such as the Potters Bar accident, the creation of Network Rail, the taking back in house of the maintenance contracts and the abolition of the Strategic Rail Authority following the publication of the White Paper of July 2004 on the future of the railways. In the following four chapters, which are new, I have analysed in detail first, in Chapter 12, the safety issues arising out of privatisation and the four major accidents, and then, in Chapters 13, 14 and 15, the rise in costs that was the most unexpected result of a privatisation which, remember, was instigated by the Treasury with the aim of cutting the level of public support for the railway. And Chapter 16 is a summary of the whole crazy story, with an attempt to point to a long-term solution.

There were a few people canny enough to predict that the taxpayers would lose out heavily once the railways were privatised, and interestingly enough one of them was the late Nicholas Ridley, who was Secretary of State for Transport in the mid-1980s. According to John Welsby,[1] BR's chief executive at the time of privatisation, Ridley 'was worried stiff that if you got this thing out into the private sector, then it might actually become a lot more difficult to control the public finance elements of it than it was if it was under an organisation that you controlled where you could sack [the chairman of the British Railways board]'. How correct that assumption has turned out to be. Indeed, whereas at the time *Broken Rails* was first published it was the continuing series of major accidents that seemed to pose the greatest threat to the future of the railways, there is now no doubt that the soaring cost of running the system is the issue that most concerns senior managers in the industry and anyone else with an interest in its future.

The story of rail privatisation is a rapidly unfolding story of unexpected events and almost continuous change. As I write, the Railways Act 2005 has just reached the statute book and the Labour government has been re-elected. It is already clear that the government's hope that the new Act will provide a framework for long-term stability is a pipedream, confirming the view of one of the great railwaymen of the post-war period, Gerald Fiennes, who wrote in 1973, 'The only certainty, past and present, is that each Railway or Transport Act ensures the next.' Further editions of this book may therefore be expected.

On the Wrong Line is aimed at the general reader with an interest in the railways, but occasionally it has been necessary to venture into technical matters when dealing with the actual operations of the railway or the intricacies of privatisation. However, I have attempted to keep such detail to a minimum so as not to interfere with the narrative.

Most of the material I have written on the railways and other matters is to be found on my website, www.christianwolmar.co.uk, through which I can be contacted.

Thanks are due to countless people in the industry, and to those who have recently left it, who must necessarily remain anonymous. I can, though, thank publicly the following who helped me either for the present book or its predecessor and to whom I am deeply grateful. In many cases, their knowledge is far greater than mine, but of course all the errors are down to me: Jo Bird, Rupert Brennan-Brown, Barry Doe, Chris Garnett, Terry Gourvish, Chris Green, Stan Hall, Nigel Harris (and all the staff at *Rail*), Mike Horne, Christopher Irwin, Howard Johnston, Juliette Jowit, Peter Kain, Brendan Martin, M A Mc, Alan Nichols, Peter Rayner, Jon Shaw, Professor Roderick Smith, Tim Strangleman, Malcolm Tunley, John Ware, Keith Porteous Wood and any more whom I may have inadvertently omitted. And of course thanks are due to my agent Andrew Lownie and my editor at Aurum, Piers Burnett.

CHAPTER 1

Government and the railways:
a terrible dependency

The railways were the most important invention of the Industrial Revolution. They changed the whole economic and physical landscape of Britain and posed a succession of difficult questions for governments. That is why the relationship between government and the railways has always been fraught. Therefore, in order to understand the present predicament of the railways it is essential to take a brief look at their history and, in particular, at the complex interplay between the public interest and private capital over the course of their development.

Britain's railways were, of course, built by private enterprise and – with a few notable exceptions – on the cheap, which is the root cause of many of today's problems, such as the large number of unnecessary curves that reduce speeds and the inconvenient location of many stations. While the early railways were highly profitable, since they clearly met a need, the second wave struggled because many linked towns of insufficient size or were built to compete with existing lines. Consequently, they suffered perennially from under-investment. Nevertheless, the construction of the railways could, arguably, be considered the finest achievement of the Victorians, a success all the more remarkable because, while the development of the whole network took some seventy-five years, the core of today's system was already in place by the end of the first 'railway mania' in 1852. By then there were 6,600 miles of railway route open compared with just 100 in 1830.[1]

It was inevitable that even Victorian governments, with their *laissez-faire* ethos, should become involved in what rapidly became the country's largest industry and one which had all kinds of social, political and economic ramifications. The politicians were, however, usually at least one step behind, legislating too late in order to remedy past ills, rather than addressing the future, not least because the railways were as new and bewildering to Victorian legislators as the internet is to Western politicians today.

In the quarter century following the first run of the train hauled by George Stephenson's *Locomotion* along the Stockton & Darlington railway in 1825, life for Britain's people was transformed by the creation of a railway network stretching from Aberdeen to Plymouth and from Holyhead to Lowestoft. George Stephenson and his son Robert were to dominate the development of new lines and technical innovation for that period. Robert was one of the driving forces behind the opening of the Liverpool & Manchester Railway in 1830, which demonstrated the railway's potential for carrying passengers as well as cargo. The Liverpool & Manchester was effectively the first 'modern' railway, linking two major towns with a double track line throughout and, unlike its smaller predecessors, eschewing the use of horses for any traction. It was partly because of the power of people like the Stephensons, who wielded an influence in Victorian Britain comparable to that exercised in the contemporary US by Bill Gates, that the government began to perceive the need for economic regulation, safety legislation and technological innovation and standardisation.

The legislature, as opposed to the government, had, of course, been involved in the railway industry right from the outset because the builders of a new line needed the power to expropriate private land, a process which involved getting a private bill through Parliament. This was a haphazard business. Although many bills were rejected, there were no clear criteria on which to base decisions and the successful passage of a bill was dependent on the ability of a strong and partisan local MP to argue for a particular scheme. Most MPs knew nothing about the railways and those who did often had a vested interest, as a supporter either of the scheme under debate or of a rival one.

The development of the railway network can be seen as a battle between the *nouveaux riches*, principally northern entrepreneurs who sought to obtain the land they needed through the compulsory procedures granted to them in the railway bills, and the old propertied classes. The government of the day did not control this parliamentary process and there was no central planning of the rapidly growing rail system as happened, for example, in Belgium where the state determined the shape of the network. Because of the vagaries of the private bill system many patently uneconomic lines, often duplicating existing routes, were approved and built. Far from imposing any strategic oversight, the government was simply overtaken by events, in the form of the explosion in new railway construction; it played no part in the major decision-making and had little influence over the ways in which the first major companies were formed or managed. The government's failure to take an active role in the planning process (which, as we shall see, has much resonance with the events of the past few years) meant that the railways were dependent upon an inefficient and expensive mechanism for their development. As one writer put it, 'In the absence of centralised state planning, the country's railway capitalists had no choice but to engage in a prolonged parliamentary free-for-all for complete incorporation, commercial territory and the power to expropriate land.'[2] One consequence was that, in a kind of dress rehearsal for the situation that prevails in today's fragmented, privatised railway, lawyers enjoyed a bonanza – one estimate suggests that by 1862 the railway industry had spent £30m on parliamentary business, much of it going to lawyers. Robert Stephenson reported that the cost of building the Trent Valley Railway in the late 1840s was 'not much greater' than the legal fees.[3]

It is worth noting here, given that much of this book is devoted to the structure of the way that railways are operated, that right from the beginning it was realised that the best way of running a railway was as an integrated system. Early railways such as the Stockton & Darlington originally allowed all comers onto its tracks, effectively acting like a turnpike road by charging for access to its line. However, this proved to be unworkable, leading to much litigation between the railway and the carriers, and the practice soon died out in the 1830s as new railway companies realised it was an inefficient way of working. As Adrian Vaughan puts it, 'The railways were a "natural monopoly", and the "turnpike" or "open access" principle was, and remains, incompatible with standardization of operating practice, essential in a public utility.'[4]

After a few years of watching from the sidelines and doing little more than imposing a tax on rail travel through the Railway Passenger Duty, the government was first gently stirred from its slumbers in 1838 when the state-owned Post Office demanded a universally fair price for the carriage of its mail, for which it was being selectively overcharged on certain routes. The Railways (Conveyance of Mails) Act became one of the very first pieces of railway legislation. More significant for the future, however, was the Regulation of Railways Act 1840, which was followed by eight similarly named acts in the subsequent half-century, and created the embryonic railway inspectorate; but safety was not the main impetus behind the legislation, as the inspectorate's principal task, initially, was the assessment of the economic viability of schemes coming up before it. However, the safety role of the new body, the Railway Department of the Board of Trade, was important and gradually increased. It included the inspection and approval of new lines for passenger use and the investigation of accidents; it also provided a means of putting pressure on the railway companies to adopt technological improvements, particularly for safety reasons.

Apart from war, famine, disease and free trade, the railways were the most controversial issue on the parliamentary agenda of the middle years of the nineteenth century. Unsurprisingly, there was no consistent government attitude towards them, as the two main political groupings, Tory (Conservative) and Whig (Liberal), did not have coherent policies towards the new industry, but simply pursued the private agendas of their more influential MPs. There was, nevertheless, a fundamental division, with much resonance still today, between those seeking increased regulation of an industry that, at times, appeared out of control and all too ready to abuse its monopoly position, and the free marketeers who felt it best left alone. In truth, that was even less possible then than it is now.

The railways were such a fundamental part of Victorian Britain that it is almost impossible to exaggerate their importance. Their advent affected every facet of life. Agriculture prospered because of the better links between town and country which allowed farmers to get most of their products, from fruit and milk to chickens and cattle, to markets more quickly and cheaply; areas of the country which could not be reached easily before were suddenly opened up; labour became much more mobile; tourism became possible; and even the fish and chip shop owes its existence to the faster transit of fish inland.[5]

The growing importance of the railways ensured that the government was forced to react in 1844 when the infamous 'railway mania' began threatening the finances not only of existing railways but of many hapless investors in new railway schemes. With the main lines already largely mapped out, the railway mania saw an explosion of speculative and ill-conceived railway projects. Between 1844 and 1847, plans were laid before

Parliament that, cumulatively, would have created 20,000 miles of new railways, many in direct competition with one another. (In fact, the whole network peaked in the Edwardian age at around 23,000 miles.) Some of the schemes had no hope of delivering a dividend to innocent investors and others were just plain frauds, like some of those promoted by the 'Railway King', George Hudson, who exploited legal loopholes to gain control of a collection of companies owning some 1,000 miles of route. He then became an MP, apparently with the sole aim of defeating rival schemes, but it emerged that he had been fiddling the books, paying his investors £200,000 worth of dividends out of the capital of their own company, Eastern Counties, and he disappeared, leaving hundreds of bankrupted shareholders. Ironically, Hudson had also been a force for the good, almost single-handedly forcing through the creation of the railway clearing house, where fares gathered by companies on each other's behalf were exchanged, and amalgamating half a dozen companies to form the Midland, one of the most ambitious and forward-looking of the Victorian railways.

In 1844 William Gladstone, then the President of the Board of Trade, tried to introduce some order into the industry and drew up a powerful bill which would have imposed strict controls, including the compulsory purchase by the state of strategic lines. The bill was also prompted by fears that the railway companies would establish themselves as monopolies whose charges would have to be controlled. However, predictably, the free marketeers, including the large number of railway directors sitting in Parliament,[6] objected and the bill was weakened during its passage. However, Gladstone's Act[7] did give governments the power to buy lines built after its passage if they made excess profits, but this clause was never put into practice and was formally abandoned on the recommendations of a Royal Commission in 1867. The Act also required railways to permit the electric telegraph to be installed beside their lines and provided for troops and police to be carried at times of unrest. Overall, however, the legislation was, as one historian put it, 'in tune with the deregulatory spirit of the age'.[8]

Gladstone's Bill was not the first mention of nationalisation. In the late 1830s the Duke of Wellington, a member of Lord Melbourne's government, had publicly expressed his concern over 'monopoly and mismanagement' and suggested state ownership. As one historian put it, 'The issue of public ownership versus private enterprise for the railways was as old as the industry itself.'[9] Indeed, some European networks were developed by the state rather than private enterprise, and even some privately created systems, like the Swiss railways, were soon nationalised, while those which continued to develop privately had government involvement in their management. In many European countries there was an additional factor, in that railways, which for the first time allowed the rapid mobilisation and movement of armies, were considered a vital strategic asset and the military took a close interest in their development. But in free-enterprise Britain, government meddling, whatever the motive, was anathema while developers continued to believe that great fortunes could be made out of the railways. In the event, however, the lines built in the wake of the railway mania, with a few exceptions, turned out to be mildly profitable at best or, in the case of most rural services, uneconomic from the outset.

Gladstone's Act did also introduce a key measure, the Parliamentary Train*, which greatly widened the market for railway travel, which had hitherto been confined to the relatively affluent. Third-class travellers, who often endured appalling conditions, had to be offered at least one train a day, stopping at all stations and averaging no less than 12mph with fares not exceeding one (old) penny per mile. While some of the railway companies exploited the potential of providing such cheap services, others responded as private enterprise so often does to regulation – in a surly, minimalist way. They timed their Parliamentary Trains poorly in an effort to deter passengers rather than seeking to attract new customers to the railway but at least the act forced them to provide the service in covered wagons, which meant poor passengers were no longer at the mercy of the elements. Despite this, some continued to force their lower-paying customers to travel in conditions that would have been cruel to livestock. The Great Western, for example, did not offer their third-class passengers the opportunity of looking at the countryside since they were 'encased in a box without windows, only permitting such light to penetrate as could find its way through the top venetians'.[10]

One beneficial side effect of the plethora of new railway projects in the

---

* Strangely, a version of Parliamentary Trains remains today. Rail companies are obliged by legislation to run at least one train per week on all their lines. There are about a dozen examples of 'ghost-trains' being run once per week along a section of line just to prevent the lengthy closure procedures from kicking in.

1840s was the establishment in 1846 of a Royal Commission on the gauge, the width of separation of the two rails. In a decision which was to affect railways across the world, the Commission decided to support the 4ft 8½ ins already used by a majority of railways in England and this size was widely adopted in a majority of countries, even those like France which used the metric system of measurements.

The railway network created by this haphazard process of development was, inevitably, not as good as would have resulted from a more rational allocation of resources by the involvement of the state.[11] The consequences such as duplication of lines created by the emphasis on competition rather than cooperation dog the network to this day and, indeed, this same misguided emphasis was to undermine the Tories' 1990s privatisation. Writing in 1846, Thomas Macaulay, the poet and historian, lamented the failure of the government to exert its influence in the face of the dominant commercial interests of the day. Indeed, he argued, the whole development of the railways could be seen as the product of government's failure to put the interests of the public above those of the railway companies. Questions affecting the convenience, prosperity and security of the public had been subordinated to the narrow interests of the railway companies: 'That the whole country was interested in having a good system of internal communication seemed to be forgotten,' he said, and while the interests of speculators and land-owners had received careful attention, 'nobody appeared to be heard on behalf of the community'.[12] This was not entirely true. In 1854, the government did impose on the railways the obligation to be common carriers – effectively to accept the carriage, at a reasonable rate, of any goods offered to them.

The lack of a visionary response to the growth of the railways on the part of successive governments is well illustrated by their failure to encourage amalgamations and mergers. While some big regional railway companies were allowed to emerge, such as the Midland and the London and North Western, in other areas, such as East Anglia, the government failed to intervene when excessive competition was clearly driving businesses that were providing an essential service into penury.

Several companies did grow through acquisition: many promoters of rural lines, often independent landowners, were happy to allow main-line operators to handle day-to-day operations and indeed most allowed their lines to be absorbed completely to escape insolvency when traffic volumes failed to live up to expectations. However, far from encouraging major amalgamations, the government actively frowned upon them: partly because self-interested railway MPs were worried that a conglomerate might gain an unfair advantage over their own companies, but also through fear of the railways establishing themselves as monopolies. Thus, when two substantial companies, the London & North Western Railway and Lancashire & Yorkshire, proposed merging in 1871 because they had similar interests in the north-west, both houses of Parliament expressed strong opposition. The companies' plans went on ice for another fifty years and they did not merge until the great consolidation of 1922. Nevertheless, the rail companies were impressively large by the standards of the day. By 1874 the four largest companies owned 39 per cent of the track mileage and claimed 47 per cent of the gross receipts,[13] but their dominance did not grow after that because of the government's reluctance to allow further mergers. Nevertheless, the largest railway company, the London & North Western Railway, had a capital value of £117m by the end of the century, bigger than that of any other business in the world.[14]

To some extent the fears that the railways might establish themselves as monopolies were justified. With canal transport painfully slow, and road transport as yet undeveloped, the railways could determine the prices for the carriage of goods, particularly perishable items and small parcels, and the hope of establishing regional monopolies was undoubtedly a motive behind many of the projected amalgamations. As Michael Freeman recounts, 'The problem was compounded by the very limited influence that Parliament exercised over railway freight rates.'[15] The issue, as he puts it, 'developed into an epic struggle', especially over the railways' habit of quoting a preferential rate for particular places, districts or even individual clients which discriminated unfairly against others. This 'remained a constant irritant in the relationship between companies and their customers right up until 1914' when the state took over the running of the railways and established clear rates for carriage (which was to cause a host of other problems). It would be wrong, however, to portray the railways solely as monopoly exploiters. They often acted in a paternalistic way, trying to encourage trade, which was in their interest, by, for example, offering special rates to encourage new industries or giving discounts for full loads, thereby passing on savings to their customers.

*

While government steered clear of involvement in commercial issues as much as possible, the state increasingly concerned itself with the improvement of safety and the imposition of standards, but only after a succession of gruesome accidents had aroused so much public concern that ministers felt able to override the powerful 'railway interest' in Parliament. In the case of many of the accidents the toll was increased as a result of the use of wooden carriages, gas lighting and even such bad railway habits as locking passengers into their compartments. Illustrious lobbyists for rail safety, such as Charles Dickens, who was deeply affected by his lucky escape in an 1865 accident at Staplehurst in Kent, helped the rapid progress on accident rates. Stanley Hall, a former railway manager and the author of a number of books on rail disasters,[16] argues that major improvements rarely resulted from a single accident but rather from a series with a similar cause over a period of several years.

There was, however, one event that proved a crucial turning point. This was the Armagh disaster on 12 June 1889, one of the worst ever on the railways. A Sunday school excursion overloaded with almost 1,000 passengers stalled on a steep gradient and the train crew decided to split the train to allow the engine to take half the carriages up the hill and return for the others. Unfortunately, the brake system on the rear section of the train, which did not have continuous brakes, was not strong enough to prevent it sliding down the hill and smashing into another train on the way up, killing eighty people and injuring three times that number.

The public outcry which followed the Armagh disaster ensured that the government had to act quickly despite the protests of the less enlightened rail companies which had been reluctant to introduce expensive safety measures. Armagh brought to a head a series of issues over safety which had been brewing for many years, and the speed with which the legislation was introduced – it came into force on 30 August, just seventy-nine days after the disaster – showed what could be done by a government acting decisively with public support. Tragically, a similar measure, the Trade Union Bill, had been tabled in Parliament by Earl de la Warr in 1876 but had been rejected by the railway directors and other vested interests.

The momentous Regulation of Railways Act 1889 codified three key improvements, the cornerstones of Victorian safety legislation, known as lock, block and brake. 'Lock' involved connecting – interlocking, as it is called on the railway – the levers in a signal box in such a way that the signaller could not set the route for a train to proceed unless the points were set correctly. 'Block' meant the adoption of a signalling system in which lines are divided into a series of blocks or sections on the principle that no two trains are allowed to be in the same section at the same time. Prior to the adoption of this system, trains had been allowed to proceed a set time after the preceding one, which often led to accidents when a train stopped unexpectedly because of a breakdown or an obstacle. As early as 1869, the Board of Trade had asked the railway companies to notify it of the proportion of their lines using the block system, a request that was received with 'explosive indignation'[17] by the railway companies who had become increasingly unpopular as a result of their perceived disregard for safety.

The key improvement to the brake system (which addressed the direct cause of the Armagh disaster) was to introduce automatic continuous brakes throughout the train, which ensured that, if the train split through some mishap, the brake would automatically be applied on both halves. As a result of this legislation, the accident rate on the railways fell dramatically, soon after its introduction, and for the first time since the creation of the railways, there were two years, 1901 and 1908, when no rail passengers were killed in a train accident.

The great railway age, when the railways were at the height of their power, stretched from 1850 to the outbreak of the First World War. If anything, the importance of the railways in the latter part of the Victorian era was even greater than in the early days of the industry. The industry employed a staggering 648,000 people, a figure which did not include those who worked for manufacturers of railway equipment either for domestic use or for export. And there were a myriad other ways in which the railways influenced the development of modern society. As Andrew Dow points out, 'The extent to which, for example, railway practices prompted the growth of professions such as accountancy and mechanical engineering may not yet have been documented in full.'[18]

The beginning of the decline of the railways coincided with much greater government involvement as the state took over the running of the system in 1914 after the outbreak of the Great War, using powers under the Regulation of the Forces Act 1871. The war was to change the management of the industry for ever. The railways, which by now had reached their peak of 23,000 route miles, were expected to shoulder the over-whelming burden of transporting materials, munitions and people, and this could only happen with government control. The railways were sweated and overused, with very little compensating investment since resources were concentrated on the war effort; by the time the armistice came, the system had been run into the ground, with a major main-tenance backlog and administrative chaos. While it would be simplistic to argue that it was entirely the government's fault, the state that the network had been reduced to after the war was to cause insuperable problems for the industry in the ensuing decades.

When hostilities ended, the government, aware of the political benefits of running the railways, relinquished control only slowly. The official wartime controls were not lifted until 1921, by which time it was evident that the businesses – 120 individual railway companies lumbered with Victorian business values and equipment – stood no chance of recovering their formerly exalted position. A mass duplication of facilities – towns sometimes had two or three stations with competing services as a result of the lack of central control and the Victorians' fear of monopoly – was clearly nonsensical when none of them could deliver a good-quality service. And, for the first time, road transport was becoming a viable alternative with the motor bus, the initial predator before the mass availability of cars, beginning to become sufficiently reliable to pose a threat.

Company amalgamations – many of them discussed well before the war – were on the agenda again, but this time the government forced the railways' hand with the 1921 Railways Act, whose principal aim was to increase national efficiency by the elimination of wasteful rivalry. War had meant that there was less interest in promoting competition, the obsession which had so dominated the Victorians' policies in relation to the railways. Even nationalisation, supported by the Labour Party and the National Union of Railwaymen, was in the air in 1919 and publicly discussed by ministers, but ultimately it was rejected because of public opinion, which was concerned, as *The Economist* put it, about the risk of putting themselves at the mercy of 'bureaucratic bunglers'[19] and 'the fact that state owned railways overseas had frequently proved dis-appointing'.[20] It was decided, instead, to create the 'Big Four' large administrative groups on a geographical basis: the London & North Eastern Railway (LNER), London Midland & Scottish (LMS), Southern

(SR), and Great Western (GWR), the last broadly unchanged apart from the absorption of a large collection of small independent South Wales systems. The Act also gave the government power to fund major improvement schemes for the railways, a recognition not only of their strategic role but also of the impossibility of making such investment profitable without at least an initial subsidy.

Government regulation of freight charging policies was also introduced, designed to deliver the same overall rate of return as companies would have expected in 1913, a year before hostilities began. The railways were put into a pricing straitjacket. They could not raise or lower prices without asking a tribunal. Road hauliers, in contrast, could not only set their own prices, they could also give a trader an instant answer, whereas the railway canvasser had to go back to head office to check what was allowed. Linking the railways' finances to a particular year fettered their commercial freedom in an arbitrary way. The railways were clearly operating in a very different way to their Victorian predecessors, yet they were still forced to be 'common carriers', which meant they were obliged to offer a range of carriage facilities on demand, whether or not they made a profit on that service, a continuation of a role first imposed on them in the Railway & Canal Traffic Act 1854 when they were a genuine monopoly.[21] Moreover, the companies were not properly compensated for the use – abuse, in effect – of their assets during the war: although a governmental Commission suggested that a reasonable claim would be £150m they were eventually given just £60m.

In the prevailing circumstances, such strict and penny-pinching government policies proved to be a recipe for financial disaster. The politicians had failed to realise that the railways no longer occupied the dominant position that they had enjoyed in the pre-war world. Both passenger and freight traffic first stagnated in the immediate aftermath of the war and then began a long period of decline. Freight suffered particularly badly in areas where a traditional industry began to collapse, like coal in South Wales. There were external threats, too, such as the lorry, which scarcely registered in the list of concerns that pre-occupied early twentieth-century railway planners. In the 1920s road hauliers, many of whom had bought cheap surplus army lorries, started to cream off local short-journey freight business, particularly in agricultural produce. The rural branch line which ran from nowhere in particular to a remote main-line junction was already becoming a redundant asset, with small bus operators able to cherry-pick routes and offer cheaper fares.

The period between the two world wars is seen by many as the golden age of the railways. This must be largely attributed to the efforts of the advertising departments of the Big Four, who created enduring images of prestigious, streamlined expresses transporting happy, prosperous families to destinations like the 'Cornish Riviera'. Seven decades later their elegant posters still adorn many a living-room wall, perpetuating this romantic image, which was still powerful enough to persuade John Major, briefly and unsuccessfully, to back a return to the Big Four as the route to privatisation in the 1990s. Until her death in 2004, Lynda Lee-Potter, the *Daily Mail* columnist, penned innumerable columns urging the return of the Great Western Railway buffet car with pressed linen tablecloths and silver cutlery which she remembered from her youth. This nostalgia is not wholly misplaced; the great expresses did indeed offer many desirable features, such as hairdressing salons, secretarial services and the renting out of headsets for radio reception, but few passengers could afford these luxuries. There was a sharp contrast between the elite services of fast expresses between large cities and the shoddy conditions on minor and branch lines, where services were often slow and dirty.

The Big Four's twenty-five-year existence can be characterised as an unsuccessful struggle to achieve profitability in competition with buses and lorries, which unlike the railways were not regulated in any way until 1930 and 1933 respectively. Inevitably, the result was a system that suffered badly from underinvestment. When the government forced through the grouping of the Big Four, it promised to maintain the companies' net receipts from freight services at 1913 levels through the regulation of charging rates. But this proved impossible to fulfil, given the fast-growing competition from other forms of transport which meant that the 1913 targets were hardly ever met, and eventually the government paid £60m to the Big Four to discharge this obligation. The freight market was the key factor in maintaining profits, but although core industries – collieries, steelworks, quarries – still relied on railways for the bulk movement of raw and finished products, they were mostly in decline while the new industries that were replacing them, such as motor manufacturing, electrical engineering and consumer goods, shunned the railways, often establishing themselves on peripheral industrial estates far from any railhead. Passengers, too, were no longer prepared to put up with shoddy service away from the main lines with corridorless trains that provided neither toilets nor refreshments.

The Great Depression which started in 1929 further worsened the financial situation of the railway companies and also depressed morale, since staff were compelled to accept pay cuts. Winston Churchill, the Chancellor of the Exchequer, did help the railways in his 1929 budget; with the aim of stimulating employment in the industry he abolished the Railway Passenger Duty that had been introduced in 1832 and was levied on all rail fares above one (old) penny a mile. The government also made funds available, in the form of repayable, interest-bearing loans for building new locomotives, stations and freight depots, and modernising equipment which the companies simply could not afford to do themselves. But increased government involvement, while welcome, also brought with it the problems that are encountered, sooner or later, by all industries that get embroiled with government. The railway companies became tools of overall macroeconomic policy and found themselves at the mercy of political whims, none of which necessarily served their short- or long-term interests. Their policies were distorted by the needs of a blinkered government which urged them to press on with, often inappropriate, investment that protected jobs. While for the first time closures began to outnumber openings, of which there were very few as the days of railway expansion were over, little effort went into achieving basic economies – such as the abandonment of duplicated routes or closure of unprofitable branch lines which had been one of the intentions behind the 1921 Act. The companies were reluctant to retrench, despite the growth of road transport, and no one, least of all the government, which feared increasing unemployment, was taking a strategic view of the railways.

Even the largest of the Big Four, the LMS, which was described as the biggest joint-stock company in the world in the 1920s, with a capital of almost £400m, did little to improve its productivity because government was reluctant to endorse the socially unacceptable policy of reducing capacity. It was certainly not a commercial decision, for example, that left the company, twenty years after the grouping, still owning three major rolling-stock manufacturing and repair factories with a combined workforce of 100,000.

The railways have consistently suffered from the inability of successive governments to set out precisely what they are for. Are they just another form of transport which therefore has to be run as much as possible on business-like lines, with maximising profits – or at least minimising losses – as the principal criterion for decision-making? Or are they there primarily to offer the community the best possible service, with a consequent need for substantial public subsidy? The GWR, for example, took the latter view. Its directors conducted a survey of all its lines in 1929 and concluded that while many were loss-making, they would not shut any because local people needed them. But the politicians have always wavered, handing out subsidy reluctantly when it is politically expedient or when job creation programmes are needed, but cutting it back whenever possible.

The lack of profitability as a result of the stagnation of traffic, both passenger and freight, meant there was always a squeeze on the money available for investment. Though some impressive schemes were pushed through, such as the electrification of many heavily used commuter routes on the Southern and, with government help, the addition of extra track capacity on the East Coast Main Line, the railways did not modernise sufficiently under the grouping arrangement. By the end of this period the LMS, for example, had undertaken very little electrification (the Great Western did none, a legacy that remains today apart from the Heathrow Express trains), and its stations were 'infrequently cleaned, seldom painted and bore a generally shabby appearance',[22] a description that will sound familiar to many of today's rail passengers.

As part of its Keynesian strategy of trying to boost employment through public works, the government made considerable loans available in the 1930s, but the money was not concentrated on schemes that addressed the railways' fundamental problem of retaining market share, but on those that maximised employment potential. The ability to invest was also hampered by the companies' need to disburse most of the small profits they did make as dividend payments to shareholders, a policy that may have looked like short-term expediency but which as private concerns, they felt they had to adopt in order to keep investors happy. Even so, the returns for ordinary shareholders were meagre and got worse as the companies decided that they had to modernise and invest in new stock to improve their service to the passengers in an increasingly competitive world. On average during the second half of the 1930s the Great Western gave the highest dividends, 2.75 per cent (and even 3.5 per cent in 1937 but only 0.5 per cent the following year), with LMS just behind at 2.7 per cent, while Southern shareholders received only 0.65 per cent and the LNER paid nothing. Indeed, the LNER was an exception, remaining 'determined to invest in its railway even in those years where the ordinary shareholder received nothing'.[23] Preference shareholders did get more – 4 per cent on the Southern in 1935, for example – but for the ordinary investor 'it took an act of faith, even of blind optimism, for anyone to consider investing in the railways'.[24]

LNER's insistence on investment paid off and instigated something of a regional golden age in the run-up to the Second World War. The company had already shown a far-sighted interest in express travel with fewer stops and tighter schedules to bring the provinces closer to London, and its new streamlined Silver Jubilee high-speed trains between London and Newcastle, launched with much fanfare in 1935, gave the railways a modern image which has since characterised the interwar period in a way that it did not entirely merit. Overall, far from the grouping representing the heyday of the railways, the Big Four were hampered by historical constraints and the lack of governmental under-standing of changes in the world of transport. As well as the inability to invest, they were constrained by the common carrier obligations and by antiquated and unimaginative fare structures. It was not all the railways' fault: as the railway historian Terry Gourvish, assessing the interwar years, puts it:

> The continued obligation to accept traffic, publish charges [which rivals could exploit], provide a reasonable level of service, avoid 'undue preference' in the treatment of customers and submit to government regulation of wages and conditions, left the railways vulnerable to their more flexible and less constrained competitors.[25]

In fact, the unfairness of the situation led the companies to launch a 'Square Deal' campaign in November 1938 demanding an end to the legal constraints under which the railways operated, such as the requirement to publish rates and treat all customers equally, but, although the government accepted the need for changes, the war intervened.

There is a cyclical pattern in British railway history which seems to determine that whenever things seem to be going even reasonably well, external factors intervene to put an end to it. Thus the Second World

War ended a bronze, if not a golden, era, just as the First had, although it should be noted that revenues had already started to plummet in 1938 because of a growing depression in trade. Later, as we shall see, the arrival of the motorway did much to wreck the massive 1950s modernisation programme, and privatisation occurred just as BR was getting its act together.

In 1939, as in 1914, the railways were taken under government control with charges being frozen and maintenance and renewal largely sacrificed to the war effort. This was done with extreme haste, the government assuming control on 31 August, a few hours before Germany attacked Poland, a recognition of the extreme importance of the railways. Indeed, this was also demonstrated by the fact that railway work was labelled a 'reserved activity' and railway employees were not sent to war but expected to remain in their jobs; in 1914 they had been initially encouraged to enlist but the government later realised this was a mistake. The railways had to move troops, like the 319,000 rescued from Dunkirk in 1940 and taken from the ports in 620 trains, carry millions of tons of munitions, construction materials for aerodromes, and fuel and bombs for aircraft. At a time when petrol for road transport had to be transported across the oceans, under constant threat of attack from U-boats, and coal-mining was still a backbone of the British economy, the railways were utterly indispensable.

Perversely, the war was the rail companies' financial heyday; they earned impressive profits, almost half of which were retained by the Treasury. However, costs were increasing rapidly while rates and fares were strictly controlled by the government, and this put the railway companies under severe pressure in the immediate aftermath of the war. Moreover, after six years of this intensive use, the railway infrastucture was in a disastrous state. During the war, investment had been negligible, leaving the companies with old wagons and carriages, many locomotives that were life-expired, the track in terrible condition with two years of maintenance backlog that led to a series of major accidents with dozens of fatalities,[26] and a major derailment, though not necessarily causing injury or death, virtually every other week.

With petrol becoming more widely available (though still rationed) and the service offered by the clapped-out railway inadequate by modern standards, competition from road intensified again. Revenues fell dramatically in the two years after the war as there was a return to more normal conditions and there was little money available for leisure travel to the seaside. Nevertheless, there was a naive expectation that passengers and freight customers would stay with the railway even though the alternatives were becoming available again. As we shall see in the next chapter, this endearing and enduring optimism was to remain a feature of the early days of BR and result in much misallocated investment.

The proclaimed policy of the Labour government which came to power in 1945 was to bring all the principal utilities under public ownership. Labour saw this as a crucial priority. It was also convenient – the government was spared the embarrassment of having to bail out a bankrupt railway industry which had not been properly compensated for its takeover by the government during the war. The decline of traditional industries was accelerating; the railways' lifeblood, coal, found itself in competition with alternative fuels, from gas to, later, nuclear power, neither of which was exactly suited for rail carriage. The more modern business practices of light industry, with its precise schedules and low-cost distribution systems, were in direct conflict with the working practices of the railways, whose staff still often believed they ruled the world and who consistently underestimated the threat of rival methods of transport.

Labour had a longstanding commitment to nationalisation of the railways, having first agreed the policy at its 1908 party conference. But it is worth noting, as the argument has contemporary resonance, that it was not only those on the political left who advocated nationalisation. Industrialists and traders, keen to move their goods cheaply, saw the railways as a public service which should not be run as a profit-making business. After the First World War, there had been a fierce debate over the merits of nationalisation and, within the coalition government, Lloyd George had intimated that he supported the idea and, according to Terry Gourvish, 'Winston Churchill, electioneering in Scotland in December 1918, suggested, somewhat injudiciously, that the government had definitely decided to nationalise the railways.'[27] As we have seen, at this time the nationalisation argument was lost, and the government decided on consolidation into the Big Four with relatively tight regulation. However, the Labour Party continued to press for nationalisation of the railways and, indeed, went further in its 1945 manifesto by advocating the creation of a national transport board to integrate all types of inland transport, an idea which eventually bore fruit with the 1948 nationalisation that brought virtually all public transport under a single British Transport Commission (BTC).

Integration was the buzz-word (as it was to be in Labour's 1997 manifesto). The Big Four, plus London Transport, were to be state-owned from 1 January 1948. A Railway Executive was established, reporting to the BTC, to manage the day-to-day rail business with the other executives charged with roads, inland waterways and London Transport.

In a scenario with powerful parallels to the 1990s, when the Tories rushed through privatisation without sufficient thought for the consequences, the Labour government used almost indecent haste to push through and implement their radical plan to nationalise not only railways but virtually all freight and public transport under the BTC. It was an unwieldy structure that would not help BR's genesis. Partly this was a result of the stroppiness of the railway boards who refused to participate in the preparation of the legislation – in sharp contrast to BR's executives who, in the 1990s, largely cooperated in their own demise. Instead, they ran a fierce anti-nationalisation campaign, which, although defeated, helped their shareholders receive rather more favourable terms for their stock than they might otherwise have done.

The refusal of many railway managers to cooperate in the nationalisation process was not only damaging because the scheme had to be drawn up without any input from industry expertise but also because it meant that most of them did not join the new set-up. At a key time the railway industry lost focus: 'The railway company directors began to lose interest in the day to day operations of their companies and concentrated instead on fighting for favourable compensation.'[28]

The three-tiered structure controlling the railways, with the BTC overseeing a Railway Executive which, in turn, was responsible for the regions, was not a happy one. The Railway Executive was perceived to be a 'collection of prima donnas with no conductor'.[29] There was managerial friction all the way down the scale. It was decided to retain much of the former company management structure in the form of six virtually autonomous regions – London Midland, Eastern, North Eastern, Western, Southern and Scottish, each with its own general manager and board of directors. They were used to running their own fiefdoms and believed their decisions should be final, without recourse to the Railway

Executive or the BTC, and it was, in fact, to be another thirty-five years before the power of the regions was broken.

Apart from the last-ditch resistance from the companies and their directors, the fundamental reason for the flawed structure was political expediency. Labour was in a hurry to nationalise the railways – and many other industries – and there was little discussion of the *transport* implications of what was being implemented – 'what mattered was political and administrative expediency',[30] a pattern repeated in the privatisation of the 1990s.

There was the inevitable parliamentary opposition from the Tories who, to a great extent, batted for the interests of the rail companies and adopted obstructive tactics, tabling 800 amendments, and much of the resulting parliamentary debate centred on detail, such as the well-founded criticism that the administrative structure of the BTC was unwieldy and subject to too much ministerial patronage. The biggest row about the nationalisation of the railways was on the terms of compensation for shareholders and the directors themselves.[31] The eventual deal was very generous to the railway company shareholders. Their holdings were valued at a staggering £927m,[32] equivalent to £24bn in today's money (contrast this with the £5.5bn[33] received in 1996/7 for Railtrack, the rolling stock and the various other BR companies). The shareholders were given a fixed level of payment, irrespective of the performance of their company. Moreover, they still, in effect, retained a stake in the railways as they were not paid in cash, but instead their shares were exchanged for government bonds on which they received a fixed rate of return, which was to be a charge on the nationalised industry, irrespective of its performance. Shareholders were thus given a generous risk-free investment. In the event, the financial performance of the railways deteriorated rapidly in the face of competition from the car and as a result of the lack of investment. This generous compensation package was to have a long and damaging effect on the future of the railways in public ownership because of the constant drain on the resources of British Railways (see next chapter).

While politicians, managers and workers jockeyed for position, they overlooked basic issues such as the state of the network. At its creation BR took on 632,000 staff (compared with a fifth of that total for the same number of passengers today), 20,000 miles of track to bring back up to standard, 20,000 steam locomotives (half of them worn out), 36,000 passenger coaches (21 per cent were over thirty-five years old, including a few gas-lit Victorian six-wheelers), 4,200 electric commuter train sets, and a staggering total of 1,223,634 low-capacity freight wagons (many of which made one journey a year, if they were lucky). And there were still 7,000 horses hauling wagons in shunting yards, a method which lasted in some areas until 1964.

Right from the outset, BR had a host of worries, ranging from the dreadful condition of its assets to the artificially low fares imposed by a socialist government. Wages now accounted for three-quarters of the fare revenue before any other bills were considered. Like its predecessor after the First World War, the Attlee government did not pay sufficient compensation for the use of the railways in the war – indeed, the Treasury even clawed back for other uses the renewals fund that the companies had set aside for investment in peacetime. BR, therefore, did not have an easy legacy or an auspicious start. Given these circumstances, its future record, though patchy, was something of a triumph, as the next chapter will show.

CHAPTER 2

Was BR as bad as its sandwiches?*

Ever since the collapse of Railtrack in the aftermath of the Hatfield crash the renationalisation of Britain's railways has been a live issue, even though Labour ministers have steadfastly refused to consider it, routinely pointing to BR's supposed poor record. Therefore, it is important to examine British Rail history in some detail, and to place the organisation's performance in the context of its legacy and the external factors that affected its ability to operate efficiently. As we have seen, BR was not nationalised in propitious circumstances. The First World War had left a legacy of underinvestment and an exhausted rail network; the situation after the Second World War was just as bad.

The early years of BR – and, indeed, most of its history – were dominated by the struggle to stem the rising losses that resulted from the fall in passenger numbers and freight carryings, while bringing the network up to modern standards. In the early years freight traffic was transferring to the roads at an average of 5 per cent annually and the BTC made no efforts to stem this flow. Many small branch-line passenger trains were running empty; losses were mounting; and the trade unions, at a time of labour shortage, were ever spoiling for a fight.

There was no easy, quick fix for these entrenched problems and, worse, there was the legacy of the way that the industry had been nationalised, which resulted in administrative disarray because of the

*BR's sandwiches were actually pretty good by the end. As many readers of *Broken Rails* have pointed out, the days of the stale curly cheese sandwich had long gone by 1996 when the industry was privatised. Indeed, BR had pioneered the idea of packaged sandwiches and had even used the services of such celebrity chefs as Clement Freud and Delia Smith to improve their wares. But the reputation of the terrible BR sandwich lives on as a kind of urban myth.

complicated structure of the British Transport Commission, and financial problems due to the generous compensation terms given to the shareholders of the former railway companies. In its early days the BTC, which was also responsible for British Road Services (BRS), the nationalised long-distance road haulage business, paid insufficient attention to the railways (or indeed to the London Underground which was also part of the organisation[1]), and decisions were confused by the three-tier management structure that controlled the industry.

During the war, the Railway Executive which ran the railways on behalf of the government consisted of the general managers of the four companies, a system which had been felt to work well. British Railways, in contrast, was perceived as a remote and formless body whose unresponsive bosses enjoyed the splendour of the 222 Marylebone Road headquarters (now a luxury hotel) and owed loyalty only to the BTC even further away at 55 Broadway, St James's Park (later the London Transport HQ).

A number of constraints hamstrung BR right from the outset. Having an integrated transport organisation like the BTC might have sounded a good idea, but it was unwieldy and the organisation made little effort to meld in or coordinate the services of the various modes for which it was responsible even though the legislation dictated that BTC had to be run as a single undertaking. In fact, BR needed to be an independent financial entity so that its investment needs could be properly identified. Second, BR had to apply to a tribunal to alter its fares, something its competitors did not have to do, and this proved to be deeply damaging to its finances since fares inevitably became a political football. The government was always reluctant to allow BR to raise fares since this was electorally damaging. There were many other mistakes, such as making BR pay £43 million for the enforced purchase of 544,000 freight wagons, privately owned by customers of the railway companies; many were in such a bad condition that they had to be scrapped immediately. Even legislation that protected coastal and inland shipping against unfair competition from the railways remained on the statute book but no protection was offered the other way around.[2]

Given the flawed structure, administrative reorganisation was always on the agenda, especially after the change of government in 1951 when the Conservatives were elected with the ageing Winston Churchill as prime minister. The experiment with widespread state control and an integrated transport policy through the British Transport Commission was to be short-lived. Road haulage had only just been dragged 'screaming and kicking into the public domain'[3] when, in the first of a seemingly perpetual series of reorganisations, the Conservatives partly dismantled the British Transport Commission through the 1953 Transport Act, which abolished the Railway Executive and appointed area railway boards directly under the BTC. This was the first of 'several defective solutions'[4] for the organisational problems of the railways imposed on the industry in its fifty-year history of state ownership, all devised by outsiders with insufficient weight being given to the views of rail managers. The key point was that BR was still not allowed to stand on its own, and it was to be another decade before the unwieldy BTC was finally abolished. The Act also denationalised road haulage, resulting in the sale of 24,000 lorries to small road hauliers who were able to compete, without any restriction on their charges, against BR which had its rates fixed by the government.

The investment programme was hamstrung by the need to make interest payments to the former shareholders, which increased losses. As David Henshaw notes in his ground-breaking analysis of the Beeching cuts, 'Whereas a private company would have paid little or no dividend in lean years, the return on British Transport Stock was guaranteed ... the railways were obliged to pay a fixed sum of around £40 million per year – even when they were making substantial losses.'[5]

That money would have been much better spent on improving the railways. According to a calculation by the Central Statistical Office,[6] the railways suffered a net disinvestment of £440m in the period 1938–53 (about £11bn at 2005 prices) – in other words, their assets deteriorated faster than they were being renewed. The disappointingly low investment in BR's early years was partly a result of the shortage of both labour and materials in the aftermath of the war but there were several other factors: narrow-minded managers often more concerned with the short-term interests of their particular section of the railway, the layers of bureaucracy – there were thirteen management levels where five were reckoned to suffice[7] – and the plethora of government controls, in particular the constant Treasury interference that was to be the Achilles heel of the railway industry for the rest of the century. Moreover, with charges, both freight and passenger, strictly controlled by the government, the Railway Executive had eschewed major projects such as electrification because they could not earn a rate of return through increasing fares.

Money was wasted, too, by the failure to understand the need for modernisation and, in particular, the urgency of replacing steam. Although some thought was given to investigating other forms of motive power, progress in implementing the idea was held up because the bureaucracy was slow and meanwhile new steam locomotives continued to be ordered. The Western Region added nearly 300 steam shunters to its stock in the first five years of nationalisation, even though diesels were known to be much more efficient for the task. The railways, therefore, missed a big opportunity. The failure to introduce either diesels – which were more expensive to build but much cheaper to run and therefore more economical in the long term – or the railbuses used widely on the continent was to prove disastrous for branch lines once Richard Beeching became chairman of the BTC a decade later. Motorway construction, first mooted in the war, had been delayed as a result of lack of finance, and this should have afforded the railways the chance of retaining their market share. Instead, without investment or clear direction, they stagnated.

However, the railways were to be given one last chance. The British Transport Commission, aware of the structural shortcomings of the network and desperate to stem losses, pressed the government to accept the case for a renewal of the railways. This was presented as the massive Modernisation Plan, published in January 1955. By then, rising costs, road competition and frequent industrial action had pushed the railways into a £22m annual loss. The Conservative administration was faced with a stark choice – modernise the railways or see them die.

The scale of the plan was breathtaking and involved a wholesale re-organisation of railway activities. It envisaged spending £1.24bn (£20bn at 2005 prices) over fifteen years to revamp the railways, including £335m on diesel locomotives and electrification, £285m on coaches and station facilities and £210m on freight services. There was to be total replace-ment of steam power by 100mph diesels, mass electrification and conversion of branch lines to diesel unit operation, while the stations, with facilities little changed in a century and many still suffering wartime bomb-damage that had been merely patched up, would be replaced by airy structures of steel, glass and concrete. (The fact that the wonderful neo-classical Euston station, designed by Philip Hardwick, was one of the stations to get this treatment was possibly the greatest act of architectural vandalism of the 1960s, a decade with several such outrages to its discredit.)

Freight, uneconomically packed into small wagons, which often went missing for weeks or never arrived at all, would be speeded up with new vehicles shunted into order in vast new mechanised marshalling yards. Oddly, however, there was little concentration on improving the main trunk network, even though, as we saw in the last chapter, the advantages of high-speed trains had been demonstrated as far back as the 1930s. While electrification of the West Coast Main Line was included in the plan, it was not prioritised, and as a result of escalating costs and a lack of commitment, the scheme – which was to prove enormously successful in boosting passenger numbers – was not completed until the late 1960s.

The aim was to make the railways profitable. Instead of having to be rescued by the government on an annual basis, BR would deliver a permanent annual profit of £85m (£1.5bn in 2005 money) within six years. Apparently hypnotised by this starry-eyed vision, Parliament approved the 1955 Modernisation Plan with little detailed debate. The Tory government was surprisingly receptive to the plan, seeing it as part of the post-war modernisation programme for which funds had, at last, started to become available. The Labour Party was more sceptical, suggesting that the Modernisation Plan was a complete waste of money. However, the party's line was not based on any cogent analysis of its shortcomings but rather on the view that the railways were finished, road transport was the way ahead, and it should be the minimum entitlement of every working man to own a motor car.

The plan was to be a once-in-a-generation opportunity to revamp the railways but it was based on a major misconception: that, given sufficient investment, people would flock back to the railways. The report's opening sentence seems, with hindsight, stunning in its naivety: 'The Modernisation Plan will win traffic back from the roads. Freight traffic will also return and grow.' As one of the few dissenting voices, H.P. Barker, a part-time member of the Commission, put it, the plan was based on the false notion that 'the present operational conceptions of the British Railways are viable in the long run, given modern equipment'; in fact, he went on to point out, 'a substantial proportion of our movement operations, as carried today, are grossly uneconomic'.[8] Indeed, it is difficult to comprehend how both politicians and railway managers persuaded themselves that there was a realistic prospect of a serious railway revival. Entering the car ownership club was now the ultimate ambition for the average family and, once achieved, the novelty would not be abandoned in favour of new trains, however bright and shiny, let alone the old stock that still rattled up and down most lines. The plan used a scattergun approach to fire investment at all parts of the railway indiscriminately with little sense of overall objectives or priorities. As well as the inherent misconceptions, the plan failed because of the BTC's inadequate appraisal of the value of the planned investments, technical problems, government interference and, ultimately, a shift in government policy.

The plan was a mixture of the sensible and the insane and its inherent flaws are, with hindsight, pretty easy to spot. One obvious example was the tendency of rail managers, seeing that money was suddenly available, to put up the most ridiculous schemes. The Eastern Region, for example, was quite right to seek to extend electrification to places such as Bishops Stortford, Ipswich and the Essex coastal towns and, later, parts of the East Coast Main Line to Newcastle. But then it got silly. The Eastern also hatched a bizarre secondary scheme for a further 1,247 miles of electrification, which included the branches to Cleethorpes, Cromer, Hunstanton, Grimsby via Boston, and Skegness. Not only did this fail to happen by 1985 as planned, but many of the lines mentioned did not even stay open that long. In similarly eccentric fashion the Southern Region, predominantly a third-rail electric suburban railway, wanted to string up masts and overhead electric wires over the 338 miles between Waterloo, Exeter, and Weymouth. The London Midland Region seriously believed that it would need 660 electric locomotives for the West Coast Main Line. Subsequently, before Pendolinos replaced locomotive-hauled trains on the WCML, it survived on far fewer than 100 locomotives. In another example of wild over-optimism the Scottish Region's requests included an unbelievable 85 locomotives just for the sparsely used former Highland Railway system north of Perth.

The new freight marshalling yards were another disaster, not only because goods were moving to the roads, encouraged by motorway construction, but because the future for rail freight lay in running whole train loads rather than individual wagons assembled by shunting engines in huge yards. The government had approved £85m (£1.6bn in 2005 prices) for 25 to 30 new or re-equipped yards of various sizes. All but four were built but within a few years it had become clear that freight would continue to haemorrhage to the roads. A massive 300,000 new wagons were ordered, but as basic products like farm produce, fish, horses, cattle and newspapers went over to road haulage, the freight business sank further into the red. BR had 1.14 million wagons in 1955 and it was discarding 8,000 each week by the early 1960s. Today, there are fewer than 40,000. The new Perth yard was the earliest casualty. When it opened in 1962 it was handling 1,200 wagons per day for 58 scheduled train arrivals, with seed-potato traffic providing a seasonal surge of an additional 250 consignments a day. Six years later the traffic had all gone and the yard was facing closure.

The plan's most visible white elephant was the Bletchley flyover, which can still be seen by passengers on the WCML. It was built for £1.6m (£30m[9] in 2005) but never put into operation as it was part of a grand scheme to use the Oxford–Cambridge line as an east–west route avoiding London that never materialised. It took six years to build and was completed in January 1962 – by which time there was no traffic to feed it.

Some of the new technology did not work as expected or proved to be unreliable. The government's insistence on certain purchases, such as domestically produced locomotives as opposed to cheaper imports, did not help. Expensive technical mistakes were made, such as trying to fit all freight wagons with compatible braking systems at vast expense, and ordering unreliable locomotives designed in haste led to an overheated supply industry. A ridiculous number of prototype diesel designs, over fifty, were tried and, because of the sudden availability of cash, many were rushed into production without the usual three-year testing programme. The result was a loss of reliability – and even occasionally the temporary reintroduction of steam – which hardly reinforced public confidence in the new technology.

The finances of the plan had always looked shaky. There was no built-in increase for wages and yet it was clear that above-inflation rises were needed to tackle labour shortages. The plan was reviewed in 1956 and it quickly became apparent that there was nothing in it to justify the notion that the BTC could achieve profitability for BR in 1970, let alone 1962. Quite the opposite. Passenger numbers were rising, with 1956 seeing a post-nationalisation peak, but the extra income was not enough to stop losses mounting. Deficits went up, reaching £90m in 1958. The financial situation had been exacerbated by government control of electorally unpopular fare rises. Twice in the 1950s, agreed rises were stopped by government intervention at the last minute, even though rail fares had risen by well below the rate of inflation since 1938.

In essence, the Modernisation Plan was little more than a series of investment schemes put up by the regions with crudely worked out rates of return based on optimistic assumptions about growth. For example, as BR's official historian put it, 'Large sums of money were committed to freight modernisation without a clear and unanimous statement of future policy.'[10] The focus was on purchasing hardware, such as loco-motives and massive marshalling yards, rather than boosting revenue through better services. Moreover, little attention was paid to reducing costs. Perhaps someone should have heeded the forthright comments of former Eastern Region chief general manager Gerard Fiennes, who later blew the lid off railway politics in a seminal book: 'The BTC's simple error was that it bought the tools before it knew what job it wanted to be done.'[11]

The fundamental point about the great Modernisation Plan was that its overarching optimism did not arise out of some political fiat but was the result of proposals presented by the most senior figures in railway management from information collected from all tiers of technical, operating and management staff. That it all got past the most senior officials in the Treasury, and ultimately a fairly parsimonious govern-ment, seems all the more remarkable. Was it that none of them foresaw the decline of the railways in competition with the car, or did they simply stick their heads in the sand, refusing to acknowledge that the century-long heyday of the railways was over?

Thus, while it would be easy to lay all the blame for the failure of the plan at the government's feet, that would be to ignore the cross errors made by the BTC and BR's senior managers. Within just five years the plan, which managed to consume £1,000m of investment – worth over ten times that sum today – was in ruins as the government turned off the cash tap. Instead of the hoped-for grand revival, passenger and freight revenues had fallen even faster than before. The government changed tack, dramatically.

In 1960, poring over the ever-worsening figures for the railways' finances, transport minister Ernest Marples decided that the railway spending roadshow had to be stopped. It had been pure fantasy to suppose that the railways could ever have made £85 million profit by 1962. The 1961 balance sheet (the last before Beeching) was a shocker. The business, affected by a mild recession, had recorded an operating loss for the year of £87m (£1.3bn in 2005 money), an increase of £19m in a single year, and it would get much worse in 1962. Add to that a further £49m in interest and fixed charges, and it is easy to understand why politicians had got fed up with the railways.

Transport politicians can usually be characterised as being either pro-rail or pro-roads, and Marples was unequivocally the latter, a keen advocate of the motorway (he had founded one of the construction companies that built the M1) and sceptical of the value of rail investment. The government had, in any case, already hedged its bets, having announced a £212m scheme to modernise the road network only days after the publication of the Modernisation Plan and the first motorway, the Preston by-pass, had opened in December 1958.

Using analysis from the United States which argued that the railway was obsolescent, Marples decided to freeze most UK railway investment. And he brought in a man cast in his own mould to wield the axe – Richard Beeching, a scientist with no experience of the railways whose previous job had been technical director of ICI, the huge chemicals company. His brief, as the new chairman of the BTC (then as chairman of BR after the BTC was rapidly abolished), was simple: make the railways profitable, whatever it takes. There was to be no consideration of the social benefits of the railway: his instructions were that if any line were not profitable, it should be hacked out.

Beeching's report,[12] published in 1963, provided a devastating but crude picture of the state of the railways. His analysis showed that half of BR's 17,830 route miles were not worth modernising as they carried only 4 per cent of the traffic; 3,368 stations generated only 4 per cent of the parcels business; coal trucks made one trip on average every three days, and of the 5,000 coal depots, 4,000 received fewer than six loads per week. Stock utilisation was so poor that some 9,000 passenger coaches stood idle for three-quarters of the year, waiting for the summer seaside business, and 2,000 were used fewer than ten times per year. It was easy to understand why road haulage was stealing all the business when Beeching found that it took a norm of two days for each wagon to deliver its consignment and that wagons were only used twenty-five times a year on journeys whose average length was just sixty-seven miles. Some wagons were lost for weeks on end. Freight locomotives spent half their time shunting in sidings and the other half hauling an average of a scant twenty wagons between marshalling yards. As Henshaw added, 'Someone had even proved that it was quicker to walk across London with a parcel than to send it by rail.'[13]

British Railways senior managers had, perhaps, been too preoccupied with the transition from steam traction to diesel and electric, and with devising a modern freight policy, to realise that one in nine families now owned a motor car, and that the other eight were saving to buy one. Now, for the first time, there was a recognition that, given the increasing popularity of road transport, it was no longer socially necessary for the railways to cover the country comprehensively. Only 10 per cent of journeys were by train (the figure now is 2 per cent, but the number of train journeys has remained remarkably stable since World War II while trips by car have increased massively).

Beeching's brutal fifteen-point solution to this situation was to put the railways into profit by 1970 by cutting swathes of lines, discontinuing most stopping services and transferring the displaced diesels to replace steam on the remainder. He proposed to shut some 2,363 small stations and 5,000 miles of track, and cut out duplicate lines. Beeching planned to damp down seasonal peaks by scrapping underutilised coaches, to coordinate suburban train and bus services and charges, and to improve the parcels and postal service. Coal and other heavy traffic would be mechanised, and rates for loss-making freight increased to the point where much would go on to the roads.

The Tories lost the 1964 election before much of Beeching's work could be completed. The new prime minister, Harold Wilson, who on the hustings had promised a thorough review of the railway closures and denounced Beeching's report in powerful terms, showed his customary duplicity by executing a remarkable U-turn after he was elected. It took some time for rail campaigners to extract a clear statement of policy from government but when they did, in March 1965, it was a great dis-appointment. Wilson claimed that he did not have the power to stop any of the thirty-eight line closures put forward by Beeching.

Of these lines, twenty-five had already been closed but far from trying to stop the process, the Labour government allowed plans for a whole series of additional closures, including ones that even Beeching had rejected, such as the Oxford–Cambridge line. Instead of being reviewed, the closure programme was speeded up: while Ernest Marples had authorised the closure of 991 miles of railway in 1964, Tom Fraser, his Labour successor, was to authorise a further 1,071 before the end of 1965.[14] However, some proposed closures, such as the Glasgow–Stranraer line and the East Suffolk line, were saved and remain in operation today. It was an arbitrary and haphazard process with little coherent logic and many of the assumptions by Beeching about lack of potential profitability were demonstrated to be wrong.

The confused state of railway policy in this crucial period is illustrated by the fact that in 1965 the Labour government received a second report[15] from Beeching which advocated concentrating investment on key major routes but, as a quid pro quo, closing vast swathes of the network. Of the 7,500 route miles which he had originally suggested retaining, only 3,000 were now to be actively developed, while the rest would to be allowed to wither away – this time around Beeching avoided the word closure. The railway would merely link a few major cities such as London, Manchester and Glasgow; Newcastle would find itself at the end of a single-track freight branch from Leeds; while the London–Leicester, Newcastle –Edinburgh and Plymouth–Penzance routes were all to be shut. Although the government rejected the report and chose not to renew Beeching's tenure at the British Railways Board, it nevertheless proceeded with a series of closures that were to prove the most damaging to the railways in the long term. When they had been completed about 10,500 route miles had survived.

Closures set out in the first Beeching Report, in fact, continued throughout the 1960s but slowed to a trickle by the mid-1970s and then dried up altogether by 1977. In fact, the attempt by BR to close major sections of the railway only ended in the 1980s with the unsuccessful and highly dishonest attempt to shut the Carlisle to Settle railway, now intensively used by freight and passenger trains and as a diversionary route.

It was the closures after 1966, by which time Wilson held a large majority in Parliament, that are most difficult to comprehend. Before then most cuts had been of structurally uneconomic lines, but the railways taken out of the network after that date caused lasting damage to the coherence of Britain's rail network[16] and reduced the system to a size which served proportionately fewer of Britain's towns and cities than comparable European systems. Although Labour's transport minister at the time, Barbara Castle, was one of the ablest ever, the civil servants who had developed the Beeching strategy were very much in control at the ministry and their views, greatly influenced by the notion that roads represented the future, were allowed to prevail. The chief casualties, which were either partially or wholly dismantled, were the Great Central which provided an alternative route from London to the Midlands and north-west, the Somerset & Dorset between Bath and Bournemouth, Oxford–Cambridge and the alternative Exeter–Plymouth line.

The failure of those who carried out the Beeching cuts to consider the railway within a wider context seems, in retrospect, almost inexplicable. For example, at the very time that the Oxford–Cambridge line was being axed, the government was busily drawing up plans to turn Milton Keynes, within easy reach of the line, into the nation's fastest growing city. The Great Central, heavily used, was an equally short-sighted closure as, at the same time, Harold Wilson was negotiating with the French to build the Channel Tunnel that would have linked in with the line, which was built to European gauge standards, able to take the wider trains used for freight on the Continent, since it was originally planned to run to Paris. The Great Central was also a classic example of BR's tactics of closing lines by stealth: cut back the timetable over a period of years, then, after passengers have fled as a result of the poor services, it becomes uneconomic, justifying closure.

The anomalies created by this indiscriminate process are legion. cross-country routes were decimated, leaving many major towns without direct links to each other or to London, while isolated communities in central and mid-Wales, the wild moorlands of Scotland, and remote areas of Cumbria, Norfolk and East Lincolnshire still have stations that can never attract more than a couple of dozen passengers a day. For example, the sizeable Lincolnshire port town of Boston, once a 'main-line station, was deprived of its direct London link and now can only be reached circuitously via Sleaford and Grantham, just to save sixteen miles of track south to Spalding. Stratford-on-Avon became an outpost of the West Midlands suburban system, which meant a complicated journey for all those tourists seeking to visit Shakespeare country from London.[17] And so on.

The short-sightedness of the policy is demonstrated by the fact that the Strategic Rail Authority, during its brief expansive mode (see Chapter

6), put forward proposals to reinstate many of the gaps in the national network left by the post-Beeching butchery such as Oxford–Cambridge and the Manchester–Sheffield line via the Woodhead tunnel, which even Beeching had sought to retain for its heavy freight potential. There was talk, too, for a time of reopening London's direct link with Lewes via Uckfield, cut to save a paltry amount of money but not safeguarded so that a road now crosses the old rail track. However, these expansionary plans have now been kicked into touch because of the railway's financial crisis following the collapse of Railtrack and these reopenings are no longer on the agenda.

Labour allowed the Beeching plan to be rushed through with little attempt to explore possible alternatives: simple operational economies such as de-manning stations, for example, or simplifying signalling, and on-train ticket sales, all of which could have played a part in seeing rural routes survive the tough 1970s and 1980s. Beeching's cuts were never going to save much money. He estimated annual savings from closures and cuts in stopping passenger services at around £30m, less than a third of the overall deficit. So little attention was paid to other ways of saving money that, as late as 1968, there were 7,000 freight guards, even though few trains still had a brake van and their role was 'not immediately obvious'.[18]

It is difficult, from the standpoint of 2005, to realise just how all-pervasive was the belief that the car represented the future. In those days before the French TGV system had been built, there was no notion that high-speed trains, even on Britain's underinvested network, would be the preferred form of travel for journeys such as London–Manchester or London–Leeds rather than the car or the aeroplane. It was that faith in road transport which underpinned Beeching's thinking and led to the massive closures, even of lines that carried large numbers of people.

Beeching's logic for line closures was largely discredited by critics. While there was obviously a strong case for some closures, Beeching, backed up by an anti-rail minister and often supported by a dubious use of figures, went much too far. He had thought of a solution and found figures to back up his case. There were well-substantiated allegations that the figures were manipulated to show the 'losses' that were required to make the case for closure. Decisions on individual lines were based on a nationwide passenger survey conducted during the week ending 23 April 1961. This was an unfair date for lines with seasonal business, but the subsequent report dismissed this as an 'irrelevant objection'. Moreover, revenue was often misallocated. Seaside towns, where few people paid their fares as most arrived with return tickets, were made to look uneconomic when, in fact, they could have been highly profitable. While it might have seemed that money was being saved by scrapping rolling stock used infrequently, the cost of retaining it to cater for such holiday traffic was, in fact, minimal.

Where Beeching so often went wrong was in his disregard for knock-on effects. Cut off the branches and the tree may die. Many local routes were slated for closure without much regard to their importance as feeders to main lines, which then landed in financial trouble. Beeching also created a climate in which the whole thrust of management was geared towards seeking closures, often by massaging figures, rather than seeking new markets and business for their industry.

Instead of looking at cheaper ways of running services through the use of railbuses or diesel units, closures were made merely on the basis of existing costs. Moreover, social benefits were not taken into account. There was no attempt at cost-benefit analysis by, for example, considering the extra road accidents caused by people travelling in cars and all the other disbenefits of motoring. The techniques for such analysis had not been developed and, in any case, logic was not part of the Beeching process. As Henshaw argues, the whole sorry episode was about achieving a shift away from the railways to roads by a pro-roads administration.

Like the Modernisation Plan, Beeching's policy was based on a misconception, albeit a completely different one – that the railways could be made profitable if loss-making branches were closed leaving a core network that could earn money. The fallacy behind this argument was explicitly admitted in Beeching's second report, which stated that even a 3,000-mile railway would not necessarily guarantee profitability.[19] In other words, the only way to ensure there were no losses was to close the railway entirely. This was borne out by the figures for BR's deficit. As BR's official historian points out,[20] the accumulated losses for 1963–73 were £775m, much higher than those for the previous fourteen years which amounted to £560m at the same prices. The Beeching plan was a failure in its own terms.

Beeching also made the mistaken assumption that people displaced from trains would be happy to travel by bus. In fact, the many substitute bus services introduced to appease opponents of closures were quickly removed since patronage was low, even where trains had previously been full. People, particularly the middle classes who are heavy users of rail services, prefer trains.

The switch in policy which had seen the Modernisation Plan replaced, almost overnight, by Beeching's swingeing cuts left the railway in a terrible state: 'The new railway system, billed as compact, efficient and modern, was really demoralised, inefficient and chronically short of investment capital.'[21]

Things did get slightly better. Barbara Castle's 1968 Transport Act, which introduced the concept of a social railway, finally made explicit the idea that railways could no longer be judged on a narrow financial basis but existed to provide a service to the public which needed subsidy from the taxpayer. Specific grants were made available for loss-making services and although, inevitably, the amounts were insufficient and calculated by a bizarre formula, there was at least a recognition of the wider role of the railways. Integration, having been promoted in 1948, but dropped in 1962, was now back on the agenda. (It featured prominently in Labour's 1997 manifesto, too, but was barely mentioned in 2001 and was utterly forgotten by the 2005 election.)

One of the great successes of the 1968 Act has proved to be the creation of self-managing Passenger Transport Executives (PTEs) in the major cities of Manchester, Newcastle, Glasgow, Birmingham, Liverpool and Leeds. This innovation worked wonders in revitalising suburban rail systems. The creation of PTEs allowed metropolitan authorities to decide transport strategies for major centres of population and also transferred financial control of these services to councillors who were aware of local needs. They were given a large measure of control, including the power to specify fare structures, integrate bus and rail services and, from the mid-1980s, buy rolling stock but their future has been put in doubt by the Railways Act 2005 that encourages the replacement of train services with buses.[22]

The 1968 Act gave BR a somewhat sounder financial footing by wiping out its historic £1,200m debt, and, boosted by the success of the West Coast Main Line electrification, the modernisation of the network, rather than its dismemberment, became the accepted aim. The Board, under the forward-looking Richard Marsh, began to develop a series of prestige projects to modernise the railways but also considered a series of closures, most of which proved politically unpalatable to implement because they were in rural areas controlled by the Tories who had won the 1970 election. The fuel crisis of 1973 ensured a renewed interest in rail as it was patently the most fuel-efficient form of transport – a two-car diesel multiple unit which can carry over 100 passengers, for example, manages four miles to the gallon.

The railways, however, had to be bailed out again when Labour returned to government in 1974. This was because there had still been no recognition that the railways needed continuing financial support, rather than just a one-off debt wipe-out. As a result, when Harold Wilson resumed his premiership he was immediately faced with a financial crisis in the railways. He allocated £2.1bn to BR, including £1,500m over five years for subsidising loss-making services , a final recognition of the need to maintain a socially useful network. This was done through the Railways Act 1974 which created the Public Service Obligation, the grant payable annually to BR that was based, rather vaguely, on the provision of a service broadly comparable with the level of service pertaining that year. There was, however, still no clear resolution as to what the railways were for. The BR Board continued to argue that a profitable railway was around the corner but that goal was never achieved.

Beeching's prediction that air would be the favoured method of transport between major cities had failed to take into account the limitations of domestic airline services. Big aircraft were not economic on short-haul routes, and capacity problems in air traffic control, as well as the hassle of travelling on congested roads to out of town airports, gave rail a competitive advantage, provided BR could speed up services. This was the big idea of the 1970s. The solution was to introduce fast diesels – the highly popular High Speed Trains (HSTs) – on some routes such as those out of Paddington and St Pancras, and to electrify others such as the East Coast Main Line out of King's Cross. Sadly, Britain eschewed the French solution of building dedicated high-speed lines, instead upgrading existing lines for higher speed travel.

Nevertheless, it was a successful strategy. The introduction of the HSTs in 1976 and the adoption of the InterCity name boosted passenger usage and radically improved railway finances. The HSTs were a low-tech solution and the plan was to replace them eventually with the tilting Advanced Passenger Train. Unfortunately, that idea foundered through the failure of the technology and a collective lack of nerve on the part of government and British Rail, as most of the glitches were on the point of being sorted out when the project was scrapped in 1986. Another scheme which did not see the light of day but on which much energy – and considerable cash – was expended was the Channel Tunnel Rail Link and the tunnel itself. Heath's Conservative government published a detailed plan in 1972 and work began but, after inevitable cost rises, it was put on hold in 1975 by Wilson, and ended up being delayed for three decades!

Under constant pressure to reduce the deficit, which had briefly been wiped out in the early 1970s but soon reappeared, BR at last grasped the nettle of efficiency, boosting productivity enormously by cutting out swathes of bureaucracy and staff made redundant by new technologies. Both Marsh, and, to a lesser extent, his successor Peter Parker, who took over in 1976, managed to drive through significant improvements in working practices which ensured the survival of many marginal services. The tide had turned on closures, with BR now more ready to take into account the contribution made by passengers starting their journeys on the branch lines but continuing on the rest of the network. By the late 1970s station reopenings rather than closures were becoming the vogue but no new major lines were being considered.

Throughout the 1970s it was increasingly evident that the railway no longer needed a cumbersome and powerful regionally based management system which bore no relationship to markets. This led to the creation of stand-alone businesses – InterCity, Network SouthEast and Provincial (later Regional) as well as freight and parcels – whose managers were expected to run them like commercial concerns by taking responsibility for marketing, investment and cost allocation. After a struggle, the powerful regions were largely phased out (though vestiges of the structure survived until the late 1980s) and the restructured railway began to assume the aspect of a modern, forward-looking business.

With the election of Mrs Thatcher at the head of a Conservative government in 1979 came an insistence that there should be greater financial discipline for the railways and that peripheral businesses, such as hotels, rolling stock manufacture and ferry services, should be privatised. The railway soon came under attack from a government with little love for an industry still seen as archaic. With modern high-speed trains and greater efficiency, BR had been booming, carrying almost a billion passengers in 1979, the highest since the start of the Beeching cuts. But recession was around the corner and the deficit was starting to rise again, going up from £692m in 1975 to £1,035m in 1982. The increasing losses, together with a prime minister hostile to the railways, led to the setting up of a commission on railway finances, a four-man committee headed by Sir David Serpell, formerly a senior civil servant in the Department of Environment, and a renewed debate about the size of the network.

On the assumption that the government still had a belief in the 'social railway', the British Railways Board had expected suggestions for a rational policy for sustaining and financing the network at its existing size, even though it was obvious that there was a need to make a major investment in track, buildings and rolling stock after decades of under-investment. Instead, Serpell produced six options for a much-pruned British railway for the twenty-first century. His infamous 'Option A' chopped the 10,500 route miles of BR down to just 1,630, comprising only the main lines from Euston to Birmingham, Liverpool, Manchester, Glasgow and Edinburgh; King's Cross to Leeds and Newcastle; Liverpool Street to Norwich; Paddington to Cardiff; and a few key London commuter lines to the Essex, Kent, Sussex and Hampshire coastlines. There would, therefore, be no railway south-west of Bristol, nothing in north or mid-Wales, or north of the Scottish Lowlands, and not a single cross-country route.

By highlighting this option, rather than some of the other more realistic ones, the BR Board managed to ensure that the Serpell Report created a storm of protest and was, therefore, quickly tossed into the bin. Instead, the Tory government surprised everyone by embarking upon a series of programmes that included modest investment in rural lines. This change of heart was the product of a fruitful relationship between the new chairman, Sir Bob Reid (the first chairman of that name who, confusingly, was succeeded by a namesake), and the secretary of state, Nicholas Ridley, which ensured that, for the first time, there was a dialogue about what the government wanted the railway to do. The benefits were seen in the form of investment in schemes such as electronic radio signalling, which scored notable successes in reducing costs in remote locations such as the West Highland and Far North lines in Scotland and in East Suffolk and, more important, the replacement of almost all the worn-out diesel multiple units and locomotive-hauled trains on regional routes, all dating back to the late 1950s, with a modern fleet, many of which were air-conditioned.

BR was set the target of making InterCity profitable, which was achieved with a bit of fiddling over the inclusion of high-revenue routes such as London–Norwich and the omission of loss-makers, such as trains to Barrow in Furness and Cleethorpes, and some creative accounting that ensured costs were stacked into the heavily subsidised Provincial Railways sector. Freight, too, was supposed to be profitable, a much harder target. From an annual loss of £100m in 1984, InterCity broke even a couple of years later and then became highly profitable in the boom years of the late 1980s. This was achieved by more intensive use of rolling stock, good marketing and better yield management – raising fares in markets that could bear it. Indeed, for the first time, fare rises were used deliberately by BR, under government instruction, to maximise revenue and bring down the deficit. Virtually every year from Mrs Thatcher's election to the mid-1990s, fares went up by more than the rate of inflation, which made sense in the narrow terms of cutting BR's losses but was nonsensical in environmental terms. Indeed, at times of boom, demand was deliberately choked off in order to damp down the need for investment in major schemes to increase capacity on the railway.

Astonishingly, at the height of the late 1980s boom, Network SouthEast, the London commuter lines, broke even despite a massive investment programme. BR was again booming, with the number of train miles having increased by 18 per cent in the three years to 1988, while costs per passenger mile had dropped by almost a third. Subsidy was a mere 0.16 per cent of Gross National Product, compared with the European average of 0.52 per cent[23] and had declined by a half in real terms between 1983 and 1989.[24] BR was now arguably the most efficient railway in the world. Indeed, according to the standard reference work, 'On statistical comparisons with almost all major European railways, showing the highest productivity and also the lowest level of funding by government. That did not affect public perception of shortcomings in service quality in some areas.'[25] In other words, the public might well have welcomed a bit more subsidy in return for a better service.

Railway economics are always highly dependent on the performance of the overall economy, and BR's new-found efficiency provided no protection against recession. Just as BR had started to get things right, it suffered a sharp decline in patronage as a result of the post-Lawson recession – numbers travelling into London each day fell by 100,000 to 350,000 over a three-year period – and the situation was exacerbated when the railways faced yet another reorganisation. Although in hindsight this prepared the way for privatisation, the decision to sell off the railways had not yet been made, but the government wanted a more business-oriented structure. The scheme, called 'Organising for Quality', resulted in virtually all aspects of the railway being devolved to the sectors. The British Railways Board would still set the objectives and standards (including safety), but the sectors would control everything else. InterCity was divided into six profit centres, Network SouthEast into eight and Regional Railways into five and these subdivisions would later form the basis of the franchising system.

Through a combination of tight management under a good run of chairmen and some, though insufficient, investment, BR had largely got it right. The management had finally got rid of the regional baronies, they had developed a competitive – or market-orientated – fares policy, strikes were reducing, the passenger's charter had been developed as a means of measuring performance – which was improving – and they had even convinced the government to allow rolling stock to be leased. As mentioned above, efficiency was the best in Europe and productivity still rising. British Rail bore comparison with any major railway operation in the world. It was 'little short of miraculous in the circumstances',[26] as another former BR board member put it: 'By that time we certainly knew more about where the money went and what cost what than we do today, ironic given that transparency was one of the arguments for privatisation.'

Chris Green, one of the most forward-looking rail managers and later head of Virgin Rail, had developed the concept of Total Route Modernisation, concentrating scarce resources on one route to improve it radically. This involved the refurbishment of the track, signalling and stations, as well as new trains in order to create what was effectively a new railway. This was done on the Chiltern line which, not surprisingly, has managed to attract massive numbers of new passengers; but the demise of BR stopped the programme. The 1994 timetable, the last written by BR, was 'reckoned to be the best ever'.[27] Despite the row over the Settle–Carlisle railway, BR was now concentrating on reopening lines, with over 200 stations opened in its last decade.

Moreover, BR had developed two instantly recognisable brand names – InterCity and Network SouthEast – and the InterCity TV advertising campaign ranks among the all-time greats. Although overall subsidy was on the rise, that was largely due to the economic downturn. As a former non-executive board member put it, 'I don't think the British railways were ever as well run as in the early 1990s.'[28]

As the first Sir Bob Reid said, 'Major organisational change is the remedy for a business which is in bad shape and ours is not.' Yet this was the point at which a government ignorant of railway realities chose to break up an efficient, publicly run, integrated railway. The recession which started in 1989 had weakened the railway and the figures looked terrible because of the fall in passenger numbers and freight tonnage carried, the collapse of the property market and the costs of an invest- ment programme predicated on a continued boom. The government failed to understand the simple economics and, pursuing its own ideological bent, embarked on its most controversial privatisation.

It would be wrong to paint BR immediately pre-privatisation as anything like perfect. There were still struggles to obtain investment and, inevitably, there were still inefficiencies and mistakes. The railways were still at the mercy of government whim and the vagaries of the economy. However, it would also be wrong to dismiss the fifty-year record of BR as a failure because of errors such as the Modernisation Plan, the Beeching cuts and the perennial problems of underinvestment. In fact, BR's record is much better than its detractors would have us believe. Its biggest problem, which many see as an inevitable feature of a nationalised industry, was its vulnerability to the stop-go investment policies of the government. The railways need a constant level of investment in order to renew and enhance the network. Successive governments of both political hues blew hot and cold. During times of boom, the railway was positively swilling with money, but deficits built up quickly once there was an economic downturn. Investment in the 1980s rose significantly and the major upgrade of the East Coast Main Line was completed before privatisation.

The period of state control was characterised by a constant paradox that was never resolved: the railway was expected to be run economically but also to cater for rather vaguely defined social needs. As BR's official historian put it,

> The BTC had wanted to modernise the railways after years of neglect. The public wanted a modern railway network of roughly the same size of 1955. The government wanted the BTC to fulfil its obligation to break even. Much

of the review activity was ... about the attempt, made under government pressure, to reconcile these objectives. Not surprisingly, it proved impossible to do so.[29]

He was writing about the Modernisation Plan and Beeching but this analysis could apply equally to any part of the past fifty years of railway history.

These last two chapters demonstrate that, over the whole history of the railways in Britain, it has proved impossible for the state and the railways to reach a mutually fruitful relationship. There has been, at various times, too little or too much interference. Victorian *laissez faire* left us with an extensive network that did not necessarily serve social needs, but the attempt to rationalise the system after the First World War failed. Again, after the Second World War, the right structure seemed to elude the policy-makers and, sadly, it was only at the end that BR and the government had got many of the basics right. However, the biggest mistake of successive British governments has been the failure to think strategically and to develop the type of grand plan whose success makes the British so envious when they travel on the French TGV system.

CHAPTER 3

The poll tax on wheels

Mrs Thatcher may rarely have travelled on a train, but her political antennae were sufficiently well attuned to detect the trouble that was likely to arise from privatising the railways. The idea of selling off the trains had been mooted as early as the 1960s by the Conservative Research Department, which rejected it as economically unviable.[1] The concept resurfaced when the Tories were in opposition in the late 1970s in a policy statement from the Young Conservatives and a pamphlet by Norman Fowler, the party's transport spokesman.[2] After the 1979 election which brought Thatcher to power, Fowler even managed to float, briefly, the idea of privatising Southern Region, but there was overwhelming opposition from his colleagues. The whole concept of privatisation was still at the fledgling stage, and clearly the time was not ripe for such a radical policy.

Contrary to conventional wisdom, Mrs Thatcher's government stumbled upon its massive privatisation programme largely by accident, and the sale of nationalised industries featured only obliquely in the 1979 election manifesto. Moreover, even the most enthusiastic privatisers recognised that there were plenty of easier targets than the railways. The first Conservative term was taken up with testing the water for privatisation through the sale of marginal state holdings like BP (5 per cent), Associated British Ports, Amersham International and British Rail Hotels, all as trade sales rather than open-market flotations. It was only in the second term, after the 1983 election, that the programme really got under way, and the next few years saw the sale of British Telecom, British Gas and the water companies, all as regulated monopolies with very little notion of competition, a fact which greatly disappointed the right wing of the Tory party, who wanted privatisation to foster the opening up of markets.

Meanwhile, a more radical type of sale was taking place in the transport arena. The late Nicholas Ridley, a clever ideologue who had the ear of Mrs Thatcher, ended up by chance with the transport portfolio in the reshuffle caused by Cecil Parkinson's amorous indiscretions which had so embarrassingly come to light during the 1983 Conservative Party conference. Following the passage of the 1985 Transport Act, Ridley set about breaking up the National Bus Company (NBC), a huge concern that ran most of the country's local bus services, into seventy separate companies, the majority of which were bought by management buy-out teams. Driven by a singular vision of small-time capitalism, Ridley could see little difference between a local corner shop and a bus, and was in the habit of going round depots asking why the vehicles were not owned by the drivers.

The break-up of the bus industry was significant for the subsequent sale of the railways because of the emphasis it placed on competition even though, by the time the structure of rail privatisation was being put in place, Ridley's much-touted belief in bus competition had been shown to be a chimera. At first, when the NBC companies were sold and the market deregulated, allowing virtually anyone to run services providing they fulfilled very basic minimum safety standards, there were fierce bus wars in many provincial towns (London escaped deregulation because the Tories rightly feared there would be vote-losing chaos). Dozens of operators thought there was a quick buck to be made by duplicating services on the profitable routes, but they were under no obligation to create the sort of network which is the lifeblood of an urban economy. They merely cherry-picked the best routes, creaming off profits that had formerly been used to cross-subsidise other services in a network.

These wars resulted in some towns like Sheffield and Manchester being swamped with battered old buses choking local people with exhaust fumes and in services that kept being chopped and changed almost daily, to the confusion of the dwindling band of bus users. Within a couple of years, however, most of the smaller operators had been driven out of business by their larger rivals, who used underhand tactics like putting on services a minute before or after their competitors, cutting fares below economical levels or even running free services. Stagecoach, the most aggressive company, found itself facing investigation by the Office of Fair Trading thirty times in the decade after deregulation; but the authorities were powerless to stop such predatory activity.

These big firms quickly consolidated and achieved monopoly status in large swathes of the country. (They were also to become the main bidders for the privatised rail franchises when these started being offered for sale in 1995.) Once they had carved out an area, they left their neighbours' territory well alone. With only rare exceptions, such as the fight between FirstGroup and Stagecoach in Glasgow, these large companies have avoided head-on battles with each other, knowing that such mega bus wars would only result in huge losses. The bus battles were, in effect, a series of massacres of the weak rather than lengthy battles between well-matched rivals.

The bus fiasco sounded a further warning to Mrs Thatcher about privatising the railways, especially as she understood the special place that chuffa trains have in the hearts of the British people. Ridley arranged a meeting with Thatcher specifically to obtain her support for rail privatisation and received short shrift. A British Rail Board member recalled:[3] 'She told him [Ridley] never to mention the words again and that was it. She said, "Railway privatisation will be the Waterloo of this government. Please never mention the railways to me again."' As well as being concerned about middle England's affection for its railways, Mrs Thatcher did not believe that privatising a loss-making industry was feasible. The Department of Transport, which had been testing the water with proposals for selling off the railways by a variety of methods, realised that the idea was politically unpalatable and abandoned it.

Paul Channon, the secretary of state for transport appointed after the 1987 election victory, managed to put the idea briefly back on the agenda by announcing at the following year's Conservative party conference that rail privatisation was being considered by the government. He even started looking at some possible models for the structure, but by the time of the next party conference he had been replaced by a rehabilitated Cecil Parkinson, who was told to play down the issue.

Thatcher finally changed her mind in the autumn of 1990, just before her demise, and Parkinson was able to tell Parliament that the government was 'determined to privatise British Rail'.[4] Her successor, John Major, shared none of her doubts and began to ask for more detail on how it could be done. He was, according to his colleagues, a more ardent privatiser than his predecessor. However, he apparently showed little direct interest in the issue – there is no significant mention of rail privatisation in his autobiography – but, in his typical bumbling way, he was open to the ideas being put forward by others without fully understanding what he was letting himself in for.

At this stage there was a key hurdle to overcome. Why privatise at all? It was bound to be a hassle since the public's attachment to the railways ensured the issue would be a political hot potato. It is surprisingly difficult to identify the political objectives behind such a key policy undertaking. There were the usual statements about the private sector being more efficient and market-focused. There was talk of extending share ownership, as with other privatisations. And there was the concept of freeing the railways from the yoke of Treasury control. But none of these are convincing given that the railways were a well-run state industry that would always be in need of government subsidy.

In fact, the drive to privatise largely came from the Treasury, whose hyperactive privatisation unit had run out of things to do as all the obvious targets had been sold off by the time Major became prime minister in 1990. A working group of ministers and civil servants, mostly from the Department of Transport and the Treasury, was established late in 1990 to decide on a blueprint for the privatisation of British Rail and the liberalisation of the rail market.

It is here that the decision that has done the most damage to the railway began to emerge. Although there were a number of different models, they can be categorised under two headings – integrated or fragmented. The adoption of an integrated model would have resulted in British Rail being sold to the private sector either as a whole or as a number of separate regional businesses, each running its own trains on its own lines. But the ideologues in the group – largely Treasury mandarins – wanted to go for fragmentation, which meant splitting off the track and infrastructure from the operations because this offered the potential for competition. They recognised that it was impossible to create competing tracks but felt that all other aspects of the railway should be opened up to competition.

The key idea was that there should be a separate 'track authority' (at that point it was still assumed that this would be BR or another state-owned company) which would provide the permanent way on which competing operating companies would bid for the right to run their trains, rather as private hauliers and bus companies pay road tax in exchange for the right to run competing services on motorways provided by the government. In the most extreme version of the model favoured by some Treasury thinkers, the train operators would even bid in monthly auctions for every individual train path to create real competition. Savour that thought for a moment; the concept would involve, say, the path for the 0800 from London to Newcastle being run by one company during that month, while the 0900 might be run by another; and then after the next auction, it could be the other way around. It was a serious suggestion that was only knocked on the head at a relatively late stage during one of the all-too-infrequent reality checks.

The Treasury, being the Treasury, also had another agenda in its sights – reducing subsidy. Averaging out the good years with the bad, the railways cost the government about £1bn per year, though, in the haphazard method of Treasury accounting, investment was lumped in with support for socially necessary routes. According to a BR board member of the time, the Treasury officials leading the privatisation drive, notably Steve (now Sir Steve) Robson who headed the privatisation unit, 'had no feel for the industry and wanted a track authority like there was no tomorrow. They thought the track authority would be free of subsidy and therefore all they'd be doing is subsidising services.'[5] This drive to save subsidy coloured all that was to follow because it resulted in a model designed to deliver reduced subsidy to a railway that was perceived as being in long-term decline.[6]

If responsibility can be attributed to any one individual for the model of privatisation eventually adopted, that person must be Robson. It was he who pushed through the track authority model, which made the rest of the debacle inevitable, and who managed to get mention of a track authority – 'one part of BR will continue to be responsible for all track and infrastructure' – into the Conservative Party manifesto for 1992. Another former BR board member[7] asked Robson how he managed to win all the arguments with the politicians, and Robson replied that all he had to do was point to the BR board, who were strongly in favour of the BR plc model – privatising BR as one company, which the Treasury saw as hopelessly monopolistic – and his view would prevail. It may seem unfair to suggest that a particular civil servant was responsible, and there are certainly competing claims. A third former BR board member[8] suggests that Sir Richard Wilson, then Robson's boss and later cabinet secretary, may have had responsibility for pushing the track authority model. And there is Sir Christopher Foster, a government adviser at the time of privatisation (as well as having been Barbara Castle's adviser in the late 1960s), who also wrote a seminal book on the privatisation of nationalised industries in 1992 and was on the board of Railtrack for its first six years.

However, the consensus shared by a large number of the people involved in the process is that Robson played the key role in driving through the model that was accepted by the government. He also, incidentally, later dreamt up the hugely controversial London Underground Public Private Partnership, the part-privatisation of the Tube which has proved to be an extremely expensive way of refurbishing the system and virtually unworkable.[9] Robson hated British Rail and its executives. He felt they were plotting against privatisation and this belief was reinforced by a story he tells about meeting Sir Bob Reid, the chairman of British Rail, by accident on a train. An 'old codger', a peer who had campaigned against privatisation, came up to them and, not knowing who Robson was, congratulated Sir Bob for having 'stuffed' the government in the debate and 'got over all the points you wanted to'.[10]

In one of his rare public forays, a panel discussion in September 2002 for a book on Japanese rail privatisation,[11] Robson outlined the aims of rail privatisation, which are worth setting out in detail in the context of the rest of this book. Robson says the motivation for privatisation was 'to improve efficiency and also to improve service to the users of the railways'. He felt there were four fundamental flaws in the state ownership model:

> First, there was a lack of clarity about the objectives of all enterprises in the state sector in the UK, and hence, there was no definition of success and so no real accountability for performance. The second problem was the interference in the activities of the enterprises by civil servants and politicians, which is obviously part of the lack of clarity of objectives. The third aspect was that the public sector generally in the UK is motivated by aversion to risk and this meant that it is motivated to avoid doing new and different things, so effectively it was motivated not to change. And finally, the finances of state enterprises in the UK are often constrained by the state's own fiscal position.

Robson went on to say that the improvement in customer service could only come about if there were competition: 'So we sought to create a structure for the railways which was not simply moving from the public sector to the private sector, but was also introducing, as far as possible, competition.' He was delighted with his subsequent efforts, oblivious to

the chaos and disarray he had caused: 'When we started the privatisation, British Rail was a monopoly employing about 120,000 people,
whereas at the end of the privatisation the only monopoly element was
Railtrack employing some 10,000 people. That was a fundamental part
of the process because it was seen as the way to get the most improvements in efficiency and customer service.'

Robson eventually left the Treasury in 2001 and admitted in an
interview in the *Financial Times*[12] that rail privatisation had not been an
unqualified success and that there were faults in the structure because
Railtrack's revenues were not tied to passenger numbers and the
operators were not given enough incentives to improve services: 'With
hindsight, that was a mistake.'

The Treasury struck at the right time. After the good times of the Lawson
boom, BR's finances collapsed in the early 1990s – the requirement for
government support rose from £700m to £2bn because of safety
expenditure resulting from the 1988 Clapham accident, the recession
which saw usage fall by 10 per cent and the costs of improvements to
lines leading to the Channel Tunnel.

The more cautious members of the Cabinet committee examining
privatisation wanted to retain a vertically integrated railway, and put
forward two alternative ways of dividing up British Rail: regionalisation,
which meant something like a return to the Big Four of 1923–48, and
sectorisation, the sale of the three passenger businesses created in the
1980s – InterCity, Network SouthEast and Regional Railways. These
suggestions, along with the idea of selling BR as one unit, were all
dismissed. It was felt that a BR plc would preclude any competition and
would not challenge the position of the strong, nationally organised trade
unions within the industry. Reducing the power of the trade unions was
one of the hidden motives for rail privatisation, expressed privately by
Tory ministers on many occasions but never boasted about in public.[13]
There was a history of bad industrial relations on the railways but while
there were some strikes, notably those over flexible rostering in 1982 and
pay in 1989, in fact there were many more threats of stoppages than actual
industrial action and the industry's record was better than the public
perception of it. In the run-up to full privatisation, however, there were a
series of one- or two-day strikes, including a series of stoppages by
signallers in 1994 which, unusually, attracted considerable public support.

Given the divergent views on the committee, it was hardly surprising that the conclusions in its report, presented to the Cabinet in mid-1991, were a compromise. The plan was to separate the infrastructure and operations on most of the railway, but to leave the London commuter area vertically integrated because the lines were full and therefore there was no scope for new entrants. The vision of the Tories that would inform the legislation was to see trains from different companies competing against each other on the same track. While in theory that sounded fine, once the logic of what was proposed began to be examined, it was patently unworkable and showed yet again just how little the architects of privatisation knew about how the rail network functions. The railway is not some kind of M1 for trains, because they have to run on tracks which have few passing loops and therefore services are greatly restricted by the availability of paths.

Although Major's Cabinet agreed the principles of the report, the secretary of state for transport, Malcolm Rifkind (the transport portfolio is a revolving door for politicians on the way up or down), began to have doubts about the model that had been suggested. He started to think that InterCity should also be a vertically integrated railway, which effectively meant that the track authority would be a hodgepodge of little-used lines that would be difficult to manage. According to one of the Treasury's privatisation team, 'Rifkind made heavy weather of whether InterCity should be vertically integrated. He was sulking in his tent and his officials hadn't been able to develop the idea [of how to privatise the railways].'[14] Downing Street then further muddied the waters by flying the kite of the regional model, which Major seemed to favour, once again. The Treasury felt this model was ridiculous as it was based on Major's strong nostalgia for the Britain of his youth, and had already rejected the idea because of the problems with trains which ran between different areas, thereby using other companies' tracks. This objection ignored the fact that well-established and workable arrangements had existed to deal with running over other companies' tracks when the railways had been in the private sector before 1948. In reality the Treasury's obsession with pushing for competition meant that no proper consideration was given to any model other than that requiring the separation of the permanent way from the rest of BR. Major was bought off with the promise that the franchises would be regional.

The Treasury also argued that 'Brussels' required such a separation and this claim was picked up and often cited by ministers at the time. Indeed, in the run-up to the 2001 election, the Tories, now somewhat embarrassed by their own privatisation of the railways, cited the European directive issued in 1991 as an excuse for breaking up the railways in that way. Tim Collins, a vice-chairman of the Conservative Party, said on BBC Radio 4's *Any Questions?*[15] that Major had wanted the Big Four model but had been prevented from introducing it by European rules:

> Separating track ownership from the responsibility for running the railway services ... was imposed by Europe rather than by the national government. What John Major wanted to do was to recreate the pre-World War II situation where you had four national companies who would have been responsible for the tracks and the signalling and the train services in those areas. He was not allowed to do that because of European regulations.

The notion of the thoroughly Eurosceptic government of John Major bowing to European *diktat* was always unconvincing, and Collins was rewriting history. Europe did indeed pass directive 91/440 just before Britain embarked on rail privatisation, which, in order to stimulate open-access competition, required railway infrastructure to be separated from operations. However, the separation needed only to be an accounting mechanism and the sole open-access operators who had to be accommodated were international freight ventures, and not, as the Tories implied, any Tom, Dick and Harry who fancied running a railway. Indeed, in the rest of Europe, state-owned companies like SNCF and Deutsche Bahn made only the minimum necessary accounting separation. A report[16] analysing the European directive and its implementation gives the lie to the Tories' excuse that they were forced into their model by Europe. The authors point out that the directive's requirements were limited to accounting procedures but that it provided the British government with 'an important resource to legitimate its risky undertaking', preparing the way for what the politicians wanted to do anyway. The difficulty for the government was 'the radical and experimental character [of the railway reform] which created considerable uncertainty and risk for political leaders'. Where better to lay the blame than Brussels, if anything went wrong?

According to the Treasury officials, Rifkind's dithering resulted in the loss of a year that should have been spent drawing up a detailed scheme to privatise the railways and this meant that the eventual scheme was implemented in much more haste than would otherwise have been the case. In order to find a coherent wording for the Conservative manifesto before the 1992 general election, Jonathan Hill, one of Major's advisers, 'walked round Whitehall saying, "We've got to have something in the manifesto on this,"' according to one official.[17] The eventual model of having a single track authority and a series of operators who held franchises to run groups of rail services seems to have been adopted at this point, although the Tory manifesto still kept options open by saying both that 'one part of BR will continue to be responsible for all track and infrastructure' and also that the new system would 'recapture the spirit of the old regional companies'.

Despite the radical but unspecific nature of the Tories' plans for Britain's beloved trains, there was precious little discussion of the railways during the April 1992 election campaign. Labour made very little play with the issue, and the media, expecting a Labour victory or at least a hung Parliament, did not examine the privatisation in any detail. This was fortunate for the Tories because, as we have seen, their scheme was not properly worked up and those senior ministers who had thought about the issue were hopelessly split over how to proceed.

After his surprise election victory, Major appointed yet another new transport secretary, John MacGregor, a pragmatic politician widely viewed in Westminster as a safe pair of hands. And so it proved, at least in the narrow sense of pushing through a controversial and unpopular policy. For the long-term future of the railways, however, he proved to be a hapless butterfingers. MacGregor realised that he had to act quickly. The imperative was to privatise the railways within the five-year Parliamentary term in order to ensure that the process was irreversible. The aim was even to try to ensure that the Tories could gain some electoral benefit from the privatisation, which meant that there was great pressure to get the sale process well under way within a couple of years of the election. Roger Freeman, the junior transport minister, talked of having privatised rail companies operating by 1994. In the event, the first privatised train ran two years later than that, but such wishful thinking demonstrated just how little ministers and their officials understood about the complexities of the railway industry. Moreover, the necessity to get things done quickly meant there was constant pressure to make decisions when there was insufficient knowledge on which to base them.

This haste was to colour the whole process and allow a deeply flawed model to be implemented, even though, as the process unfolded, many Tories realised that it was by no means an ideal solution.

In fact there was still time to stop the disastrous separation of track and operations. MacGregor had a meeting with Sir Bob Reid, the BR chairman and John Welsby, the chief executive, shortly after the election at the St Ermin's Hotel near St James's Park. Welsby argued cogently and powerfully for an integrated solution, saying that all the aims of privatisation could be achieved with the model that had been created through the Organising for Quality restructuring – except, of course, open access which would not really be possible if the same company owned the track and the services. Welsby stressed to MacGregor that his system was not going to work, but his pleas fell on deaf ears. A second meeting with BR's top twenty-seven managers was arranged and every one of them spoke against the proposal to separate the track from operations. Rather than listening to the professionals' advice, ministers were determined to ignore it and throughout the rest of the process of privatisation they never again asked for the views of BR managers – indeed, some consultants working on the project were barred from talking to BR.

Chris Green, a former InterCity and Network SouthEast director who later ran Virgin Trains, argues:

> The unique feature of rail privatisation is that the nature of the new structure was not decided by the experts working within the industry but by people from outside such as consultants, politicians and civil servants. They were acting out of a genuine desire to create economic freedom, competition and to break union power, though they could not say that publicly, and a belief that the industry was too big, unmanageable and inefficient.[18]

Amazingly, the civil servants at the Department of Transport knew that a completely flawed structure was being created. A decade later Sir Patrick Brown, the permanent secretary, told a BBC4 TV programme: 'I don't think any of us in the Department of Transport thought that open access as described could have any part in the privatisation. But you couldn't say so.'[19]

Indeed, civil servants do not rock the boat. Especially when, as Brown confessed, open access was a 'totem' for his colleagues in the Treasury. So Brown pushed on with a policy he and everyone in his department knew to be ridiculous, and as we shall see, unworkable. (Brown's scepticism over the model did not prevent him doing very well out of the privatisation as he has been on the board of Go Ahead, one of the companies which has obtained rail franchises, since 1999 and is currently its non-executive chairman.)

There was no time for the niceties of a Green Paper, the consultative document which normally precedes a White Paper for such an important policy. Instead, realising he had been left with the task of implementing a policy for which there was no blueprint, MacGregor quickly cobbled together a White Paper called *New Opportunities for the Railways* which was published in July 1992. It was a thin, badly drafted and inadequate document which outlined, in very broad terms, the way the industry would be privatised. It set out, for the first time, the concept of franchising – inviting different operators to bid for the right to run a set of services for a fixed period – but with just 100 short paragraphs it begged more questions than it answered. The paper explained that franchises were to be based on the provision of minimum service levels and quality standards, and that BR would continue running those services for which no bidder was found, a recognition that ministers were terrified that there would be insufficient private-sector interest. In launching the document, MacGregor said there was no 'universal template' for a franchise, as this would depend on the requirements of the private sector. More worryingly, he refused to rule out the possibility of closures and gave no assurances that the rail network would be preserved in its existing form.

While the White Paper promised that 'network benefits' – such as through-ticketing and a national timetable – would be retained, it then contradicted itself on the next page, which said: 'It will be for train service operators to make arrangements to accept each others' tickets.' In other words, the operators could choose not to, which would have broken up the whole network. Moreover, there was no guarantee that the various railcards such as those for pensioners, young people and off-peak travellers in the south-east would be retained, though the government said it believed 'operators will find it in their commercial interest to offer a range of discounted fares and travelcards'.

A separate company (which later became Railtrack) would be set up within BR to take over ownership of the track and related facilities and to collect the track charges paid by the train operating companies; like the other quasi-monopoly industries it would be regulated by an independent regulator who would ensure that the various operators were treated fairly by Railtrack and who would set the charges they paid. Another new regulatory body, the Office of Passenger Rail Franchising (OPRAF), would be created to manage the business of letting the franchises to the train operating companies. Most of the services the franchisees would be operating were expected, initially at least, to be loss-making and it was OPRAF's job to negotiate with bidders to see which would offer the best deal – i.e. accept the lowest level of subsidy.

Obviously, if franchises were to be let for a limited period, the train operators would not be willing to buy their own rolling stock – what would they do with the trains which have a working life of at least thirty years if they lost their franchise after, say, just seven? Separate rolling-stock companies (later dubbed roscos) would therefore be set up within BR and subsequently sold to the private sector. They would take over the existing rolling stock and lease it, first to the existing BR profit centres and then, after privatisation, to the new train operating companies. The engineering companies, responsible for maintenance and renewals within BR, were also to be hived off into separate businesses which would again be sold off to the private sector. As for freight, the idea was to create three principal competing companies, as well as a separate container business and another which ran the overnight mail trains. All five were to be sold off separately, though in the event all but the container business were bought by the same US railroad, Wisconsin Central.

The spurious emphasis on competition remained. The franchises were to 'be designed, wherever possible, to provide scope for competition'. Even more radically, the White Paper specifically suggested allowing open access to the rail network for any private company that wanted to operate trains. Despite the fact that this notion was patently unworkable, the structure of privatisation and the legislation that created it were very much built around the idea of open access. It was a blueprint for a madcap free-for-all on the railways based on a complete lack of understanding that the network was an integrated system with coordination and cooperation, rather than competition, as its bedrock. As a civil servant who went to Brussels frequently during this period to explain the ideas to his European counterparts said, 'I spent the whole time emphasising that the railways were a business and not a service. I was met with blank incomprehension.'[20]

The outline scheme set out in the White Paper was much more radical than the model eventually adopted and some of the former ministers who drew up the plan now claim that this was part of the political game. Fly a kite about killing all the first born, and then, following the resultant outcry, say that you will only bump off one in ten and you will sound almost reasonable. Thus many of the more ridiculous aspects of the scheme were dropped as the legislation was dragged through Parliament and then implemented. For example, transport minister Roger Freeman suggested at first that there would be thirty-five or forty franchises, in order to maximise the potential for competition, but this was later reduced to twenty-five, largely based on BR's existing profit centres, because of the sheer complexity of dividing up the railway into so many parts. The notion of selling off stations separately by creating a Stations Authority was also quickly dropped.[21] The possibility of allowing the private sector to determine whether the various railcards were retained proved too unpopular, and guarantees that they would be kept had to be provided. Ticket interavailability, a key plank of the network, was also retained in the face of widespread opposition to its withdrawal, but operators were given the right to issue cheaper tickets for use exclusively on their own trains.

These retreats were helped along by a guerrilla movement from within BR. Key papers outlining the battier aspects of the plans kept on being leaked to the media. One BR member of staff said:

> There were certainly some active attempts to sabotage privatisation by middle managers within BR. I came across a number of confidential privatisation papers circulating about fare levels and the impact on through and multi-modal tickets. These, when leaked (and they all implied fare rises and loss of multi-operator tickets), were, I think, instrumental in forcing the Tory government to regulate real fares downwards reversing the trend they had applied on BR. The movement to save the London Travelcard was greatly helped by a document, the revelation of which obliged Steve Norris [the junior transport minister] to guarantee its future by making it a franchise requirement.[22]

Indeed, fares regulation was one of the great victories for opponents of the privatisation. The original plan had been to regulate fares only where train operators had a virtual monopoly – such as on the London commuting routes and in rural areas – but ministers were keen to make privatisation more palatable and eventually, late in the process, a scheme to regulate season tickets, savers and some other fares was implemented as a sop to passengers. It was a marked reversal from BR's policy of using fares to restrict growth but, as with all aspects of privatisation, the implications for the economics of the railway were not thought through.

After a series of very confused messages from the government, which resulted in ministers contradicting their own civil servants at a Commons committee hearing, John MacGregor was forced to concede what any A-level economics student could have told him – open access was not compatible with the idea of selling franchises. Steve Norris, the sharpest of the transport ministers, had understood this straight away:

> It was clear that no franchise for train operations could be let unless there were guarantees about where the potential revenue came from. If there were the prospect that any other operator could come along and cherry-pick the best bits, you've destroyed the basis on which you can make the bid.[23]

Norris adds that one consequence of total open access would, of course, have been much higher levels of subsidy for loss-making routes. The other objection to competition is that people do not want to be saddled with a ticket that is not useable on some trains. They do not care who the operator is – they just want to get on the first train heading for their destination.

But Norris's colleagues were slower to cotton on to these contradictions. It was not until January 1993, when the Railways Bill was already in Parliament, that MacGregor realised somewhat belatedly that a free-for-all on the railways was both impractical and had the same potential to cause chaos as it had in the bus industry. He announced to a railfreight conference, 'If some franchises have to be exclusive in whole or in part, then they will be made so.'[24] There was, however, no explanation about how what came to be called 'moderation of competition' would be achieved. Instead, the buck was passed to the first rail regulator, John Swift QC, who was appointed in January 1993. He recalls that in his initial meeting with officials he asked: since Railtrack was a monopoly and it was being proposed to moderate competition, how was he supposed to fulfil that part of his remit which was to 'promote competition'? Swift relates, rather amusingly, that the permanent secretary asked the deputy secretary who in turn put the matter to the under-secretary, who mumbled something about it being 'a question of time'.[25]

After much consultation and backroom negotiation, Swift came up with a system which prevented Railtrack from selling train paths for journeys already provided by an existing operator. This was supposed to be relaxed in stages over the next six years but it was clear that this could only be done in a very limited way (and, in any case, Labour, which took over in 1997, showed no interest in promoting on-rail competition). This was essentially a tacit admission that the whole basis for the creation of the complex model that involved separating the track from the operations was a mistake. Open access, the Treasury's totem, was quietly dropped from the agenda. The policy that justified the railways being broken up would now not be implemented. As John Welsby later put it, 'all the operational and managerial problems that derived from splitting off the infrastructure from the operations were being incurred for no benefit'.[26] It is a scandal for which the Treasury officials like Robson and the Tory ministers such as MacGregor have never been held to account.

John Prescott, Labour's transport spokesman, spotted the contradiction straight away: 'If the [government's] proposals will not lead to competition in the provision of services ... instead of the public monopoly about which the government are so concerned, we shall have what the secretary of state calls "exclusive service" – in other words a private monopoly.'[27] But Labour nevertheless held back from trying to wreck the legislation.

The process of blunting the sharper edges of the policy continued throughout the Bill's passage through Parliament and the subsequent detailed implementation of the policy. The Bill, in fact, was widely criticised for providing few details as to how privatisation would work in practice. Oddly, it made no specific mention of Railtrack because the government was still hedging its bets over what sort of model would eventually emerge and the door was being left open to have vertical integration in some areas. Eventually, with the exception of the tiny Island Line on the Isle of Wight, this idea was dropped. The gaps in the Railways Bill demonstrated yet again the extent to which ministers were making it up as they were going along.

The government did not have a monopoly on daft ideas. In January 1995 John Swift, the rail regulator, came up with the notion that there should only be a requirement for operators to sell through tickets at 294 core stations rather than the 1,300 where tickets were currently available. The press quickly picked up the issue and Swift was ridiculed in Parliament by Labour's shadow transport secretary, Michael Meacher (who took over from Prescott in 1993), who pointed out: 'Under the regulator's proposals, there will be an 88-mile stretch between Salisbury and Exeter, with Yeovil at its centre, with no core station. Thus a passenger wishing to travel from Yeovil to Birmingham will have to detour to Bristol or to Swindon to get a through ticket.'[28] Swift denied that this had been his intention and rapidly abandoned the notion of core stations. The episode demonstrated the ease with which opponents of privatisation could inflict political damage and showed Swift the perils of the treacherous minefield into which he had ventured.

Despite growing awareness that the Bill was deeply ill-considered, and the almost universal opposition, there was no question of the Tories abandoning what was now so obviously a flawed piece of legislation. They fought tooth and nail to push the Railways Bill through Parliament. It had a stormy passage; indeed, had it not been for the untimely death in the summer of 1993 of a key Tory opponent, Robert Adley, the Bill might not have got through without major changes. Adley, an old railway buff with a deep knowledge of the system, was a formidable opponent in a key position and his untimely demise was a major piece of good fortune for the government. The man who had coined the term 'poll tax on wheels',[29] widely picked up in the media, he was the chair of the Commons transport committee, which produced a couple of reports that were surprisingly damning for a Tory-dominated group commenting on a key Conservative policy. The interim report produced in January got right to the heart of the contradiction over franchising and open access and may well have prompted MacGregor to drop the latter. The final report, in April, raised the fundamental point that the government had not set out how it saw the railway's role within the context of its wider transport policy.

The committee also expressed fears about fare rises and recommended that they should be regulated and tied to the rate of inflation. Surprisingly, this was later agreed by the chancellor, Kenneth Clarke, despite the fact that it meant that operators had to be offered higher subsidies before they could be persuaded to take on the franchises. Key fares such as the saver return and season tickets were controlled, a move which, again, was part of the process of buying off the opposition to what became the most unpopular of all the privatisations.

The prospect of line closures, too, was dropped in order to soothe the opposition. The Bill introduced a closure procedure that was even more tortuous than the legislation it replaced. The difficulty of trying to make even small cuts to the timetable within the context of privatisation was demonstrated early on when Roger Salmon, the head of the Office of Passenger Rail Franchising (OPRAF), made the mistake of trying to shut down a service, which served only to inflame the opposition to the whole privatisation process. He had identified the sleeper services to Fort William as deeply loss-making and barely used, calculating that the subsidy amounted to £450 per passenger – a figure that was widely challenged – and announced, in an unnecessarily provocative gesture, that he would not include these trains as part of the franchise process. In other words, there would be no subsidy available to pay for them.

It was just the sort of move that the opposition had been waiting for. A variety of pressure groups, backed by much of the media (including *The Times*, whose correspondent dubbed the train the Deerstalker Express because it was used by the gentry going to the Highlands on shooting trips), rallied around the cause and initiated a legal challenge.

Salmon, a political tyro, was trying to convince the Treasury of his credentials as a careful disbursor of government funds:

> One of the signals I wanted to give the Treasury and everyone else was that we were going to run this thing with some sort of coherent and sensible basis, and my thinking at the time was that if we conceded to the Scottish lobby over Fort William, how could we ever say no to anyone else wanting their local service?[30]

And so it proved. The attempt to scrap the service was lost in the courts on a technicality and Salmon quietly coughed up the extra subsidy in exchange for a revamped service. The row showed that, given the public's hostility and distrust regarding privatisation, it was impossible for the government to use the process to make cuts in services. The skirmish also highlighted the way that rational discussion of rail services had become impossible. The carriage of a few affluent but heavily subsidised visitors – the service is too expensive for locals – had no transport or social relevance. That is why wider questions, such as whether the affluent south-east commuters should benefit from subsidised rail services, were never discussed. Even the Treasury understood the lesson of the Deerstalker Express and, as we shall see below, greased the path to privatisation with large amounts of extra cash.*

*A similar battle was brewing in summer 2005 over the planned scrapping of the Paddington–Penzance sleeper service.

After that little fiasco, Salmon retrenched and did not try to cut any services. He did face a more important legal action, however, which nearly scuppered the whole process. The draft franchise contracts virtually replicated the existing timetable on all loss-making routes. Privatisation, therefore, far from threatening marginal services, enshrined them in stone at great cost to the taxpayer. On profitable services, however, the required frequencies were reduced, since Salmon argued that the service would be safeguarded by the self-interest of the operators who would wish to run as many trains as possible in order to maximise revenue. He was challenged by a union-backed group called Save Our Railways, which won a partial victory in court in late 1995, just before the announcement of the letting of the first franchises. The court setback required a rapid redrafting of the regulations by the new transport secretary, Sir George Young, but did not cause any further delay to the privatisation timetable. As it turned out, Salmon was right. The profit-making services, principally InterCity, did not need protection as operators have increased the number of trains since privatisation, quite dramatically on lines with some spare capacity such as Midland Mainline out of St Pancras and GNER out of King's Cross.

Robert Adley's death in the summer of 1993 removed the lynchpin of the Tory MPs' opposition to rail privatisation and, without a leader, their campaign subsequently waned. Given the tiny Parliamentary majority, MacGregor had been forced to spend a lot of time in the lobbies and bars of the Commons persuading sceptical Conservative MPs that the privatisation proposals were sound, but it proved to be more difficult to win over the Tory peers. Opposition on the Conservative benches was remarkably widespread, with even that old right-winger and former transport minister Nicholas Ridley, now elevated to the Lords, expressing doubts about the feasibility of the project, with a Delphic pronouncement in an article in the *Evening Standard*: 'I do not believe it is possible to privatise the railways. Nor does the government.'[31]

Oddly, opposition in the Lords centred on the right of British Railways Board to bid for franchises. A former transport minister, Lord Peyton, moved an amendment to this effect but ministers were opposed because they felt it would reduce interest from the private sector. In a cunning political coup pulled out of the bag just as defeat in the Lords seemed inevitable, the government granted this concession subject to the discretion of the franchising director. Since the franchising director was a creature of government who acted under the instruction of ministers, this was a rather dishonest ruse, but Peyton and his allies were fooled. They must have felt stupid when, later, Salmon began to let the franchises and simply barred any bids from BR.

The Labour opposition did not distinguish itself during the privatisation battle. It was easy for the party to capitalise on the public opposition and its string of spokespeople during that Parliament – Prescott, Michael Meacher, Brian Wilson, Clare Short and Andrew Smith – made all the appropriate noises and pressed the right buttons. Remarkably, Tony Blair was even moved to make one of his most radical-sounding speeches when he promised to restore a 'publicly accountable, publicly owned railway', and yet, when asked precisely what this meant and whether a major renationalisation was on the agenda, he prevaricated.

BR's position throughout this process was hopelessly muddled. As we have seen, there were some insiders trying to sabotage the process but, according to one, they were in a minority: 'Most people protect their own backsides. Only a very small proportion of us made any real contribution, but some were in quite influential positions.'[32] This individual feels that most of BR's senior staff agreed with him privately:

> I had made my position as a dissident known to John Welsby [the chief executive] and Bob Reid [the chairman]. In effect they agreed with me, saying the proposed structure was not one they supported, but as it was government policy, it was their duty to work with it and try to get pragmatic changes made. The only alternative was resignation, and that they felt would play into the government's hands as they would be replaced by people less experienced and more compliant, to the further detriment of the industry. I am not sure I agree with their analysis, as I think their resignations would have severely shaken the process.

In fact, the government had long lost faith in Sir Bob Reid (the second incumbent of that name) but the departure of Welsby, who was eventually very helpful in smoothing the path to privatisation, might have held up its progress.

As we have seen, British Rail was in an optimistic phase. It had sorted out its structure and there were a lot of very good senior managers running the railway. Sir Bob Reid was himself strongly opposed to the way that privatisation was evolving, even though he had been appointed by Cecil Parkinson from the private sector (Shell) to oversee the sale. Sir

Bob favoured a much more gradual approach, involving the contracting out of all peripheral activity, such as renewal and maintenance, while leaving the core service in the hands of the public sector. He even went on radio to express his doubts, causing a furore, but although the tone of his remarks implied extreme disenchantment with the process, he remained in his post for the reasons cited above.

Most BR staff were implacably opposed to privatisation, not just out of fear of redundancy, but also because of a genuine belief that the plans would be bad for the railways. Others, however, saw the potential for making money out of privatisation through management buy-outs which were actively encouraged by the government. Indeed, it is remarkable that the railways kept running during the run-up to the sell-off given how many managers were drawing up management buy-out plans while simultaneously running services as well as restructuring the railway for privatisation. The unions, too, made little real fuss. They fought pitched battles over pensions and staff travel, but did not make any real attempt to stop the process, not least because ASLEF, the drivers' union, quickly realised that it was on to a winner.

The civil servants at the Department of Transport and their ministers felt that BR was being obstructive and quickly decided to ignore any arguments put forward at meetings by BR's managers, thus ensuring that the eventual structure failed to take into account the needs of the railway. There was, indeed, a bias against using anyone with railway expertise in the process. The regulator, Swift, and the head of OPRAF, Salmon, were both outsiders with no railway experience – a competition lawyer and a merchant banker respectively – and railway staff appeared to have been systematically excluded from the appointment process for these posts. Whenever expertise or advice was needed, consultants were called in. According to a Parliamentary answer,[33] a staggering £450m was spent just by the government on consultants (not including the amounts paid out by BR and Railtrack) during the run-up to privatisation and many of these consultants had no prior knowledge of the industry. It was a case of the blind advising the deaf.

There were some real opportunities for Labour to stop the whole process had it really wanted to do so. If the party's spokespeople had, unequivocally, said that the railways would be returned to public hands, then privatisation would have been stopped in its tracks. Labour was consistently ahead in the opinion polls throughout the 1992–7 parliament and private-sector investors would certainly have been deterred by such a threat. Moreover, popular opinion was clearly against privatisation.

In fact, thanks to Labour's posturing coupled with inaction the taxpayer got the worst of both worlds. Clare Short, the shadow transport secretary, warned, 'Anyone contemplating bidding for any part of the rail network should know that there will be no gravy train for fat cats out of this one and that Labour intends that the rail system should remain in public ownership.'[34] This deterred bidders for the lucrative rolling-stock companies (roscos), the first major part of British Rail to be put up for sale, and significantly reduced the amount of money which was obtained from their disposal. Indeed, Short's sidekick, Brian Wilson, even gloated when NatWest, a bidder for the rolling-stock companies, pulled out: 'I warmly welcome this decision by NatWest which I am sure other key investors will follow. Labour's message is that they should stay clear of this high risk and totally unwanted privatisation.'[35]

This guerrilla war on the privatisation process would have been perfectly valid if Labour had really intended to stop the sale. But it did not. New Labour, as it was now calling itself, wanted to distance itself from its old image of being hostile to the private sector. The crunch moment came during the sale of Railtrack (described in the next chapter) scheduled for the spring of 1996, when there was a genuine opportunity to undermine the process fatally. In the run-up to the sale, Labour's transport team, led by Short together with Prescott, Geoff Norris from Tony Blair's office, Lord Williams of Elvel and Andrew Smith from Gordon Brown's team, cooked up a scheme to stop the flotation of Railtrack. The plan was simple. Labour would announce that, once in office, it would swap Railtrack's shares for preference shares, which, like bonds, only pay a fixed rate of interest, rather than dividends that depend on the company's performance. Williams had checked out the scheme with City experts who pronounced it watertight. But it had to be inserted into the Railtrack sales prospectus that was to be issued in May and Gordon Brown vetoed the idea because it represented a public expenditure commitment. Interestingly, following the collapse in value of Railtrack's shares after the Hatfield accident in October 2000, the chairman of the company, John Robinson, privately suggested a similar idea to the government.

Labour's cries of 'wolf' had, however, cost the taxpayer dear. The three roscos had taken over all of BR's 11,260 locomotives and coaches and represented about half of BR's assets. But their sale turned out to be deeply disappointing, with very few bidders coming forward despite a massive and expensive round-the-world sales pitch by Hambros, the merchant bankers in charge of the marketing operation. Partly this was a result of Labour's opposition which the politically naive City and, in particular, the large American leasing companies, unable to spot a bit of grandstanding, wrongly perceived as a genuine threat.

Sandy Anderson led the management buy-out team for the £526m purchase of Porterbrook which, only six months later, was sold to Stagecoach for £300m more, allowing him to pocket around £40m for a personal investment of just £120,000. He is in no doubt as to who to thank for his good fortune: 'If anybody says to me, why was I able to get Porterbrook so cheap, I say I'd like to thank the Labour Party.'[36]

Anderson is being a bit glib because, despite Labour's dishonesty, the main culprits were, of course, the Tories who cut a lot of corners to ensure that the roscos were sold quickly. They had been desperate to boost their rail privatisation programme with a big sale in order to show that it could be done. Moreover, the rolling-stock companies, along with Railtrack, represented the Treasury's best chance of obtaining a substantial chunk of cash for the public purse. But selling quickly, as the subsequent National Audit Office (NAO) report into the sale demonstrated, would result in a lower sale price. One reason was that the bidders would not know who their customers were going to be since the franchises would not have been let, although if the City whizz-kids had been cannier, they would have realised that most of the rentals were guaranteed by the government in any case. Another was that the roscos had only just been carved out of BR and divided up arbitrarily into three companies in order to provide competition, and therefore they had no proven financial track record to provide a basis on which bidders could determine a price. To compound this uncertainty the government never even bothered to obtain up-to-date valuations for the three roscos because, according to the Department of Transport, this was impossible, a view challenged strongly by the NAO.

By the completion of the bidding process there were only four companies in the race – three management buy-out teams and one outsider, GRS Holding Company, a consortium including Babcock and Brown. Although the NAO says Hambros managed to keep the lack of bidders secret, there were rumours flying around the industry and this absence of competition must have affected the eventual price. In the event, the three roscos went for £1.8bn in early 1996, and within two years all had been resold for a total of over £2.65bn. The NAO estimated that even on moderate assumptions about the state of the market, the Department should have been able to get £2.5bn – £700m more than was obtained. The requirement that no company should be allowed to buy more than one Rosco meant that GRS's higher bid for Porterbrook had to be rejected, at a cost to the taxpayer of £55m.

The roscos were highly profitable because they had been deliberately fattened up to make them sellable, a strategy which became a consistent feature of the rail privatisation process, used, for example, in the sale of Railtrack and the thirteen companies which maintained and renewed the track (see next chapter). The fact that, in the longer term, this meant extra subsidy and cost to rail travellers was irrelevant. The Tory government was only interested in short-term capital receipts rather than in the long-term financial viability of the industry, let alone any wider considerations such as the need to boost rail travel for environmental reasons and to reduce congestion on the roads.

The flawed sale of the roscos was the greatest scandal of privatisation in terms of cost to the taxpayer but cannot be blamed entirely on the politicians. It also exposed the weakness of the market for rail companies, none of which, by definition, had any independent financial record. The sale demonstrated the City's wariness of new markets and its failure to understand that the roscos were an excellent deal with a guaranteed income flow and virtually no risk. The aspect which had most concerned the City was the fact that the leases were relatively short while trains have a thirty- to forty-year life-span. Potential backers were worried about what would happen when the leases ran out. They did not understand that since the trains had to keep on running, the train operators would most likely sign new leases – there was not likely to be a supply of idle trains waiting for someone to come along and lease them. Instead, in estimating the worth of the roscos, many City firms simply assumed that the trains had only a token value at the end of their leases. This 'residual risk' problem dogged the whole sale and reduced the number of bidders. In fact the roscos were terrific bargains at the prices achieved, even if the residual values were assumed to be zero.

*

Despite the failings of the rosco sale and the paucity of bidders, with £1.8bn in the bag, the government felt sufficiently confident to go full out on the sale of the twenty-five rail franchises. Three sets of lines – Great Western, South West Trains and London, Tilbury and Southend (LTS) – had been selected as the first to be sold. Although the government claimed that thirty-eight potential purchasers had prequalified, many of these were no-hopers going along for the ride and, in fact, there were very few solid bidders for these initial franchises. While the transport secretary, Brian Mawhinney, who took over briefly from MacGregor, was gung-ho in public, saying the high number 'was a vote of confidence in rail privatisation', behind the scenes, according to Roger Salmon, the franchising director, there was a state of panic: 'We were short of bidders. There was a terror that there were not going to be enough bidders, like with the roscos.'[37]

The sale of the roscos had little public impact and the government was in a desperate hurry to get the franchising process going to demonstrate to the electorate that privatisation would become a reality. MacGregor had said, rashly, that half the railway would be franchised by April 1996. This was an empty politician's promise based on unfounded optimism and the forlorn hope that there could still be benefits of privatisation to present to the voters at the next election. The impossible target led to a major rift between Salmon and ministers, who felt he was not moving quickly enough. Indeed, only ministers' concern that sacking Salmon would delay the process prevented them from showing him the door. In the event, Salmon, sick of the pressure from ministers, announced his departure as soon as the franchising process was under way.

Opposition to the whole process continued unabated, putting ministers under continued pressure. The official watchdog, the clumsily named Central Rail Users Consultative Committee which represented passengers' interests, was very wary of the whole privatisation process and, in his swansong, the outgoing chairman, the steadfastly non-political Major-General Lennox Napier, said that while he did not oppose privatisation, the model chosen by the government was wrong and financial problems were likely to arise: 'So I end rather looking at a pantomime. Pantomimes should have a happy ending. At the moment there isn't a Prince Charming called Finance or Investment yet in the script.'[38] Sir George Young, who as transport secretary was responsible for appointing Napier's successor, was incensed and hit back, arguing, 'Privatisation offers the opportunity for stronger investment and better services.'

Given this political climate, ministers were so terrified by the prospect of not having any interest from business that they gave special incentives to encourage the management buy-out teams to bid. Despite much behind-the-scenes arm-twisting among supporters of the Tories, the major players in the City and industry could not be induced to bid. Even companies in other transport industries which the government had hoped to attract, such as the airlines and shipping companies, largely stayed out of the process because they saw it as too complex and unremunerative.

The government was, however, saved by the bus companies created, as we have seen, by the Tories' own mid-1980s privatisation. Stagecoach in particular was prepared to go where others feared to tread and was richly rewarded with a highly profitable franchise, South West Trains. Created by a buccaneering and aggressive brother-and-sister team from Perth, Brian Souter and Ann Gloag, Stagecoach had earlier had its fingers burnt over rail privatisation when it tried to launch Stagecoach Rail, the first private main-line trains in fifty years, which offered cheap seats for overnight travellers between London and Scotland. The initiative had failed miserably, partly because of lack of cooperation from BR, but principally because of a severe misreading of the market. Undeterred, Stagecoach, which along with the French conglomerate CGEA was the only substantial outside bidder for the first franchises, ultimately bid for them all, though very conservatively, which meant the only other one it acquired was the tiny Island Line on the Isle of Wight.[39]

The first three franchises were eventually put out to tender in May 1995, and in November that year news leaked out that they would go to Resurgence Railways (Great Western), Stagecoach (South West Trains) and the management buy-out team (LTS). In the event, of these three operators, only one, Stagecoach, finally took over its franchise, compounding the sense that the privatisation process was spinning out of control. Resurgence quickly fell away when the company, a start-up venture created by a Thatcherite former BR freight manager, Mike Jones, failed to obtain the required bank guarantees. It was not helped by a report in the *Financial Times* revealing that its finance director had headed up a double-glazing firm that had gone bust. The franchise had to be hastily awarded to the under-bidder, the management buy-out team which had backing from FirstBus (later renamed FirstGroup).

The media coverage remained implacably hostile, with much fun being made of the fact that the first privatised train due to run, early on Sunday 4 February 1996, was, in fact, a bus running on a substitute service for Great Western. And it got worse for the government when, just as the management team for LTS was about to take over, an auditor uncovered a petty little scam that involved creaming off revenue from London Transport to the nascent rail company. This was leaked to the BBC by one of BR's fifth columnists in time to maximise embarrassment for the government. Sir George Young, the patrician aristocrat who had replaced the universally disliked Brian Mawhinney as transport secretary, had no choice but to pull the plug on the management buy-out team's deal and relaunch the whole bidding process for the line.

The collapse of Resurgence and the LTS fiasco meant there was a miasma of sleaze which so infected the privatisation process that the government never managed to clear the air. Nor did Stagecoach's reputation help matters. The company's already dreadful image was made worse by the publication of a 1995 MMC report on its activities in Darlington, where Stagecoach had run free buses that had proved the final straw in bankrupting the ailing but long-established local municipal firm. The MMC described this practice as 'deplorable, predatory and against the public interest'.

Despite the constant mantra from Sir George Young, who described every franchise announcement as 'great news for the taxpayer and for passengers', there was only one criterion for determining the winning bid – the lowest level of subsidy being demanded by the bidder. Stagecoach's success on SWT set the tone. The OPRAF press release struggled to say anything exciting about it and merely mentioned a couple of bus links, a tighter passenger's charter and 'improved customer information on stations'. A few franchisees, like Midland Mainline, made some obvious improvements, such as doubling the number of trains between London and Leicester, but there was no overall strategy or any attempt to try to boost numbers using the railways.

The process speeded up in 1996 and the machine which Salmon created became adept at letting out the franchises. Encouraged by Stagecoach's involvement, other established companies like Sea Containers and National Express successfully entered the fray, while Prism, another start-up created specially to bid for franchises, picked up four.

Most of the franchises were for seven years, a compromise between the Treasury, which had wanted very short ones, and the bidders, who had lobbied government for much longer terms in order to provide stability (and profits). A few of the deals, requiring the leasing of new rolling stock, were for periods of up to fifteen years but the franchisees were not otherwise committed to provide any investment. Indeed, the train operating companies bear little resemblance to other transport businesses: they do not own the rolling stock, the stations or the track, merely having a licence to run services for the duration of their contract. They had no incentive to invest, nor to provide any extra services beyond those which could be squeezed out of their existing rolling stock.

The one truly exciting scheme was for the West Coast Main Line but this had needed a total refurbishment in any case. However, Virgin had bravely signed up for a deal which meant that by the year 2012, rather than receiving £76m in subsidy (as it did in 1997/8), it would be paying the Exchequer £227m (in 1997/8 prices) for the right to run main-line services along the route. There were to be new trains on a completely refurbished track but the deal, as outlined in detail in Chapter 15, was a chimera and would prove to be very expensive for taxpayers. It was always unlikely that Virgin would pay that amount in premium which, in any case, would have represented a tax on rail use, something which the government was supposed to be promoting. It was a marked contrast to the near-identical service on the East Coast Main Line whose franchisee would not be paying a large premium.[40]

The contracts all required subsidy levels to decline over time in this way, putting enormous pressure on the operators to cut costs even though BR, as we have seen, was relatively efficient. Cutting staff was, therefore, essential and many middle managers found themselves redundant, a loss to the railway that would later affect performance. Frontline staff were cut, too, which meant that far from enjoying the promised improvements, some passengers found that even more stations became unstaffed.

Labour had a final opportunity to stop the franchise process at this stage and retain at least part of the railway in public ownership. Most of these late franchises involved Passenger Transport Executives in the large conurbations like West Yorkshire, Greater Manchester and Tyne and Wear, which funded commuter and suburban services (through government grants). OPRAF could not have let these franchises without the agreement of the PTEs, which were all Labour-controlled. Given that negotiations stretched into early 1997 with the increasingly desperate OPRAF officials making more and more generous offers, it would not have taken much for the local Labour politicians to sabotage the deals or delay the process until the election, which had to be held that spring. But they were under instruction from Andrew Smith, who had inherited the shadow transport role from Clare Short, to reach accommodations on the best possible terms because Labour did not want to be saddled with a hybrid railway after the election.

After the initial reluctance of many companies to bid, the later franchises, much to the delight of ministers, were the subject of fierce competition as more players entered the fray, seeing the opportunity to make what they felt would be easy money. They made a classic mistake, however. The later franchises were mainly those that required the most subsidy, covering regional and rural lines. Most of the income, therefore, came from the taxpayer; but OPRAF, under orders from the Treasury, nevertheless built sharply declining levels of subsidy into these franchises. This was to cause problems for several operators (see Chapter 6).

Most of the twenty-five franchises went to bus companies whose focus was on managing declining businesses through cutting costs and staff and who overestimated the similarity between the two industries. Only three management buy-out teams managed to get a stake in a franchise, the rest being defeated by their lack of access to cheap capital. However, most of the managers who led unsuccessful bids were retained by the new franchises because of their experience of running trains. Therefore it is hardly surprising that there was very little of the much-promised innovation which the Tories said privatisation would bring to the railways and few benefits to passengers, apart from the ubiquitous – and often horribly garish – new liveries for the trains.

There had also been a damaging hiatus in new train orders, a gap of nearly three years, which not only caused massive financial hardship to the rolling stock manufacturers but also meant that many older trains in desperate need of replacement were still running on the tracks.

The biggest irony was that, in order to coax through the privatisation of the railways, the Treasury was prepared to throw money at them and double the initial subsidy paid to the train operators in order to ensure that private companies would take them on. The figures are somewhat difficult to decipher because the proceeds from privatisation are not separately listed in the government accounts but were merely used to offset grants from the Treasury; but in broad terms the grant to British Rail in 1993/4, the last year before the break-up of the railway in preparation for privatisation, was £1.1bn, which almost doubled to £2.16bn the following year.

Under the franchise plans the level of subsidy was scheduled to drop to just under £1bn by 2002/3 but the Labour government's ten-year transport plan, announced in the summer of 2000, reversed that decline and, indeed, promised unprecedented levels of financial support for the industry. Given that several rail operators had already got into trouble meeting their financial targets even before the Hatfield accident and its aftermath, it is doubtful that those 'savings' were ever realistic, but they looked good enough on paper to allow the Tories to argue that privatisation saved money in the long term (see Chapter 12 for a fuller assessment of the financial impact of privatisation). BR managers were incensed by the level of largesse disbursed to smooth the path for privatisation, arguing that had they been given this amount of money, they would have been able to create a modernised railway without the disruption engendered by privatisation.

Ministers were too concerned with ensuring that the whole edifice was broken up and sold in time for the 1997 election to bother much about the short-term financial effects or the long-term robustness of the structure they were creating. The fact that they succeeded in disposing of the railway so quickly was, in many respects, a remarkable achievement since it was the most complex of all the privatisations. However, any chances of making political capital out of the sale – which had always been pretty thin anyway – were lost when Stagecoach, which had taken over the South West Trains franchise, found it had allowed too many drivers to claim redundancy and started cancelling hundreds of trains. The debacle started in February 1997, just as the prospect of a general election was heating up the political climate. Over the next two months, the company was forced to cancel 2,000 trains and, instead of apologising, the Stagecoach chairman, Brian Souter, poured petrol on the fire by suggesting that some of his customers had nothing better to do than write letters of complaint in office time and wondered whether their bosses knew they were doing this.[41] The new franchising director, John O'Brien, threatened to fine the company £1m, and passengers even staged a takeover of a train being taken out of service. Eventually

Stagecoach managed to wriggle out of paying the fine because the enforcement regime was so weak, but the political damage had been done.

The early part of the franchising process was proving unpropitious. But this did not deter the Tories from proceeding with the even more controversial sale of Railtrack, an episode that would prove to be a complete disaster.

CHAPTER 4

Compounding the catastrophe: the sale of Railtrack

Railtrack had deliberately been left out of the original plans for the privatisation of the railway. When the White Paper was launched in 1992, John MacGregor, the transport secretary, intimated that Railtrack would remain in public hands until after the following election. There were good reasons for this. Railtrack was not an easy candidate for privatisation. Hived off from BR in 1994, it was the owner of a national asset, built up over 170 years, which was difficult to value and much of which had long been written off anyway. Moreover, Railtrack was a monopoly dependent on subsidy and responsible for a massive programme of investment largely funded out of public money. Even the most enthusiastic privatisers in the Tory party realised that selling Railtrack would be difficult.

Therefore, as we have seen, public attention during the passage of the Railways Bill in 1993 was largely focused on the passenger services and there was little mention of the fate of the infrastructure, not least because Railtrack, as explained in the previous chapter, was not even mentioned in the Bill. The feeling within the Department of Transport was that Railtrack would remain in the public sector while all the other parts of the railway were sold off. The model envisaged was not unlike that of London Transport buses, where a central public-sector organisation determines the routes and frequencies and owns the infrastructure but the buses are actually owned and run by private firms. Railtrack was therefore little discussed or considered during the long debate over privatisation.

However, this step-by-step transition to private ownership was to be quickly undermined once Railtrack had been carved out of British Rail, and Bob Horton, an aggressive oilman previously sacked by BP, was appointed as its first chairman in February 1993. Horton had a reputation as an abrasive but strong-minded manager, and he immediately started lobbying for the privatisation of Railtrack, which he was convinced was essential:

> I always felt that the long-term funding requirements were for the infrastructure and we would not get these amounts of money unless we were privatised. I started lobbying ministers, strongly pointing out that it was likely that there would be a change of government and that this would leave Railtrack in the public sector. This would mean that the whole point of privatisation – the renewal of the system – would not be achieved because Railtrack would still be constrained by government rules.[1]

The creation of Railtrack was not easy. Horton, who had little railway experience, having been on the BR board only since December 1992, had the task of separating out the organisation very quickly, as the government wanted the company to become free-standing, although still state-owned, by April 1994. It was a massive logistical task, with the lawyers playing a prominent role as they had to draw up the contracts to govern relationships between Railtrack and the 100 other businesses created out of BR. These relationships had previously been informal and the key task was to change the industry from being a command structure, where orders were passed down clear hierarchical lines, to one where everything was set down in contracts. It was a Herculean task that absorbed hundreds of millions of pounds in fees. John Edmonds, Railtrack's first chief executive, recalls, for example, that setting up the freight access agreements required 224 separate legal documents.[2] The creators of this paper mountain argued that its construction was no more than a necessary formality, as, once signed, the contracts would remain in the bottom drawer; but clearly they failed to grasp the nature of such arrangements or to appreciate that the basis of interaction between the various players in the industry would necessarily change from cooperation to conflict.

When Railtrack became a legal entity in April 1994 it assumed ownership of 11,000 route miles of track, with associated signalling, 40,000 bridges, viaducts and tunnels, and 2,500 stations. It was done in extreme haste and, necessarily, corners were cut. As Richard Middleton, the technical director of Railtrack, put it, 'When they did the same thing of separating out the infrastructure on the Austrian railways, they took five years over it.'[3]

Again, outside advisers played a central role in the development of the structure with little input from old BR managers, not least because most experienced railway staff were opposed to separating the track from the services. Middleton, while supporting the creation of Railtrack because he felt it would be better able to manage the expansion of the railways, nevertheless accepts that the changes were made too hastily: 'Our industry was not ready for it. They tried to change too much too quickly.'[4]

No sooner had Railtrack been carved out of BR and started operating independently than the process of preparing it for privatisation began. Horton's lobbying had been successful, although a formal announcement about the proposed sale was not made until November 1994. Unlike the other businesses carved out of BR, Railtrack was not simply to be sold off; instead it was to be floated on the stock market, a considerably more complicated process and one whose outcome was far more difficult to predict because the public had to be induced to invest in its shares. This was a novel venture and the company had no past financial record since it had been tied into British Rail. However, the idea of involving the public was appealing to the Tory politicians whose previous privatisations had, indeed, resulted in wider share ownership.

It had not been only Horton's efforts that had brought about the change in policy. A former senior civil servant in the Department of Transport recalls that there was a strong push from civil servants, eager to please ministers, to get Railtrack privatised:

> Key officials like Steve Robson at the Treasury and Nick Montagu at Transport pushed very hard for the sale of Railtrack because they were exasperated by the lack of progress, which, they felt, was down to a lot of ex-BR managers who were sabotaging the process. They argued that, without privatising Railtrack, the whole thing would get bogged down because the managers would ensure that progress was halted. It was a 'sod it, let's get the bastards' kind of attitude. They lobbied hard and were successful. Indeed, during the whole process Robson nearly always got what he wanted.[5]

As another very senior servant in the Department at the time put it, 'A decision was taken to privatise Railtrack and it was kept very tight. There was not much consideration of it. It was driven by Robson and Montagu. They were clever men on a self-indulgent and very dangerous rank. It looked fine on paper but not in practice.'[6]

Horton and his allies in the Department were, in any case, pushing at an open door as far as ministers were concerned. While the long-term implications for the industry of a privatised Railtrack did not figure in the debate, there was the prospect of a short-term cash bonanza. Indeed, Kenneth Clarke, the chancellor of the exchequer, soon realised that the flotation offered the potential for a sizeable capital receipt and this was quickly incorporated into his budget plans, setting in stone the plan to sell Railtrack in 1996.

Imperceptibly, therefore, the model for the privatisation of the railways changed, but not for reasons that had anything to do with the better operation of the railway. As the former civil servant quoted above remarked, 'There was not much discussion about what was a very significant change. Just, suddenly, it was going to happen.'[7]

Separating Railtrack from the rest of the industry was crazy enough. But trying to turn it into a conventional profit-making company was even madder. Railtrack was an infrastructure provider, highly dependent on subsidy and only able to make money from selling train paths, whose price was arbitrarily determined by a regulator and ultimately subsidised by government through payments to franchisees via OPRAF. The most pertinent comment on the idea came from a rail executive from Japan, where the railways have been successfully privatised as integrated entities. He wrote – before the Ladbroke Grove accident and so with remarkable prescience – about the British privatisation:

> The first point I have difficulty with is that Railtrack, which had been expected to run up deficits, is making profits, paying dividends and has listed its shares on the stock market. Operation of infrastructure resulting in profits is unthinkable in Japanese railway operations. If profits by Railtrack have resulted from high levels of usage rates, the UK government should reduce its subsidies to operating companies and insist on cuts in track usage fees, as would certainly be the case if this happened in Japan. If the profits of Railtrack have come about by cutting costs required for upkeep and mainte-nance of infrastructure, *there would be problems regarding operational safety.*[8] [my italics]

Even before Railtrack was put up for sale, another crucial mistake was made in the way that the railways were being carved up, which was to have a deeply damaging effect on their performance. When Railtrack was created, the thirteen track maintenance and renewal companies – British

Rail Infrastructure Companies, or Briscos – were not included as part of its structure; for they were also in the process of being separated out from BR and put up for sale.

The arbitrary division of the Briscos into maintenance and renewal companies was another error which contributed to the lack of control that Railtrack had over the management and maintenance of its own assets. This little-noticed decision was, again, an ideologically driven move to break up any potential remaining union power which had no historic basis in the way that the railways traditionally functioned. The Tories wanted to break up the unions. They feared that if Railtrack had included the Briscos, that would have created an organisation of around 40,000 employees, which would mean the unions retained their strong central bargaining position. With maintenance and renewal devolved to thirteen regional companies, the position of the unions was greatly weakened. As a manager involved in the creation of Railtrack commented, 'This was the unspoken agenda. Ministers told us in private that they wanted to break up the unions, but of course they did not say that in public.'[9]

Again, the combination of haste and political opportunism meant that the needs of the railway industry and, ultimately, those of passengers did not come into the equation. The government forced on BR the separation of the maintenance and renewal functions, an artificial division that was widely seen as 'inappropriate'[10] and which greatly weakened Railtrack's ability to maintain the railway to a good standard. Several Railtrack managers had resisted this separation, trying to keep as much of the industry together as possible. Indeed, this strict distinction between renewals and maintenance had not existed under BR – though there had been some contracting out of major renewal projects – and it further complicated the process of getting work done. As Steven Marshall, the chief executive of Railtrack from November 2000, explained: 'If a rail needs replacing, the maintenance company has to go to us and ask us to agree that the work needs doing. With only limited information, we have to decide whether it was the result of poor maintenance or because it was simply worn out by age. Then we have to pass the work on to the renewal company which has to fit in the work with its existing programme of possessions [temporary track closures].'[11]

There was even a set length of replacement track which determined whether the work was carried out by the maintenance or the renewal company – 60 feet for jointed rail and 600 feet for continuous welded rail. For other work, maintenance contractors carried out work worth up to £25,000 per job and bigger contracts are put out to the renewal contractors. It was all extremely time-wasting and costly. This system also meant that it was impossible for Railtrack to make proper judgements about when rails should be replaced or maintained. As one insider put it, 'While the amount of investment going into the industry rose after the first two years of privatisation, there was no way of knowing whether that money was being spent wisely because so much was wasted by putting work out in this way.'[12]

A compromise, which Middleton says was a better option, would have been for Railtrack to have inspection and monitoring resources to identify what work was needed and then call in contractors to do it. However, that would have required an engineering department and it was felt that there were not enough good, qualified engineers within the old BR to staff a Railtrack department as well as leaving sufficient people to run the Briscos. Until the reorganisation prompted by the Hatfield crash, therefore, Railtrack did not have an engineering department. Instead, it had to take on a lot of contract managers, mostly from outside the industry, to oversee the engineering work.

As with the rolling-stock companies, the Briscos had to be fattened up in order to make them saleable. This was done by granting them seemingly generous contracts with Railtrack. Not only were these regionally based companies guaranteed to be the sole contractors within their areas for between five and seven years, but Railtrack had very little control over how the work was carried out. Indeed, one former Railtrack manager explains how it was impossible for the company, still state-owned, to get information out of BR about the nature of the contracts it was entering into on Railtrack's behalf: 'BR were saying that the contracts were commercially confidential. They didn't want us to know what was in them. Eventually, we won a bit of a concession as we were given auditing rights over them.'[13] In other words, BR, under instructions from the government, was determining the terms of contracts between two third parties, Railtrack and the Briscos.

In order to make the Briscos saleable, the terms of the contracts had been progressively weakened as the sales process got under way. Incredibly, according to Middleton, by the end of the process 'The contracts were so weak that Railtrack was not even allowed to withhold payment if work were not done. The infrastructure companies decide what is done, how it's done and where. We have no power to tell them, for example, to replace a specific set of points.' Railtrack was therefore saddled with contracts over which it had very little control and which it did not have the resources or ability to monitor.

At first Railtrack did not even check the work carried out by the engineering companies after it was finished, raising serious concerns about safety (see below). While a checking process was gradually introduced during the first couple of years after privatisation, it was still greatly inadequate. Some of those involved in the process argue that the contracts might have been sufficient had Railtrack monitored them as intended. As one put it, 'We were under constant pressure from Norman Broadhurst [Railtrack's finance director] and the regulator to cut costs and that meant not having enough people to do the checking. Only one of the ten zones audited the contracts properly.'

Other former insiders argue that the contracts were fundamentally flawed in that the auditing and monitoring provisions were not sufficiently robust. As early as 1998, Railtrack had begun to recognise that the contracts were unworkable, but it could not impose changes without incurring massive losses. Instead, the company began drawing up a new form of contract involving a partnership between contractors and the company, with both benefiting from cost savings. However, these new contracts, which started taking effect in 2000, still placed an emphasis on cost-cutting rather than ensuring that the railway was in the best possible condition.

While the terms of the contracts were loose, not even specifying set outputs, and by the same token virtually unpoliceable, they were also insufficiently profitable for the contractors because the level of payments for the contracts had started from a relatively low base. Under pressure from the Treasury, BR had cut back on maintenance and renewals in its last few years, knowing that it was to be privatised. The maintenance contracts were let in 1995 with the price set at the old BR cost, which was thus a historically low figure. Therefore, the contracts were underpriced; moreover, increases were capped by the regulator to a level of 3 per cent below the rate of inflation per year, a substantial cut in real terms, particularly as wages were rising.

The contracts were 'closed book', which meant that Railtrack had no idea what the real costs were, nor how much profit the contractors were making. The maintenance contractors had no incentive to ensure the track was in the best possible condition. They made their profit by spending as little as possible to meet the vague standards set out in the contracts, which, for example, specified the intervals at which work had to be carried out. The contractors were under constant pressure to make a profit which meant that Railtrack's contracts managers, according to a former Railtrack executive, 'spent all their time dealing with claims and variations, rather than making sure that delays were being kept to a minimum, or, indeed, that the system was safe.'[14]

The Briscos were mostly bought by established engineering companies such as Tarmac, Jarvis and Balfour Beatty, who were experienced at making the most out of such deals and arguing over every variation and claim. This combination of unpoliceable contracts and the pressure to reduce costs proved to be lethal, as is shown by the story of the Hatfield crash, outlined in Chapter 8.

The sale of the Briscos eventually brought in a paltry £169m but as we have seen, money was not the principal motivation behind that sale. Without the Briscos, Railtrack was a very lean company with just 10,000 employees, around two-thirds of whom were signallers. This leanness made the company much more attractive for privatisation. Indeed, had it included the 30,000 people who worked for the Briscos and all the associated problems, some City analysts reckon Railtrack would have been unsaleable, since there had already been concerns over the disruptive strike by signallers in 1994.

Nevertheless, there were still problems in making Railtrack attractive to private investors. A roadshow toured the City institutions and was relatively successful because the Railtrack team and their advisers stressed the potential for cost reduction in the new company. However, the City was less convinced about the company's growth potential, and the government decided that at least one major project, Thameslink 2000, had to be included in the prospectus to demonstrate that the shares would be a growth stock.

Again, haste and political expediency overrode the aim of maximising revenue for the Exchequer or, indeed, any consideration of what would be best for the railway. Ministers clearly wanted a scorched-earth policy that left no part of Railtrack in public hands. S.B.C. Warburg, its advisers, recommended a 100 per cent sale, as retaining a minority stake would lead to worries among investors about whether this might be a

Trojan Horse for subsequent renationalisation by a future government. Moreover, such a residual stake was perceived as a way that the government could influence the company, in particular pushing it towards expensive investment schemes.

The subsequent National Audit Office report[15] suggested that proceeds of the Railtrack sale – which grossed £2.5bn if debt transferred to the company is included – would have been increased by a quarter (£600m) had the government retained a 20 per cent holding in the company at the time of the flotation in May 1996. A 40 per cent stake could have enhanced proceeds by an impressive £1.5bn, almost doubling the amount received by taxpayers, because the share price soared in the months following the flotation. The NAO also pointed out that the fears set out by Warburg could easily have been allayed. A new government, it said, would require primary legislation to renationalise the railways and legislation would have protected Railtrack's private shareholders against adverse effects of government pressure to overspend on investment.

Taxpayers also lost out through the timing of Railtrack's privatisation. Under pressure from the chancellor, and concerned about their wafer-thin parliamentary majority, then being eroded at every by-election, the Tory ministers pushed for the earliest possible sale. The problem was that Railtrack did not have a financial track record, though Norman Broadhurst, the finance director, cobbled one together by going through the BR accounts, with some difficulty because they had been drawn up on a completely different basis. But the City, which is slow to adapt to new markets and very risk-averse, still did not really understand the rail industry. As the NAO report put it, 'The timing of the sale may have had an adverse impact on the value achieved, since it was carried out at a time when the market was only beginning to understand the new commercial and regulatory structures within the rail industry.'

The NAO was told by institutional investors that a higher price 'would have probably [been] obtained for the company'[16] had the sale been postponed just for a few months. Such a delay would have allowed investors to learn more about Railtrack's business and the complicated regulatory regime. The Department of Transport told the NAO that it believed that market confidence would have been damaged by a delay until the autumn, putting at risk both the flotation and the privatisation scheme generally but, in the measured language that is used for these reports, it is clear that the NAO completely disagreed with the department's analysis: 'In our view, a delay to the sale of Railtrack, even only to the autumn of 1996, would have been helpful to institutional investors and analysts as it would have enabled them to gain a better appreciation of Railtrack's business within the privatised rail industry.'[17]

Another obstacle on the course to a successful sale was the large burden of debt carried over from British Rail days. Right from the outset, it was clear that the company could not be saddled with large amounts of BR's historic debt, as this would make the share offer too unappealing. According to the NAO, Railtrack owed £1.5bn to the public sector, which was cancelled on privatisation and replaced with new debt of £586m – a write-off of around £900m, equivalent to half the eventual receipts for the company. The reduction in debt was partly a result of Railtrack's hard bargaining over the Thameslink 2000 project. The government had wanted to show that privatisation would boost investment but Railtrack was anxious not to take on the burden without compensation. After protracted negotiations, the level of Railtrack's debt was reduced further by £225m to cover much of the cost of the project, with the Department arguing, disingenuously, that Railtrack's value would be boosted by £240m because of lower debt payments and a boosted share price due to investors' enhanced perceptions of the company's growth prospects. However, when the NAO spoke to investors, most said that the Thameslink 2000 project 'did not have a significant influence on their valuations'.[18] The NAO reckoned, therefore, that of the £225m additional write-off £125m was wasted. At the time of writing, summer 2005, the Thameslink project is still on the drawing board, with little prospect of development, and the money earmarked for the project has long been lost somewhere in Railtrack or Network Rail's accounts.

The most blatant fiddle was the way in which Railtrack was compensated for another potential risk which might have made it more difficult to sell. In an effort to improve punctuality and reliability, a performance regime was introduced in April 1995 based on the passenger's charter, which recorded the percentage of trains that were cancelled or which were more than five minutes (for short distances) or ten minutes (for longer journeys) late. Under the new system every delay was to be allocated either to Railtrack, if the problem was with signalling or track work, for example, or to the operator, if it was a result of, say, a train failure or an absent driver. The system measures the delays not just at the end of the journey, but also at various points *en route*. Railtrack became responsible for the fault attribution, although train operators also took on staff whose sole function was to quibble over who should be penalised for particular delays. In an extraordinary decision the rail regulator John Swift, under pressure from ministers, sweetened the pill for Railtrack by allocating the company an extra, inflation-protected £75m in track access charges to compensate for any possible losses on the performance regime.

This was done largely to 'correct', from the ministers' point of view, a measure that Swift had introduced earlier. Originally, the level of track access charges had been determined by a group of civil servants and Swift had realised that it was too high, potentially allowing Railtrack to be too profitable. So he had announced that there would be a reduction of 8 per cent for 1995/6 and that, in subsequent years, Railtrack was to be allowed a maximum increase of inflation minus 2 per cent. The cut in charges angered ministers and officials in the Department of Transport, who were worried that it would jeopardise the flotation of Railtrack. So the addition of the supplementary access charges, supposedly to cover for the performance regime, was a compromise between Swift and the government with, yet again, the taxpayer footing the bill.

In the event, Railtrack performed well in 1996/7, and therefore it received £111m out of the performance regime, money which again largely came from taxpayers and most of which (£77m) was the result of these supplementary access charges. It was, in effect, a 'heads Railtrack wins, tails Railtrack wins' kind of regime which removed some of the pressure on the company to improve performance. As with all Swift's decisions, he was hamstrung by the fact that he had to ensure that he did nothing which actually jeopardised the flotation of Railtrack – as opposed to eliciting whinges from Railtrack's managers – because part of his remit was to ensure that the company could be privatised.

Track access charges were Railtrack's principal source of income, worth, at the beginning of privatisation, around £2.3bn annually and paid by the train operators who, in turn, received subsidy from the government (a total of £1.8bn in 1997/8 which declined to £1.15bn by 2001/2). The access charge regime, which was necessarily complex and arcane, highlighted the arbitrary way that privatisation had been designed. Swift did not particularly like the system that he had inherited but he could not change it as there was not sufficient time. Although too complex to describe in detail, the system essentially determined how much Railtrack should invest in maintaining and renewing the railway and then set the access charges to ensure that the company had sufficient funds to do the work and to reward its shareholders. It was very unwieldy and the amounts were largely fixed, with only 9 per cent of the charges being variable. In other words, Railtrack got very little extra money (and in many cases none at all) when additional trains were run on its tracks, a situation which was to cause the company much grief when operators started putting on many new services in the late 1990s. The privatisation was supposed to make the whole of the rail industry transparent and to expose the costs of running the railway in order that rational economic decisions could be made on the viability of many marginal services and lines. However, the way that Railtrack was valued meant that this transparency never emerged from the fog of railway economics.

The regulator proved to be equally generous towards Railtrack in its decision about what should happen to the company's income from property sales. Here, the government had learnt from previous privatisations, notably the sale of the bus companies where purchasers had made large, quick profits by flogging off town centre bus stations, and ensured that the company only took on operational railway land while property that could no longer be used for railway purposes was left to be sold by the British Rail Property Board, which remained state-owned.

However, this still left Railtrack with many sites that had great development potential, which, along with rental income, was expected to bring in £250m in profits over a five-year period. Rather than imposing a blanket clawback clause, Swift allowed Railtrack to retain 75 per cent of any extra profits beyond the £250m, with the remaining 25 per cent going towards reducing access charges. This was another climbdown by Swift, as ever under ministerial pressure, as he had earlier intimated that Railtrack would only be able to keep a small proportion of these windfall profits. Horton, however, had lobbied hard to be allowed to retain the bulk of the proceeds, arguing that it would boost the image of Railtrack as a high-yielding utility with the added spice of potential development windfalls. Critics saw the move as encouraging Railtrack to focus on its property portfolio rather than on its main task as the infrastructure provider for the rail industry.

In fact, the way the industry was regulated gave little encouragement for Railtrack to invest. Indeed, the most amazing omission in the new structure of the industry was that there was no obligation on Railtrack to spend money to improve the railway. Although the track access agreements included specific items of investment that Railtrack was obliged to carry out, it was under no obligation to follow an investment plan set out by the rail regulator. In other words, he had no powers to direct Railtrack to carry out particular bits of work or, most important, any enhancements. This omission was later remedied by the addition of licence Condition 7, agreed between Railtrack and Swift in 1997, which specified Railtrack's duties in maintaining and improving the network, but this was still a vague requirement. The regulator had no power to force Railtrack to invest in particular projects.

All these decisions were taken in order to make Railtrack more saleable and to allay the fears of Horton and his colleagues as they prepared for the sell-off. As we saw in the previous chapter, the Labour Party had threatened to stymie the sale but its statements of intent became progressively weaker as the time for the privatisation approached. Even as late as February 1996, just three months before the eventual flotation, Brian Wilson, Labour's pugnacious transport spokesman, said: 'Without public ownership of the infrastructure, a Labour government would be hamstrung in its determination to expand and develop the railways. ... These practical considerations must dictate our view on Railtrack.'[19] Yet despite the clear message that renationalisation was on the agenda, by the time the statement had to be drawn up for the Railtrack prospectus a couple of months later, Wilson's boss, Clare Short, had dropped any commitment to renationalise the railways in a speech setting out the party's position in relation to the flotation, arguing it would be 'irresponsible'[20] for Labour to threaten potential investors that, once in government, the party would take back Railtrack.

When the prospectus was issued in the run-up to the sale, Labour's U-turn was all too evident. The attempt to put flesh on Blair's commitment to a 'publicly owned, publicly accountable railway' still left the bones exposed. While criticising the privatisation and arguing, 'We do not believe that increased investment and a more intensive use of rail can be achieved with the current structures proposed for the privatised Railtrack,' Short only promised tighter regulation and, bizarrely, 'reconstituting British Rail' to encourage and foster partnership between public and private finance in the rail network. On the big question of renationalisation, the formula was hardly threatening and contained more weasel words than the average lawyer's briefcase: 'Dependent on the availability of resources, and as priorities allow, seek, by appropriate means, to extend public ownership and control.' In other words, given big Gordon is not going to prioritise buying back the railways, we'll let you get on with it.

This removed any remaining doubt about the flotation. The price of the shares was set relatively conservatively at 390p, after a bookbuilding exercise – involving investors being approached individually – had proved successful. The company was sold in May 1996 for £1.9bn, although, since it assumed the debt of £586m, the total receipts were almost £2.5bn. The offer was seven times oversubscribed, which led the NAO to criticise the fact that the share price had not been raised during the bookbuilding process. Since, as we have seen, around £900m had been written off by the government, the net receipts were £1.6bn and the company was receiving around £1bn per year in subsidy (via the track access charges paid by the train operators, who were being subsidised by OPRAF), Railtrack was not so much sold as given away.

Railtrack quickly began to attract much of the opprobrium that had been levied at British Rail, made all the fiercer by the fact that its share price was soaring and its directors were paying themselves inflated salaries. The public sensed that Railtrack was not acting in its best interests and the company quickly became the target of widespread criticism. As I put it in the *Independent on Sunday*, 'Railtrack has succeeded where generations of British Rail managers failed: it has made BR popular.'[21] In the autumn of 1995, for example, it had produced its first 2,100-page *Great Britain Passenger Railway Timetable*, having taken over the task from British Rail; there were so many mistakes that two supplements totalling over 300 pages had to be produced simultaneously, a fiasco which led Barry Doe, a timetable expert, to say, 'I have timetables going back to the 1950s and this is by far the worst I have ever seen.'[22] To make matters worse, Railtrack had charged each train operating company £100,000 to produce the timetable. Eventually it pulped the whole 80,000 print run and offered previous purchasers a free copy of the revised version on production of the old cover.

Everything that was wrong with the railways was being blamed on privatisation and, quite often, on Railtrack. Remarkably, even Her Majesty's Inspector of the Constabulary joined in. In his 1996 report he wrote that there was 'a direct link between the increase in crime [on the railways] together with the reduced number of detections and some of the changes that had occurred within the railway industry'.[23] He cited reduced staffing, open access to premises and reluctance of staff to 'patrol some late night services'. In fact, in fairness, all of these trends had developed under BR, and the inspector seemed to be jumping on the anti-privatisation bandwagon.

Even the relatively pliant John Swift found Railtrack's behaviour intolerable. As he commented, 'Railtrack "got greedy" sometime in 1997.'[24] He detected an unwillingness to invest which he found troubling and this is what led him eventually to introduce the new licence Condition 7.

While the sale was a success within its own narrow terms, having been achieved on time with 665,000 applications for shares, Railtrack's early behaviour in the private sector was disastrous for the railway. As a company with a conventional structure, its legal duty was to its share-holders and, freed from government control, Railtrack's directors decided that they only had one purpose in life – to satisfy those shareholders and maximise their dividends.

But the directors didn't know what to do with their new-found freedom. There was no strategy, no vision, not even an idea of precisely what Railtrack was for. Edmonds, the chief executive until the autumn of 1997, was an experienced railwayman but not a good delegator, and he ran the organisation as his own fiefdom. A pompous man with a penchant for expensive French wines, he used to insist that his regular train to Sandy ran on time, whatever the consequences for the rest of the timetable. Moreover, he had a long-term dislike of engineers that was to prove very damaging to the company. He did not share his vision, if he had one, with his colleagues. As Richard Middleton, who was a zone director at the time, put it, 'We pottered along. After privatisation, we did not know what to do next. People were dabbling in this or that, but there was no clear sense of corporate purpose. We hadn't decided it was a growing business and therefore there was no objective to deliver growth.'[25]

Railtrack never set out a corporate strategy, or even figured out what its role was. The early Network Management Statements, the agenda for investment which the company was obliged to produce, reflected that. They were thin documents full of banalities: 'Over the next ten years, we will spend more than £1bn annually to make our vision of the world's best railway a reality', and 'Our privatisation freed us from public-sector constraints on spending.'[26] (As we shall see in Chapter 15, in reality Railtrack became even more heavily dependent on subsidy than BR, as evidenced by Railtrack's 1999/2000 annual report, which said: 'It is clear that the level of government subsidy for the railway will need to rise.'[27])

Initially, investment of £10bn was promised by Railtrack over the first ten years. While that sounded a big number, it was only sufficient to ensure the track and infrastructure remained in the same condition without any improvements. Indeed, in the 1996/7 statement, maintenance was forecast to go down from £740m to just £500m a decade later; and renewals were scheduled to be at the same level of £600m in 2006/7 as in 1995/6, with a bit of extra expenditure during the intervening years.

In the absence of any other guiding purpose, profit maximisation became the holy grail. Gerald Corbett, who replaced Edmonds as chief executive in the autumn of 1997, was swept up by that agenda. Corbett was a conventional big-company executive, having previously been financial director of GrandMet (now Diageo), and therefore did not question Railtrack's ethos. As he stated to the House of Commons Transport Sub-Committee in late 1998, 'We believe very strongly that profits and investment are two sides of the same coin. The more profitable Railtrack is and the stronger Railtrack is, the more money we can raise and the more we can get done.' The purpose of the company was to manage the infrastructure to reduce delays which were attributable to Railtrack so that it could make a profit out of performance. The view of Railtrack executives was that it was a separate company from the rest of the industry with a limited remit to do its bit. Corbett believed that Railtrack's job was to manage the assets in such a way that the company maximised profits, and he initially went about that task aggressively before he realised that Railtrack's remit included a wider public agenda.

Railtrack's management systems were rudimentary for a company that, overnight, became a member of the FTSE-100. Corbett said that when he took the job he was told there was a target to improve performance by 15 per cent:

> I asked what the performance plan was. The managers said it was 15 per cent. So I said, 'What's the plan?' And they said, 15 per cent. But, I said, 'How are we going to get there?' – blank look. There was no plan. There was no sugges-

tion of how you might want to do it, or how you could go about it. There was
no thinking about what they were capable of achieving. Some of the better
ones put a few things down on paper, but the others just exhorted the troops
to do better.[28]

Corbett set about trying to change this with a massive operation devised
by McKinsey's, the management consultants, named Project Destiny,
which was an attempt to formulate a plan about what Railtrack should
do and how it should set priorities for investment. There were some
improvements – investment increased and performance got better – but,
as we shall see in Chapter 9, the strategy was flawed.

Not surprisingly, the City loved all this. Railtrack became one of the
great privatisation successes, with its share price soaring to reach a
record level of £17.68 by the end of 1998, over four times the original offer
price. Railtrack's managers clearly got overexcited, ordering that a daily
notice with the previous evening's share price be posted on every signal
box noticeboard.

To be fair to Corbett, he eventually understood that Railtrack could
not simply aim to maximise its profit without regard to wider social
issues, and he changed his tune completely. In April 2000, in an interview in the *Observer*,[29] he said: 'We have moved completely off the profit
agenda and the shareholder agenda. After we were privatised, we stayed
on a profit and shareholder agenda for too long. We have now gone over
to the public service obligations agenda as agreed with Tom Winsor [the
rail regulator].' This was, in part, a clever ploy. Corbett set up a
regulation department with twenty-five people whose main task was to
ensure that Winsor (who took over from Swift as regulator in 1999) gave
the company a favourable settlement in the access charge review. In this
he was successful: Winsor agreed to a 50 per cent rise in access charges to
give Railtrack a total of £15bn over five years. But even this was not
enough to save it from financial collapse in the wake of Hatfield.

Safety was the dog that did not bark – at least initially. Throughout the
privatisation process there had been fears expressed by trade unionists
and other anti-privatisation groups that safety would be compromised by
the fragmentation and privatisation of the railway. John Edmonds later
wrote: 'While the financial elements could be manipulated to meet the
demands and expectations of the market, a single serious accident

involving loss of life would have scuppered the entire process and all those closely involved were well aware of this.'[30] By chance – or perhaps mischance – the fatal accidents caused by privatisation were to happen after the sales process had been completed.

The break-up of the industry necessitated a completely new approach to the management of safety on the railways. Traditionally, under BR, the industry had been largely self-regulating. Her Majesty's Railway Inspectorate (HMRI) investigated accidents, but it was a tiny organis-ation staffed by former senior army officers with barely half a dozen inspectors and it had no day-to-day role in relation to safety, which was seen as the responsibility of everyone in the industry. BR employed inspectors to cover all aspects of its work.

Safety improved gradually in the railways through the rather crude but effective process of learning from accidents. All the major improve-ments in safety came as a result of applying the lessons from disasters and through investment in new safety measures. The prevailing philo-sophy was that there was no such thing as absolute safety, but that it should be the aim. However, it was also recognised – which is a point that the public is less prepared to accept today – that, however much effort the industry put into preventing them, there would be accidents, and even fatalities.

The management of safety began to change after the Inspectorate was criticised by the Fennell report into the 1987 King's Cross disaster for not taking on a pro-active role in preventing accidents. The Clapham disaster the following year resulted in the Hidden report, which was also critical of HMRI. Stan Hall, author of several books on railway disasters, feels Fennell and Hidden misunderstood the role of HMRI, initiating changes which led to the bureaucratisation of the safety process in the industry: 'HMRI was not responsible for overall safety. Its remit was to investigate accidents and trends, to oversee, gently, any works and to keep ministers informed. The industry was self-regulating.'[31] But, insists Hall, the system worked because there was mutual trust, a culture of pride in the railway and great respect for the inspectors.

This came to an end when BR and the government accepted the Hidden recommendations and, as a result, HMRI was incorporated into the Health and Safety Executive (HSE). Safety then became the responsibility of an outside body with a large bureaucracy, and that process was extended further with privatisation, which necessarily led to a massive expansion of this bureaucracy.

With privatisation, there was no longer any question of the industry being self-regulating, given the fragmentation of what had been BR into so many parts. The government commissioned a report from the Health and Safety Commission (which oversees the HSE) to work out how safety could be regulated in a fragmented industry. Called *Ensuring Safety on Britain's Railways*, the document recommended that every company involved in the railways set out a safety case, which involved assessing all the potential risks and putting forward strategies for keeping them to a minimum. This was a concept developed successfully in the nuclear and offshore oil industries and would now be applied to rail.

On the recommendation of the HSE, another controversial decision was made without proper consideration of the implications. Following the Clapham accident, British Rail had set up a Group Standards Organisation which set standards for all aspects of British Rail's operations, ranging from driver training to the maintenance of locomotive wheels. There was a fierce debate over whether this should remain intact as an independent unit or as part of the HSE. Oddly, the HSE did not want it, suggesting instead that Railtrack should take over the organisation, creating what became the Safety and Standards Directorate (SSD).

This idea was opposed by many people in the railway industry because of fears that the company would be influenced by commercial considerations when making decisions on safety requirements. Moreover, it gave one commercial company, Railtrack, a role over others in the industry, something that neither party would be happy about. Railtrack felt it was being burdened with a role for which it was not suited; the other companies feared that Railtrack could exercise control over them by masking commercial considerations under the guise of safety considerations. Nevertheless, the government adopted the HSE's suggestion, partly allaying fears over the profit motive by ensuring that part of Railtrack's licence condition was to fund SSD adequately and that it was to be independent of Railtrack's commercial business. It was an arrangement that failed to recognise that perceptions about the management of safety were almost as important as the reality itself. Inevitably, therefore, the status of SSD as part of Railtrack was highlighted in the aftermath of the Ladbroke Grove disaster and it was quickly hived off into a separate subsidiary, Railway Safety (see Chapter 7).[32] Railtrack was thus given the role of monitoring the safety cases of all the other companies working in the industry, while its own safety case was vetted by the HSE. While the safety case system is considered to be robust, there is a tendency for it to lead to 'ticking boxes' and an attitude which sees the objective as fulfilling bureaucratic requirements rather than improving the safety of the industry.

Even before privatisation, Railtrack's safety management had become the subject of criticism from the Health and Safety Executive. In a report published in March 1996,[33] following the HSE's most extensive inquiry ever carried out on the railways, the deputy chief inspector of the railways, Vic Coleman, warned that there were severe weaknesses and poor management in Railtrack's safety systems. He argued that Railtrack's position at the heart of the railways' safety system was constantly undermined because it was not seen as an impartial player and because it had a lot of responsibility without any real power.

Safety was considered to be a given to such an extent that it was not included as a measure of the performance of the railway in the same way as 'minutes delay'. Therefore, the performance regime outlined above did not measure or reward the safe running of the railway but focused only on punctuality and the number of cancellations. This created a potential conflict between safety and performance that was to contribute to the Hatfield disaster (see Chapter 8).

But first there were two other major disasters soon after privatisation, both caused by trains going through red lights, the first of which was at Southall in September 1997.

CHAPTER 5

Southall: a moment's inattention

The disaster which Railtrack's first chief executive, John Edmonds, had feared would halt the sell-off never happened. The major accidents which are examined in this book all occurred after the completion of the privatisation process. There was one serious accident near Watford in August 1996 when a passenger train went through a red light and hit an empty one crossing its path, killing a woman passenger, but the train operating company, North London Railways, was still operated by BR at the time and the issue of privatisation never came into play.

Nevertheless, despite the superb record of the railway in the early and mid-1990s, the question of safety did become a key issue in the privatisation debate as critics of the process expressed concerns that the fragmentation and sale of the railways would increase the risks to rail passengers. It was not only the many opponents of privatisation who raised this issue; far more importantly, they were also given resonance by the highly critical report from Her Majesty's Railway Inspectorate[1] (HMRI, part of the Health and Safety Executive) published in March 1996, which said weaknesses in Railtrack's systems 'cause concern' that rail travel could become less safe as a result of the changes. In particular, the Inspectorate highlighted the system of contracts and legal agreements that was at the heart of the new way of running the railways. The report, the biggest single project in HMRI's history, listed a series of incidents in which management failures had led to safety defects. In one, remarkably, a signal was not reinstated after work on the track. More systematically, the report said that, while Railtrack was dependent on technical audits to monitor the performance of the railways, the HMRI 'found little evidence of technical auditing taking place'. Vic Coleman, the then deputy chief inspector of the railways, said: 'We have found a management system which does have a number of weaknesses and we believe that those weaknesses need attending to.' As the Hatfield crash was to show, Railtrack did not sort out a lot of these weaknesses and, indeed, possibly exacerbated them over the subsequent years.

There was also evidence that Railtrack was taking a more commercial attitude towards safety issues. In the 1996/7 annual safety report from the Health and Safety Executive, the chief inspector of railways, Stan Robertson, criticised Railtrack for its nit-picking approach to safety. He cited the example of Railtrack's appeal against an improvement notice seeking better fencing on the Foord viaduct in Kent. Railtrack, he said, 'spent almost as much money on assessment etc. to avoid compliance as would have been necessary to provide the additional safety feature required by HMRI in the first place'.[2]

The derailment of a train at Bexley in February 1997 raised further concerns about standards of maintenance and of communication between Railtrack and its contractors (see Chapter 8 for details of this incident, which highlighted issues similar to those raised by the Hatfield disaster). This was the inevitable result of creating a railway where relationships between various parties were based on contracts rather than on established hierarchical procedures.

The bigger question that naturally arose from all these incidents was whether privatisation was affecting the trend towards better safety on the railways. This long-term improvement had been a feature of rail travel almost since its invention because of the way that lessons were learnt from disasters. There were fewer deaths in railway accidents in each post-war decade than in the previous one: the 344 deaths in the 1940s and 337 in the 1950s compare with just 75 in the 1980s and 46 in the 1990s. In fact, until the two accidents on the main line out of Paddington – Southall in 1997 and Ladbroke Grove in 1999 – the 1990s had been an excellent decade for rail safety, with three years in which there were no deaths and a total of just eight in seven years.

Privatisation occurred in 1996/7 and the two disasters after that killed a total of thirty-eight people. It would be a misuse of statistics to place too much emphasis on the fact that the two major incidents of the decade occurred in the three years after privatisation, but nevertheless it is a disturbing point, especially as the next major post-privatisation disaster, Hatfield in 2000, was unequivocally caused by the new structure of the railway (see Chapter 8) and there are clear indications that the next one, Potters Bar in 2002, also had its roots in the way the industry was privatised.

At the time of writing (summer 2005), there have been six major rail accidents in the post-privatisation era, which exhibit a strange symmetry: three have been on the Great Western, relatively close to London, and three have been on the East Coast, two near to London. Moreover, two (Southall and Ladbroke Grove) were caused by drivers failing to stop at red lights, two (Hatfield and Potters Bar) by problems with the track and two (Great Heck and Ufton Nervet) by vehicles on the line.[3] Great Western has been involved in three (twice blameless) and GNER in two, both times utterly blameless. Fate deals an odd hand. Indeed, this strange series of accidents shows that commentators should be wary of jumping to simple conclusions on the basis of a handful of rare events such as rail accidents. Coincidences are often just that.

The rail network and the management of safety within it was the product of 175 years of steady evolution. The privatisation and fragmentation brought about an unprecedented upheaval. Of course, there had been changes and reorganisations before but nothing on the scale of those of 1996/7, which were revolution rather than evolution. As a lawyer would put it, privatisation has a prima facie case to answer, which will be examined here and in Chapters 7, 8 and 10.

On the face of it, the accident at Southall on 19 September 1997 appears to be a run-of-the-mill railway disaster that could have happened at any time under British Rail. But on closer examination it is clear that the recent fragmentation and privatisation of the railways contributed in several ways to the collision.

The accident involved a Great Western high-speed train from Swansea to Paddington which smashed into a goods train crossing its path at Southall in West London. Seven people died and over 100 were injured. The immediate cause was the inattention of the driver of the high-speed train, Larry Harrison. With the train travelling at its maximum permitted speed of 125mph, he had failed to notice first the double yellow and then the single yellow signals which, on British railways, always precede a red. By the time he saw the red, which was protecting the junction that the goods train was using to cross the high-speed train's path, it was too late. Although Harrison applied the brakes, a collision was inevitable and the passenger train smashed into the middle of the goods train, which consisted of empty aggregate hoppers, at a combined speed of between 80 and 90mph.

Driver Harrison clearly should not have passed the red signal – in the industry this is called a SPAD, a signal passed at danger, which, interestingly, is one of the few technical railway terms to have gained currency among the general public. But, as with nearly all major transport disasters, the underlying causes are much more complex. The Uff report into the accident, published in 2000, highlighted, in particular, the absence of the Automatic Warning System (AWS) as a key factor, but there are several other issues worth examining. The AWS is a device that alerts drivers when they are approaching yellow or red signals. Between the rails, a couple of hundred metres before each signal, there is a box containing magnets and this triggers off the warning device in the cab. If the signal is green, a bell rings and a black aspect is shown on a little display in the driver's cab. If the signal is double yellow, single yellow or red, a horn sounds and there is a yellow and black 'sunflower' shown to the driver. The sunflower is displayed until it is reset to black by the next green signal, thus giving the driver a visual reminder that he or she should proceed with caution. If the driver does not acknowledge the horn, by pressing a reset button, the brakes are applied automatically. Crucially, on the day of the Southall disaster the high-speed train's AWS had been 'isolated' – turned off.

The background to why the AWS was not functioning is both very complicated and highly revealing of the way that the massive changes in the industry had unexpected consequences relating to safety. A fault in the AWS in locomotive 43173, which was at the front of the high-speed train when it hit the goods train, had occurred the evening before the accident when the train was pulling into Oxford to pick up passengers. The driver, Allan Taylor, found he could not reset the system after it was triggered by the red light at the end of the platform and consequently the train came to a halt halfway along it. Taylor then isolated the AWS in order to be able to proceed and was allowed to take the train, with passengers, to Paddington, even though the safety device was not working.

At this point there occurred one of those little oversights, insignificant in themselves, that might have made all the difference as to whether or not the name of Southall joined the roll call of rail disasters. At Oxford, driver Taylor had told the station supervisor (who worked for a different company, Thames Trains) that the train had stopped because of the AWS. The supervisor then passed this information to Richard Parker, the signalman (who worked for Railtrack), but Parker remembered only that the brakes had come on and did not recall anything being said about AWS. Consequently, he did not pass any information to Operations Control in Swindon (run by Great Western Trains), which would then have logged the failure onto the fault reporting system, known as RAVERS, which in turn would have been picked up by the depot at Old Oak Common in West London where maintenance is carried out. Taylor did make an entry in the defects repair book on the train which said, 'AWS isolated, unable to cancel', but when he took the train to Old Oak Common after the journey to Paddington he failed to fill in a defect report form or an incident report form as required by the rules, both of which would have ensured the fault was logged onto RAVERS.

The train was due for an 'A' examination at Old Oak Common, a series of checks carried out every three to four days. However, as a result of the failures by driver Taylor and signalman Parker to report the fault, the only record of the problem with the AWS in locomotive 43173 was contained in the defects book on the train and the fitters only came to it late in their shift since they had other faults to fix.

Old Oak Common had been the subject of a reorganisation after Great Western Trains took over its operation from British Rail in February 1996. The number of staff had been reduced and, as Professor John Uff put it in his report on the Southall accident, 'The men were working under more pressure, and cannot have been motivated to spend more time than the minimum necessary to carry out the required tasks.'[4] In fact, there were only four fitters on duty as opposed to the six who had been employed prior to the 1996 reorganisation.

GWT's post-privatisation reorganisation had already given rise to concerns about its impact on safety. While the history of problems over the standards of Great Western's maintenance work stretched back to BR days, its roots were in the separation of Railtrack from the operations in April 1994. Sloppy maintenance at GWT had caused a train fire at Maidenhead in September 1995 which resulted in the death of a passenger who fled from the fire into the path of an oncoming train. The fire had started when the rear fuel tank on the front locomotive fell off after its retaining nuts worked loose due to insufficient maintenance. The following year there was renewed concern from Railtrack about a series of nine incidents between June and November 1996 attributed to defects in GWT's rolling stock. The subsequent investigation, carried out by an independent safety auditor, David Parkes, found, according to Uff, that 'key activities had lapsed and key safety posts had been withdrawn without adequate resources being provided'.[5] A new internal audit system covering fleet maintenance was introduced early in 1997 as a result of these concerns, but it was allowed to lapse in August 1997, just before the Southall accident.

Moreover, the depot still showed signs of bad management. Training was inadequate and haphazard, with poor record keeping. There was a lack of clarity about precisely what work should be included in standard maintenance procedures such as the 'A' examination. Uff was scathing about the failings at Old Oak Common: 'It must be concluded that maintenance procedures at Old Oak Common were far from robust. Whatever the effect of the reorganisation of 1996 ... there was, in September 1997, a lack of attention to details, some of which were safety-critical.'[6] Uff is careful not to blame any particular individual but, instead, focuses on the failings of management which had allowed the depot to become so badly run.

As a result of only finding out about the faulty AWS in 43173 during the latter part of their shift, the maintenance engineers gave it a cursory examination which found that it was functioning normally. In fact, it would have taken a much more detailed test to reveal that the problem was caused by a rogue bit of polish on a contact whose presence the inquiry and investigators never managed to explain.

So the train left Old Oak Common with what appeared to be a fully functioning AWS. On the morning of the accident, driver James Tunnock took the train to Paddington using the locomotive 43173, which was at the London end of the train. The AWS was functioning normally and at Paddington he shut the engine down and walked to the other end, locomotive 43163, where he found the guard/driver buzzer was not working. He went back to 43173 and it was at this stage that he found, like driver Taylor the previous night, that he could not cancel the AWS. Again, there was further minor sloppiness which contributed to the accident. Tunnock claimed – and Uff believed him – that he phoned Operations Control at Swindon to alert them to the problem. But no proper record of that call was taken.

The confusion over the messages and precisely who was responsible for 'control' became an issue in the inquiry. The rule book made frequent references to 'Operations Control' but, as it had not been updated since privatisation, the precise meaning was unclear. In the days of BR, of course, the driver, signaller and control staff were within the same organisation and part of the same hierarchy. As Uff put it, 'One of the potential difficulties created by privatisation was the split, first between the driver and signaller, who would work respectively for the train operating company and Railtrack; and secondly, between the signaller and Control, which might refer to either Railtrack or the train operating company.'[7] There was, in fact, a Railtrack control and a Great Western control. While the two were in contact, as Uff pointed out, this was not recognised in the rules and added to the confusion over who was responsible for reporting and dealing with faults.

Back to the train. Tunnock drove it to Swansea as the 0700 service from Paddington, with the AWS working as there was no problem with 43163. However, when he arrived a few minutes before 10 a.m. the fitters he expected to find waiting for him on the platform were not there. His message to Swindon that he needed fitters to fix both the guard/driver buzzer and the AWS had never been passed on. Tunnock contacted the station services manager who in turn telephoned the GWT Landore depot ten minutes away and the fitters arrived around 10.15, just seventeen minutes before his scheduled departure. They were not able to fix the guard/driver communication system but, more importantly, they did no work on the AWS because they were not advised that it was out of order, although Tunnock believed they had previously been advised of the problem.

So a series of mishaps and minor mistakes contributed to the fact that the train started off from Swansea with no AWS. The fault in the AWS could not, in fact, have been repaired at Swansea, as it needed to be worked on from a pit, for which the train would have had to go to a depot. But the train could have been taken out of service or turned around.

Here we have to consider the ambiguity in the rules surrounding AWS, which requires a quick look at the rule book. AWS is a relatively simple and crude system that was introduced over the space of thirty years following disasters at Harrow and Wealdstone in 1952 and Lewisham in 1957 which killed 112 and 90 people respectively, and which were both caused by drivers going through signals at danger. Although not foolproof, because drivers get into the habit of unconsciously resetting the device, and also less effective than it could be because both yellow and red signals trigger the same sound, it has played an important role in reducing the number of SPADs. However, AWS has never been made mandatory, having been installed gradually and almost imperceptibly on the great majority, but not all, of the signals on the rail network.

Back to 43173's fatal journey. One other way of dealing with the faulty AWS would have been to adopt the simple expedient of turning the train around. Here we get into theoreticals but they are, nevertheless, worth considering. If the controllers had been warned about the faulty AWS, would they have ordered the train to be turned around so that the functioning AWS could be used? This was an easy manoeuvre at Swansea as there is a triangle of tracks allowing trains to turn around, but the answer is 'probably not' because of the industry's ambivalent attitude towards the importance of AWS. Moreover, while in BR days turning a train would have been easy, now Great Western would have incurred charges from Railtrack for using up an unscheduled train path, and, had this caused a delay, possible penalty payments as well. In other words, there were built-in obstacles to carrying out a simple manoeuvre that would have prevented the disaster.

The rules governing what should have happened when the AWS was not working were unclear. While operators were keen to ensure that the safety system was functioning properly, they were also desperate to avoid taking trains out of service unnecessarily, especially as, since privatisation, that put them at risk of financial penalties as well as loss of revenue. The rule book for drivers, devised by British Rail but passed on to Railtrack, said at the time of the accident that 'a traction unit must not enter service if the AWS is isolated' and a bit later that 'if it is necessary to isolate the AWS the driver must inform the signalman at the first convenient opportunity. The train *must be taken out of service at the first suitable location without causing delay or cancellation*' [my italics]. As Professor Uff put it in his report, 'These provisions are, and were perceived to be, ambiguous.'[8] It is unclear whether they mean the train should have been taken out of service once its AWS was found not to be working. Indeed, at the inquiry hearings, various experts even differed about precisely when the train 'entered service'. Did it 'enter service' that morning at Paddington when the first passengers boarded, or at Swansea when it began the fateful return journey that was never to be completed?

The root of the problem is whether AWS was regarded as simply an aid to drivers' vigilance or as a vital piece of safety equipment without which trains should not run. The former view was the historic conventional wisdom but gradually managers in the industry had started to realise that AWS was essential for the safe running of trains. As Uff commented, wryly, 'No one was to be heard justifying the decision to allow [the train] to run normally between Swansea and Paddington with its AWS isolated. Yet, with very few exceptions, such concerns were not expressed before the accident.'[9]

In his conclusions, Uff said that the responsibility for the non-functioning of the AWS on the train 'rests firmly with GWT, first in having inadequate maintenance procedures to eliminate known faults, and secondly through inadequate procedures for communicating and taking action following AWS isolation'.[10] However, he also blamed Railtrack for the 'existence of ambiguous and confusing rules as regards action to be taken in the event of AWS isolation', and says that the company should have initiated a review on this issue.

Another post-privatisation change which had a bearing on the accident was that the requirement to have a second driver at speeds over 110mph had been negotiated away with the unions. The tradition came from steam days when there was a driver and a fireman; the latter sometimes helped with spotting signals, though the evidence about the safety benefit of having a second person in the cab is ambivalent, as the two people can distract each other. At the Cowden accident, for example, where five people were killed in October 1994, the guard, who had ambitions to drive trains, was, contrary to the rules, in the cab with the driver, and both were killed.[11] Uff is equivocal on the issue and, indeed, seems to contradict himself: 'The [Southall] crash would probably not have occurred had there been two men in the cab, but it would not be right to conclude that the adoption of single manning above 110mph was itself a contributory cause of the accident.'[12] Nevertheless, in the specific circumstances of a train with a malfunctioning AWS, having a second person in the cab would reduce risk and, indeed, such a change was recommended by the internal railway inquiry into the Southall accident.

Driver Tunnock's duty ended at Cardiff and he was replaced by Larry

Harrison, a driver with a good but not unblemished past record. There were a couple of incidents in the 1970s when Harrison went through signals at danger at slow speeds and one in 1996 when he started a train without the proper signal from the guard. Nevertheless, he was categorised at the highest level of competence. Driver Harrison drove routinely from Cardiff towards London, although the inquiry heard that passengers at both Bristol Parkway and Swindon reported that he was driving with his feet (or a foot) up on the console.

There was one more safety device which could potentially have prevented the disaster – Automatic Train Protection (ATP) – but it was not functioning. It is replete with irony that, although only two lines in Britain were fitted with ATP, both the Southall and the Ladbroke Grove accidents happened on one of them. The reason why Harrison did not have a functioning ATP was not a technical one, as with the AWS, since the ATP on both the train and the trackside was working, but an administrative and political one.

Again, a bit of history is required here. ATP is a system that physically prevents a train from going through a red light. The device constantly monitors the speed at which a train is approaching a red signal and ensures that it can stop in time. In the case of Southall, Harrison's train would have been slowed down before ever reaching the red signal that was protecting the goods train.

The report of the Hidden Inquiry into the 1988 Clapham train disaster recommended the network-wide installation of ATP, a rather strange decision given that Clapham was not caused by a SPAD but by the faulty wiring work of a signals engineer. However, the Hidden Inquiry also looked at two other accidents, Belgrove and Purley, both in March 1989 and both caused by a signal passed at danger. Indeed, even before Clapham the British Railways Board had already approved plans for the development of an ATP system, and it seemed that it would be only a matter of time before the device would be introduced throughout the network. Subsequently BR chairman Sir Bob Reid made a commitment to ATP at the Hidden Inquiry into the Clapham disaster, which was reiterated by his successor, the second Sir Bob Reid, in the board's safety plan for 1991.

Two routes, parts of the Great Western between Paddington and Bristol and of the Chiltern line out of Marylebone, were selected for pilot schemes. At first, development progressed well. Driver training started in August 1991 and the equipment began to be fitted to locomotives and to the trackside. There were, of course, teething problems, notably those caused by slipping on the wheels of the high-speed trains which could result in unnecessary emergency brake applications. The antennae under the trains were frequently damaged by flying ballast because there was nowhere suitable to put them. And retrofitting – putting the equipment on old rolling stock – proved much more difficult than installing ATP on new trains such as the new stock for Heathrow Express and Chiltern. However, by April 1994, when Railtrack was separated out of BR, the trackside infrastructure was largely complete: all GWT's locomotives had been fitted and it only remained for the full pilot scheme to be put into operation.

Then privatisation intervened. The estimated costs of installing ATP across the network were proving much greater than expected – £750m, possibly £1bn[13] – and the newly separated Railtrack began to express concerns over this. However, the British Railways and Railtrack boards knew that dropping ATP would lead to public criticism in the event of an ATP-preventable accident. A memo to the Railtrack board written in December 1993 by Simon Osborne, the company secretary, and Andrew Sim, its legal adviser, warned of the potential risk of manslaughter charges in the event of an accident, and suggested that 'At the end of the day, the most difficult question which may have to be answered is why many foreign administrations have introduced APT [sic] but the British network has not.' The memo reveals that Railtrack's intention was simply to get out of BR's commitments to network-wide implementation of ATP. It concludes that the risk of manslaughter charges could, 'with care', be reduced and, therefore, 'These risks, per se, do not warrant the board taking the line that it is already committed to ATP.'

How the Railtrack executives, so eager to privatise the company, must have cheered. As Peter Rayner, a former BR manager who has been highly critical of the post-privatisation safety regime put it, the meeting held to discuss the memo was 'taking up public funds to protect the backs of people who are already trying to find ways and means of not implementing ATP'. The Railtrack memo recommended a series of actions to reduce the risk of a future manslaughter charge, including a 'meticulous study of the benefits of ATP based not only on trials in the UK but also the experience of ATP in foreign administrations', a consideration of cheaper alternatives to ATP and a full cost-benefit analysis. In the event, only the last was carried out because there was not time to do a more detailed study as ATP was threatening to disrupt the privatisation timetable. The memo, however, makes it clear that this was not an open study to assess the value of ATP but one which was being used to endorse a decision which had already been made – the dropping of the network-wide commitment to ATP. The cost of implementing ATP was clearly an unwelcome obstacle that had to be overcome on the road to privatisation.

On the day before BR formally handed the infrastructure to Railtrack, Sir Bob Reid sent the cost-benefit analysis of ATP to the Department of Transport and also set out what BR would have done had it still been in charge. He said the Great Western and Chiltern pilots would have been put into full operation and that ATP would have been installed on any new high-speed line.

The BR report which accompanied his letter raised doubts over the cost of ATP, suggesting that it would cost £10.9m per life saved to install, well above the norm of £1m usually applied for such safety schemes. For selective implementation on the busiest lines, the most likely estimate was £5.5m per life saved, still well above the industry norm.[14] (See Chapter 12 for a fuller explanation of the cost-benefit analysis process.)

British Rail's report on the economic viability of ATP was referred by the government to the Health and Safety Commission which, after some backroom dealing, backed the decision not to proceed with Hidden's recommendation for network-wide implementation of ATP. The HSC, however, warned that it was not entirely satisfied with the remit of the BR report. In his letter to Brian Mawhinney, the transport secretary, Frank Davies, the chairman of the HSC, said that the calculations only applied to the forms of ATP that were being trialled on Great Western and Chiltern and 'do not necessarily apply to the generic concept of automatic train protection'. Moreover, he warned that the report did not take sufficient account of the wider damage caused by major disasters: 'What does seem clear is that in any catastrophic accident, the damage in terms of public confidence, additional costs, and harms and risks to people quite aside from the number of deaths is substantially greater than damage connected with the generality of risks to individuals.'[15] In other words, a much higher price per life saved might be worth paying because of the long-term damage caused to the industry by catastrophes. Davies was being prescient because, of course, there were to be three such ATP-preventable disasters, Watford, Southall and Ladbroke Grove, within three years of each other.

Mawhinney, an impatient man not noted for his careful consideration of issues, brushed aside any such doubts and used the HSC report to dispose of the ATP problem. He received the report in December 1994 but took three months to issue a press release which killed off ATP as an aspiration for the whole network. The press release made the statistical point that 'Accidents involving SPADs, overspeeding and buffer stop collisions which ATP could prevent are infrequent and account for about 3 per cent of fatalities and injuries (excluding trespassers and suicides).'[16]

That figure was totally meaningless. In his response, Mawhinney had lumped together all train incidents, including passengers being run over by trains or falling over drunk at stations, and all injuries, even very minor ones, to reach the figure of 3 per cent. In fact, of deaths in major train crashes in the previous five years, according to Stanley Hall, the author of several books on rail safety, about a third would have been prevented by ATP.[17] Despite the abandonment of ATP on such flimsy grounds, there was no commitment to introduce a cheaper system, but merely a statement: 'Railtrack is giving high priority to the development of appropriate techniques for analysing the costs and benefits of all safety projects addressing [the] risks associated with signals passed at danger, overspeeding and buffer stop collisions.' This was not so much kicking ATP into touch as completely out of the stadium.

Having abandoned ATP, Railtrack showed no sense of urgency about looking for a cheaper alternative. British Rail had been developing a Train Protection and Warning System that would greatly reduce the number of SPADs (and the impact speed of those it did not prevent) but Railtrack merely asked for assessments about costs rather than trying to ensure progress in the development and installation of TPWS (which is discussed fully in Chapter 7).

Although ATP had been dropped as a national objective, all the parties involved said they were committed to ensuring that the two trials, Great Western and Chiltern, would be fully implemented. Uff, however, is pretty sceptical about this commitment. He wrote: 'Privatisation remained contentious and inevitably the abandonment of ATP altogether in 1995 would have had political implications. ATP pilots represented enhanced safety on Great Western and Chiltern, there was no realistic alternative to their going ahead.'[18]

In other words, it was politically unacceptable to drop the trials, but no one was particularly interested in pursuing them since they were a BR initiative and BR was dead. For the manufacturers there was no longer the prospect of a highly lucrative national scheme. The train operator, Great Western Trains, run since February 1996 by the management buy-out team, was, from the outset, lukewarm about the whole project, which its managers saw as a hassle and a cost with little discernible benefit. That lack of interest from train operators was to contribute to both the Southall and Ladbroke Grove disasters. Furthermore, implementation of ATP became much more difficult with fragmentation. Whereas previously only BR had been involved, now there were three parties – the rolling-stock companies, Railtrack and the train operators. Therefore it would have taken extra effort to ensure that the system was fully implemented.

And GWT was not prepared to make that effort. Quite the opposite. This was made clear at the Southall inquiry by the testimony of Richard George, the GWT executive who made £3m out of the sale of Great Western to First Group (see Chapter 4) and who was responsible for safety. George, who happened to be a passenger on the ill-fated train, denied that GWT had shown no commitment but admitted the company had not been very interested in pursuing the ATP pilot. He told the hearing: 'I will say again that we could and should have shown greater commitment to the project than we did.'[19]

George highlighted the way that the fragmentation of the railway made such investment much more difficult to justify, given that there were now shareholders and a whole host of complex contractual agreements. He told the hearing that the privatised railway had created an environment where everything had to be set out clearly on a contractual basis or else 'there is no legal basis for expenditure'. Therefore, in 1996, when it was found that £350,000 was needed to pay for modifications to the ATP antennae, Great Western baulked at having to foot the bill. So did Angel Trains which owned the locomotives. A memo of a meeting on the subject, read out at the hearing, said that 'GWT expressed clearly that they would not, at this stage, fund any part of the modification programme as the system belonged to Railtrack.'[20] George claimed that this was a negotiating ploy in order to ensure there was a 'strategic understanding' of progress on the scheme and, in the event, it was agreed that the cost should be shared between Angel and GWT – but no order was actually placed for the antennae. At a meeting just a week before the crash, GWT reiterated its complaint that the unreliability of the equipment was the major obstacle to its wider implementation but, as Uff found, 'Lack of driver training was the sole reason why ATP was not able to prevent the crash.'[21]

This lack of commitment to ATP at management level percolated down to the maintenance staff. A report into the ATP project by Electrowatt highlighted the situation, saying that while staff at one depot, Landore, were enthusiastic about ATP, 'They are [a] minority in the company [as the] general view is that ATP is at best an inconvenience to the running of trains services and, at worst, an unfair imposition on the company. It is tolerated while its use remains at the present low level, about 13 per cent of train services overall.' That low level of use showed just how little regard was being paid to ATP by GWT. Uff commented that the ATP project 'came close to being abandoned before the Southall crash'[22] and, indeed, Railtrack was preparing to ditch the project before the publication of the Electrowatt report which recommended its full implementation.

The neglect of the ATP trial was also demonstrated by the absence of a coherent training programme for drivers. Various witnesses, whose statements were read to the inquiry,[23] related how ATP training was not listed as a particular competence for drivers and therefore no attempt was made to match suitably trained drivers with trains that were due to run using ATP. Amazingly, the resource centre that allocated drivers' duties had no record of which drivers were capable of using the system. Moreover, the driver training manager for the period prior to the accident was not even ATP-trained himself and therefore could not train people in the use of the equipment. ATP refresher courses had stopped entirely in January 1996, and were not resumed until after the Southall accident.

In a way it is unfair to be too harsh on George, who had the good grace to admit that there was no 'sense of urgency' about the ATP trial. He had a good reputation as a railwayman within the industry and was deeply affected by the accident and its aftermath, bursting into tears at the inquiry hearing. He just happened to be in the right (or rather wrong) place at the right time to be seduced by the bright lights of privatisation and the opportunities which it afforded a few lucky managers like him.

The new structure meant that decisions were no longer taken in the general interest of the railway. Viewed narrowly, of course, the ATP trial was a hassle and, as it was no longer to be implemented nationally, why should GWT and its managers have taken much interest? They were little people for whom the big picture was an irrelevance. That is why the failure to have a fully functioning ATP on Harrison's train was not really George's fault, but that of the system of which he was part. There was no ownership of the project and therefore no one was thinking that ATP could actually be a vital back-up should AWS not be working.

So back to the hapless Larry Harrison, getting into his train at Cardiff. Despite the host of technical difficulties which had dogged the ATP trial, the train which Larry Harrison took over at Cardiff had a functioning ATP system. But Harrison did not turn it on for several reasons. First, he felt he was not properly ATP-trained. He had been on a course some years previously and claimed to have asked for refresher training, though Uff did not believe him. He had, in any case, never driven a train unsupervised with the ATP switched on. Secondly, GWT's rules actually prevented ATP being switched on en route. When the ATP system was switched on, according to the rule book, there had to be a four-minute start-up test to ensure it was working properly. This led GWT to tell drivers that the system should never be started up at an intermediate station because of the delay the start-up process would cause. By 1997 there was no reason to maintain the rule since the start-up test had been reduced to two minutes and therefore would not create any appreciable delay; but, again, the implications of a set of changes had not been thought through because of the lack of management of the project, which, as Uff puts it, 'lost its urgency and impetus'. He concludes that 'The willpower and commitment to take the steps which can now be seen to have been required to bring the ATP pilot into full operation simply did not exist before the Southall crash.'[24] He found that there was not even a proper legal framework for the continuation of the ATP trial.

Uff's conclusion is, perhaps, too general when viewed in the context of what happened in neighbouring Chiltern, the other line used for an ATP trial, albeit with different technology. There, much better progress was made with the system, not least because the management showed commitment to it right from the beginning. Although Chiltern had newer rolling stock and the initial fitment was 'significantly less troublesome than the Great Western trials',[25] the attitude of the new private management contrasted very strongly with that of Great Western. The company that took over the franchise, M40 Trains, had an immediate commitment not only to retaining ATP but to extending it, despite the cost. Adrian Shooter, the gangly and genial managing director who was a career railwayman, stresses that 'my first job has always been to run a safe railway and to make sure that we do everything we can to make it safer'.[26] Although the trial had been 'drifting' when M40 took over in July 1996, Shooter says, 'We got hold of it by the scruff of the neck. We knew we had a system that was a valuable safety feature and that we had to make it work.' Moreover, when, soon after taking over the franchise, Chiltern became the first of the privatised franchises to order new trains, the company insisted that they must be fitted with ATP. According to Shooter, 'That raised a few eyebrows as people had expected us not to because of the cost.' And the cost ran into hundreds of thousands of pounds because there was only one possible supplier of the equipment 'who had us over a barrel'. Chiltern's already strong commitment to ATP was reinforced after the Southall accident, and the company now has a policy of taking trains out of service if the ATP is not working.

Uff appears rather naive when assessing the role of privatisation in the lack of commitment to ATP. He says, 'It has been suggested that Railtrack's cost-benefit analysis of 1994 was inspired by anticipation of privatisation.'[27] Indeed, the memo to Railtrack's board shows that this is undoubtedly true. Uff, however, goes on to argue that such an analysis of the costs of ATP would have taken place anyway. That may be the case, but it would have been politically impossible for a government to abandon the scheme in the face of opposition from BR, whose chairman, Sir Bob Reid, and director of operational standards and safety, David Rayner, had given specific undertakings for its fitment. In any case, the letter from the second Sir Bob Reid, written on the eve of Railtrack's separation, makes clear that the commitment to the ATP trials was solid.

Would the various circumstances which led to the Southall accident have arisen under BR – or, more pertinently, had the changes in the industry been slower and less dramatic? The answer is almost certainly no. There are minor caveats. Some of the failings arose from practices that had their roots in BR days and, moreover, the commercial pressures which played a key role in the disaster were not solely a result of privatisation since BR, too, was becoming more business-focused. That said, it is impossible to get away from the fact that the Southall crash has its roots in the fragmented railway created by privatisation. Under BR the depot would not have been reorganised in that way; the train might well have been turned around or taken out of service under BR; there would probably have been a second driver; the development of ATP would undoubtedly have proceeded more coherently; the confusion over 'control' and the split between the driver, the signaller and operations would not have existed; and so on. There were other factors too; for instance, privatisation put pressure on greater use of rolling stock – sweating the assets as the bean counters call it – and there were fewer spare sets, so taking a train out of service was likely to be more disruptive, and therefore implicitly discouraged.

Another decision resulting from the break-up of the railways whose wider implications were not properly considered was the change, instituted by the regulator, in the priority given to different types of trains. Under BR, high-speed passenger trains always had priority over goods trains, which sometimes sat in sidings for a long time before being allowed to proceed. John Swift, the first regulator, changed that after consultation with the industry, creating a system of minimum overall delay. This was, as Uff points out, 'driven, to an extent, by privatisation and the perceived need for commercial equality in the face of the penalty payment system'.[28] The change was introduced without any risk assessment having been undertaken, a failing which was highlighted by several parties at the inquiry hearings, but, surprisingly, there was little controversy over its introduction. Railtrack, keen to minimise the cost of delays, ran 'track access awareness' sessions for signallers, which outlined the penalty system. The new rule Swift introduced said that various factors had to be balanced in train regulation, including 'protecting the commercial interests of Railtrack and each affected train operator'. While there is little evidence that signallers considered commercial matters when making decisions and Uff judged that the 1996 regulation policy did not have safety implications, Tom Winsor, who became regulator in 1999, clearly did have such concerns. He told the inquiry that this requirement had been put in against his advice in 1995 (when he was legal adviser to the regulator) and, as regulator, he promptly removed it in November 2000.

While Uff was reluctant to rule definitively on the role of privatisation in causing the accident, presumably because he felt that the issue was somewhat beyond his remit, the evidence is unequivocal. The most compelling evidence is that demonstrating how the structures of privatisation contributed to the disaster. The break-up of the clear decision-making process that had been a key safety feature of BR's operation, and the difficulties over interfaces between the various players, are both factors that emerge several times in the story of the Southall accident. Even with all the safety case paraphernalia, decisions were taken in isolation from one another, as there was no one to consider the whole picture. So, for example, the decision about having a single driver for high-speed trains should have been considered in relation to what happened if the AWS were not working, but there was no one to suggest that there would always be a second driver should the train not have a functioning AWS. As Uff notes, when the requirement to have a second person at high speeds was removed, 'no consideration was given to running High Speed Trains without operative safety systems and the EQE [the technical consultants] report appeared to place some reliance (which was quite misplaced in the circumstances) on the availability of ATP'.[29]

Moreover, privatisation put Great Western Trains in charge. While it had the same management team as when it was part of BR, its remit changed because the directors were working to shareholders rather than a government-owned board. That they misused the freedom which their new positions as railway bosses gave them is not in doubt.

It was little solace to the relatives that in July 1999, before the inquiry was held, Great Western had been fined £1.5m – a record for any health and safety matter – after pleading guilty to breaches of the Health and Safety at Work Act 1974. Driver Harrison had originally been charged with manslaughter but the Crown decided not to proceed with the prosecution. Charges of corporate manslaughter against GWT were rejected on legal grounds by the judge, Mr Justice Scott-Baker, much to the fury of victims and the bereaved. As presently constituted, British law makes it difficult to proceed with corporate manslaughter charges, because there needs to be a 'directing mind' who is clearly identifiable. To have proceeded against Harrison without pursuing GWT's rich executives would have seemed patently unfair to the victims and bereaved, as well as to the general public. The Home Office is currently (summer 2005) reviewing the law on corporate manslaughter, which may have a significant impact on the operation of the railways. It has published a consultation paper that suggests there should be a broader test that 'looks more widely at failings within the senior management of an organisation' but legislation is likely to take several years to reach the statute book.

Unfortunately, the Southall Inquiry, which did not start until the autumn of 1999 because of the criminal proceedings, was overshadowed by the Ladbroke Grove crash, which occurred just as the inquiry had got under way. It was, as Chapter 7 shows, another accident in which privatisation played a key role.

CHAPTER 6

Labour fails to grasp the nettle

It was not only safety that had been compromised by the rushed privatisation of Railtrack. The railway was suddenly transformed from a relatively well-functioning integrated service into a fragmented business, but at least initially the terrible damage that had been inflicted was not apparent, largely because managers and staff continued much as before, ignoring the full implications of working in a new contract-driven structure.

There was, too, hope that much of the change could be reversed. The Labour party was always the favourite to win the general election eventually held on 1 May 1997, and it had promised a 'publicly accountable, publicly owned' railway, whatever that meant. Which was not much, as it turned out, even though in the election Labour triumphed so convincingly that it seemed, for a while, as if anything were possible.

Labour had been so critical of the privatisation in opposition that the new government was expected to introduce rapid changes to the rail industry. However, the party's election manifesto had been guarded, an early indication that Labour was preparing to hoist the white flag in the battle over privatisation of the railways. The manifesto recognised that 'the process of rail privatisation is now largely complete' (omitting to say, as we saw in Chapter 4, that the party had helped along the process itself) and suggested there would be no major changes to the structure or ownership of the industry: 'Our task will be to improve the situation as we find it, not as we wish it to be.'

John Prescott, the deputy prime minister, was given a brief that suited his girth and his ego as head of a specially created department which combined environment, transport and the regions. Gavin Strang was, briefly, made minister of transport, also with a place in the Cabinet, which suggested that transport would be high on the new government's agenda.

But it was not. Transport has never been perceived by New Labour as being a key political issue. Tony Blair had shown little interest in transport in opposition and he largely ignored the subject after the election, which, as ministers later admitted privately, was a big mistake. Transport policy is a long-term business and not doing anything much in the first couple of years of what turned out to be a four-year parliament was short-sighted. Mistakenly, Prescott did not press the issue. He wanted time to draw up a White Paper, get the transport legislation through Parliament and then obtain the money. He managed to do this, but it took all four years of Labour's first term and therefore there were to be precious few achievements in those four years.

Unpopular road schemes would be scrapped or 'reviewed', as promised by Labour in opposition in order to garner the environmental vote, but nothing much else was on the agenda. In any case, the railways could not be reformed without primary legislation and it quickly became clear that none would be forthcoming in the first two years of Labour rule. Instead, a White Paper on transport was commissioned, with the promise that it would set out a vision for 'integrated transport', an oft-repeated but ill-defined slogan. The Tories had already produced a quite commendable Green Paper, which, surprisingly, had little emphasis on building roads and stressed the need for public transport, but this was consigned to the dustbin.

The development of a coherent transport policy was not helped by a series of spats between Prescott and Downing Street over the nature of the policy. Blair was terrified of frightening the ever-powerful motoring lobby and his policy team at No. 10 actively briefed against Prescott's carrot-and-stick approach, aimed at encouraging people out of their cars and onto public transport through a mix of extra charges on road use and improvements to rail and bus services. The differences between Prescott and his boss came to a head in a TV interview by the deputy prime minister when he referred to Geoffrey Norris, the forty-something who held the transport brief in No. 10's policy unit, as a 'teenybopper'.[1] The put-down was a response to Norris's temerity in writing to Prescott to warn him that the prime minister was concerned that the proposed White Paper on transport was too green and too anti-car.

Prescott, in need of allies, instead wooed Gordon Brown, the chancellor, and won some key concessions from him – but at a heavy price. Prescott managed to persuade Brown to allow councils the right to spend any money they raised through congestion charging on local investment schemes for transport, including rail and bus as well as roads. He even obtained a promise from Brown that any future revenue from the fuel tax escalator would be earmarked (hypothecated) for national transport spending, but this was to prove a Pyrrhic victory, since the automatic escalator was abolished in the 2000 budget and then buried by the fuel tax protests that autumn. Moreover, congestion charging was a long-term prospect and needed legislation before it could be introduced.[2]

The price Brown extracted was Prescott's agreement to two controversial part-privatisations, of the London Underground and National Air Traffic Services. While the latter is beyond the scope of this book, the Tube has relevance because the Public Private Partnership (PPP) proposed was similar to the railways, in that the infrastructure was to be separated from the operation of services, although in the case of the Tube the infrastructure was split and privatised, with three private-sector infrastructure consortia responsible for three or four Tube lines each, while the operations remained in the hands of the publicly run London Underground. However, there was concerted opposition to the scheme, particularly in the wake of the Hatfield crash, led by the mayor, Ken Livingstone, who was elected in May 2000. A lengthy political battle ensued.

Just as the campaign for the June 2001 election got under way, the government made a big concession, allowing Livingstone's appointee, Bob Kiley, to take over the runnning of the Tube and the negotiations with contractors over the terms of the PPP. However, Kiley was soon sacked from this role after the election as ministers continued to push through the scheme despite widespread opposition. Transport industry experts were remarkably united against the scheme and few could understand why the government was so intent on pushing through the plan despite the fact that the Hatfield crash (see Chapter 8) had demonstrated the disadvantages of separating the management of maintenance from the running of services. However, despite this concerted opposition, the PPP was driven through by the government and has shown every sign of being a very expensive way of improving the infrastructure of the London Underground.[3]

Prescott tried to disguise his inability to do anything much on transport by making a lot of noise, the usual politician's trick of masking lack of action with words. He rashly announced in a press conference that he would persuade people out of their cars and made a commitment that few thought he would ever be able to keep: 'I will have failed if in five years' time there are not many more people using public transport and far fewer journeys by car. It's a tall order but I urge you to hold me to it.'[4] So far as the railways were concerned, given the retreat from renationalisation, Prescott was forced to tinker at the margins. Soon after the election new instructions were issued to the franchising director which removed the requirement to push privatisation, and, importantly, this was replaced by a new emphasis on growth. But a more radical move, regulation of the rolling-stock companies in order to control prices, was blocked by the rail regulator, John Swift, who argued that it was unnecessary.

Instead, Prescott took his aggression out on the train companies, barracking them rather impotently from the sidelines and taking every opportunity to criticise them. When FirstGroup, the large bus company, took over Great Western Holdings' three franchises from the management buy-out team in March 1998, the original directors, former BR managers, became instant millionaires. The managing director, Richard George, saw his £40,000 investment turn into almost £3m, while Brian Scott, the chairman (who had once fiercely opposed privatisation), received £4m for his stake of £37,000 just two years after the franchise had started operating in the private sector. This was all the more galling for Prescott because, as we have seen, it had been Great Western whose driver was at fault in the previous year's Southall crash. Prescott tried to stop the takeover but ultimately he was told that he did not have the power to do so. Instead, he extracted a few new coaches and a stricter performance regime out of FirstGroup, which, along with other measures, were optimistically valued at £75m.

Much to Prescott's consternation, there followed a steady trickle of news about the creation of yet more rail industry fat cats and massive profits for rail companies. It was the rolling-stock company executives who did the best out of privatisation, which is why Prescott had tried unsuccessfully to regulate them. John Prideaux, a former head of InterCity, made a staggering £15m from the sale of Angel Trains to the Royal Bank of Scotland, and Andrew Jukes, the managing director of

Eversholt, did even better with £15.9m when the company was sold to Forward Trust – though neither of them became as fat a cat as Sandy Anderson, who, as we have seen, made around £40m when the third rolling-stock company, Porterbrook, was bought by Stagecoach in the summer of 1996, barely half a year after it had been privatised.

Railtrack, too, was booming, with annual profits of £339m announced in June 1997 for its first year in private ownership. Prescott let it be known that he had told the company's chairman, Sir Robert Horton (who had been rewarded with the knighthood he apparently craved in John Major's final honours list), that 'Railtrack must no longer put the needs of its investors above those of the taxpayer.'[5]

Even in abandoning the renationalisation commitment at the 1997 conference, Prescott had attacked the new railway barons: 'To purchase Railtrack would cost over £4bn,' Prescott said, and 'not a penny piece of this money would go into investment or indeed rail safety. It would go into the pockets of Railtrack shareholders. I don't believe you really want me to use public money next year to make fat cats even fatter.' In order to defeat a rail unions' motion calling for renationalisation, Prescott suggested that there might be a role in future for the public sector in running the railways, but this was clearly an empty gesture since all franchises ran at least until 2003 (and when the refranchising process eventually started in 2000 there was no suggestion that any would return to the public sector). He went even further in his criticism of the rail companies at the following year's Labour Party conference. After many delegates had been delayed by a series of mishaps on Virgin trains, he departed from his planned speech to call the train companies 'a national disgrace' and later summoned them to a rail summit.

Prescott's attacks on the rail companies were widely seen within the industry as just hot air from a man who everyone knew was hamstrung by his leader's fear of alienating business. Given a free hand, Prescott would have renationalised the railways, cost or no cost, but he knew that that was impossible because of Blair's conservative approach. As Steve Norris, the former Tory transport minister put it, 'Prescott doesn't like the private sector. He tolerates it. He is one of those dangerous people who actually think the public sector runs things better than the private sector.'[6] Instead, sullenly, Prescott used every opportunity to criticise the railways, a futile gesture which damaged morale in an industry that was already the target of a disproportionate number of media attacks.

But the system was against him. The Tories had deliberately engineered much of the government's role out of the railways. Prescott therefore saw his White Paper, the first on transport for twenty years, as the instrument through which he would regain control of the industry. By the time it was published, in July 1998, the lacklustre and taciturn Strang was already on the way out, to be replaced by John Reid, a sparky *bon viveur* Scot who was on the fast track to the Cabinet. (Reid was followed a year later by Helen Liddell, who lasted barely a couple of months before being replaced by Lord Macdonald, a technocrat who was good on TV; by now it was clear that the revolving-door policy for transport ministers, long operated by the Tories, had been retained by Labour. Prescott remained throughout Labour's first term, but he had little time for detail given that he had to deal with everything from global warming and aviation to rural policy and local councils.)

The White Paper, *A new deal for transport: better for everyone*, lacked clarity and, as its wordy title implies, a hard edge. It was a typical piece of Blairite inclusive politics that eschewed the hard choices that must be made in a complex policy area such as transport. Prescott wanted to present it as a radical shift away from the old emphasis on roads, but he could not be seen to be too radical because of Blair's fear that Labour would be labelled anti-motorist. The use of public transport, walking and cycling were to be encouraged, whilst, overall, the need for travel would be reduced through better land-use planning and technological innovation. The White Paper announced plans to allow congestion charging and taxes on company car parking, and there were plenty of other good ideas and suggestions, but it was short on firm commitments. While the White Paper represented a marked shift away from the 'predict and provide' model of road building – whose ultimate logic was the paving over of much of southern England – a few radical edges had been knocked off on Downing Street's orders, such as a suggestion to tax supermarket car park users. More importantly, there was no date for implementation since there was no commitment to a Transport Bill for the 1998/9 Parliamentary session. As the *Daily Mail* accurately observed: 'A quick reading could lead to the impression that the Paper contains hard and decisive policies. Unfortunately, closer examination suggests there is less to his proposals than meets the eye.'[7]

Rail was to be at the heart of the programme, with investment and improvements inducing people out of their cars and on to public transport. As Reid put it, 'If we don't have a decent train system, we can't handle the other problems in creating an integrated transport policy. Train is the central element in solving all our transport problems.'[8] There was to be a Commission for Integrated Transport to act as a government advisory board and, for the railways, the White Paper confirmed the creation of the much-trailed Strategic Rail Authority (SRA). The idea was that this new body would inject some long-term thinking into the industry, a function blatantly absent in the Tories' model, and would also take over the role of disbursing subsidies. The SRA was presented as a way of bringing together a fragmented industry, but this was not strictly true. It was, rather, an addition to the panoply of organisations with their fingers in the railway pie and its power to crack heads was limited, as events after the Hatfield disaster were to show.

Yet Prescott was desperate to be seen as doing something for the railways and much play was made of the creation of the SRA. A draft bill was published in the summer of 1999 but this was only a fig leaf to cover up the fact that legislation would not pass through Parliament until the following session. In fact, because the creation of the SRA became part of a complex Transport Bill, it did not actually reach the statute books until the autumn of 2000, over three years after the Labour government had been elected.

Not only did the hapless Prescott fail to obtain any legislation until three-quarters of the way through Labour's first parliamentary term, he also had no money to improve train services. The Tories had set subsidies for the train operators at sharply declining rates, with the level of payments reducing by £200m and £300m per year from the initial level of £1.8bn in 1996/7. That meant the train companies faced a constant squeeze on their finances. Nor was there was any prospect of extra money, since Gordon Brown had pledged Labour to sticking to the Tories' tight spending plans until April 1999.

Well-targeted Tory taunts that Prescott had done nothing for transport apart from the publication of the White Paper prompted him to announce the preparation of a ten-year transport plan, which was eventually published in July 2000. The headline commitments in the document, *Transport 2010: The 10 year plan*, looked, at first glance, impressive. The staggering sum of £180bn, split three equal ways between roads, rail and other modes of travel, would be spent on transport in the first decade of the new century. However, as with all such documents, closer examination revealed a less generous picture, not least because the figures included increases for inflation.

While both the White Paper and the ten-year plan contained measures aimed at making significant improvements to the railways, the delay in producing them, together with the fundamental policy differences between Prescott and No. 10, resulted in Labour losing the political initiative on transport. With such a large majority, Labour had a brief opportunity to launch radical policies whose benefits would have begun to percolate through in time for a general election. Instead, Labour got the worst of both worlds because its relatively radical rhetoric, even though it had not been backed up by corresponding action, helped provoke a backlash. By the time they left office the Tories had realised that a transport policy based solely on making life easier for the motorist was counterproductive, but under a more right-wing leadership the party now reinvented itself as the motorists' friend. Their supportive rottweilers in the tabloid press could be unleashed at the slightest whiff of anti-motorist policies.

The roads lobby, that powerful coalition of interests representing bodies as varied as the Automobile Association, car dealers and truckers' organisations, had been relatively silent in the final years of Tory rule. Margaret Thatcher had feathered their nest with the country's biggest road-building programme but the plans had ground to a halt during the late Major years as a result of concerted opposition from local residents and roads campaigners, combined with the Treasury's realisation that most schemes were not good value for money. When the Tory party changed its tune after the 1997 election, the roads lobby returned from the wilderness and quickly pointed its guns at 'two Jags' Prescott, who was seen as an easy target, not least because he did own two Jaguars. He bore the brunt of many attacks provoked by, for example, his idea of creating a bus lane on the M4 near London and his spectacularly stupid 200-yard drive along the Bournemouth sea front at the 1999 party conference, allegedly because his wife, Pauline, had been worried about her hair blowing about, although Prescott claimed it was for security reasons. The M4 bus lane proved, later, to be a great success, reducing journey times for both bus passengers and cars, but that never made any headlines. (Pauline's hair, meanwhile, remained immaculate.) The ease with which the roads lobby could whip up support was illustrated when both the *Daily Mail* and the *Daily Express*, reporting the 1999 Queen's

Speech, ran front-page stories declaring a 'war on the motorist',[9] merely because Tony Blair said the forthcoming Transport Bill would include measures that would 'reduce road congestion'.[10]

The backlash culminated in the great petrol-price revolt in the autumn of 2000. A group of pasty-faced farmers and beer-bellied truckers brought the country to its knees on the ludicrous premise that petrol prices were excessive. In fact, the overall real cost of motoring had remained virtually unchanged for two decades but a hike in the world price of oil combined with the fuel-tax escalator, which ironically had been abandoned in the previous budget, had led to record prices at the petrol pumps.[11] The government dithered and for inexplicable reasons the tanker drivers felt unable to cross the picket lines at the depots while the police behaved with kid gloves, in marked contrast to their confrontations with the miners during the 1984 strike. The country almost came to a standstill as the pumps ran dry and, despite a few local hiccups where operators found themselves short of fuel, the railways enjoyed a momentary boom (only to lose their new-found customers a month later following the Hatfield disaster), while many people enjoyed the freedom of the relatively traffic-free streets for a few days.

The petrol-price revolt exposed the lack of coherence in Labour's transport policy. Its ministers, Tony Blair included, refused to go on the offensive and argue for the need for high prices to protect the environment. Instead, Labour politicians justified the high price of fuel on the basis that it paid for schools and hospitals, a simplistic argument which the public saw through.

By the time Labour went into its successful 2001 election campaign, its transport policy was utterly incoherent. While the railways were scheduled to benefit from the ten-year plan, roads would do even better and, unlike the rail passenger, the motorist could see that the investment was already beginning to come through. In December 2000 the government announced a £1bn programme of by-passes and dual carriageways, including many schemes which had previously been postponed in the roads review carried out in the wake of the 1997 election. Blair's pandering to the motoring lobby ensured that Prescott's grand schemes for getting motorists out of their cars and for massive investment in 'integrated transport' were stillborn. During the whole 2001 election campaign, Tony Blair made no significant mention of public transport.[12] The bankruptcy of Labour's ideas on the subject was shown by its manifesto, which had barely half a dozen paragraphs on transport, based on the promise to 'improve and expand railway and road travel' – did that suggest Labour wanted to see more cars on the road? Despite the collapse of Railtrack's share price during the election campaign, the issue did not feature at all in the hustings.

Even more than Blair's lack of interest, Prescott's muddle-headedness blighted the first Labour government's policy towards the railways. Prescott was a fan of the railways but could never contain his hatred of the companies that ran them. So he never talked up the industry and its successes, such as the sharp rate of passenger growth, or provided what Gerald Corbett, Railtrack's chief executive, referred to as 'air cover' when there were disasters such as Southall and Ladbroke Grove. Instead, by allowing a damaging briefing by Alastair Campbell, the prime minister's official spokesman, in the aftermath of the Ladbroke Grove accident (see Chapter 7), he not only undermined Railtrack but encouraged the overly conservative response of the industry in the aftermath of Hatfield.

Prescott seemed to act like an opposition politician in relation to the railways. Twice, for example, in 2001 he criticised fares rises – by Silverlink and then Virgin – and yet did not attempt to impose more regulation of fares, which was in his power through the Strategic Rail Authority and the refranchising process. As one rail insider put it, 'Prescott undermined the industry rather than supported it.'[13] He appointed a regulator, Tom Winsor, who was more interested in warring with Railtrack than regulating it, and he also made the mistake of thinking the SRA could pull together the fragmented industry, when, in fact, the events after Hatfield showed that the structure was wrong. In short, the industry felt that the government had always asked for the impossible and then criticised the rail companies when it was not delivered.

While the railways toiled, the roads blossomed. Labour's road-building programme was potentially even more ambitious than that of the Tories during their whole eighteen-year rule. As two academics put it at the Royal Geographical Society in early 2001, Labour's support for roadbuilding was 'completely inconsistent' with the party's earlier support for integrated transport.[14] The railways were no longer at the centre of transport policy as John Reid, the long-departed transport minister, had promised; now this priority for railways had been lost. Instead, Prescott had taken the easy way out, promising lots of money for all modes of transport. The ten-year plan was a step forward, but the numbers in it were not sacrosanct beyond the Treasury's usual three-year spending horizon and, indeed, the whole plan was thrown into disarray as a result of the explosion in railway costs described in detail in the latter part of this book.

Labour ministers invested a good deal of political capital in the Strategic Railway Authority, which was supposed to give direction to the privatised industry. Its creation was the inspiration of Prescott who, when in opposition, had discussed plans for some kind of rail authority to direct the government's policies in the rail industry. Sir Alastair Morton, the former chairman of Eurotunnel, who was widely credited with having saved the channel tunnel project from bankruptcy, was appointed as its part-time chairman. Labour ministers repeatedly claimed that the SRA would be the vehicle for bringing order into the fragmented rail industry but this was patently overambitious, and a great irony given that they killed it off within five years.

The SRA took over the functions of OPRAF on franchising, but had the added responsibility of trying to coordinate investment in the industry in a 'strategic' way. With the industry owned by so many different players pulling in different directions, this task proved virtually impossible. Sir Alastair immediately tried to reassure the industry that he would not try to run it from Whitehall. He stressed that he was not seeking 'command and control' of the industry but instead to 'lever in resources and skills' from the private sector into the industry through 'partnerships'. But there is an inherent contradiction there – if you do not attempt to control an industry, it is difficult to impose a direction on it.

It was a muddled agenda that soon became bogged down in the realities of an uncoordinated and fragmented industry. Sir Alastair's stated aim was to maximise 'investment, investment, investment', as he put it, emulating Tony Blair's catchphrase on education. Realising that Railtrack was never going to be able to supply all the investment needed, he tried to get the train operators to put forward schemes to improve the railway. As an inducement, the successful bidders were to be offered twenty-year franchises, rather than the mostly seven-year deals in the first round of franchising, which would provide the stability the operators needed to be confident enough to make substantial investments.

A policy document, *The Strategic Agenda*, had long been promised and was finally published by the SRA in February 2001, after several delays.

But far from setting out a coherent programme, it was a sparse paper, providing a brief *tour d'horizon* of the state of the railways and a list of potential projects, with no prioritisation, all interspersed with the thoughts of chairman Morton. Indeed, the Strategic Rail Authority's approach to investment, together with the much-hyped promises of privatisation, created a fantasy about the potential for an improved railway without proper consideration of the realities of railway finance and the government's ability to pay for what Railtrack executives liked to call 'a world-class railway'. Even with the most generous settlement from the rail regulator, Railtrack was never going to be in a position to fund much more than £6bn–8bn worth of enhancements in the five-year period from April 2001. Morton therefore had the idea of creating 'special purpose vehicles' (SPVs) to tackle big improvement projects, a common feature of other industries in which he had worked such as oil.

Special purpose vehicles were to be consortia of investors and engineering companies who would carry out improvements to the rail network and, probably, sell on the schemes to Railtrack to operate. The advantage was that this would create extra sources of capital for the railways but the disadvantage, as Railtrack was quick to point out with much justification, was that it would lead to further complexity on an already highly fragmented network. Indeed, carrying out major enhancements on a working railway is a risky business and was almost impossible without the active involvement and support of Railtrack. And Railtrack would not play ball. Morton's plan was strongly opposed by Gerald Corbett, Railtrack's chief executive, who argued that to design and deliver major projects separate from the day-to-day management of the railway was not feasible.

The notion of creating special purpose vehicles over the head of Railtrack was pure fantasy. And so was the SRA's belief that everything was possible. Under Morton, the SRA steadfastly refused to prioritise between the many options being suggested or to set a realistic agenda defining the kind of railway it wanted to see and even, as a wider consideration, what type of journeys it wanted to encourage. There was no attempt to address the big questions such as 'what are the railways for?' or 'on what markets should they focus?' A former executive of the SRA said: 'Alastair rejected any attempt to set out a clear plan. He just didn't see it as our job. The whole basis of the refranchising exercise was based on investment ideas, rather than on what was feasible. You end up with batty ideas.'[15]

With some £2bn of subsidies for services to allocate each year, the SRA could have encouraged inter-city travel through targeting investment on the main lines, or it could have made it easier for commuters by investing in their services. But there was no such debate. Nor was there any discussion of how safety factors were distorting investment priorities.

Sir Alastair's strategy was based on a false premise. Train operating companies (TOCs) are bizarre constructs which actually own no assets – they lease trains, rent stations and are given a contract to operate services by the government. They are, as the Treasury adviser Shriti Vadera put it in an unguarded memo, 'thinly capitalised equity profiteers of the worst kind'.[16] Therefore, what can they invest in? Sure, they can order more coaches, but it is actually the rolling-stock companies which take the risk and provide the capital, while investing in stations or the track should have been Railtrack's responsibility.

The SRA's strategy led to TOCs submitting all kinds of outlandish bids which, in turn, resulted in the complete paralysis of the refranchising process. The bidders were mostly the existing franchisees, but with a few newcomers such as Serco, Group 4 and foreign railways (the Dutch, French and Swiss, ironically all state-owned). Now they were encouraged to come forward with all manner of expensive schemes such as new high-speed lines between London and the North, tunnels under London, double-decker trains and rebuilt stations. But who was going to pay for all this? By asking bidders to come up with their ideas, Sir Alastair had misunderstood the relationship between the private and public sectors. Private companies want Christmas every week and they acted as if there were an infinite amount of money available. Yet the bulk of these ideas would have had to be underwritten by the taxpayer because such schemes are never commercially viable.

There was an even more fundamental question about this whole strategy: why should these bidders know better than government? Franchisees are in reality only transient contractors who do not have a long-term interest in the railway.[17] Even if they had a twenty-year deal, it could be rescinded by the SRA should they not perform properly. Moreover, most of the franchisees and bidders were bus companies with little imagination or experience of working in an expanding industry. Despite widespread criticisms and pressure from within the industry, Sir Alastair refused to set out clear proposals for where he wanted to take the railways. Instead, he sat back while the bidders tried to outdo each other in the scale and imagination of their schemes, without much concern about the cost. It was quite the opposite of a strategy.

To make matters worse, the SRA failed even to clarify the precise boundaries of the franchise areas. At first, the SRA had announced that it wanted fewer franchises in order to simplify the rail network, but again its plans foundered on the complexities of redrawing the franchise map. The highly cerebral Sir Alastair, and his more down-to-earth chief executive, Mike Grant, were finding it very difficult to make decisions, much to the frustration of franchise bidders, the government and Railtrack, all of whom wanted some certainty about what was happening on the railways. The Treasury was not amused. The mandarins felt that Sir Alastair was not doing his sums and, as one commented at a meeting, 'He likes big numbers but doesn't seem to care whether they are black or red.'[18]

Sir Alastair had only accepted the job on the basis that the Treasury would support major investment initiatives. He had been promised that over the next decade the railways would benefit from a £60bn investment plan which would transform the network. But Railtrack's incompetence, together with the Treasury's reluctance to release the money, and then the Hatfield accident and its aftermath, ensured this was to be a pipedream. The Treasury started to give Sir Alastair and his crew a hard time by blocking the signing of franchise agreements. Sir Alastair had, at first, promised to get the eighteen franchises which ran out in 2003/4 re-let by the end of 2001 and managed to announce his first deal in the summer of 2000, the relatively easy decision to allow Chiltern to remain with the John Laing group. Details of a couple of other deals, including booting Connex out of the large SouthCentral commuter franchise and retaining Stagecoach for South West Trains (initially on a twenty-year deal, see Chapter 13) followed, but essentially Morton was getting nowhere. Several franchise processes were delayed, most notably the loss-making Central which was halted in February 2001 when the SRA said that the two remaining bids were not good enough, infuriating the companies concerned, National Express and Group 4, who had spent hundreds of thousands on putting them together.

Far from setting the agenda, therefore, the SRA seemed to be chasing everyone else's ideas, and making decisions was never its strong point. Now it was busy trying to let out the franchises without an overall plan for the railway – a topsy-turvy way of doing things, as the bidders were desperate for a clear statement of what the SRA – and therefore the government – wanted from a particular franchise to enable investment plans to be developed. Railtrack was faced with trying to cost and develop investment schemes for every hare-brained idea that any bidder suggested on the back of an envelope. On a railway with limited capacity this inevitably led to conflicts between different operators, both freight and passengers, using the same lines. With the SRA unwilling to use its strategic role to sort out such issues, Railtrack was left in an impossible situation. As a Railtrack insider put it, 'Railtrack can only respond to different demands by offering the lowest common denominator. No one has the power to impose what to do in terms of the railway. Trying to please all parties is impossible. Franchise propositions should have been clear about what investment was needed, and then offered out to bidders.'[19]

The SRA's task was much more difficult than that faced by its predecessor, OPRAF, during the initial franchise letting process in 1996/7. Then there had been only one criterion – price. Now, the SRA was trying to let out franchises for a growing railway on terms that would maximise the amount of investment. But it also wanted to reward the past efforts of good franchisees, improve standards for passengers and, where possible, increase the number of services. But if two competing bids offered very different types of improvements, choosing between them was virtually impossible.

This was the problem that caused the refranchising of East Coast Main Line to develop into an almighty fiasco that highlighted the flaws in the SRA's 'let's try all flavours' approach. The incumbent, Sea Containers, which operated under the name Great North Eastern Railway and had a pretty good reputation, saw tilting trains – which it had mooted for the first franchise but which had never materialised – as the solution to the overcrowding on the line, as they would allow services to go faster. Virgin, its rival, wanted instead to put extra diesel engines on the trains in addition to the electric locomotives to speed up acceleration and, crucially, suggested around 100 miles of new parallel, high-speed line to improve capacity.

The SRA was paralysed. It did not know what to do because it had not developed a way of comparing such disparate proposals. After some hesitation it commissioned a study into the proposal for a new line and tried to get the two companies to put in bids on a comparable basis. The issue was further confused by a vicious public spat between Railtrack and the SRA over the costs of upgrading the East Coast line. In February 2001 the SRA seemed to discover that the cost of the proposed upgrade was £3.4bn rather than the original estimate of £1.9billion, and possibly much more as the details of the scheme were worked up. This was not due to Railtrack's incompetence or inefficiency but was principally related to the perceived risks of the project, which always add considerably to privately funded schemes. However, rather than quietly having it out with Railtrack, the SRA went public, pulling the franchise process and arguing that Railtrack was trying to exploit its monopoly position by increasing the costs. The company responded by saying that it wanted a clear franchise proposition from the SRA so that it could know what investment plans would be needed.

Accusations of duplicity and double-dealing were thrown about by both organisations and the episode degenerated into farce, infuriating ministers and the Treasury. Railtrack responded with a press release that said the cost increases were 'not unusual for a project at this early stage'[20] and eventually the SRA seemed to accept this view. After a three-week delay, peace broke out, rather unconvincingly. However, the row hardly reinforced public or, more importantly, City confidence in the ability of the railway to handle major investment projects and the SRA's understanding of the private sector.

In fact, the SRA's battle with Railtrack over the East Coast was part of a wider war between the two organisations over how improvements to the railway were to be brought about. Sir Alastair had long been highly critical of Railtrack's inefficiencies and its lack of discipline over costs, which, as we shall see, was a perfectly reasonable accusation.

Neither special purpose vehicles nor the grand plans for the East Coast ever got off the ground. Following the 2001 general election and the replacement of John Prescott by Stephen Byers, the whole franchise process was put on hold, including the notion of twenty-year deals. Instead, Byers sought to get two-year extensions in order to obtain quick gains for passengers and Morton, who was now disliked by both the Treasury and the transport department, was clearly on the way out. In July 2001 the government finally announced its decision on the ECML.

Or rather it didn't. Byers instead said the twenty-year franchise decision would be put on ice and that Sea Containers would be granted a two-year extension, provided it offered more passenger benefits. The full rebidding process on the East Coast did not start until the end of 2004 and then the Treasury made clear there was to be a plain vanilla deal, with no costly enhancements or service improvements. The new franchise deal was finally announced in March 2005, with GNER regaining it at the cost of having to pay £1.3bn in premium payments over the ten-year life of the franchise, with just £100m promised for investment. It was precisely the opposite of what Morton, by then sadly dead,[21] would have wanted. His other dream, the Special Purpose Vehicle concept, also died when Railtrack went into administration, scuppering the only major scheme that had been created, which was supposed to have improved the London–Brighton line.

As I put it at the time, the SRA should have been called R because it had no strategy and no authority. Indeed, its failure during the first two years was not only an embarrassment to Morton, the man who had successfully bludgeoned through the Channel Tunnel project in the face of hostile bankers and rapacious contractors, but also to the government, which had invested its hopes for the railways in the organisation.

But its failure cannot by any stretch of the imagination be laid solely at Morton's door. It was also a demonstration of the difficulty of bringing any coherence to the fragmented rail network. The root cause of the latter's semi-paralysed state was the failure of the Labour government to set out any clear aspirations for the railways and, inevitably, also the constant meddling of the Treasury – which had never gone away – over investment plans. In private, Sir Alastair complained constantly of Treasury interference. Moreover, a secretary of state with greater determination and strategic vision than John Prescott would have been able to drive through some of these projects more quickly. Instead, ministers seemed to think that the mere creation of the SRA would solve the problems caused by the fragmentation of the railways. Inevitably, it failed.

There was, of course, one other crucial factor. By 2001, Railtrack, which had been riding so high when Morton first joined the shadow SRA in the summer of 1999, was looking like a corporate basket case, and rail users, rather than looking forward to a 'world-class railway', were wondering when, if ever, services would be restored to the standard that they had enjoyed just twelve months earlier. This dramatic reversal of fortunes was attributable to the two major accidents that had occurred in the interim: Ladbroke Grove and, to a much greater extent, Hatfield.

CHAPTER 7

Ladbroke Grove:
disaster at signal SN 109

The crash at Ladbroke Grove on 5 October 1999, the worst railway accident since the Clapham Junction disaster eleven years earlier, can, like Southall, be linked directly to the changes made as a result of privatisation and fragmentation. Thirty-one people died and 425 were injured when an inexperienced Thames driver, Michael Hodder, unaccountably ignored a red light and went down a prohibited piece of track. Hodder's 8.06 a.m. Thames Turbo train bound for Bedwyn smashed head-on into the Great Western High Speed Train Cheltenham Flyer just a couple of miles out of Paddington station.

The aftermath of the collision was one of the most horrific ever witnessed on a British railway track. The combined impact speed was reckoned to have been 130mph, at that time[1] the highest ever on British railways, and the front coach of the Turbo quite literally disintegrated. Visiting the floodlit site that evening, I was particularly struck by part of the side of the Thames train which hung gruesomely over the largely intact middle coaches of the HST. The aluminium-built Turbo, weighing a total of 90 tons, never stood a chance because the leading vehicle of the HST was a heavy, wedge-shaped locomotive pulling a 400-ton train that brushed it aside like a bird bouncing off a car windscreen. All but seven of the dead were in the Turbo, mostly in the front coach. All the dead in the HST, apart from the driver, were in the leading coach, first class carriage H, which quickly became engulfed by fire. The report[2] on the accident by Lord Cullen contains much detail about the crashworthiness of the vehicles involved and consideration of the means of escape but such matters are largely an irrelevance. No trains can be built to withstand impacts of this speed and, indeed, it is a great tribute to the solidity of the HST carriages that everyone outside coach H survived, though, of course, there were many very severe injuries. The high death toll – at one point the police suggested it might reach over 100 – and the proximity to London's media HQs – the BBC's Television Centre is a mile down the road – turned Ladbroke Grove into one of the biggest news stories of the year which, in turn, ensured a powerful political involvement. This, as we see below, was to prove highly damaging to the railways. Of course, even if the accident had happened somewhere more remote, there would have been extensive coverage, but there is no doubt that the location, along with the fact that it took nine days to recover the bodies and remove the last coach, heightened and prolonged media interest.

The primary cause of the accident was, of course, the fact that Hodder went through a red light, but, as with most accidents, there were many other contributory factors, several directly related to the way that the industry had been fragmented and privatised. The key issue was the high incidence of Signals Passed at Danger (SPADs) in the Paddington 'throat' in the six years since it had been remodelled and electrified with overhead line equipment in order to accommodate the Heathrow Express trains. According to Lord Cullen,[3] there had been sixty-seven SPADs in the area in that period, many more than would be expected, even for such a complex section of track.

Most significantly, the signal which driver Hodder went through at red had been passed no fewer than eight times during that period. SN 109 was an unusual signal in that it was shaped as a reverse L, with the red not, as is usual on Britain's railways, at the bottom of the set of lights but to the left at the same level as the lower yellow lamp. This unique set-up had come about because of concerns about the signal's visibility; it is partially obscured by a bridge, a problem that had not been recognised until the equipment was actually fitted.

While four of the SPADs at SN 109 involved only tiny overruns, such a spate of incidents clearly pointed to the fact that this was a more than averagely troublesome signal. The four other SPADs all gave cause for concern. In February 1995 a Thames driver admitted that he misread an adjacent signal as relating to him and he told the inquiry how the signals were difficult to see because of the bridges and that he would normally count across from the leftmost signal to check which one related to him. He passed the signal by 105 yards before bringing the train to a halt. Another incident, in March 1996, also involving a Thames train which overran by 146 yards, was put down to 'driver inattention', a conclusion which train companies were all too ready to reach, in the same way that airlines like ascribing accidents to pilot error since it implies that no significant changes to systems need be made. The report of the last incident, in August 1998, an overrun of just three yards, is also highly relevant because, as driver Offen later told the Cullen Inquiry,[4] the signal was obscured by the bridge: 'It didn't register as well as it should have done ... The moment I seen [sic] SN 109 I reacted to it ... I realised it [SN 109] was there and red as it come [sic] into view under the bridgework.' In other words, from these accounts, it is clear that this was a very difficult signal because of the bend and the bridge, a fact that was confirmed by the post-accident research into the visibility of the signal.

However, the most significant incident, which was almost a dress rehearsal for the disaster, took place on 4 February 1998, twenty months earlier. This involved a Great Western HST whose driver mistakenly thought he was on the main line, where he would have expected a clear set of greens, rather than on the track controlled by SN 109. Fortunately, the driver, having confidently accelerated to 70mph after the previous yellow, spotted 'six signals in a line'[5] and realised his error but only managed to stop 432 yards after the signal. The oncoming train, a Heathrow Express shuttle, had, by then, also come to a halt as the signaller managed to turn its signal, SN 120 – just a few metres away from the collision point of the Ladbroke Grove disaster – to red. While the cause of the driver going through the red light was investigated, crucially no one noticed that the near miss highlighted the potential danger of a SPAD at SN 109 – that the way the track was laid out and the points were set meant that a train going through that signal would end up directly in the path of an oncoming train.[6] (See diagram overleaf.)

The high incidence of SPADs in the Paddington area led, almost inevitably by the law of averages, to one collision. This occurred at Royal Oak, less than a mile outside the station, in November 1995. It was not SN 109 but a similar gantry signal, SN 74, which was passed at danger. A Thames driver, approaching the station, thought that a neighbouring signal referred to him and, although he realised his error and managed to stop, he did so too late to avoid a low-speed collision with a Great Western High Speed Train heading for Swansea. There were no injuries but an inquiry was held which made fourteen recommendations in March 1996.

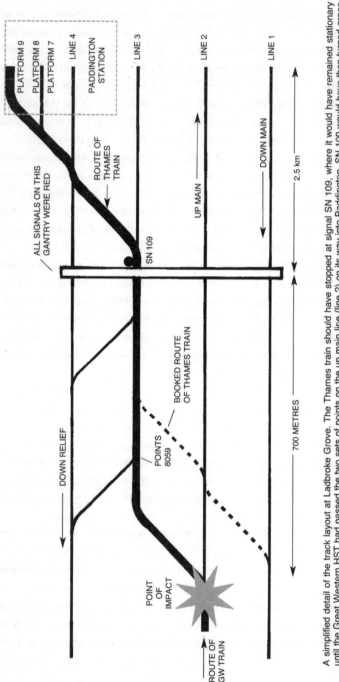

A simplified detail of the track layout at Ladbroke Grove. The Thames train should have stopped at signal SN 109, where it would have remained stationary until the Great Western HST had passed the two sets of points (line 2) on its way into Paddington. SN 109 would have then turned green allowing the Thames train to proceed on its booked route, taking it across line 2 and onto line 1, the down main. Had points 8059 been set towards line 4, the down relief line, there would have been a risk of a train passing SN 109 at red hitting a train going the same way on line 4, but no danger of a head-on collision. In fact, the points were set the other way because, first, that route provided a slightly longer, 700-metre, safety overrun and, second, as line 3 ceased to be bi-directional after points 8059, it was assumed that any driver passing them would realise he or she was going the wrong way on a one-way track.

It is here that the first clear evidence of Railtrack's failings emerges: the company had no procedure to ensure that the recommendations of such inquiries were implemented. Of the nine Royal Oak recommendations accepted by a safety review group, Railtrack failed to implement seven. While a couple were not proceeded with because other events made them irrelevant, the others seem to have disappeared into an administrative black hole, not actioned or followed up by the person given the task, who, in any case, did not know that he was responsible. Several of these recommendations involved improving the visibility of signals in what was recognised to be a difficult area for the drivers. Similarly, four of the five recommendations arising from the inquiry into the very serious February 1998 SPAD were not followed up, including the suggestion that there should be a risk assessment of bi-directional working – the practice of using the same lines for trains travelling in both directions – in the Paddington throat.[7]

At that time Railtrack was divided into seven zones, and the Great Western zone, broadly covering the routes out of Paddington, had a troubled history with frequent senior management changes and a poor reputation among train operators. Cullen found that the zone simply had 'no procedure for the tracking of recommendations'. His report's account of the action taken on the recommendations following that SPAD seems to have been taken out of a manual on how not to run a successful organisation: 'Recommendations 3, 5 and 6 were allocated for Mr Wiseman [Railtrack Great Western zone's business development manager]. He was unaware of this fact until over eighteen months later [i.e. after the disaster, suggesting that he would never have found out had it not occurred], apparently as a result of Mr Sutton [the zone's performance services manager] failing to notify him. Recommendations 4 and 7 were allocated to Mr Wilkinson [the zone's production manager]. It appears nothing was done.'[8]

Wilkinson told the inquiry that the recommendations were simply sent to headquarters and he did not attempt to progress them. Sutton, the zone's performance service manager, claimed that it was impossible to follow all recommendations since the zone was swamped with 400–500 of them. Cullen, however, says this was an exaggeration and that there was nothing like this number of recommendations to be dealt with. Nor did the zonal manager responsible for following up such recommendations do so. He was, in any case, described by Chris Leah,

Railtrack's director of safety, as 'more of a register and not a chaser and closer down of recommendations'.[9] Revealingly, Leah confessed to the inquiry that the system was flawed and that the problems with it would not have been uncovered had it not been for the evidence given to the inquiry.

It is worth noting that the very title of Peter Wiseman's job – business development manager – betrays much about what was wrong in the way that Railtrack was structured. Implementing safety recommendations, which necessarily implies adding costs to the production process, is hardly compatible with the notion of 'business development'. There is a strong parallel here with the circumstances surrounding the Hatfield accident (see next chapter), with engineering decisions being made by contract managers who knew nothing about how the railway functioned. While it is wrong to suggest, as the tabloid media often do, that commercial considerations cannot play any part in decisions relating to railway safety, Railtrack's structure was such that responsibility for safety and other issues was too often placed in the hands of managers whose primary function was commercial. Of course commercial issues have to be taken into account — it is just that they must not be allowed to dominate in the way that clearly they did within Railtrack.

It is impossible to pinpoint any single recommendation made prior to the disaster whose implementation would have actually prevented it. But it is clear that there was a fundamental failing in the way that Railtrack dealt with safety recommendations arising from incidents; and it seems likely that, had all the recommendations been put into effect, the thirty-one lives lost at Ladbroke Grove would have been saved.

Given that Railtrack did not even manage to implement recommendations of a formal inquiry into an accident, it was hardly surprising that the series of SPADs at SN 109, none of which had resulted in a collision, failed to trigger an adequate response. This part of the background to the accident shows widespread failings in the way Railtrack was managed and has even more direct relevance to the accident. The fact that SN 109 had been passed at danger eight times in six years should clearly have rung alarm bells throughout the zone. Indeed, there are set procedures for calling signal sighting committees – a team of experts – to assess the visibility of signals if they have been repeatedly passed at danger. According to the rules, a signal sighting committee should be called when a signal has been passed at danger more than once within a year, or three or more times in any three-year period. If this rule had been followed, six of the eight SPADs at signal SN 109 would have resulted in the convening of a signal sighting committee. None was called, even though a meeting of the SPAD action group on the day after the February 1998 incident concluded that committees should be convened for both SN 109 and another signal, SN 63, within a month.

The reason for the failure to convene a signal sighting committee could, again, be taken from the manual of how not to manage: there was no one charged with that responsibility. A number of Railtrack witnesses to the inquiry thought that it was the job of Symon Murrant, the zone's train operations liaison manager. Murrant admitted to the inquiry that he had tried to call these committee meetings, but he was not aware it was actually his responsibility and was just attempting to show the train operators that he was trying to do something. His bosses were unaware that signal sighting committees were not being held and Murrant gave the inquiry three explanations as to why he had not convened them: difficulty in obtaining safety permits for possession of track; the lack of qualified people; and the absence of a clear direction from senior management. However, on being pressed, he admitted that he had never tried to get any possessions, nor had he made much effort to find suitable people. Cullen totally dismisses the third explanation, saying that convening the meeting was not an option but 'mandatory' and therefore nothing to do with the view of senior management. Cullen concludes that the whole episode 'betrays a culture of apathy and lack of will to follow up promised actions'.[10]

It would be wrong to single out hapless junior managers like Murrant, since on further investigation the story gets far worse. When internal auditors from Railtrack Assurance and Safety came to visit the zone, six months before the disaster, a random sample for the report revealed that sighting committees had not been convened following SPADs at SN 63 and SN 109. Moreover, the zone was found to be the worst performing of Railtrack's seven zones in terms of safety matters. But the auditors were reassured by the fact that a larger exercise, checking all the signals in the two miles out of Paddington, was being undertaken. 'This and other initiatives by Great Western zone,' they reported cheerfully, 'demonstrate a pro-active stance on this issue.'[11] If only. In fact, what the auditors were referring to was a plan by Bernard Melanophy, the operations manager, to commission W.S. Atkins to review the signalling between

Paddington and Ladbroke Grove. Unfortunately, as Cullen says, the auditors were under a mistaken impression, 'since Mr Melanophy did not in fact commission W.S. Atkins or anyone else to review the signalling'.[12] In other words, someone pulled the wool over the auditors' eyes. The auditors said there should be a signal sighting committee but this was still ignored by the local managers and a follow-up audit in September 1999 again found that no action had been taken. However, Chris Leah, Railtrack's director of safety, must have also been misled because in December 1999 he told an employment tribunal hearing, which was appealing against the Health and Safety Executive's post-accident decision to shut down signal SN 109, that such a meeting had been held after the February 1998 SPAD.

Cullen concludes, 'The failure to have signal sighting committees convened was persistent and serious ... [and] was due to a combination of incompetent management and inadequate process.'[13] Cullen is being too kind. The behaviour of various managers in the zone seems to reflect an appalling lack of concern about safety in what is, above all, a safety-critical industry. Treating inquiry recommendations as if implementation were optional, persistently failing to take a course of action which was clearly set out in the rules and misleading the company's own auditors is symptomatic of a culture of almost wanton ineptitude and perhaps even deliberate dishonesty.

The real tragedy is that the convening of a sighting committee was not a mere technicality but would very likely have prevented the accident. As Cullen says, it would have led to changes, possibly including the replacement of Gantry 8, the one holding SN 109, and of other signals on the routes out of the station. This is because, as the subsequent investigation revealed, the signal broke all the rules. Right from the beginning there should have been a signal sighting committee for SN 109, which was first commissioned as part of the new Paddington layout in 1993 before the overhead wires were installed. Twice, subsequent changes should have led to a signal sighting committee: first, in the following year, when the signals on the gantry were lowered because the view was being obscured by Golborne Road bridge which is 100 metres in front of the gantry;[14] and secondly when, in 1995, overhead line equipment for the Heathrow Express was installed which further obscured the view of the signals on Gantry 8. The presence of the overhead line equipment meant that, from the driver's point of view, the signals disappeared temporarily and then reappeared. The experts who carried out the signal sighting exercise after the accident found that SN 109 was not compliant with the rules, which specified that it should be seen for at least a full seven seconds from the cab of a train approaching it at the line speed of 6omph. Moreover, they concluded that, because there were five other signals on the gantry, the situation presented to drivers was very confusing. Of course, as driver Hodder was killed in the crash, one can only surmise why he missed the red aspect, and Cullen draws no conclusions, except to point to the difficulties of seeing the signal.

There are few heroes in this story, but one of them is Alison Forster, First Great Western's director of operations and safety (and now managing director). She persistently expressed concerns over the series of SPADs in the Paddington area in a series of letters and tried to get Railtrack to do something about them. The fact that her efforts proved futile demonstrates the extent to which Railtrack was impervious to outsiders' concerns. Her evidence to the inquiry was chilling, perhaps more harrowing than any of the other evidence for the survivors and the relatives of the dead. She spoke of meetings where lots of ideas were generated but no follow-up was instigated. There was a lack of clarity about who at Railtrack was supposed to deal with reducing SPADs and, worse, many of her letters were simply ignored. In August 1998, for example, she wrote to Les Wilkinson, Railtrack's production manager, about signal SN 109, asking if 'you would advise me as a matter of urgency what action you intend to mitigate against this high risk signal',[15] and she told the inquiry, 'I have never received a full response to that.'[16]

Overall, Forster said, Railtrack took a narrow view of safety concerns: 'The organisation does not look very often at some of the big-picture issues. They tend to be reactive to incidents and single-issue problem-solving processes ... and sometimes not taking a broad risk-based approach to the management of safety, which I do not think is helpful for long-term improvements that we need to see ... they do not seem to be a learning organisation.'[17]

Forster was not listened to because, as an employee of a train operating company, her role in the privatised and fragmented railway was simply that of a customer. Her warnings to Railtrack were dealt with in much the same way that retailers' 'customer relations departments' fob off complaints from people seen as pushy. One can almost hear Railtrack's reaction – 'Oh, it's that bloody Great Western woman again, send her standard letter B this time.' Tom Winsor, the rail regulator, would argue that there was a legally enforceable contract between the two companies. But the real world does not work like that. Railtrack was supposed to provide a properly functioning and safe railway to its clients, but working out the precise meaning of such vague requirements is impossible for middle-ranking executives such as Ms Forster. How could she press her case? Had she been working for the same organisation under a unified structure, then she would have found it much easier. There would have been clear lines of communication and responsibility. Her warnings would have carried extra force and her superiors would have known precisely how much weight to give to her expressions of concern. There would have been the in-house expertise to assess them and to carry out the work if it were considered necessary. Instead, Railtrack with its 'business development managers' and its commercial concerns had its attention focused elsewhere.

One consequence of separating the track from services was that there were no longer any 'Fat Controllers' – general managers, as they were in the earlier days of BR, and later directors of sectors such as InterCity – who were responsible for all aspects of the railway. Had there still been someone in this role, he or she would have realised that in addition to the signal sighting problems, there were fundamental flaws in the layout at Paddington (see diagram p. 140); these received insufficient attention in the Cullen report. After SN 109, the line on which the Thames train was travelling extended for a distance of 700 metres before it merged into the up main line on which the Cheltenham Flyer was travelling. About halfway between the gantry and the junction there is a set of points – 8059 – which, had they been switched the other way, would have taken the Turbo back on to the down relief line from which it had come. That might, conceivably, have led to a collision, though this would have been unlikely and, in any case, would have involved a side-on impact at a much slower speed.

The lengthy overrun of the Great Western HST in February 1998 would have alerted the Fat Controller to the major flaw in the layout, which is that a down (away from London) train passing SN 109 at red is routed into the path of an oncoming up train with nothing in between to stop it. The logic behind that layout was that it gave a longer safety overlap than if 8059 were set in such a way that the train was routed back towards the down relief line. The assumption was that no driver would ever go through SN 109 by 700 metres because they would realise they were going down a prohibited piece of track. But this failed to take into account what would happen if a driver did make this mistake and, crucially, the difference between the relatively benign consequences – either a side-on crash or a rear-end shunt – if the points were set to return an errant train to the down relief line, compared with the appalling risk of a head-on collision. It is quite possible that Hodder, at this stage, was lost, which would explain why he actually accelerated after passing the signal and, unaccountably, cancelled his AWS.

Two principal reasons for the failure to provide what is called 'flank protection' in the industry were given to the inquiry: that the alternative offered a longer overlap and, second, that the line was expected to be imminently provided with Automatic Train Protection. As we shall see below, Thames trains were not fitted with ATP and, once this was realised, there should have been a reassessment of the decision, but by then, with the fragmentation of the industry, there was no chance of such a reconsideration ever getting on to the agenda, despite the frequent SPADs at SN 109. Even more astonishingly, Railtrack did not even implement its own logic and consistently opt for the longer overlap; points 8059 were simply left as they had been used by the last train. Had a train gone that way previously, then the accident would never have happened.

Cullen's conclusion on this issue is particularly lame. He merely says, 'It is, of course, necessary to make a comprehensive assessment of not only the need for flank protection but also the risks to which its use may give rise. For that reason, it is not possible for me to determine that it should have been provided or should not be provided.'[18] In other words, the issue was too complicated for him to consider properly.

The other criticism of Railtrack by Lord Cullen was directed towards the signallers in the Slough control centre and the failure to ensure they were prepared for such an emergency. Until recently, the only way of contacting a train had been through the signalling system and when there was a SPAD the standard reaction was to put all signals to red. Following other accidents, a system called cab secure radio was installed in most trains in order to improve communication, but the signalling procedures had not really changed to take account of this technological improvement. Therefore, it would have theoretically been possible for the signallers to send a stop message to driver Hodder after his train had passed SN 109.[19] However, no such action was taken until a second or two before the crash. It took the ill-fated train twenty seconds to travel the 700 metres between signal SN 109 and the point at which it smashed into the HST. Could the signallers have done anything in time? Cullen certainly thought so, but only if they had been properly trained. He calculated that by the time they could reasonably have realised that the train was heading for disaster, they had between 7.35 and 9.25 seconds in which to send the vital message to Hodder to stop the train, which might have reduced the speed of the accident or even prevented it altogether. Instead, the signaller in charge, David Allen, decided to 'monitor' what happened, only taking action at the very last moment.

The issue is confused by the fact that the various signallers in the control centre at the time gave misleading accounts of their actions, which Cullen does not entirely trust. Cullen, however, does not blame the individual signallers for their actions but rather the way in which they were managed and trained. Indeed, he suggests, 'It is surprising that [these] deficiencies were not picked up by senior management.'[20] It emerged clearly that the signallers were not properly trained. Even though there had been an average of a SPAD per month in the area covered by the Slough control centre, there was no proper training of the signallers on how to deal with them or any attempt to learn the lessons of previous incidents. The use of the radio was not really properly considered because of this lack of training and no signaller had received any training in the use of the radio in emergencies. Cullen concludes, 'The general picture which emerged was of a slack and complacent regime, which was not alive to the potentially dire consequences of a SPAD or of the way in which signallers could take action to deal with such situations.'[21] The attitude of the signallers was very much that SPADs were a matter of driver error and nothing to do with them. While this was a legacy from BR culture, clearly the fact that drivers and signallers now worked for different organisations did not help to create a shared awareness in the signallers that they were the last line of defence against errors by their fellow railway workers. Moreover, Cullen's judgement on the signallers is harsh. They faced a very difficult situation and really had very little time to do anything.

*

Railtrack was the subject of most of the criticism in relation to the Ladbroke Grove accident, in both the Cullen report and the subsequent media coverage. But this too was unfair. The primary cause was the fact that driver Hodder went through a red light, and the role played by Thames Trains, who allocated him to the most complex and difficult layout in Britain without proper training or knowledge of the route, is as significant as Railtrack's failings. Hodder was only two weeks into his job and on only his twenty-first trip out of Paddington when he made his disastrous mistake. He was by all accounts a model pupil, having previously been in the Navy, although one of his references was from a relative and the other was not taken up. He was never asked to fill in an application form and therefore did not disclose a recent minor conviction arising out of a fight. This readiness to ignore the proper procedures was a result of the fact that Thames was desperate for drivers and had only recently started recruiting from outside the industry when Hodder applied in February 1999.

Under British Rail, there had been a minimum training period of forty-three weeks and most drivers were already experienced rail workers, familiar with the railway and its rules, but after privatisation there was no set period for driver training. Instead, there was a Group Standard to ensure basic competence but each train operator individually certifies its drivers when they are judged to be competent. Incredibly, in the privatised industry there was no independent assessment of driver competence.[22]

Thames had already been criticised in the Royal Oak Inquiry, which found in March 1996 that 'The methods of route learning into and out of Paddington appear very informal.'[23] The inquiry also recommended that SPAD briefings should be held for drivers, including the use of videos. However, at the time, Thames was not recruiting and, as Cullen puts it, the company's 'corporate memory was weak' in that it failed to heed these recommendations when it started taking on drivers again over two years later.

Indeed, very little attention seems to have been paid to SPADs in the training programme, even though, for example, six of the eight SPADs at SN 109 were perpetrated by Thames drivers. Again, the auditors, this time the Railway Inspectorate, had the wool pulled over their eyes when Thames claimed in September 1996 that all drivers were receiving briefings on SPADs as part of the strategy to reduce them.

In reality, Thames's programme was lax in the extreme. No particular consideration was given to the fact that recruits from outside the industry would need different training from those who already knew about the railways. There was no clear syllabus and, most amazingly, there seemed to be no coherent assessment of the trainee's performance. As an expert, Professor John Groeger of the University of Surrey, told the inquiry, 'There were no specific criteria ... to determine whether the driver had competently handled a situation; [and] there was a lack of definition as to how frequently the driver should have to perform in similar situations before being assessed as competent.'[24] As Cullen put it, the praise for Hodder was all very well, but it was in the context of the fact that 'His teachers were working with a less than perfect programme.'

The training programme was particularly deficient in relation to warnings about the risks of SPADs. Terry Worrall, Thames's director and general manager, admitted to the inquiry that the course had failed to instruct '[Hodder] directly about the risks of SPADs at particular signals like SN 109', or to ensure 'that his route learning assessment specifically covered the area between Paddington and Ladbroke Grove'. Nor had Hodder attended a SPAD awareness day.

The most astonishing admission came from Ray Adams, Hodder's instructor, who said that route learning was not a matter for him: 'I was not there to teach Michael the routes. I was totally [*sic*] to teach Michael how to drive a Turbo.'[25] Hodder started training on 1 February 1999 and took his first solo shift on 22 September, thirty-three weeks later, some ten weeks less than the BR minimum. This whole pattern suggests the operation of Thames's course was tailored not so much to ensure competence as to meet their need for new drivers. Thames had abandoned driver training and then, suddenly aware that there was likely to be a shortage, recreated a programme that was clearly inadequate. It was no comfort to the victims and their families that, even before the accident, Thames had realised that its procedures were sub-standard and that subsequent trainees were on a much improved course.

The other aspect of Thames's culpability which arises from the privatisation is the fact that its trains were not fitted with Automatic Train Protection. As we noted in Chapter 5, it is a quite bizarre coincidence that the two worst crashes caused by SPADs post-privatisation should have happened on one of only two lines in Britain fitted with ATP equipment as part of a BR experiment, and that on both occasions the equipment was not functioning. In the case of Southall this was a result of a failure to train drivers in its use and a general lack of interest on the part of Great Western, and a similar nonchalance was shown by Thames.

The fact that Thames trains did not have ATP, even though all the trackside was fitted and there was even space earmarked for the equipment in the Turbos, seems unbelievable. As we saw in Chapter 5, BR's trial Automatic Train Protection programme had lost its way as a result of privatisation. Thames seems to have shown as little interest as Great Western in continuing with the pilot. The management buy-out team took over the franchise in October 1996 and within a few weeks the management executive of the company decided that ATP should not be fitted to its trains. Following the Southall crash in early 1998 Thames decided to reconsider this decision and commissioned a study from W.S. Atkins to establish the costs and benefits of installation. Atkins found that it would cost £9m[26] to fit, operate and maintain ATP between Paddington and Oxford. The study suggested that, statistically, it was probable that only one life would be saved by fitting ATP, which meant that in terms of the standard value (which was then around £2.45m) ascribed to a life in the rail industry when considering such schemes, it was too expensive. Thames was happy to concur with this decision.

Clearly the Thames directors failed to consider the wider repercussions of an accident and the particular dangers of the Paddington throat. A subsequent analysis of the Atkins study performed for the Cullen Inquiry by Det Norske Veritas found that it lacked robustness and had not sufficiently taken into account the possibility of a major catastrophe. Some of the figures, too, underestimated the benefits and exaggerated the costs, though not sufficiently to bring down the price to less than the £2.45m per life used by Railtrack. Indeed, Thames's decision to commission the W.S. Atkins study has all the hallmarks of a back-covering exercise to ensure that Thames could continue to eschew ATP despite Southall. Of course, it was unlucky for Thames that its driver made a disastrous mistake that cost thirty-one lives, despite having a fully functioning Automatic Warning System which he cancelled properly, but the company's failure to consider the wider implications was an inevitable consequence of the way that the industry was fragmented. Oddly, despite the flaws in the Atkins methodology, Cullen accepted Thames's argument for not fitting ATP, even though, as we saw in

Chapter 5, neighbouring Chiltern, an equally small company which operates the same type of trains, was prepared to spend the money because its directors realised what an enormous benefit the system represented above and beyond the narrow financial considerations. There were essentially two ways of approaching the ATP issue: a 'can do' approach of trying to sort out the problems and an attempt to seek excuses not to do the work because ATP was a hassle. Chiltern chose the former, Thames and Great Western the latter.

One of the factors that influenced Thames's decision not to fit ATP was that, at the time, the company expected the new Train Protection and Warning System (TPWS) to be fitted relatively soon. TPWS is an extension of the Automatic Warning System, described in Chapter 5, which will stop most trains from going through red lights. It works via a device about 350 metres in advance of a signal that will monitor the train's speed and ensure that it is not going too fast to stop at the signal if a red is showing. Because of the technical limitations of the system, trains travelling above 70mph may not be stopped in time to avoid a collision but they will be slowed down considerably.

In 1995, after the Tory government effectively abandoned ATP in the run-up to privatisation, Sir George Young, the transport secretary, announced that trials of TPWS would take place the following year and that 'the aim is to start wider installation in 1997'.[27] Inevitably, the timetable slipped. The trials, on Thameslink, took longer to implement. Eventually, in early 1999, a report recommending the adoption of TPWS found its way on to John Prescott's desk but he dithered for seven months until August 1999 before making a decision to implement the system across the network by the start of 2004 (a target that was eventually realised). TPWS, then costed at £310m (but which came out at almost twice the cost), would have prevented Ladbroke Grove (but only slowed down the Southall impact), but, of course, it would not have been fitted in time, even if Prescott had not prevaricated.

The government's delay over TPWS had a bizarre side effect that was to have a highly damaging consequence in the aftermath of the Hatfield accident. On the Saturday after the Ladbroke Grove crash, a high-level meeting, which included Tony Blair, John Prescott, Lord Macdonald and their respective press officers, decided to try to hijack the news agenda by letting it be known that the government intended to remove the safety role from Railtrack. The group had got wind of the fact that Prescott might be under the cosh for having hesitated over the implementation of TPWS and were fearful of critical coverage of the government's role in the following days' papers; they suspected the hacks would not be sophisticated enough to realise that, even had Prescott given an immediate go-ahead, the accident would not have been averted.

The press officers promptly briefed Sunday newspaper journalists suggesting that a report due to be published imminently by the Health and Safety Executive would say that Railtrack's safety responsibilities should be taken away. In fact, the HSE report recommended no such thing, merely stating that the issue needed to be looked at. This was confirmed on the following Monday in Parliament when Lord Macdonald merely said the government was 'minded' to make the move. The spinning, however, had done its trick, focusing press attention on Railtrack rather than Prescott, and it showed Railtrack just how dirty the politicians could play. Indeed, the knowledge that ministers were so ready to attack the industry to protect their own backs contributed to Railtrack's extremely conservative response in the aftermath of Hatfield. How could Railtrack executives take any risks when they knew that there was no 'air cover' – to use Gerald Corbett's term – from government? It was a disgraceful episode that continued to sour government relations with the industry, which had already been damaged by Prescott saying, in an interview at the accident site, that money was no object in ensuring safety on the railway. This was one of those knee-jerk responses which can never be challenged at the time but which are, in fact, a blatant lie. Prescott did not make it clear who would foot the bill when, in truth, safety measures always have to be paid for by government.

In the event, an inquiry was set up to decide how to restructure the safety role of Railtrack and it recommended that Railtrack's Safety and Standards Directorate should be hived off into a separate subsidiary,[28] Railway Safety, operating completely independently of Railtrack Line, the main business. However, in September 2001 the second part of the Cullen report recommended the setting up of a new investigation organisation to examine accidents, filling the same role as the Air Accident Investigations Branch in the aviation industry, and the separation of Railway Safety from Railtrack to form a new, independent rail industry safety body,[29] both of which were later carried out.

*

So, as with Southall, the question of the role of privatisation and fragmentation in the accident needs to be addressed. Would this accident have happened if BR had still run the railways? And again, the evidence is very strong that it would not. One can argue that here were two utterly incompetent sets of management who, between them, got a rookie driver into an area with an appalling history of SPADs without proper training or appraisal. It took the involvement and failings of both companies to bring about this disaster because had either of them done their job properly, the crash would never have happened. Both companies were artificial constructs, bits of the railway hived off for reasons that had nothing to do with improving services or safety. Railtrack we know about already. Thames was a small train operator, initially a management buy-out which was later sold on, making the original managers millionaires. Such a small company clearly could not have the large-scale and well-resourced training programmes such as those run by BR.

To suggest that the same set of circumstances would have come about under BR is fanciful. It is inconceivable that the whole fatal sequence of mistakes would have occurred under the unified structure: the failure to call signal sighting committees; the lack of response to Alison Forster's concerns; the inadequacy of the driver training programme; the failure to spot the flaw in the track layout; and the unwillingness to install ATP. An alternative scenario on any of these issues would have produced a completely different outcome. More importantly, in BR days there was a 'Fat Controller' or general manager who was responsible for every aspect of the railway including all engineering, civil, mechanical and signal and traffic, and who would have dealt with the concerns of the likes of Alison Forster.

Above all, there was the failure to follow recommendations of inquiries into incidents. The old railway culture – both BR and pre-nationalisation – was about learning from mistakes and trying to reduce the number of small ones so that there was less chance of having a big disaster. There is no doubt that an accident of this type would not have happened in the tighter and more disciplined BR culture where, moreover, safety responsibilities did not end up with 'business development managers'. Railtrack's Great Western zone's culture of ignoring recommendations resulted in a deliberate failure to prevent the recurrence of the situations which had already put lives at risk. Ladbroke Grove was, quite literally, a disaster waiting to happen.

CHAPTER 8

Hatfield: the accident that broke the railway

'The accident at Hatfield was not caused by a broken rail. It was caused by total mismanagement by Railtrack and its contractors. The broken rail was the result of complete incompetence by the management somewhere between Railtrack and the contractor, Balfour Beatty.' Those are the words of Chris Garnett, the chief executive of GNER, the company which ran the train that derailed at Hatfield. Indeed, Hatfield was the perfect example of an accident caused by the way that the railways had been fragmented. Broken railways, broken rail. There is a poetic neatness about it, but not for the families of the four men who were killed.

They were travelling on the 1210 from King's Cross to Leeds, which came off the rails on a curve between Welham Green and Hatfield station at 115mph, the maximum speed allowed on that section of the line. (Actually, it was travelling at 117mph; and the locomotive was in the hands of a trainee driver who shouldn't have been at the controls because she hadn't completed enough weeks of her course. Neither of these facts had any bearing on the accident, but they are just two more examples of the sloppiness that seems to be all too common in this tale.)

The locomotive and the first two coaches stayed on the track but the other seven and the driving van trailer were derailed. The four unlucky men were in the buffet car, which, because it smashed into one of the stanchions supporting the overhead line electrical equipment, was the only coach that was severely damaged. Of the other 178 people on the train, seventy were injured, four seriously, and it was only the strength of the modern BR-designed Mark IV coaches that prevented a much higher death toll.

After the accident, following early speculation about a bomb or a broken axle, it quickly emerged that the cause of the derailment was a broken rail, which was later revealed to have smashed into 300 pieces. Some 90 metres of line, in two sections, had totally disintegrated leaving, oddly, 44 metres of mostly intact rail in between. The line was closed for twenty-four days and panic about the condition of the track led to disruption throughout the whole network worse than anything previously encountered on Britain's railways. Indeed, Hatfield would have remained no more than a footnote in British railway history had it not been for the subsequent imposition of thousands of speed restrictions that caused chaos for rail travellers and hundreds of millions of pounds in compensation claims by the train operators. The reasons why Railtrack panicked, and the far-reaching consequences of this overreaction, are explained at the end of this chapter, but first let us look at the causes of the accident.

The deterioration of that piece of track into such a disastrous condition was the result of a series of decisions by people at two very different levels. In the months prior to the accident there were several errors concerning the maintenance of the part of the track that failed and led to the disaster. But while, at first glance, this accident seemed to have been caused by the failings of the maintenance company and Railtrack, in fact its roots are to be found in the privatisation process described at length in this book. In the case of the Ladbroke Grove and Southall accidents, the interactions between privatisation and the causes of the accident were extremely complex; at Hatfield the part played by the fragmentation and sale of the railways is very clear. The whole ghastly tale of mismanagement, greed and incompetence that caused the Hatfield disaster was a result of the crazy structure for the railways created by John Major and his ministers, aided and abetted by civil servants and, worse, railway managers who should have known better. Hatfield was the epitome of the failings created by rail privatisation. It was also privatisation's epitaph, given that Hatfield turned Railtrack from a profitable company into a financial wreck that had to be bailed out by the government. At the time of writing (summer 2005), the trial of five middle managers, two from Balfour Beatty and three from Railtrack, together with their companies, is taking place. Manslaughter charges were dropped part way through the trial, leaving the defendants only facing offences under health and safety legislation. Charges against more senior staff in the two companies were also dropped because no clear line of responsibility linking them to the faulty rail could be established.

From evidence given at the trial, along with material obtained for my earlier book, *Broken Rails*, a picture of what happened at Hatfield has begun to emerge, but a completely definitive account is impossible until the completion of the court hearing and the subsequent release of documents by the various parties involved. It is known, however, that the problems on this piece of track had been reported long before the crash. According to the opening prosecution statement by Richard Lissack QC, a fault had been discovered at the site twenty-one months earlier and at the time of the crash a new rail had been lying beside the defective section of track for six months ready to be installed. Lissack outlined how some 200 faults had been discovered in the first 43 miles out from King's Cross and how a meeting of Balfour Beatty and Railtrack, which included the accused, had agreed, in June 2000, to set the clock back so that 'all the faults that were overdue for repair were wiped out in the sense that fresh time limits were brought in to address the backlog'. According to a former executive of Railtrack, the backlog had built up because of failings by local Balfour Beatty management and could have resulted in the total closure of the line for repairs.

As with all these accidents, it was an accumulation of little mistakes that built up to cause a disaster. Before getting into a consideration of the broken rail and what caused it, there is an interesting side issue that may have contributed to the accident. There is evidence that it was not the 1210 which actually broke the rail but an earlier train, which had damaged it sufficiently for it to have snapped, but in such a way that for a short period of time wheels could still pass over it without derailing. This evidence comes from the track circuit, a system which involves a small current being run through the rails to keep signallers informed about the location of a train. When the circuit is broken because of a split rail or some other impediment, the train effectively disappears off the signallers' panel and when it returns at the next track circuit, it comes on without its train describer – the unique set of numbers and letters which identifies every train. When this occurs an alarm sounds in the box to alert signallers. According to a signalling source, this alarm – a Non Description Alert (NDA) – sounded frequently in the King's Cross control centre, but because of a fault on another section of line, not the Hatfield one. On the day of the Hatfield crash four trains sounded NDAs before the one that derailed. However, because NDAs had become almost routine on the nearby North London Lines section, the signallers failed to take any action or even to alert more experienced managers; instead they merely cancelled the alert. Another source sent me a leaked memo, issued in the aftermath of Hatfield, which confirmed that the cause of these alerts should be analysed by technicians and not merely ignored; this suggests Railtrack may previously have relaxed company policy in relation to NDAs. Railtrack refused to comment on this matter but it illustrates how minor decisions relating to safety can lead to major incidents.

The accident itself could have been prevented if either of the two inspection regimes undertaken by Balfour Beatty for checking the track had been carried out properly. Unfortunately neither was. Although both Balfour Beatty and Railtrack had known for a long time that there was a problem with this section of track, neither clearly realised – at the right level of management – how bad it was; had they been aware of the situation, a speed limit would have been imposed. Various people seemed to be aware that there was a crack which needed sorting out properly but either their appeals for action fell on deaf ears or they were not prepared to push hard enough to ensure the work was done. Most remarkably, while the track inspector, Andrew Preston, walked along the track every Tuesday afternoon to check its condition, he had not been told that the rail was so bad that it had been scheduled for replacement. The accident happened on a Tuesday morning and it may be that he would have spotted the break that afternoon, but we will never know. Week after week, his reports – the last dated 10 October, precisely a week before the disaster – reported nothing untoward about the track, and yet some of his managers were preparing schemes to rerail that section because of its poor condition. Preston told Railway Safety, which produced a report into the accident,[1] that he had never been trained about gauge corner cracking – the type of damage that had affected the rail – nor about how to spot it or assess its gravity. The gauge corner is the top inner corner of the rail that is in contact with the wheel flange and is subject to the most stress, since it must absorb lateral forces as well as bearing the weight of the train.

But even if the hapless Preston had been properly trained, he would not have been able to see the damage. In addition to the track inspector, rails are inspected by teams of labourers walking by the side of the track to check their condition. Busy lines like the East Coast Main Line are walked every week, often by the same people. There are four sets of track on this part of the railway; these are, going from east to west, the down slow (conventionally, down tracks lead away from London, up tracks towards it), down fast, up fast and up slow. Balfour Beatty, responsible for the day-to-day maintenance through its contract with Railtrack, had got into bad habits, prompted by cost-cutting. The way that the railway was privatised meant that both Railtrack and its contractors had to reduce costs by 3 per cent per annum in order to retain the same level of profits. Instead of teams of four or six people, which would allow the vital look-outs at the front and back, the gang consisted of just two men. This meant they could not venture onto the six-foot – the gap between each set of up or down lines – or the ten-foot – the gap between the down and up lines – because, even with a ten-foot width, it is simply too dangerous, given the prospect of two 115mph trains from different directions bearing down on these vulnerable track workers.[2] There are four sets of rails to check and the men walked on the cess (the railway's name for the trackside path, not a pit) alongside the track rather than risk their lives on the track. Moreover, according to the Railway Safety report, the track inspectors lacked clerical back-up, which suggests that their reports may not have been sufficiently monitored.

They went up one cess and down the other, but this did not give them a good view of all the rails. Indeed, as far as the crucial Welham Green curve was concerned, they might as well have saved their blisters. On the bend the rails are canted – set at an angle – in order to keep friction to a minimum. The cant meant that the top of the rail at the bend was not visible when the inspectors were walking in the nearer cess, and too far away to be clearly seen when walking in the further one. The gradual deterioration as the crack – already noted in 1998 – dug its way into the rail went unobserved. Even when a manager came to inspect the line in July 1999, he stayed in the cess but, because he knew what he was looking for, spotted cracking and suggested that replacement should be considered.

There was a second type of testing, ultrasound, using a machine which is pushed by hand along the track and which beams sound down on to the line and records it bouncing back in order to detect any cracks. That this device did not alert the company to the dangerous rail was a combination of failure by both man and machine. In the term used by safety inspectors, the equipment was not 'fit for the purpose'. The machines could not measure the sort of crack – gauge corner cracking – which was propagating rapidly through the rail. The standards for these machines had been inherited by Railtrack from British Rail and not updated, even though there was growing evidence round the network of gauge corner cracking. Railtrack was 'slow in adopting best practice in ultrasonic inspection',[3] as a report into the broken rails problem later pointed out, largely because the company was simply not prepared to find the money to invest in modern equipment.

The inadequacy of the equipment meant that, although the track was tested by ultrasound every three months, the results were difficult to interpret. There was, moreover, no proper evaluation of the results and the rail was not rechecked when no reading was recorded. In November 1999 the test found that there was a 'loss of rail bottom' – in other words, the equipment was not able to get a measurement of the depth of the crack. In April 2000 that section was found to be untestable, and two months later there was, again, total 'loss of rail bottom'. Then on 5 October, just twelve days before the crash, the equipment for the third time found 'loss of rail bottom'.

Such readings should have prompted immediate attention. The fault was categorised as 3G, which meant the rail needed to be replaced within three months. But, in fact, not only did the reading on the machine indicate it should have been a 1A – which requires the instant imposition of a speed limit and replacement within 36 hours – but somehow, instead, the tester merely wrote on the form that the action required was 'retest'. Clearly, somebody should have rechecked that part of the line manually and, in the meantime, imposed a temporary speed restriction. Moreover, the 'loss of rail bottom' should have alerted the supervisor.

However, even if the information had been properly recorded, there are doubts as to whether this information would have found its way to managers. Investigators found that there were serious gaps in the record-keeping and, moreover, the whole story reveals that the lines of accountability both within and between Balfour Beatty, Jarvis Fastline – which was responsible for renewals in that Railtrack zone – and Railtrack were so unclear that while certain managers were busy trying to replace the damaged rail, others knew nothing about the problem and the poor track inspector on the ground had no idea of its state because no one had bothered to alert him.

There was a series of missed opportunities and a timetable of events which, in hindsight, make painful reading. In 1998 Vernon Bullen, Balfour Beatty's area maintenance engineer, said he was aware of gauge corner cracking in the area. He recommended grinding for early in 1999 which never happened. In mid-1999 he proposed to Railtrack the rerailing of ten sites, with the Welham Green curve as top priority – rather than any time in the following year, the normal expectation for renewals. However, Railtrack seems not to have understood the urgency of the situation and the scheme was sent back to Balfour for prioritising. In January 2000 Jarvis was asked to survey the up fast line but it examined the wrong line and only undertook the correct work three weeks later. In March 2000 Jarvis and Railtrack agreed to a rerailing schedule but, as we see below, the work was not carried out in time. Somehow the sense of urgency which built up at various times was lost in the bureaucracy and the interface between the three companies. A quote from the Railway Safety report perhaps explains why: 'Any item requiring to be done to a tighter timetable [than a year] i.e. outside the bounds of normal planning, would be flagged as an emergency because of its potential impact on maintenance costs or its effect on train performance resulting from a Temporary Speed Restriction, or both'.[4]

Furthermore, there were clear conflicts of interest between the three firms. As explained in Chapter 4, the task of keeping the track in good order was arbitrarily split at privatisation between renewal and maintenance companies. Under Railtrack's standard RT1a contracts, there was a set but arbitrary rule about when 'maintenance' should be upgraded to 'renewal': any continuously welded rail longer than 600 feet that needed replacing had to be done by the renewal company – in this case Jarvis Fastline – rather than the maintenance firm, Balfour Beatty. The way that maintenance and renewals were separated was another bit of privatisation madness. The maintenance contracts were fixed-price and therefore any work that could be passed on to Jarvis was good news for Balfour Beatty; it was also good news for Jarvis as the company was paid on a job-by-job basis, which meant that the more work there was, the more money it received. Railtrack therefore had an interest in ensuring that Jarvis got as little work as possible and was anxious to keep disruption to the network, which reduced its performance payments, to a minimum. As a former Railtrack manager quoted in the *Financial Times* related, the arguments between the three parties at times almost became physical: 'It was a constant battle ... At some of those meetings with contractors, we nearly came to fisticuffs because we, at Railtrack, were having to deny them the access they required.'[5]

A Balfour Beatty inspection sheet dated 11 January 2000[6] reported that 'gauge corner cracking' was 'showing bad' and said the rail needed replacing. After Railtrack had inspected the site in February, it was decided to replace the rail, but Welham Green was only one of ten sites which needed rerailing. A request to do all the work was turned down by Railtrack's senior project manager for the North East zone, Amanda Henderson, because, according to the Railway Safety report, she said it was 'considered impossible to deliver without deleting half the existing track renewal programme'. However, the Welham Green section was reckoned to be a priority. It was given P1 status, which means replace within a month but, amazingly, the Railway Safety report says that Ms Henderson did not understand this appellation. By March, however, the zone engineer was in a position to go to the Black Tower – Railtrack's ugly black headquarters next to Euston station – and put a business case to Asset Management for the cash and authorisation to carry out the work. This department kept a check on cashflow and had to give permission for all major work on the network. Railtrack claimed to the *Guardian*, 'The cost of rerailing the track is never an issue where safety is concerned'[7] but this is not true. Requests were made by zone directors for replacement of rails and these had to be slotted into existing timetables of possession and to the budget. Risk assessments were made as in any safety-critical industry.

In this case, it was agreed to replace the rail, but then the request was passed on to Possession Management in the zone for the work to be scheduled. (When I explained this process to a senior executive of Amtrak, the US passenger railway, he said: 'You're kidding? If we have a rail that needs replacing, the chief engineer just orders the work to be done.') The job of Possession Management was to work out the 'rules of the route', the schedule for when parts of the network could be closed – normally at weekends – in order for major repairs to be carried out. There are routine closures determined two years in advance with all the operators, both passenger and freight, but Railtrack tried to avoid having extra possessions – closures – because it had to pay compensation to the train operators for the disruption. However, Possession Management seemed to have grasped the urgency of the situation because it agreed to a special 27-hour closure of the line on 19 March in order to replace the dodgy rail.

The whole Hatfield tragedy and its appalling aftermath would not have occurred without another of those seemingly inconsequential little mistakes: it took four attempts to deliver the rails before they all reached the site and by then the lengthy possession had been lost. The first train – in one of those further complexities of fragmentation, it was operated by Jarvis but staffed by Railtrack – was late and then the second was the *wrong sort of train*: it could not unload the rails without fouling the overhead line equipment. At the third attempt, in early April, half the rails were dropped off and finally, on 28 April, the rest were delivered. Replacement was carried out on neighbouring sites but Welham Green could not be done because the site needed the longest possession. Possession Management, by this time none too pleased with the delay, refused to sanction another emergency closure, particularly as the busier summer timetable was now in operation and disruption would have caused delays to more trains, incurring greater penalties. According to John Ware, who made a BBC *Panorama* documentary on the crash, Jarvis was seeking five 8-hour possessions to do the work and this was not acceptable to Railtrack which offered only two, each for just 4 hours and 20 minutes. It was not a question of money but simply that the work could not be done in such a short period of time, as it takes an hour to turn the power on or off, leaving insufficient time for any rerailing to be carried out. The new rail sat there alongside the old one, gently rusting.

There was, though, another factor which did involve money. The reluctance by Railtrack to close the line during the busy and lucrative summer period was clearly a result of financial pressures. Payments to Railtrack from the train operators under the performance regime were dependent on keeping the line open at all times, except during scheduled possessions. Moreover, this pressure may also have been felt by some individual managers as, according to an engineer,[8] 'You should never underestimate the influence of bonuses. Everyone's bonus was based on not going outside the agreed possessions. When a Railtrack zone beats its performance regime, then the zone directors get bonuses. It's done on a [four-week] period-by-period basis.' In the summer, moreover, the skilled workers such as welders required to do the work were also in demand from the construction industry, meaning that contractors found it harder to find sufficient workers, and had to pay them more.

Consequently, as a result of these pressures and a failure to under-stand the seriousness of the condition of the track, the work was rescheduled for November – two years after the cracks were first discovered and a month after the Hatfield disaster.

The biggest unanswered question remains why no speed limit was imposed. It is routine to place temporary speed restrictions on damaged sections of track. There were literally dozens of people who must have realised that there was a rail in poor condition. Obviously, the failures of the inspection regime, both the ultrasound and the patrol, meant that no one quite knew the extent of the damage to the rail. Those failures are a damning indictment both of how the railway was privatised and of the incompetence of the companies that took over from BR.

Leaving aside the failings of the inspection process, how did the rail get into that state anyway? Of course 20-20 hindsight is an easy science. But the likelihood of a rail breaking was frighteningly predictable; if the accident hadn't happened at Hatfield, it would very probably have occurred on some other part of the network with similarly dramatic consequences because the events that would lead to Hatfield had been set in train several years previously by the privatisation process.

Hatfield was the first accident caused by a broken rail since the Hither Green disaster on Guy Fawkes night in 1967. There, a break at the fish-plate – the fitting which connects rails, now largely redundant because of continuous welded rails – led to a broken rail, causing a derailment at around 75mph and killing forty-nine people in a crowded Sunday night train travelling into London from Hastings.[9] The Hither Green accident was caused by a phenomenon known as starcracking, which was allowed to propagate into the rail due to inadequate maintenance. Improved maintenance ensured that starcracking never caused another accident.

In the intervening years, under BR, rail maintenance standards had improved enormously, but with privatisation came immediate doubts about Railtrack's ability to keep the track in good condition because of the way that all work was done through contractors. In order to assess the impact of the creation of Railtrack on safety, Her Majesty's Railway Inspectorate (HMRI, part of the Health and Safety Executive) conducted its most comprehensive ever study into railway safety.[10]

The report specifically highlighted problems with the relationship between Railtrack and its contractors and the way in which the company ensured compliance with its safety case. In the words of the then deputy chief inspector, Vic Coleman, 'There were weaknesses in the way that Railtrack seeks to maintain health and safety,' some of which 'cause concern'.

The report pointed out that the outputs for Railtrack's maintenance contracts were very unspecific. They set out broad objectives such as ensuring the track met certain standards, rather than more specific aims/requirements such as that a set of points would be out of action for only a given amount of time per year. Therefore Railtrack needed very efficient monitoring and control systems, but the HMRI report found cases of contractors who did not have safety cases approved by Railtrack and 'many examples of contractors not meeting Railway Group Standards'.[11] According to a manager involved in setting up the contracts, 'The monitoring and auditing requirements were set out in meticulous detail in various documents. But, with possibly only one exception, none of the Railtrack zones did enough monitoring and made sure that work was carried out.' Here again money was at the root of the problem: 'We were under constant pressure from Norman Broadhurst [Railtrack's finance director] and the regulator to cut costs. They didn't give us the resources to carry out the checks. It became just a ticking box exercise.'[12]

The systems for selecting, managing and controlling contractors were also not being followed correctly. While these matters may have appeared minor, the HSE was clearly very concerned. Coleman concluded that while Railtrack had made great efforts in putting in the right systems to manage its contractors, 'We were disappointed that greater progress has not been made.' While Railtrack assumed that the contractors were self-auditing, the HSE clearly did not trust them to do the work without extensive monitoring. That fundamental difference of approach seems never to have been satisfactorily resolved.

An accident to a freight train at Bexley in February 1997 highlighted the disparity between theory and practice in the way that this horde of new contractors on the railway were being controlled by Railtrack. The train, operated by English, Welsh and Scottish Railways, the main privatised freight company, was carrying old ballast from track renewal work when part of it derailed on a viaduct just after passing Bexley station. It was travelling at around 55mph, considerably faster than the 40mph which was the maximum permitted speed for freight on that line. Seven wagons were completely derailed, and six of them smashed through the small wall protecting the track and toppled eight metres onto the yards underneath the viaduct, seriously injuring four people.

The train had not only been travelling too fast, but the track renewal contractor, Southern Track Renewals Company Ltd (owned by Balfour Beatty), had overloaded the wagons causing extra pressure on the rails. This would not have mattered had they been in good condition, but they were not. They had spread as a result of rotting timbers that were in a very poor state of repair. As the accident report[13] showed, the timbers had sunk deep into the ballast and there was evidence of botched repairs using bitumen and incorrectly fitted tie bars. Indeed, as the investigators discovered, the local track maintenance company, South East Infrastructure Maintenance Company Ltd (SEICML, again owned by Balfour Beatty), had long known about the appalling condition of the track. As far back as August 1995, a bridge examiner had reported finding serious decay in the timbers. Inexplicably, nothing was done and a consultant's report drawing up a replacement programme in December 1996 was also ignored. As the report puts it, 'Because of poor organisation and a breakdown in communication within SEICML, no one arranged for the work to be done.'[14] The local section manager again recommended, in February 1996, that the timbers 'needed renewing' but again nothing was done. Meanwhile, the weekly patrollers continued to report defects, stressing that the timbers were in 'very bad condition' and needed changing.[15]

As for the track renewal company, its managers clearly had no understanding of the relationship between weight and volume. The wagons were originally used for transporting steel but when they were filled with a dense material like ballast, they were grossly overloaded – some 30 per cent according to the investigators.[16]

The most worrying aspect of the accident was the fact that it showed Railtrack had failed to remedy the defects in its management of contractors identified in the 1996 HSE report, despite having introduced a new system of controls and checks. As the report put it, 'The HSE accident investigation found very little evidence of the new standards having been implemented. Railtrack were unable to produce an audit plan for the twelve months leading up to the accident.'[17] Again, money was at the root of the failure: Railtrack had simply not budgeted for the cost of extra controls since 'the resources available to the Railtrack Permanent Way Engineer were insufficient to enable the end product checks to be done'.[18] In other words, Railtrack had never intended to ensure that its monitoring was improved.

As no one was killed, the Bexley accident and its aftermath attracted little attention, even though a major disaster had only been avoided by sheer luck – the wagons could easily have fallen on people, cars or even buses. Moreover, because of prosecutions by the HSE, which resulted in fines and costs of nearly £200,000 for the two firms (both, as we have seen, owned by Balfour Beatty), the subsequent report was not published until March 1999, which delayed its recommendations (or 'lessons', as the report calls them, because clearly the HSE realised it was dealing with companies whose managers needed to go back to school) being put into effect.

Essentially, however, those 'lessons' merely reiterated what the 1996 HSE report had already recommended. The multiple failings which led to the Hatfield crash demonstrated that these lessons had still not been taken on board eighteen months after the publication of the Bexley report. The failure of communication in relation to the cracked rail at Hatfield between Balfour Beatty and Railtrack and the fact that Railtrack appeared unaware that Balfour Beatty's inspection teams were inadequately staffed, in clear breach of group standards, is a clear illustration that little had changed.

Bexley was not the only accident involving sloppy practices by Balfour Beatty that resulted in the company receiving heavy fines. Balfour Beatty was one of the biggest players in the 'Infraco' market. It bought three of the thirteen Briscos originally put up for sale by the government, seeing them as a bargain because of the guaranteed contracts they had with Railtrack. The company's previous record, however, was unenviable. Already, before taking up these contracts, Balfour Beatty had been responsible for the collapse of the Heathrow Express tunnel in 1994, leading to an enormous hole emerging in the middle of the airport into which a small office block collapsed. Fortunately, no one was killed but the firm was later fined £1.2m, then a record for Health and Safety at Work offences. The subsequent HSE inquiry found that 'The collapses could have been prevented but for a cultural mind-set which focused attention on the apparent economies and the need for production rather than the particular risk.'[19] Then, just six months after the Bexley derailment, another freight train went off the rails at Rivenhall in Essex as a result of faulty working by the contractor. Again, Balfour Beatty was given a heavy – £500,000 – fine and an admonishment from the judge in Chelmsford Crown Court, who said that the men working on the track were 'not properly monitored or supervised with the result that a serious risk to health and safety was created'.[20]

The 1999 annual audit of Railtrack by its own Safety and Standards Directorate (later to become Railway Safety) highlighted a key change that seems to have exacerbated the failings over the management of maintenance on the railway. Railtrack, on the advice of management consultants McKinsey, was implementing a new strategy by the name of Project Destiny, which was based on the idea of replacing assets only when it was necessary rather than at set time intervals. According to the audit, however, this 'just-in-time approach led to major shifts from track renewals to maintenance'. In other words, it was a 'patch and mend' rather than replace approach which resulted in 57 per cent of proposed renewals being either postponed for a year or put into maintenance. The Railway Safety report into the Hatfield accident confirmed the impact of this policy. The report quoted the Balfour Beatty manager who had been in charge of the East Coast Main Line as warning that the rate of track renewal had been 'too low' for the previous two or three years: 'The strategy [was] inappropriate for the heavily trafficked and high-speed East Coast Main Line.'[21] The report attributed this to the recommendations by McKinsey.

Long before Hatfield, the problem of a rise in broken rails had already been identified as having the potential to cause a disaster by the Health and Safety Executive. With frightening prescience, in the press release accompanying the annual rail safety report, the chief inspector of the railways, Vic Coleman, said, 'We took a snapshot look at the state of the tracks at the end of June 1998. This showed us that track quality was getting worse ... If this decline is not reversed it will have an effect on safety.'[22] His figures showed that rail breaks on the Railtrack infrastructure had risen from 2.75 to 3.31 per million train-miles, an increase of 20 per cent, in 1998/99.

The energetic new rail regulator, Tom Winsor, who took up the post in July 1999, was already on the case. Barely a month into the job, he had noted that an HSE report[23] had uncovered a sharp increase in the number of broken rails, a 21 per cent rise to 937 in 1998/9 compared with 755 in 1997/8 and a Railtrack forecast of 600. One of Railtrack's licence conditions, which are policed by the regulator, is to ensure that its assets are managed properly and safely, and Winsor felt that the rise in broken rails was evidence that there might be a breach of licence. On 12 August

1999 Winsor wrote to Gerald Corbett, Railtrack's chief executive, in tough terms, demanding more detailed information about rail breaks and, in particular, clarity about Railtrack's policy on what was the acceptable level of breaks. Winsor had spotted that in Railtrack's 1998 *Network Management Statement* – the annual report on its proposed investment strategy – the forecast numbers of broken rails for the next two years were 525 and 400. Yet in the 1999 statement those predictions had risen to 770 and 700. Now Railtrack's target had gone down to 600, which suggested Railtrack was accepting that a higher number of broken rails was going to occur and seemed not to care.

Winsor also referred to a spat between the Health and Safety Executive and Railtrack over rail maintenance in the four-mile-long Severn Tunnel, Britain's longest, which seemed to be symptomatic of the company's attitude towards rail replacement and of its bellicose attitude towards the safety authorities. Historically, in this wet tunnel, which requires a continual pumping operation in order to remain usable, rails had been replaced every six years, about eight times more frequently than normal. No science had been called on, no textbooks consulted. It was just that the old BR engineers knew that the conditions required such frequent replacements or otherwise there would be broken rails. There had been none in the tunnel for many years.

Railtrack changed that. The local zone director decided to save 50 per cent of the costs by fitting a new type of rail that was thought to require replacement only every nine years. But the old type were also being left in longer and suddenly, in a seven-month period there were four broken rails, all involving sections that were more than six years old. It was only through good fortune that no major accident was caused.

That was bad enough. But even more amazing was Railtrack's attitude to the subsequent complaint about the Severn Tunnel by Her Majesty's Railway Inspectorate. In April 1999 the Inspectorate complained about the situation but Railtrack, not taking sufficient account of the consequences of a derailment and possible collision in the network's longest tunnel, said it was too difficult to replace the rails before October because of the disruption to the service and suggested 50mph restrictions with daily inspections instead. Infuriated, Vic Coleman, who had by then become chief inspector of the railways, took the very rare step of issuing a formal notice to require Railtrack to do the work, and, in the meantime, imposed a 20mph limit on the tunnel, causing prolonged delays on train services to and from Wales. Many trains had to be diverted via Gloucester, adding an hour on to journey times. In taking this action Coleman may well have prevented the Severn Tunnel from being the name that resonates through the rail industry in the way that Hatfield, sadly, now does.

Coleman even went on the radio to explain his actions, a rare move since the HSE is usually happier doing things behind the scenes with quiet words in the right people's ears. The rail regulator[24] joined in too, demanding a report from Gerald Corbett. Then, suddenly, like some backstreet car mechanic offered a fat tip, Railtrack found it could, after all, do the work, and promptly replaced the rails in June, four months ahead of schedule.

Coleman identified the key issue at the heart of the problem. Railtrack's Project Destiny was intended to ensure that assets were maintained and renewed when they became life-expired, rather than at set intervals of time. Therefore, for example, heavily used points should be replaced more often than those on less busy routes. This all sounds very reasonable except that this strategy was based on the premise that Railtrack knew what its assets were and their state of wear. However, Railtrack – incredible as it seems – did not have an asset register. The company did not know what it owned or anything about the condition of its assets. The zones had some knowledge but each one worked on a different basis. As Tom Winsor later put it, 'There's nothing wrong with replacing your assets on the basis of condition, as long as you understand their condition.'[25]

So Coleman was extremely concerned that Railtrack's lapse over the Severn Tunnel was not a one-off, but the symptom of a systemic problem: the company was cutting maintenance costs without having enough information to base rational decisions on what to renew and what to leave. This was a clear example of how policy changes which at board level sounded reasonable created extra risks at the sharp end. The authors of a report into the broken rails situation were incredulous, recording that Railtrack 'does not keep central statistics'[26] and was therefore unable to plot trends about defects in its rails, even though contractors were required to maintain such records.

Like Coleman, Winsor, the rail regulator, was also worried that this type of event was evidence of a systemic failure rather than a one-off. Railtrack responded to his 12 August letter by arguing that the increase in breaks was partly a result of the rise in the number of trains on the network and partly of 'rail nearing the end of its life in high tonnage routes'.[27] Winsor was not satisfied, even when in subsequent correspondence Railtrack categorically rejected the suggestions that the backlog of track defects had built up through lack of maintenance. To sort the issue out Winsor commissioned a report from the US consultants Transportation Technology Center Inc., a subsidiary of the American Association of Railroads, and its findings were critical of Railtrack's management of the network. There was one major problem with the TTCI report – it was published nearly a month after the four men were killed in the Hatfield disaster, having been completed on 25 October, just eight days after the accident. Winsor's attempt to rein back the damage caused by Project Destiny had, through no fault of his own, been too slow. Hatfield, according to one jaundiced train operator, 'was McKinsey's finest hour'. The TTCI report outlined several reasons for the increase in rail breaks, attributing them mainly to changed practices on Britain's railways and a failure to take account of the changing nature of their use. It found that the condition of the track had deteriorated dramatically in 1995 and 1996, and despite subsequent improvements, 'has not yet consistently reached the 1994 levels'.[28]

Railtrack's inspection methods were criticised; amongst other failings, in 1995 the company had mothballed BR's Ultrasonic Testing Train because it argued that 'hand testing' was more accurate, even though the train was much quicker. The TTCI report looked at the experience in Europe and found that much more sophisticated equipment was being used, with ultrasonic trains capable of covering 150 miles in a shift. The authors of the report said: 'All the comparison railways inspect primarily using inspection vehicles, with manual methods used mainly for verification tests and tests at special areas like switches and crossings.'[29] In other words, Britain was in the railway dark ages. Again, after Hatfield, Railtrack sought to make good its error, dispatching Richard Middleton, who was hastily appointed technical director in the aftermath of the accident, having previously been commercial director, with a blank cheque to buy as much testing and grinding equipment as he felt necessary – a far cry from the penny-pinching days of the late 1990s when Railtrack's sole agenda was to cut costs.

The virtual abandonment of the rail-grinding programme in the run-up to privatisation was another major factor in the deterioration of the quality of the track highlighted in the TTCI report. Rail grinding smoothes off the top of the rail, preventing small cracks from spreading further into the rail. BR had run down its rail-grinding regime and by 1991/2 had just one machine working, operating some 120 shifts per year.[30] In the following two years, BR's last and Railtrack's first in charge of the infrastructure, there was no grinding at all. Throughout the period 1994/5 to 1998/9, Railtrack had that one machine back in operation, at a cost of just £1.1m per year, and it was only in 1999/2000, as part of Railtrack's belated attempt to reduce the number of broken rails, that more resources were beginning to be devoted to grinding rails, with a new machine doubling capacity and a further two ordered.

This was, of course, too late to prevent the Hatfield disaster. According to an expert on rail damage, Stuart Grassie, rolling contact fatigue (of which gauge corner cracking is one type) was a growing phenomenon on many European railways. Ironically, the best research on the problem had actually been undertaken in Britain at Cambridge University and British Rail Research during the 1970s and 1980s. BR Research was privatised along with the rest of the industry and sold to AEA Technologies and much of its expertise was lost because the companies which took on the railways had no commitment to such research. This again was a gap left by privatisation since the importance of research and development was not taken into account by those who privatised the railway. (In contrast, in Japan, where the railways are also owned privately, rail research is funded by the government.) Belatedly, Railtrack, along with Corus and Schweerbau UK, had agreed to pick up the cost of some of this research as the problems of broken rails became apparent before the Hatfield accident, but as Dr Grassie put it, 'Regrettably the benefits of this work will come too late for the families of the four people who died at Hatfield ... and perhaps also too late for Railtrack itself to benefit fully from maintaining its rails rather than simply replacing them.'[31]

According to Dr Grassie, the main way of preventing rolling contract fatigue is through regular grinding, which was carried out in Europe at a far higher rate than in Britain. Rails always develop tiny cracks as trains pass along them, and these are generally ground out naturally as more trains pass over them or by treatment from grinding machines. The cracks are initially shallow and at a small angle towards the direction of travel. It is only when they turn down at right angles from the top of the rail, after about 10mm, that they begin to pose a danger. Network Rail has now reintroduced an extensive rail-grinding programme.

In another awful blunder Railtrack got round to grinding the rail that caused the Hatfield crash on 4/5 September, just five weeks before the accident. Unfortunately, it was, as Railtrack now concedes, quite possibly 'the wrong treatment at the wrong time', because the cracks were, by then, too deep to be remedied by grinding (which, incidentally, was carried out by yet another contractor, Serco). The section of track at Hatfield was, in fact, subjected to very heavy grinding that may well have weakened the already damaged rail even further, although the Railway Safety report was inconclusive on this question. It did, however, confirm the possibility that the heavier trains in use on the line since the completion of its refurbishment in 1989 could have weakened the rails over time.

Railtrack suggested to the TTCI researchers that the main cause of the rise in broken rails was the increase in the number of trains on the network and changes in rolling stock design which had unexpected consequences. Certainly, both of these explanations formed part of the story and contributed to the spread of gauge corner cracking. A Railtrack insider said: 'I'm convinced that it was a change in wheel profile initiated by BR which caused the outbreak of gauge corner cracking. However, the phenomenon had existed for a long time; as I recall there was a rail showing signs of it at Warrington in the 1970s and it had to be replaced.'[32]

The intensity of use, particularly the rise in numbers of freight trains, involved sweating old assets and inevitably led to more breaks. There was an increase of some 1,200 passenger trains per day between 1996 and 2000 (a 7 per cent rise in services, which, because they were mostly long-distance trains, represented an 11 per cent rise in mileage[33]) and many additional freight services (the amount of freight carried on rail grew 41 per cent in the first four years of privatisation[34]). Because of the way that the industry was structured, Railtrack had no incentive to ensure that the track could cope with this influx of new traffic, as its track access charges were largely fixed and train operators were allowed to provide 8 per cent additional services without paying any extra money to Railtrack.[35] There was much anecdotal evidence, too, that there were more wheel flats (a wheel that is out of shape after being damaged during braking or sliding) on the network than under BR, possibly because train operators reduced maintenance to cut costs after privatisation. While this is difficult to prove, the TTCI report noted that wheel flats might be a major contributor to rail damage, as flats place enormous stresses on the rails.

This was symptomatic of the fact that no one was in charge of the 'wheel-rail' interface. (Indeed a high-level committee, the excitingly named Wheel-Rail Interface Authority, was created to deal with this issue by the industry after the Hatfield crash but, astonishingly, could not function properly because, according to the Railway Safety and Standards Board, 'it could not obtain economic public liability and professional indemnity insurance' and had to be wound up in 2004, though the work carried on through a 'systems interface committee'.) Under BR if a particular train or type of train was causing damage to the track, the engineer would quickly track it down and ensure that the operations manager sorted out the problem. But with three different companies involved in the wheel-rail interface – Railtrack, the operator and the rolling-stock leasing company – there was no one to ensure that this key relationship was working safely. In the aftermath of the accident Railtrack chief executive Gerald Corbett said that one of its causes was that no one was managing that interface. Dr Grassie's research supports this contention by highlighting a counter-intuitive reason for the increase in gauge corner cracking: 'RCF has become more prevalent not only because ever-greater loads are borne by the rails (and wheels) but also because wear has been greatly reduced, primarily as a result of more effective lubrication.' In other words, better lubrication prevented the wheels operating as a kind of huge polisher. This was precisely the sort of unexpected consequence of technological changes that might have been spotted in an integrated railway but had no hope of being discovered within the fragmented structure.

Tellingly, the TTCI report found that Railtrack estimated that 400–600 miles of track were affected by gauge corner cracking, although the 'full extent of the problem is not known',[36] as events following Hatfield proved only too clearly. At one site gauge corner cracks were emerging on rail just one year old, according to TTCI. If, as is clear, Railtrack had known about this problem for some time before Hatfield, and indeed instances were recorded as far back as the 1970s, why was the company not doing more to tackle it? The TTCI research backs up the suggestion that had the Hatfield disaster not occurred, it is highly likely that the same kind of accident would have occurred elsewhere on the network, with more or less disastrous consequences.

Professor Roderick Smith, who was quickly hired by Railtrack to investigate the problem of gauge corner cracking and the wider pheno- menon, rolling contact fatigue, in the immediate aftermath of the disaster, is convinced that the abandonment of an extensive rail grinding programme was the key factor in the spread of gauge corner cracking: 'No one knows why Railtrack abandoned its grinding programme. If the railway had been in tip top condition, it would have been possible to have a maintenance holiday for a few years. But the railway was not in tip top condition and therefore it was the stupidest thing they could do.'[37] While heavier loads, the extra trains, the increase in wheel flats and the standardisation of the wheel profile, which meant the same part of the rail tended to be used by every train, all contributed, Professor Smith says, 'It was the absence of grinding which was the key element.'

There was another possible cause of the deterioration of the quality of rails across the network. In its early years Railtrack simply did not buy enough new rail. The decline in orders for new rail had started as part of BR's rundown in preparation for privatisation and continued under Railtrack. Richard Hope, the veteran rail journalist, had obtained figures from British Steel for the Commons Transport Sub-Committee showing that the rail replacement rate was just 0.8 per cent per year, implying that rails would have to last 125 years. To show the absurdity of this, Hope pointed out that had no rails ever been replaced since the railways were first built, the average rail life would have, at the time, been precisely 125 years. This compared with an average of forty years in the major railways of Europe such as the French, Italian and German systems. As the TTCI report concluded, 'Reduced rail purchases over the years have led to increasing rail age and a consequential increase in rail fatigue. That is, there has been a prolonged under-investment in rail.'[38]

Railtrack's explanation, given to the Committee by David Rayner, the director of safety and standards,[39] was that BR had been 'living on its inventory' but, in fact, when Railtrack published its 1996 *Network Management Statement*,[40] setting out its investment plans, the same rate of rail replacement was forecast, just 250 kilometres per year over the next ten years. This compared with a rate of 402 kilometres per year during the previous four years under British Rail. Railtrack explained in the NMS, rather unconvincingly, that it was able to achieve this reduction because of 'recent technical advances'.

Railtrack had inherited from British Rail the British habit of making do and exacerbated the problem with its parsimonious approach and its adoption of McKinsey's recommendations. The TTCI authors noted that there was a higher tolerance of broken rails on the British railways than on other systems, and Railtrack had seemed happy to go along with this traditional acceptance of a high rate of rail breaks until 1999, when it began to increase its purchase of new rail. The researchers estimated that there were a staggering 25,000–30,000 track defects around the network, something like one for every mile of track. While rail breaks were counted because they were part of Railtrack's performance regime, defects – including cracks – were not a measured output. There was no incentive built into the system for Railtrack or the maintenance companies to keep the level of defects down, except the vague requirements of the contracts, which stipulated that the track had to be maintained to an adequate standard. There is always a problem with a management system based on targeted outputs rather than one that takes a holistic standards approach – everyone goes for the targets and other factors are ignored, particularly when there is considerable financial pressure. It was of little comfort to the relatives of the dead that in the six months prior to the Hatfield accident Railtrack, reacting to the increased pressure on the issue, had reduced the number of broken rails by 30 per cent.[41] It was too little, too late.

Railtrack might have been able to cope with these pressures had there been a strong culture of engineering within the company. However, as Corbett explained just before he was sacked, the structure of Railtrack created for privatisation marginalised the role of engineers:

> The way the maintenance was contracted out broke the engineering chain and, at the time, no one realised that. Under British Rail, the engineering function was very strong. There was a chain going right down to the local area engineer. The local engineer was in charge of the system and optimising the wheel-rail interface and the chain of command went up to the top engineer. But when maintenance was broken off, a load of engineers went into the maintenance companies and some stayed with Railtrack, but the interface stopped being an engineering interface. *It became a commercial interface*, with all the problems.[42]

Railtrack's de facto head of engineering (though his title was actually head of asset management as there was no chief engineer), Andy Doherty, was therefore not on the board and, amazingly, the area engineers did not report to him. They reported, instead, to infrastructure contract managers (ICMs) who were not engineers but commercial people, often from outside the industry. There was only a 'dotted line relationship' between the area engineers and Railtrack's head of engineering in HQ. In other words, these local engineers did not report into Railtrack's corporate engineering structure and there was no direct link between the two, an extraordinary anomaly. There was another complexity, too, which prevented quick and effective decisions from being made. The ICMs worked with their counterparts in the maintenance companies but, as a Railtrack insider put it, 'you would have another chain of command in the contractor, with all its different layers, and somewhere you would find an engineer, but that engineer, talking to Railtrack's engineer, would be a terribly vague relationship. In BR, there would have been a direct chain from that person up to the top.'[43]

Railtrack's emphasis on making profit undermined everything else. As one former executive put it, 'I thought that Railtrack had learnt from Ladbroke Grove and that there was more emphasis on safety. Hatfield showed they hadn't. There was still too much emphasis on profit and the lessons of Ladbroke Grove had not been learnt.'[44]

Tony Roche, a career railwayman and president of the Institution of Mechanical Engineers, is convinced that Railtrack's focus on money prevented it from fulfilling its engineering role: 'There are a number of factors which make a successful operation or business. Money is always there ... but for the railways, key issues are engineering and people. ... Engineering was not understood because people didn't look at inputs – they didn't actually understand, from the risk assessment point of view, the importance of all things working properly.'[45] He feels that the huge number of interfaces between the various companies that had once made up BR generated a 'culture of confrontation' rather than cooperation. Corbett told the Commons Transport Sub-Committee inquiry that the financial pressure from the regulator to reduce delays affected the whole culture of the organisation and put the wrong priorities at the top of the agenda. Corbett, who in his three years at the head of Railtrack had begun to understand the flaws in the way the industry had been privatised, became convinced that the Hatfield accident was not only a managerial aberration but a result of structural weaknesses. He told the Sub-Committee that he felt 'There is a conflict between performance and safety.'[46] He went on to say that the fundamental question for the investigators in the Hatfield crash was to understand why a speed restriction had not been imposed and whether the decision had been influenced by concerns about performance:

> I think we do have to understand whether or not there is not an issue at the front line in the maintenance contractors and within Railtrack ... we do need to understand better on the front line what the impact of the drive for performance is ... I think it is harder to balance the safety/performance equation if you have a set of external pressures on you that are focusing on one particular bit of it.[47]

Corbett pointed later to the random nature of the regime: 'To take, say, £20m costs out of the system is quite hard work, but to make it out of the performance regime is relatively easier. But it is haphazard, though, largely dependent on the weather.'[48] So the whole highly ingenious regulatory regime was dependent on how much it rained and snowed. Railtrack estimated that without Hatfield the flooding of the autumn of 2000 would, in any case, have cost the company £150–200m. This was against the background of constant pressure from the regulator. According to 'Insider', the anonymous rail executive who writes a column in *Rail* magazine, Railtrack had been set an impossible task: 'Where the Regulator got it 100 per cent wrong, was an insistence that overall costs were reduced while network use was growing ... The cut in permanent way staff is at the heart of what went wrong [at Hatfield] and this was caused by the cost reduction targets the regulator had said must be achieved.'[49]

Tom Winsor, the regulator, disagreed, which was hardly surprising given that it was his performance regime that Corbett felt was at the root of the potential conflict between safety and performance. Winsor argued that the two went hand in hand and that a punctual railway was a safe railway. While this is undoubtedly true, Winsor, with a mindset based on legal contracts and regulation, may have missed the wider point made by people like Roche and Corbett – that an emphasis on performance had infected the culture of the railways and its staff.

Any emphasis on performance completely disappeared in the aftermath of the accident. The panicking Railtrack executives arbitrarily placed hundreds of speed restrictions on the railway, effectively causing the collapse of the network and wrecking the train service. The process by which those speed restrictions came to be imposed provides a fascinating insight into the way in which Railtrack was managed and the extent to which privatisation had affected its ability to run the railway by depriving it of experienced railway people and replacing them with newcomers who lacked knowledge of what is a unique and highly technical industry.

The Railtrack executives huddled in their bunker in the Black Tower on the night of the accident faced a fundamental question: was the poor condition of the rail at Hatfield a one-off or was it symptomatic of deterioration across the network? A properly run railway organisation would have had the knowledge and ability to make such a judgement. Railtrack did not, and the consequences of that were devastating.

The problem the Railtrack board faced was highlighted by the fact that it included just two engineers, and the most senior, Richard Middleton, the commercial director, was responsible for dealing with the train operating companies and therefore not in a position to exercise influence over engineering decisions. Moreover, the company did not have a research department; a small amount of R & D was subcontracted to outsiders but none was carried out directly by Railtrack. BR had been one of the world leaders in railway research but that expertise was lost at privatisation when BR Research was effectively disbanded. Without in-house expertise, Railtrack was at the mercy of outside consultants, who, as one insider put it, 'always have their own agenda, which is often to ensure that as much work as possible is needed'.[50]

The fundamental problem for Railtrack was that it had no idea of the extent of the problem with the track. BR had never compiled an asset register and, as we have seen, Railtrack, despite injunctions from the regulator, had failed to do so. In BR's case the lack of an asset register was less serious because the knowledge was in the heads of its workforce, who passed it on down the generations, but the privatisation process had broken that chain. Moreover, Railtrack had no method of recording defects centrally, for it was the maintenance contractors who were supposed to be aware of the condition of the network. The contracts gave Railtrack only a loose form of control and it was therefore inevitable that Hatfield caused panic among Railtrack's executives, who had no way of knowing how much of the network for which they were responsible might have been affected by gauge corner cracking, let alone how fast such cracks might propagate through a rail to the point at which they posed a threat.

Within a few hours of the crash, speed restrictions were placed on eighty-one sites across the network. These were sections of track where there was evidence of gauge corner cracking and where, as at Hatfield, a decision had been taken to rerail, though this may have been scheduled for up to two years ahead. But, given that Railtrack knew that gauge corner cracking was present at many other sites, the managers in the black tower worried that this was not sufficient.

The task of responding to the crisis was made more difficult by the fact that Jonson Cox, Railtrack's director of operations, the executive with the day-to-day responsibility for running the railway, had joined the company only seven weeks before the disaster. Cox had been brought in by Railtrack to help the chief executive, Gerald Corbett, who was struggling under the weight of running a difficult company in the face of tremendous political, media and operational pressures. Cox had a reputation as a doer, a man who would make a difference, and Corbett gave him the role of director of operations, even though Cox had never worked in the railway industry.

The head of track was David Ventry, who had the legal responsibility for its condition, and he reported to the head of asset management, Andy Doherty. Under Railtrack's safety case (the document which sets out the company's assessment of risks and the steps taken to control them, and which has to be approved by the Health and Safety Executive), Ventry, a relatively junior manager, was responsible for preparing the guidelines for imposing speed restrictions. Cox was put in charge of Operation Response, the team quickly set up to deal with the implications of the gauge corner cracking issue. Two other directors, Chris Leah, the safety director (and Cox's predecessor as director of operations), and John Curley, the performance director, both veteran career railwaymen, were also in the group, which met daily and conferred by conference call with the seven zone directors, all experienced railway managers. A senior engineer, Andrew McNaughton, at the time head of the Great Western zone, was quickly summoned to head office to help deal with the crisis. Significantly, Corbett, the chief executive, was not part of the committee.

After the imposition of speed restrictions on the initial eighty-one sites, Ventry recommended that restrictions should also be placed on all other sections of tracks where there was evidence of gauge corner cracking. McNaughton argued that the restrictions should be at two-thirds of line speed, whereas Ventry suggested 20mph for all of them.

The basis of McNaughton's argument was that a speed restriction of two-thirds of (the maximum) line speed is safer because that is the speed at which the weight of a train on a curve is equally distributed between the two rails. The rationale for a 20mph limit was that that is the maximum speed at which, it is assumed, a train can be expected to remain upright even if it is derailed; 20mph, therefore, represented the accepted limit at which risk was reduced to a minimum.

The difference was crucial. Even though no one knew the precise extent of the problem, it was expected that several hundred sites would be involved, and the imposition of 20mph limits on all of them would cause immense problems throughout the rail system. Over the weekend after the crash, Ventry prepared a memo, which was sent out to zone directors together with a covering note from Cox and Leah. It later became known as the 'meltdown memo' because it almost brought the network to a halt.

There was much debate within the organisation over whether to send out a hard or soft memo. Crucially, McNaughton was not around that weekend. The atmosphere in the Black Tower was frenetic and totally unbusinesslike. According to one executive: 'There was much buck passing. All the zone directors had signed off certificates saying their assets were safe back in April as they did every year, and that meant they wanted to cover their backs, too. Moreover, it flushed out a lot of information the local people had known but had not fed up to HQ. There was a feeling there was a lot to worry about.'

Ventry's guidelines said that any site with cracks longer than 30mm (just over an inch) should have an immediate emergency temporary speed restriction of 20mph. As a result, the Scottish zone director, Janette Anderson, after checking with head office that the instructions were correct, closed the West Coast Main Line because she would have had to impose so many restrictions that the passage of the trains would become impossible. It was reopened a day later.

The implications of the decisions taken by the Operation Response team now became clear: they had effectively set the rules without anyone knowing how many sites would be affected. The best early estimate had been around 300 places where the track was showing signs of gauge corner cracking; ultimately there turned out to be 6,821. Not all the cracks were severe enough to require the imposition of speed limits, but temporary restrictions, mostly of 20mph, were suddenly popping up around the network like mushrooms on a rotting tree. At the peak, about a month later, there were 574 restrictions imposed as a result of the Hatfield crash (in addition to the 500 or so routine restrictions placed on sections awaiting repair), and overall, by 21 May 2001, there were 1,286 sites where restrictions had been imposed at some point following the accident. Given that many of these were on busy parts of the network and that Railtrack did not have the resources to deal quickly with such a high number of inspections because each one needed a team of engineers, the result was the worst set of delays to the trains in the history of the railways, other than those caused by industrial action.

Railtrack justified the decision to impose so many temporary speed limits on the basis that it had no alternative – it was, according to a press release,[51] 'an appropriate and necessary response to the phenomena [*sic*] of gauge corner cracking'. The official line was that Railtrack could not risk the possibility of another rail break, which would have drastic repercussions for the company (though possibly not quite as dramatic as those resulting from the speed restrictions). But the vast majority of people in the industry felt that Railtrack had been far too cautious, pointing out that no rail in the same poor condition as the one at Hatfield was ever found in the course of the thousands of inspections prompted by the accident. For example, Sir Alastair Morton, the chairman of the SRA, told ITN that the closure of the West Coast Main Line was an 'overreaction' and said the railways had suffered a 'nervous breakdown'.[52] Many engineers concurred. The drastic reaction was, many felt, a result of the company's lack of engineering expertise.

Interestingly, one zone director stood out against the guidelines. Michael Holden of Southern, a long-time railwayman, realised that Railtrack had massively overreacted and simply ignored the restrictions, saying the lines in his zone had a speed limit of 100mph anyway. That is why commuters south of the Thames largely escaped the chaos. Had they not, there would have been even more pressure on Railtrack and its executives. As it was, Tony Blair soon became involved, summoning Railtrack executives to Downing Street on 27 October, a mere ten days after the crash. He had another meeting with them exactly a month later. The extent of chaos in the organisation was illustrated by the fact that the presentation was finished so late that one of the executives had to leg it to No. 10 after his taxi got stuck in a traffic jam half a mile away. Blair was well briefed and on both occasions pressed hard for the speed restrictions to be relaxed or removed. Indeed, according to evidence given by Ventry at the Hatfield trial in March 2005, Blair put Railtrack under considerable pressure to increase the speed limits, something Ventry feared might cause another crash.[53]

As Holden's successful resistance suggests, it seems unlikely that such a policy of imposing blanket speed restrictions would have been adopted under British Rail. There would have been a team of managers running a region or sector of the railway covering such disciplines as civil engineering, rolling stock, operations, marketing and personnel. They would have reported to the director or general manager who made the ultimate decisions. Therefore, civil engineers would probably never have even dared to suggest blanket 20mph speed restrictions and, had they done so, they would have been given short shrift. The general manager would have balanced the needs of the engineers with those of the other directors and the requirement to keep the railway running.

But, as Blair was told, once the process unleashed by Operation Response was under way, it was impossible to rein back. Although the imposition of a speed restriction did not need the sanction of the Health & Safety Executive, through its railway arm, Her Majesty's Rail Inspectorate (HMRI), removing any of them did. The inspectors – again taking a very conservative view – ruled that, before any restriction could be lifted, Railtrack had to carry out a risk assessment of that particular site and provide detailed guidance on the criteria it was using to impose and remove speed restrictions. Despite the evidence of chaos all around it, Railtrack was remarkably slow in changing its guidelines on speed restrictions. Eventually, it slipped out in May 2001[54] that the company had 'changed the guidelines based on the extra information about causes and risks of the problem, and how to deal with it, accumulated since Hatfield'.

In the meantime, the result for the train operators was chaos. On the second weekend after the accident, as the number of restrictions spiralled out of control, the trains literally ground to a halt. The rail companies resorted to advising their customers not to use their services. A Midland Mainline spokesman, Kevin Johnson, told a Sunday newspaper: 'We have been told the disruption is going to last for at least two weeks but on Sunday I would suggest people do not travel at all.'[55] The suggestion that the disruption would last only two weeks was, of course, to prove ridiculously optimistic.

The railways quickly reduced passengers to despair. Journey times were doubling or worse, forcing many people used to taking a day trip from, say, London to Manchester to travel overnight and stay in a hotel. The InterCity services were particularly affected. It was frequently taking five hours to reach Manchester or Liverpool from London. Bristol to Glasgow became a nine-hour marathon.

Then the skies opened, ensuring that 2000 would become the railway traveller's *annus horribilis*. Within a couple of weeks of Hatfield, the persistent autumn downpours created widespread flooding, the worst for many years. The GNER line north of York was closed for several days and many lines in outlying areas such as Wales, the West Country and Scotland were shut for weeks. The train companies were so overwhelmed that on some routes they did not even offer replacement bus services. Public transport was, in effect, suspended, a poor advertisement for the rail industry's wares which was to have a long-term effect.

Operators began drawing up a series of temporary timetables, a process that would normally take six months but was now being done on a weekly or fortnightly basis. Extra restrictions were being added every week as new hairline cracks were discovered, which meant that these updated timetables were unworkable as soon as they were produced. Conveying this new information to passengers proved hard, even with the use of the internet. For example, it took three days for a new timetable to be loaded into Railtrack's public timetable and therefore website visitors would get misleading information. People who relied upon the National Rail Enquiry Service would frequently turn up at the station to find no trace of the service they had been advised to take.

Gradually, Railtrack began to realise that the basis on which it was making decisions was too conservative, but the process on which it had embarked was unstoppable. After two weeks, gauge corner cracking was reclassified into severe, medium and mild, though severe was still reckoned to be anything 30mm long or more, and yet the number of temporary speed restrictions continued to rise. This was because both Railtrack and maintenance contract people on the ground had by now got into the habit of taking very conservative decisions about the potential danger of cracks. The whole of Railtrack had become focused on avoiding another catastrophe caused by a broken rail rather than trying to run a railway.

Figures for punctuality and reliability had gone off the scale.

Punctuality normally hovered around the 90 per cent mark, but several companies, such as Great Eastern (normally one of the best in the country), West Anglia, Great Northern, Virgin West Coast and CrossCountry and GNER, had fewer than one in four trains running on time[56] in the month after Hatfield. According to the Strategic Rail Authority's figures,[57] just under half of long-distance trains arrived on time during the last three months of 2000. Even those figures underestimate the number of delays, as many of them were calculated against temporary timetables based on journey times that had already been substantially extended. Complaints reached record levels.

By early December, according to Railtrack, there were still 553 speed restrictions, of which 401 were 20mph. Around 10,000 trains out of 18,000 each day (55 per cent) were running late. Temporary timetables meant that many journeys were still taking twice the normal time, and a quarter of passengers had abandoned the system to use other means of transport or had given up travelling altogether. Not surprisingly, while airline ticket sales soared, train companies' revenues shrunk commensurately. Some companies, particularly those operating long-distance services, such as GNER, lost half their revenue for a couple of months.

The sense of chaos within the industry in general, and Railtrack in particular, was not helped by the sacking of Corbett a month after the Hatfield accident. He had tendered his resignation on the day of the crash, but the board, influenced by the surprising amount of public support for Corbett, rejected it, only to change its mind a month later. The trigger appears to have been his outspoken comments to the Commons Transport Sub-Committee suggesting that the structure of the rail industry needed to be changed, but there was also a dislike of Corbett among some of his fellow executives, who, according to one, felt he ran the company like 'a medieval court'.[58] The non-executive directors (one of whom was Jennie Page, whose recent lacklustre record included running the Millennium Dome and being on the board of the ill-fated Equitable Life) organised a coup by persuading the ineffective and weak chairman Sir Philip Beck to sack Corbett. He was replaced by the finance director, Steven Marshall, also a man with little experience of the rail industry since he had joined Railtrack only a year previously from GrandMet (now Diageo).

Corbett's departure just made things worse for Railtrack. He was one of the railway's few class acts and, after a bad start, he had earned respect within the railways for standing up for the industry in the aftermath of Ladbroke Grove. On Corbett's departure the rookie director Jonson Cox was promoted to chief operating officer, leaving Britain's railways in the hands of two forty-three-year-olds with barely a year's railway experience between them. Richard Middleton, the commercial director and the sole engineer on the board, was now made technical director. But even this move was carried out with some reluctance. Initially, Marshall had suggested that Middleton report to Cox, but Middleton baulked and threatened to walk out, leaving the new board even more bereft of railway savvy. In addition, another engineer, Andrew McNaughton, was appointed chief engineer – though not given a place on the board – in order, according to the Railtrack press release, to 'ensure that engineering is given proper priority by the company'. Despite this promise, even after the accident, only two of Railtrack's seven executive directors had extensive rail experience – Middleton and Chris Leah, the safety and environment director.

As the implications of Hatfield and its aftermath began to sink in, it soon became apparent that the biggest single victim of Railtrack's ineptitude was going to be the company itself. The problem was not just the direct costs of the accident and the subsequent disruption, though these were certainly bad enough. In mid-January 2001 the company accepted that they would amount to £600m, and by the time it announced its losses for the financial year 2000/2001 the figure had risen to £733m, and was still going up. The more fundamental – indeed, as it would turn out, the fatal – casualty was Railtrack's credibility. Not only had Hatfield demonstrated, in the most public way possible, that Railtrack lacked the management and skills required to carry out its basic functions, it also caused the market to lose the faith in its future that had carried the company's shares from £3.90 at flotation to a peak of over £17 at the end of 1998; less than a year after Hatfield, the value of the shares slid below the flotation price.

Hatfield was not the only factor contributing to this loss of confidence. It had become increasingly clear that Railtrack was likely to lose its responsibility for major improvements to the network and with it most of the potential for the growth of its business. The costs for its two biggest projects, the improvement of the West Coast Main Line and the cross-London Thameslink 2000, were spiralling out of control and both would, it was clear, require substantial further subsidies from the government if they were to be completed; as a result, the SRA, out of whose budget such subsidies would come, was advocating that Railtrack surrender its responsibility for major capital projects to new 'Special Purpose Vehicles' (see Chapter 6). All in all, Railtrack had ceased to look like a glamorous growth stock and was now perceived as a rather dismal utility company with an unhealthy dependence on government subsidy.

Railtrack tried to counter this perception by paying a dividend to its shareholders in May 2001 in order to maintain its 'access to the capital markets', even though it had declared a loss of £534m. This decision was both foolhardy and counterproductive. Not only did this move attract a further torrent of ridicule and abuse from the media, it also left Railtrack in an indefensible position, since the company had only very recently been obliged to ask the government to advance £1.5bn that it was due to receive as part of its investment programme between 2006 and 2011. The company said thanks by immediately recycling 10 per cent of this cash to its shareholders.

The request for the additional funds had been made through the rail regulator, Tom Winsor, whose responsibility it was to ensure that Railtrack had the money to carry out its agreed investment programme. Since Winsor had only comparatively recently agreed with Railtrack a financial settlement for the five-year 'control period' 2001–2006, which some analysts felt was exceptionally generous to the company, the government could be expected to extract its pound of flesh in return for advancing the £1.5bn – it duly did so. Railtrack had to agree to tie any growth in dividends over the next five years directly to earnings and to accept a non-executive director who would represent the public interest on the company's board. Both these concessions were considered bad news by the markets and Railtrack shares fell further. Shortly before the general election of June 2001, Railtrack was back, insisting that it needed another £2bn. This time Winsor had had enough: he curtly advised the company 'to put away its begging bowl'[59] and get on with running the railways.

After a long search for candidates with more relevant experience, John Robinson, another non-railwayman whose previous job had been as chairman of Smith & Nephew, a medical devices company, was appointed as chairman from July 2001, further adding to the sense in the City, government and the rest of the industry that the company had lost its way. Robinson quickly attempted to signal a new direction by sacking

Cox and publicly accepting responsibility for the Hatfield crash at the company's AGM, but, as we shall see in the next chapter, he made a fatal mistake in going directly to the government to ask for more money, prompting the demise of the company.

Railtrack was ultimately destroyed by the Hatfield accident and its aftermath, and it is not an exaggeration to say that the accident completely wrecked the Tories' model of privatisation by highlighting its fundamental flaws at the cost, however, of four lives. Railtrack's overreaction, which was to prove its death warrant, was a result of the company's lack of confidence in its own ability to handle the engineering task that was its basic function.

There was a final irony. One of the reasons why Railtrack did not have access to the right information after the crash was that the British Transport Police speedily impounded Balfour Beatty's files, thus preventing Railtrack from seeing them. Had Railtrack been able to get immediate access to Balfour Beatty's ultrasound reports, and interpreted them correctly, then it would have discovered the very exceptional circumstances that led to the Hatfield rail break. Of course, if the maintenance had not been contracted out, the files would already have been in Railtrack's possession and the information would have been readily available. Had it not been for this, the immediate panic, and the subsequent repercussions of Hatfield, might not have been so great and much of the enormous and unsustainable cost escalation in the industry discussed later on in this book would have been avoided. But then there are an awful lot of ifs in this story.

CHAPTER 9

Railtrack: suicide or lynching?

When Tony Blair returned in triumph to No. 10 to begin his second term in June 2001, Railtrack had few friends in or out of Whitehall. The company had become an object of hatred and ridicule to passengers. It had caused grave financial damage to its customers, the train operating companies, and had lost any credibility in the City. The regulator, Tom Winsor, who was responsible for determining how much money the company received from government and through access charges from the train operating companies, had made it clear that his patience was exhausted. Responsibility for new large projects had effectively been taken away from Railtrack; even those on which work was proceeding had an uncertain future. The new Secretary of State at the Department of Transport, Local Government and the Regions (DTLR), Stephen Byers, had been warned by his officials, and their colleagues in the Treasury, that Railtrack seemed to have an insatiable appetite for cash and a more or less foolproof method for extracting it from the public purse. For the brutal truth was that no government could afford to stand by and see the railway system grind to a halt. So if Railtrack could persuade the regulator, whose remit obliged him to provide the company with sufficient funds to carry out its functions, that it needed more money, there was very little the government could do except cough up. Certainly, the regulator was supposed to make sure that the company had been operating competently and efficiently, but this was a near-impossible task given the complexity of the structure of the privatised railway. Privatisation, it had now become evident, far from freeing government from the financial burden imposed by the railways, had, instead, removed much of its ability to control and limit that burden.

It was therefore somewhat unlikely that when John Robinson, who had recently taken over as chairman of Railtrack from Sir Philip Beck, walked into the headquarters of the Department of Transport on 25 July 2001, he expected to get a particularly warm welcome from Stephen Byers. And even less likely that he would emerge with promises of lots of extra lucre. Nonetheless, his company's plight was dire and he wanted the new minister's help. Having been so recently told by the regulator not to put out the begging bowl, he tried to bypass Winsor by appealing to ministers directly. He asked for what Byers would later describe as a 'soft letter of comfort' addressed to Railtrack's banks and a three- to four-year suspension of the regulatory regime. That was a demand to which ministers could never have acceded, even though the government would also have got a new type of share in the company in return for the risk it was taking on. It would have meant, in effect, that Railtrack would have permanent and unlimited access to the Treasury's back pocket: the company would have been able to threaten to close lines if insufficient money was forthcoming from the government and there would have been no regulator to ensure that the company was operating efficiently and competently.

Robinson felt he had little choice but to throw himself upon the government's mercy. (In fact, he might well have done better by going to Winsor, who might have granted the company extra funds in the light of Hatfield.) Despite the dividend paid in May 2001, supposedly to ensure the company had continued access to the capital markets, Railtrack was now perceived to be so much of a financial lame duck that institutions only felt comfortable lending it money if its debts were tacitly underwritten by the government. Robinson hoped that such an assurance could form part of a long-term plan that would secure Railtrack's future, and he felt confident of a positive response. Regardless of Railtrack's dire financial performance, the government, as he saw it, had no alternative to bailing out the company. Indeed, Byers had repeatedly talked of the industry needing a period of stability, and his boss, Tony Blair, had repeatedly ruled out renationalisation. So what alternative was there to the government effectively rescuing the company yet again?

Byers, however, saw the matter differently. For him it was the last straw. Being new to the job, he was prepared to look at alternatives that would put an end to the constant demands for money from the hapless Railtrack executives. Robinson, a Yorkshire engineer for whom the term 'bluff' might have been fashioned, was a political tyro; he knew Byers from the minister's days as Trade and Industry Secretary and had deliberately chosen to make his pitch in the context of a man-to-man chat in Byers's office. Unwisely, he went in without any other Railtrack executives or aides to provide advice or back-up and he even asked for no note to be taken of the crucial part of the discussion, which meant that the Department subsequently had to cobble together a record of this vital meeting from the recollections of those in the room.

That is one reason why the two parties have subsequently differed sharply in their interpretations of their discussion. Robinson believed he was going to advise ministers that there was a significant but soluble problem; Byers took his words to mean that the company was in deep trouble. Moreover, as Byers admitted to the Railtrack court hearing in July 2005, disscussions about putting Railtrack into administration were already underway. Robinson agreed to a series of sessions between his advisers and government officials at which the latter would be given access to a report prepared by Credit Suisse First Boston, who had recently been appointed as advisers to Railtrack. From Robinson's point of view this was a fatal mistake. The report, prepared secretly on his own orders, and codenamed Operation Rainbow, was highly critical of the company's management and its failure to control costs. The consultants argued that change was inevitable and suggested three possible courses of action: restructuring Railtrack, which would have involved abandoning the way that the company's funding was determined through the regulator, which would, in turn, mean giving it lots of extra cash, estimated later at some £3.5bn; renationalisation, which would have given ministers direct control of the railway, something that would have gone against the whole thrust of government policy on increasing private involvement in public services; or, third, putting the company into receivership,[1] which is what eventually happened through a process defined in the Railway Act 1993 as 'railway administration'.

Robinson's second visit to Byers came on Friday 5 October that year, when he was called in by the minister to be told that Byers's department intended to apply to a judge that weekend to put the company into administration. The events that took place between the two meetings are the subject of fierce political controversy and a legal challenge brought by shareholders and other interested parties in a case whose result in due in October 2005.

At the four-week court hearing in July 2005, the shareholders contended that Byers was guilty of misfeance, by effectively renationalising Railtrack without paying compensation to the shareholders who, under European law, would have been entitled to around £9–10 per share, based on the average share price in the previous three to five years. While the issue of compensation remains a matter for the courts, the chain of events leading to Railtrack's demise suggests that it was as much a result of an assisted suicide as the corporate lynching of which Byers has been subsequently accused, although the minister certainly schemed in an attempt to avoid paying shareholders much more than the price of the shares on 5 October. None of the parties involved, however, emerge with much credit from a set of events that had more to do with base politics and the Treasury's concern about money than with the future well-being of the railway.

Robinson's first visit and the Project Rainbow report, together with advice from across Whitehall and the rail industry, prompted Byers to set up a rival project, Ariel, to examine the possible alternatives for the future of the company. He appointed Schroder Salomon Smith Barney as his financial advisers to examine the alternatives and, later, as it turned out, to help draw up a scheme to place the company into administration. In public Byers kept on saying that the railway needed a period of stability, as he was obliged to do because any alternative inference would have led to the collapse of the share price. In private he was busily looking at the possible options.

Railtrack subsequently argued that Byers misunderstood the Credit Suisse First Boston report. It was not, the company contended, intended to set out alternatives for discussion, and only included a mention of railway administration and renationalisation by way of identifying all possible outcomes facing Railtrack plc and in order to give both sides the opportunity to rule out these options for clear and compelling reasons. Railtrack reckoned that at the outset of the discussions the Department's advisers gave the impression that these were not realistic options.[2] At best this demonstrates that Railtrack's executives were badly advised; at worst that they were extremely naive.

On 23 August, Byers appointed Ernst & Young as potential administrators, starting the process that was to lead to the takeover of Railtrack. He later stressed that this did not mean a decision had been taken, but that, since various alternatives were being considered, he had to prepare for the possible implementation of any one of them. Although Byers continued publicly to stonewall in response to any questions about major changes imminent in the rail industry, there were tell-tale signs that something was afoot. On 7 September, Bob Linnard, director of railways at the DTLR, announced radical changes to the organisation of the department's railways directorate, greatly expanding both its personnel and its role. Indeed, as early as 12 September, according to the shareholders' particulars of claim for the court hearing,[3] Byers told Pam Warren, the leader of the Ladbroke Grove survivors, to 'watch out for around the 8th to 10th of October when you will have some news that will be very pleasing to you'. If it was murder that was being planned, then the conspirators were assembling, though the victim appeared blissfully unaware of any danger.

An even stronger indication came on 2 October, when in his major speech at the Labour Party conference, Tony Blair, while defending privatisation generally, singled out parts of the privatised railway as a 'disaster'. Everyone knew what company he had in mind. I had happened to bump into Byers the previous evening in a bar at the conference and he told me to keep my diary clear for the weekend but would not elaborate. Yet Railtrack's shareholders remained in the dark, although the steady downward drift of the share price suggests that some of the cannier investors guessed the game was up.

By this stage it was also clear that the upgrading of the West Coast main line was totally out of control, with projected costs increasing almost daily (see Chapter 15 for more details). Although the regulator had agreed to fund part of the extra cost of the investment from the public purse, the City perceived, rightly, that the risks of the West Coast project were too great. Railtrack's share price tumbled and the company could no longer raise capital; its days were clearly numbered. Without Hatfield, Railtrack might have lingered on longer or even been allowed to continue in a different form, but the accident, its aftermath, the subsequent losses and, in particular, Railtrack's naive and politically fatal reaction in trying to protect its shareholders from the effects of its mistakes ensured its demise.

The mechanism which was to push Railtrack into administration had already been triggered by the time Blair spoke at the party conference. On the day before his speech, Railtrack had been due to receive a grant of £162m from the government. This was part of the £1.5bn bail-out agreed in April 2001, bringing forward money that originally was going to be paid to Railtrack in the 2006–11 control period, which would have allowed the company to leverage in a total of £445m.[4] But the deal was contingent on the creation of a new organisation, Renewco, basically an accounting device that would allow the government to keep the investment off its balance sheet by implementing a complex plan to smooth out the very lumpy payments over the five-year period. The creation of Renewco had got into difficulties, according to Byers, because no way had been found to keep the expenditure off the government's balance sheet. Therefore he blocked the £162m payment. Railtrack thought that the money had been guaranteed under the terms of the April bail-out, but Byers later said that the government had only promised to use 'its best endeavours' to ensure Railtrack got the money.

Byers's decision to hold back the money instantly transformed Railtrack from solvency to insolvency and became the key issue in the ensuing controversy. Railtrack's finance director, David Harding, had begun to get a bit anxious about the money but not enough for the company to worry about what the government might be planning. So when Robinson was summoned to Byers's office with virtually no notice at 4.45 p.m. on Friday 5 October (a time carefully selected because the markets had closed for the weekend), he had no inkling of what was in store for his company. Byers told him that he would petition the High Court for Railtrack to be put into 'railway administration', a special procedure that allowed the government to appoint administrators to allow the company to keep running despite the fact that it was insolvent. According to the *Mail on Sunday*,[5] Robinson asked wanly whether there was any option: 'No,' Byers replied.

Amazingly, the Railtrack chairman left that meeting with the offer of a new job. Byers asked him to take over the chairmanship of 'NuTrak', the non-profit-making company limited by guarantee that Byers wanted to emerge when Railtrack was eventually taken out of administration. Robinson should have realised immediately that he was in no position to accept such a post. As chairman of a plc, his role was to act in the best interests of the company, which generally means protecting the shareholders, who, according to Byers, were going to lose virtually all their money. But if Robinson took the new job, he might well find the interests of NuTrak conflicting directly with those of the Railtrack shareholders. He eventually recognised this and turned down the job after the weekend, but by then he had lost all credibility.

When Byers told Robinson that there was no alternative, he was being slightly economical with the truth. Railtrack's passage into administration was by no means a fait accompli. The previous visitor to Byers's office that Friday evening had been the rail regulator, Tom Winsor. As we have seen, Winsor determined Railtrack's income by setting the access charges and taking into account any other sources of revenue. The charges were reassessed every five years and the latest review, announced days after the Hatfield train crash in October 2000, had taken effect from April 2001. However, as the regulator had a duty to ensure that Railtrack has 'sufficient funds for the competent and efficient operation, maintenance and renewal of the network', there was a procedure for carrying out interim reviews should the company get into financial difficulties. It was in order to prevent Winsor starting such an interim review that Byers had summoned him.

Winsor, arriving without any prior knowledge of the purpose of the meeting, was astonished to find that Byers threatened to abolish the independence of the regulator. Byers told Winsor that Railtrack was insolvent, which the regulator found strange since the company was about to benefit from a 50 per cent rise in its income, thanks to the increase in its access charges he had just sanctioned. Indeed, in the court hearing, the shareholders pointed out in the particulars of claim that Railtrack made a profit of £292m in the six months to the end of September 2001 and that its assets exceeded its liabilities by £1bn.[6] Moreover, Winsor reminded Byers that Railtrack could ask for an interim review of access charges at any time. Byers told him that the government had thought about that and would table emergency legislation to prevent the regulator pumping extra money into the company through an interim review. Winsor was apoplectic. He later told the Commons Transport Sub-Committee that, 'after pausing to consider if I had really heard what I had just heard', he had warned Byers that neutering a regulator in this way had implications way beyond the railways.[7] Removing his independence, he said, would destroy private investors' confidence not just in the rail industry but in other infrastructure projects and entire industries where regulation was an important factor, such as telecoms and the utilities. He warned Byers that this decision would undermine the government's programme for getting private money into projects for schools, hospitals, prisons and many other capital projects, a central tenet of government policy. Byers ignored him; and, crucially, he did not reveal to Winsor that he was not going to pay Railtrack the £162m.

The mere possibility of an interim review would have undermined the government's case for putting Railtrack into administration, because the outcome of the regulator's decision would have been uncertain and, to obtain the administration order, the government had to show that Railtrack was no longer solvent. With Winsor potentially able to allow Railtrack hundreds of millions of pounds extra in income – or even billions as turned out to be the case when an interim review was eventually carried out in 2003 – the judge would have been very unlikely to grant the order. Indeed, Byers later admitted to Parliament[8] that if Winsor had merely announced an *intention* to commence an interim review, it would have been very unlikely that the judge would have made the administration order. Yet, the judge, sitting in emergency session on the Sunday, rubber stamped the government's case for the order, barely considering the fact that Railtrack could have asked for an interim review. Winsor did not attend the hearing, mistakenly assuming that his fellow lawyers would explain the legal position relating to an interim review.

In fact Winsor did not launch an interim review for the simple reason that Railtrack never asked him for one. Why its executives failed to do so is one of the mysteries of this strange episode. Byers's approach to Winsor had not deterred him, Winsor is an independently minded Scottish lawyer who enjoys a fight and thinks he can outwit any opponent. Legally, he was still a free man until the threatened legislation was passed. An interim review seemed the obvious lifeline for Railtrack but by the time its executives phoned Winsor on the Saturday evening, they seemed already to have given up the ghost. The conference call initiated by Robinson and Steve Marshall, the Railtrack chief executive, opened with the latter saying that they were contacting Winsor 'as a matter of due diligence' which suggests they were going through the motions to show their shareholders that they had done the right thing, rather than making any real effort to save the company.

Marshall asked what would happen 'if we were to apply for an interim review?'[9] Winsor responded with a series of questions: 'Why, when and how much extra money was needed?' The answers took him aback: the review was required because of 'Hatfield and the gap' – the difference of

£1.2bn between what the company had demanded in access charges for the five-year period starting April 2001 and what Winsor had decided; it was needed by Monday. Winsor responded that it was impossible to undertake such a review on such complex grounds so quickly but that he could start one provided he was given more information. Robinson, however, seemed defeated already, his resolve perhaps weakened by the offer of the chairmanship of NuTrak. He told Winsor that the review had to be done that quickly or not at all, because otherwise the government would overrule him. Winsor tried to point out the difficulties the government might encounter, but Robinson would have none of it: 'I still think they will do it,' he kept on repeating.

Railtrack did not come back to Winsor that weekend and failed even to contest the administration order made on the Sunday, even though that would have bought two precious days' delay. One party to the events that Sunday said: 'They were only worried whether they would be sued by their shareholders for having failed in their due diligence.'[10] Railtrack and its legal advisers seem not to have recognised that it is one thing for a minister to threaten emergency legislation and quite another actually to get it onto the statute book. An emergency bill would have required the cooperation of the opposition, which it would certainly not have got. In reality, such a bill would have been strongly opposed in the Commons, might well have been defeated or delayed in the House of Lords, and would undoubtedly have not gone through speedily, as Byers had suggested. Indeed, the mere prospect of the furore that such a bill would have raised in the City might well have deterred ministers from carrying out Byers's threat.

Railtrack missed several other opportunities to fight back on that famous weekend. The Railtrack executives could even have threatened to resign en masse, which would have stopped all rail services since they had a legal responsibility for safety. Instead, the company had already prepared a press statement saying there was no 'credible alternative' to administration. The Conservative opposition later accused Byers of threatening Winsor and brutally assassinating Railtrack, and there were widespread calls in the media for the minister's resignation. But Byers could argue that, in strictly legal terms, all he had done was to inform Winsor of his intentions; he pointed out that, although Railtrack could have acted in its own defence, it had failed to do so.

Thanks to a bit of bluffing and the good fortune of Railtrack's incompetence, Byers got away with it. He then made the mistake of playing to the gallery, effectively implying to Labour backbenchers that he had renationalised the company. Byers needed their support. He knew already that he was about to face one of the biggest political scandals of Blair's second term, the infamous 9/11 email from his special adviser, Jo Moore, suggesting the attack on the twin towers provided a good opportunity to 'bury bad news', and it suited Byers to bank support from his fellow MPs in anticipation of the furore.

Initially, his plan seemed to have worked and his move was seen as courageous and welcomed by most Labour MPs. But he soon found himself at the centre of a storm of protest. One of the perceived advantages of administration over renationalisation was that the shareholders did not have to be bought out. As far as the government was concerned, the shareholders' equity had been wiped out and there was no point propping up Railtrack since that would merely have given money to the shareholders which they did not deserve. On the evening of Friday 5 October, the last time at which they were traded, Railtrack shares stood at £2.80. But under the European Convention on Human Rights, had the government opted for renationalisation, it might have had to pay the average price over the past three to five years. That is the basis of the shareholders' claim and it was hardly surprising that parts of the City went berserk at what they saw as Byers's cynical ploy. For the City and the shareholders, niceties such as the fact that Railtrack was not viable in the long term are irrelevant and they saw Byers's move as an act of governmental banditry, a Stalinist takeover and plain old daylight robbery.

That is why the Treasury was infuriated by Byers's grandstanding in Parliament. It was precisely because the Treasury feared this kind of reaction, which would dent City investors' confidence in the Labour government, that it had agreed a strategy to present the plan in a completely different way. According to one source, the Treasury's line would have been: 'Railtrack is no longer viable, this is the structure we are going to propose and we are going to accompany that with other reforms in the industry.'[11] In other words, administration would be presented as a regrettable but inevitable step that had been forced upon the government. However, there appears to be some rewriting of history here. Byers would not have been able to proceed with his plan had it not been supported by the Treasury and to suggest that he threatened Winsor off his own bat stretches credulity. Gordon Brown, the Chancellor, and Prime Minister Tony Blair approved of the plan to foreclose on Railtrack[12] but the way that Byers did it, effectively boasting that the shareholders would get nothing, inevitably stoked up a furious controversy. Byers also later admitted in court that he had lied to the Commons Transport Sub-Committee over whether he had planned to do away with Railtrack before the 25 July meeting with Robinson.

The point often lost sight of in the row over the manner of Railtrack's dispatch is that shareholders, as opposed to lenders, earn a higher rate of return precisely because they take a greater risk. Railtrack, an inherently loss-making company in constant need of subsidy,[13] was always at the mercy of government whims, and therefore 'political risk' should have been one of the considerations of those who invested in it. As Nigel Harris pointed out in *Rail* magazine: 'The pundits, financial advisers and city institutions who howl so loudly do so, I suspect, partly to mask their own embarrassment, for they have been guilty of passing several clearly-sighted signals at danger.'[14]

Belatedly, Railtrack hit back. Steve Marshall promptly resigned, although he said he would serve out his six months notice, and issued a series of stern rebukes to the government that belied his reputation as a placid accountant who had never sought to place himself in the public spotlight. Marshall said the government's behaviour had been 'shoddy and unacceptable'. Why did Robinson and Marshall, having evidently acquiesced in Railtrack's demise, make such a fuss afterwards? One explanation is that, as Winsor pointed out to the select committee, he was under a duty to ensure that Railtrack had sufficient funds only if the company was competent and efficient. Since Hatfield was unequivocally the company's responsibility and Winsor had already decided that he was not going to pay Railtrack the full amount it had demanded in the access charge review, perhaps Marshall and Robinson felt they were unlikely to get enough cash off him. And that might explain why Robinson went behind Winsor's back to ask for Byers's support at that meeting on 25 July rather than using the proper procedure of asking the regulator for an interim review.

In retrospect, it seems clear that Byers acted with unnecessary haste. Railtrack was doomed anyway, as its share price had been plummeting while its liabilities soared. Back in June 2001, the Dutch investment bank ABN Amro had said the shares were only worth 58p, a comment which had hastened the slide down to below the original sale price. The government could probably have just left the company to die quietly and then intervened when the value of the shareholders' equity had been wiped out. That would have had the added advantage of not leaving its replacement, Network Rail, with such a huge debt.

Instead, because Byers pushed Railtrack into administration without having properly prepared for what was going to happen afterwards, the company ended up being in administration for a year, which proved to be a very expensive temporary solution. Moreover, to assuage the shareholders' wrath, as we see in Chapter 11, they had to be given extra money.

Winsor got a partial revenge. Byers asked his civil servants to draw up legislation which would effectively fetter the freedom of the regulator by merging his office with the Strategic Rail Authority but Winsor managed to head off that move by obtaining the support of the major private sector companies in the industry. Moreover, as we see in the next chapter, his interim review was to allow Network Rail far more money than envisaged under the government's spending plans. The independence of the rail regulator was, for the time being, guaranteed, though after Winsor's departure it was to be restricted by the Railway Act of 2005. And Byers ended up being publicly exposed as a liar, ending any hopes he might have entertained of returning to ministerial office.

Irrespective of who held the dagger when Railtrack was put out of its misery, the company's short life was testimony to both its own failings and those of the flawed structure of the industry created by privatisation. Its behaviour in the aftermath of Hatfield highlighted all the mistakes that had been made in creating the company as an outsourcing organisation with few in-house engineering skills and no research capacity, and after the accident its demise was inevitable. Once Railtrack died it was certain that other changes would follow suit, such as eventually the abolition of the SRA and changes to the regulatory structure. In the first instance, however, the government had to work out how to replace Railtrack and the process of establishing its successor proved slower than hoped for, a delay that contributed to the cost explosion in the industry. And during that interim period came the fourth – and hopefully last – of the accidents that can be traced directly back to the privatisation process.

CHAPTER 10

Potters Bar: the strange case of the 'railway saboteurs'

The Potters Bar accident is important, not only because it once more highlighted the new risks introduced by privatisation, but because it led to a significant reform which promises to eliminate some of these dangers, the reintegration of maintenance back into Network Rail, the not-for-profit company that replaced Railtrack. Indeed, the principal side effect of the disaster was to wreck the finances of Jarvis, the company responsible for the maintenance of the track on which the accident occurred. However, the financial demise of Jarvis resulted not so much from its failings over the maintenance of the line as from its attempt, when faced with a rapidly plunging share price in the immediate aftermath of the crash, to shift the blame to unknown 'saboteurs'.

It is not possible to piece together the sequence of events that led to the crash in the same way as the other accidents described in this book, because there is a complete lack of information on precisely what happened leading up to the disaster. Precise details of what maintenance gangs were on the track in the weeks before the accident and what work they undertook there have not been made public and in some cases were not clearly recorded. The bare facts show that only a great deal of good luck prevented the accident becoming one of the worst disasters in the history of British railways. Seven people died but it could have been many more.

The crash occurred on Friday 10 May 2002 when the 1245 West Anglia Great Northern King's Cross to King's Lynn service derailed at a set of points just south of Potters Bar station. The four-coach train, with around 140 people aboard, was travelling at 100mph when the rear coach derailed at the points. The first three carriages stayed upright and came to rest nearly half a mile along the down fast line on which it had been travelling, largely undamaged although the rear bogie of the third coach had derailed.

The fourth coach and its passengers, however, were not so fortunate. The coach detached itself from the rest of the train, slewed sideways, skidded along the track, and ended up under the canopy of the station, having destroyed a waiting room on the platform. Although the coach did not break up on being detached, apart from losing one of its bogies, internal fittings and furniture were wrenched loose, windows were shattered and several passengers were thrown out of the carriage.

There were several elements of luck, however. Had the derailment occurred in the rush hour, the platform would have been jammed with commuters who would have been crushed to death by the detached carriage. Alternatively, if another train had been travelling in the other direction, more than likely at over 100mph, it could easily have been derailed by the impact, multiplying the number of deaths several times. Or, quite simply, the whole train could have been derailed by the rogue points, again causing much more mayhem. That said, the accident was a severe one. In addition to the seven deaths, which included an unlucky old lady who had been walking under the bridge and was killed by debris dislodged by the train, there were seventy-six people injured, thirty-two of whom required hospital treatment.

The investigators quickly ascertained that the points, numbered 2182A, were the cause of the accident. Unaccountably, the points had started to move across as the train passed over them and caught the wheels as if trying to route the train across to the slow line. Points, of course, are not supposed to move once locked into position and, indeed, are interlocked with signals in such a way as to prevent there being a conflict between the route shown by the signal and the path selected for the train by the signaller. So there was no way that any action by the signallers could have triggered the movement of the points while the train was passing over them. Moreover, only one of the two blades of the points moved across, suggesting there was something very amiss with their geometry. The right-hand blade of the points had moved because the horizontal bar linking the two blades at the front of the points had snapped. That rod, called a lock-stretcher bar, was the only one holding the blades at the right gauge (4ft 8½ins), but it was not designed to do so. There should have been two adjustable stretcher bars holding the points at the right tension but neither bar was in position because the sets of

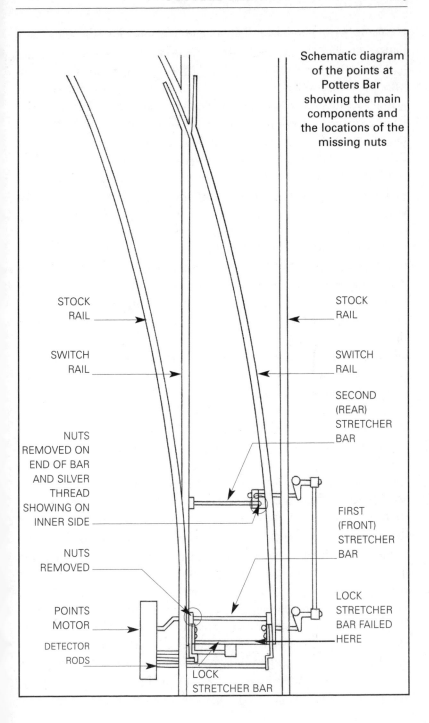

Schematic diagram of the points at Potters Bar showing the main components and the locations of the missing nuts

STOCK RAIL

STOCK RAIL

SWITCH RAIL

SWITCH RAIL

SECOND (REAR) STRETCHER BAR

NUTS REMOVED ON END OF BAR AND SILVER THREAD SHOWING ON INNER SIDE

FIRST (FRONT) STRETCHER BAR

NUTS REMOVED

LOCK STRETCHER BAR FAILED HERE

POINTS MOTOR

DETECTOR RODS

LOCK STRETCHER BAR

nuts at one end of each of the bars had been undone, rendering them useless. Most oddly, the investigators discovered that the two sets of nuts had been left lying neatly next to the rails. The strange state of the points meant that they could not have got in that condition merely through the normal passage of trains but, rather, that someone appeared to have adjusted them in that way. The mystery remains as to who did that and whether it was done maliciously to cause an accident or whether it was maintenance work that had not been carried out properly.

Unlike Hatfield, where the sequence of events leading to the disaster is well understood and the problems with the track were quite obvious, the exact reasons behind the Potters Bar crash are not – and probably never will be – known. Examination of nuts on other points in the area by the Health and Safety Executive revealed that 20 per cent of them had not been properly tightened, though its interim report said 'none of the points inspected were in the condition found at Potters Bar'.[1] However, an article in *Rail* magazine pointed out that finding that many nuts had 'not been properly tightened' was a red herring, since the HSE admitted that it had not tested the points with a torque wrench and therefore it was impossible to assess whether this was correct.[2] The condition of points 2182A was, therefore, inexplicable, and although there were hundreds of points of the same design on the network, none of them was in a similar state.

The investigation, however, was overshadowed by an extraordinary claim by Jarvis, the company which had taken over the maintenance of the East Coast Main Line from Balfour Beatty in April 2001 by bidding much lower for the prestigious contract worth £50m per year. Given Balfour Beatty's role in the Hatfield crash, Railtrack must have been glad to have found a different contractor, but it was a decision both companies would regret.

Jarvis, which had been a near-bankrupt business in the mid-1990s, had grown rapidly to have a turnover of £700m and employ 8,000 staff by 2001, thanks to a policy of bidding aggressively for contracts. The railway was a core part of the business, contributing over half its turnover – to most of which Potters Bar would put a sudden end. Jarvis's shares started plummeting in the days following the crash, and its executives were desperate to stem the haemorrhage. There was genuine confusion within the company as to how the points had got into that condition and the various senior managers assembled at a meeting at the company's York headquarters settled on a sabotage theory.

At first the theory was widely touted in the newspapers and Jarvis's attempt to deflect attention from its own role as the maintenance contractor for that stretch of track seemed to have worked. On the Sunday two days after the crash, the papers were full of headlines mentioning the possibility of sabotage and several stories continued in that vein during the week. At briefings for journalists, Jarvis presented photographs in which, supposedly according to their own experts, shiny bits of thread on the bolts proved that the nuts had only recently been undone as otherwise they would have been tarnished. Jarvis said its staff had not been on the tracks in the three days before the accident, while the steel bolts would normally oxidise within a day after being exposed to air. This suggested that the points had been deliberately tampered with.

However, the other parties involved, such as the police, the Health & Safety Executive and Railtrack, were privately briefing journalists to be cautious about the sabotage theory, and gradually the strategy rebounded on Jarvis because the evidence appeared so thin. Jarvis admitted that its staff had not been allowed onto the site to examine the points themselves and therefore only relied on the photographic evidence to make the sabotage claim. The victims were getting angry about what they saw as an attempt by Jarvis to pass on the blame and there is one fundamental rule of disaster PR management – never get into an argument with those who have been directly affected by the accident.

Ignoring the doubts, Jarvis went big on the sabotage theory. One of its directors, Steve Norris, a very experienced communicator since he was a former Tory transport minister and London mayoral candidate, decided to stick his neck out. Norris, who later became chairman of Jarvis, went on television stating that sabotage was the likely cause: 'There is real *prima facie* evidence of sabotage. It's pretty clear – certainly for anyone who understands the railways – that some tampering has been going on here.'[3] It was to prove an almost fatal error for the company.

There were all sorts of counter-arguments. Why should anyone do such a thing? How would they have known how to alter the points in that way? And why would the vandals have chosen a set of points so near a station where they were likely to be seen? After all, there were plenty of points that could be sabotaged where those carrying out the crime would be at far less risk of being noticed. Moreover, the way that the points were adjusted would have unpredictable results and it was only through bad luck that the stretcher bar broke, causing the derailment.

Far from saving Jarvis and its share price, the sabotage theory resulted in the constant media hounding of the company. Any incident on the railway during the ensuing months which involved Jarvis attracted publicity while other companies' errors were ignored. Since Jarvis was at the time the largest single contractor on the railways for both maintenance and renewals, there were bound to be some errors and so bad publicity was inevitable.

Moreover, Jarvis's cause was not helped by the fact that it was involved in a series of further incidents in the eighteen months following the Potters Bar crash, several of which attracted widespread publicity. The most serious were a couple of potentially disastrous mistakes when sections of track were left missing, causing derailments. In the first, at Aldwarke Junction near Rotherham, on 10 November 2002 – coincidentally six months to the day after Potters Bar – Jarvis had removed a crossing without making sure the points could not be moved. Poor communication with the signaller resulted in the derailment of a freight train, which fortuitously happened at night when no other trains were passing so that nothing ploughed into the wreckage. The company was later fined £400,000 for breaches of the Health and Safety legislation arising from this accident.

While this incident received little publicity, the second occurred in September 2003 on the day Tony Blair was opening the new Channel Tunnel link. The accident happened when Jarvis workers forgot to replace a 1.5m length of rail outside King's Cross, derailing a GNER train and causing the closure of the station for the day. Again there was poor communication between the signallers, who of course worked for Network Rail, and the Jarvis people on the track. There was widespread condemnation of the company in the extensive media coverage which the incident attracted. There were several other minor incidents in this period, notably a major dispute with Network Rail over its failure to properly stress newly fitted rails which had been replaced as part of the West Coast refurbishment work.[4]

The continued bad publicity led Jarvis to throw in the towel. In October 2003, the company announced that it was pulling out of its three rail maintenance contracts – pre-empting by just a few weeks Network

Rail's announcement that it was taking back all rail maintenance. Chris Garnett, head of GNER, could barely conceal his delight at getting rid of Jarvis as contractor for much of the line on which his trains ran. He said on the day of the announcement: 'The King's Cross derailment was just one thing too many, I think the fact that they're going is very good news for all our passengers and for all our staff.'[5] Nevertheless, Jarvis retains its renewal contracts in the rail industry.

It was not only Potters Bar and the other railway incidents that destroyed Jarvis's credibility. The company had got into trouble over a lot of its Private Finance Initiative contracts for schemes such as building schools or providing student accommodation. According to one estimate, 'Jarvis controlled about 10 per cent of the £35.5bn PFI debt which the government has raised across the public sector'[6] for PFI deals with schools, universities, hospitals and GP surgeries. However, Jarvis, under its maverick chief executive Paris Moyaedi, had bid too cheaply for many of these contracts and not been able to deliver on them. The pattern was the same throughout the company's divisions and suggests just how ill-suited the company was to work in the rail industry where cutting corners inevitably raises safety issues. Geoff Allum, an analyst with stockbrokers Investec, summed it up neatly:

> Jarvis under Paris Moyaedi has been overtrading for years – taking on far too many things without the knowledge, or the experience, or the expertise to deliver. Its contractors have been complaining about what or how quickly they are paid by Jarvis. If they go offsite because they are not being paid, this leads to delays in the projects [and] Jarvis starts getting penalised ... That means you have to keep pricing aggressively to win new contracts. You end up in a vicious circle.[7]

However, the railways and, particularly, the company's disastrous PR strategy in the wake of Potters Bar, were definitely Jarvis's nemesis. Interestingly, while Jarvis did make several mistakes, it had also invested quite heavily in the railway and its travails were greatly exacerbated as a result of that enormous PR gaffe. As a former adviser to the company put it, 'there is only one way to handle PR communications following a disaster like Potters Bar. You have to express sorrow for the victims and say you are doing everything to find out the cause of the incident, and to make sure that it will not be repeated. No one wants to hear excuses or that it was not your fault.'[8] Jarvis, as the adviser put it, 'became symbolic of everything that was bad with private involvement in the railways'. Indeed, Jarvis suffered far more for its involvement in Potters Bar than Balfour Beatty did for its role in the Hatfield accident and all its prior mishaps. Quite apart from the ill-fated sabotage theory, Jarvis was perceived as a bit of a fly-by-night operation which had grown too rapidly, whereas Balfour Beatty is a major, long-established civil engineering contractor.

Jarvis belatedly apologised for having touted the sabotage theory. In April 2004, two years after the crash, the chief executive, Kevin Hyde, accepted that the company had made a fundamental mistake in promoting the sabotage theory. In a letter to passengers and bereaved relatives, he apologised for the 'hurt and anger' Jarvis had caused by blaming sabotage for the crash. He said: 'In the aftermath of the crash, when Jarvis was under great pressure to explain itself, we were drawn into a debate about the possible causes of the crash. On behalf of the company and my colleagues, I would like to apologise for the hurt and anger our actions in responding caused ... I will not try to justify our thinking other than to say I truly believe we tried to act responsibly.' The company also accepted liability, jointly with Network Rail, which was a great relief to the survivors and relatives.

But it was too little, too late. The company barely survived, disposing of many of its contracts outside the railways and retrenching to York, its business reduced to a small rump of its former glory days. In 2004, its turnover had halved to £356m and it made a loss of £283m. Its shares, worth £2.50 on the day it was announced that Jarvis had won the East Coast contract in early 2001, had plummeted to 6.5p by June 2005, less than 3 per cent of their former value.

A year after the accident, a report[9] was published by the Health & Safety Executive which suggested that little real progress had been made in uncovering the precise cause of the accident. However, while the results of '23 technical reports' had certainly not led to an explanation of what went wrong, there was much evidence of shoddy maintenance.

The report concluded that 'no evidence has yet been established to support speculation that sabotage or deliberate unauthorised interference was the direct or root cause of the derailment'. It went on to say that the investigators were 'satisfied that an explanation can be given for the failure of points 2182A based on evidence of the poor condition of these points to an extent that they were not "fit for purpose"'.[10]

The accident itself remains something of a mystery. The Railway Safety and Standards Board, in a statement[11] issued nearly three years after the crash, concluded: 'the panel was not able to establish with certainty how the front and rear adjustable stretcher bars came to be in the condition in which they were found following the derailment'. The report drew attention to the fact that maintenance procedures introduced in the days of British Rail to tighten and secure the stretcher bars may have resulted in loosening them but there was no explanation on why no other points had been found that were in a similar condition. The thrust of the findings was that the proper method for maintaining the points had not been sufficiently explained to the track people carrying out the work, but overall there was no satisfactory account of what had led to the accident.

Potters Bar was to prove the last straw for the maintenance companies. The new managers at the top of Network Rail, who had more engineering and railway experience than their predecessors at Railtrack, clearly considered right from the outset that contracting out all the work did not make sense, and that the arrangement by which contractors did all the work and were essentially self-checking was inherently flawed. Even the somewhat tighter contracts introduced under the Corbett regime still left far too much flexibility in the hands of the contractors, who were able to make hefty profits for work that was often unsatisfactory and overpriced. The decision to take back maintenance was always, albeit privately, part of NR management's game plan. In January 2003, just three months after assuming control of the infrastructure, John Armitt, the chief executive, announced that maintenance work in three areas, about 15 per cent of the total, was to be taken back in-house. At the time it was stressed that this was an experiment to allow benchmarking of costs, but in fact it represented the end of maintenance outsourcing. While in public Network Rail's bosses argued that taking back the maintenance was principally an attempt to reduce costs, there is no doubt that safety considerations had been taken into account as well, prompted by Hatfield and Potters Bar, as well as the series of less disastrous but significant incidents.

By October 2003, when Jarvis announced its decision to hand over its three contracts to NR, NR had privately made the decision to take back all the maintenance work on the railway. A couple of weeks later, in a prearranged coup, NR leaked to the BBC that all maintenance, worth

£1.2bn per year, would be taken back, though the company would continue to let out contracts for renewals. The move meant bringing in-house 18,000 staff from the various contractors, which included big names such as Balfour Beatty, Carillion, Amey and Amec, by the summer of 2004, a target that was successfully achieved. The unions, of course, were delighted as they thought the move would greatly strengthen their bargaining position.

In explaining why Network Rail decided to make the change, Armitt made a point that had been plain to all but a few ideologues who had imposed the crazy system on the industry. Asked why such contracting out could work in aviation or shipping, but not on the railways, he said: 'Everything that's done to the railway day to day is done out there – it's not done in a hangar, it's done in the full fury of the elements and you've got to get out there, and sort the problem, the instant it happens.'[12] Having various contractors working to different objectives and reporting to separate management hierarchies was clearly a recipe for extra expense and lack of coordination. Instead, Armitt stressed, the workforce 'will only be concerned with what we are trying to do as a company'.[13] Contracting out had made the relationship between management and the 'orange jackets' on the track fuzzy and introduced unnecessary risk, as well as inefficiency. Moreover, with a labour force under its direct control, Network Rail would no longer have to fit in with arbitrary boundaries between contractors and would be able to move its workforce around at will to cope with unexpected events. No savings targets were issued at the time, but NR hoped that the move would meet the regulator's target of reducing costs by a third over a five-year period.

It was, of course, a major step towards the recreation of a nationalised railway since NR is effectively in the public sector but, naturally, the company refused to acknowledge that and ministers simply peddled the line that it was a purely administrative move to improve efficiency. As Alistair Darling, the Transport Secretary, told Parliament in a brief statement a few days after the announcement of the decision, 'The issue is not about private companies working on the railway; rather, the issue was the nature of the contracts set up by the then Government at the time of privatisation. Network Rail is determined to control costs, to improve performance and to ensure that the very large sums invested in the railways are used to the best possible effect – something that Railtrack conspicuously failed to do.'[14] However, the truth was all too obvious, as Richard Wachman, summing up City thinking in *The Observer*, put it: 'The decision by Network Rail to take all maintenance work in-house has shattered any illusion that the company is anything but an arm of Government. No matter how many times ministers may say the opposite, the railway system in this country is being renationalised by stealth. And most people are heartily relieved.'[15] It was, in effect, the first major step toward putting the railway Humpty Dumpty back together again.

CHAPTER 11

Rebuilding the railway (sort of)

While Jarvis was desperately trying to evade responsibility for Potters Bar, and the folly of outsourcing maintenance work was becoming increasingly apparent, the new body responsible for co-ordinating Britain's railways was taking shape. Railtrack was killed off before there was any detailed strategy in place for its replacement. The period of administration was supposed to last only a few months, but in the event it took a year and an extra pay-off to the shareholders before the phoenix Network Rail could emerge from the ashes.

Tony Blair had publicly rejected the most obvious solution, straightforward renationalisation, and a small team of officials from the Department of Transport and the Treasury had worked behind the scenes over the summer of 2001 on an alternative strategy for the railways. The key figures were Shriti Vadera, an adviser to Gordon Brown, Dan Corry, Stephen Byers's special adviser at Transport, and Tony Grayling, a senior research fellow at New Labour's favourite think-tank, the Institute of Public Policy Research. Grayling had written a pamphlet[1] suggesting the replacement of Railtrack with a not-for-profit 'company limited by guarantee', which would be ultimately controlled not by shareholders but by a group of stakeholders. Interestingly, Grayling first presented his ideas in the pamphlet at a seminar in February 2001, soon after Hatfield, and clearly he already had the ear of ministers as he was invited to demonstrate his ideas at No. 10 that September. Grayling argued that 'a not-for-profit company or trust would have advantages over a traditional state owned industry in terms of access to private finance and the accountability of its board to stakeholders, including passengers and the industry'.[2]

As there were to be no shareholders, there would be no potential conflict between profit and safety. Any profits would be reinvested to improve the network and instead of the profit motive, the new company's objectives 'could include maximising the use of the railways by passengers and freight and high standards of safety'.[3] It was a solution that had been used for another capital-intensive industry, water, with the creation in Wales of Glas Cymru, also a company limited by guarantee.

The Grayling plan had become the government's preferred option before Byers moved in on Railtrack, but ministers had to pretend that they were considering other possibilities. So when a German state-owned bank, West LB,[4] began to take an interest in bidding for the benighted company, ministers were forced to consider the offer seriously because they had a legal duty to ensure that they got the best possible deal for the shareholders. West LB suggested that refinancing, efficiency savings and the sale of non-railway assets could improve Railtrack's cash flow by £2bn per year. It wanted, too, a kind of vertical integration with operators being allowed to take responsibility for parts of the infrastructure, but in truth the whole idea was based on an unrealistic analysis of the railway's finances and simply got in the way of the government's plans.

The period of administration was expensive, adding about £1bn per year to the cost of running the infrastructure, because, not surprisingly, Ernst & Young, the administrators, did not know how to run a railway. Fearing any sort of accident like Hatfield, they were very risk-averse, and therefore ensured that work was carried out to the highest possible standard. Indeed, insiders confirmed that it was gold-plated in order to minimise risk. The administrators themselves were also expensive, charging £250 per hour for even relatively junior staff, and costs soon mounted up. It was ironic, of course, that having turned down Railtrack's request for extra money the government was now having to cough up a significantly greater figure in order to keep the railway going. Moreover, as we shall see, these costs would carry on for years after the permanent way had been transferred to Network Rail and extra payments had to be made to ensure that the deal was acceptable to shareholders.

The delay in wrapping up the administration and installing a replacement for Railtrack was partly due to the fact that the government had not really prepared its alternative in sufficient detail. Moreover, everything had to be done by the book because of the intervention by West LB and the hostility of the Railtrack shareholders, backed by many newspapers who gave their case very favourable coverage. West LB eventually faded away and Network Rail, the new company-by-guarantee organisation tucked away in a small office in Tottenham Court Road, a couple of hundred yards away from Euston, eventually put in its bid on 25 March 2002. The sweeteners to win over the shareholders included a government grant of £300 million which was, as Byers put it, 'to reflect the value and benefits of early exit from administration'.[5] This was, of course, the same Byers who had said in the immediate aftermath of Railtrack's collapse in October 2001 that there could be no question of compensating the shareholders. How realpolitik hurts! Network Rail would also, he announced, pay £500m to Railtrack Group as compensation for assets which it was taking over, money that it would borrow as part of a bridging finance loan of £9bn. While that loan would not officially be government debt, since it was a requirement of the exercise that the new company should not be in the public sector, the loan was effectively supported by the state through the Strategic Rail Authority. Railtrack shareholders also benefited from £370m that was in the coffers of the company at the time of the takeover, as well as £400m for the sale of the concession for access charges for the Channel Tunnel Rail Link, then under construction. These bits and pieces dug up from various parts of Railtrack in order to pay compensation really represented a fig leaf for the government to protect Byers's assertion that there would be no compensation for shareholders. The shareholders were to receive around £2.50 per share, not far short of the £2.80 at which the shares stood when Byers made his move. However, this did not stop them from embarking on the legal action mentioned in the previous chapter.

Network Rail was vested with a unique structure. The company is run by the directors, who, with the exception of one appointed by the SRA, are chosen by the members, the 113 'stakeholders' who are, in turn, selected by the government. There are two types of members; thirty represent the industry, while the others are drawn from the general public. However, in practice they cannot exercise much power, merely holding meetings twice a year and having only notional control over appointment of directors and their remuneration. They are also required to oversee the accounts and vet any changes to the NR constitution but they do not have the same powers as shareholders, who would normally be expected to focus on the share price and therefore have a vested interest in the financial health of the company.

This weakness – the absence of what was termed an 'equity buffer', shareholders who could win or lose a lot of money depending on the performance of the company – was a constant target for criticism, notably from Tom Winsor, still the rail regulator at the time of NR's creation, who was highly sceptical of the members' ability to exercise control over Network Rail. As the National Audit Office report put it, 'Network Rail's members all have the aim of getting a better rail network but there could be disagreement on how "better" is defined'.[6] The Commons Transport Committee was equally unimpressed by the members' role: 'Network Rail did not convince us that the members of the company were exercising an effective control of the company'.[7]

Unlike Railtrack, the new company at least had a strong engineering element on its twelve-strong board, including the chief executive, John Armitt. The chairman, Ian McAllister, had previously been a senior executive with Ford, the motor manufacturer, and the other key member of the team was the deputy chief executive, Ian Coucher, who had formerly been chief executive of the Underground infrastructure company Tube Lines. Salaries were definitely set at private- rather than public-sector levels, with Armitt getting £450,000 per year and Coucher £400,000, before the payment of any bonuses (which amounted to around £100,000 for both men in the first year of operation of NR, even though one of the key targets, on performance, was not met). This was, of course, far more than a BR chairman ever received, even taking inflation into account.

The intention of the board was demonstrated at the outset by its adoption of the mission statement 'Engineering excellence for Britain's Railway', which suggested that spending money, rather than value for money, was the organisation's game plan (it was later quietly dropped, as a rather embarrassed Armitt admitted to me in a press conference in May 2005). Initially, when NR was first set up in March 2002, McAllister told the press that the company would soldier on with the amount of money that had previously been allocated to Railtrack by Tom Winsor in the access charge review that covered the five-year period from April 2001 but this was clearly unrealistic, and Winsor was asked to embark on a review, which led to a 50 per cent rise in the company's income.

The deal finalising the transfer went through in October once the procedures for the takeover had been gone through in sufficient detail to ensure that the unwanted intervention from West LB was seen off. Network Rail took over Railtrack's debt, £7.1bn, which was covered by the £9bn bridging loan. On top of this, Network Rail was sheltered from cost overruns and other unexpected expenses by a standby loan facility of £4bn from the SRA, which effectively took the risk previously borne by shareholders. The new company was also expected to borrow more money over the next few years, up to a maximum of £21bn.

This huge sum meant that much effort had to be expended by the architects of the Network Rail structure in the Treasury to ensure that the company was kept off the government's books despite the fact that the SRA, a government body, was acknowledged by the National Audit Office to be the 'ultimate risk bearer'. The obscure 'Public Sector Classification Committee' of the Office of National Statistics (also called, just to make things even more difficult, the National Accounts Classification Committee) is the body charged with deciding whether organisations should be treated as part of the public or the private sector for the purposes of the government accounts. The issue is fiendishly complicated and readers may understandably want to skip the next couple of paragraphs, which are only included because the question is of great importance and involves billions of pounds of our money.

The Committee initially, in June 2002, gave a provisional view that the putative Network Rail would start life as a public body because of 'government involvement in the initial appointments that were necessary to establish the company'.[8] However, much to Gordon Brown's relief, the Committee ruled that the organisation could be reclassified as private from the date at which 'certain criteria' regarding its independence had been met. Therefore, on 16 August 2002, still well before the date at which it took over the operations of Railtrack, Network Rail was quietly reclassified as a 'private non-financial corporation' – i.e. a private-sector company.

In February 2004, the Office of National Statistics announced in a statement that it had 'new evidence' which showed that the SRA had 'temporarily retained more influence over Network Rail' than previously assumed. Specifically, this related to the original management incentive plan (i.e. in plain English, extra bucks for the managers) which was an 'exceptional and temporary arrangement' used for the first six months after Network Rail had taken over Railtrack. The Committee therefore retrospectively amended the reclassification date from 16 August 2002 to 1 April 2003, the date at which Network Rail's remuneration committee approved a new version of the management incentive plan.

Of course, with the abolition of the SRA (see below), the government will take over the role of 'ultimate risk bearer'. Yet, thanks to the legal niceties of the way the organisation has been created, for the moment at least Network Rail will remain off the balance sheet. Whether that is sustainable in the long term is uncertain. The Office of National Statistics has said it will review the situation once the SRA has gone. While in a way the issue is of more importance to the Treasury than the railways, if the debt does go back on the government's books it will not only blow a hole in the government accounts but also put added pressure on the railways to cut back on expenditure.

The fact that the issue remains in balance is demonstrated by a bizarre joint statement[9] issued in 2002 by the Office of National Statistics and the National Audit Office in which clearly they agreed to disagree over the issue. The NAO takes the view that 'the guarantees and stand-by loan facilities being extended to Network Rail will also represent contingent liabilities in the resource accounts of the Department for Transport' and essentially should count as government expenditure. However, the ONS says that international accounting standards do not require such contingent liabilities to be included as part of government expenditure. The SRA has no day-to-day control of Network Rail and therefore its spending and borrowing can remain off the government's books unless the SRA had to 'use its powers to gain control in the event of Network Rail's financial failure'. Then the whole weight of NR with its debts (£15.6bn at the end of March 2005) would land on the Chancellor's desk, upsetting his whole handling of the UK economy. The joint statement ended with a hilarious attempt to show that really they were both of a like mind: 'The financial statements of central government and the National Accounts are each prepared for different purposes and under different sources of guidance. They are not therefore alternative views on the same issue but fundamentally different activities undertaken for separate purposes, and hence can lead to different conclusions.'

The uncertainty of the status of Network Rail meant that the government deliberately drew up the legislation for the Railways Act 2005 to take into account its possible transfer to the public sector. This is made clear in a document on the rail review leaked to me in June 2004, a month before its publication: 'If Network Rail is reclassified to the public sector, the Government should be able to reinforce its control via the contract, with the urgent need to create a statutory corporation', i.e. a new British Rail.[10] The document also said that there should be government- and train-operator-nominated directors of Network Rail, but this did not emerge in the subsequent White Paper.

These Jesuitical debates over the status of NR would be amusing if they did not cost taxpayers dear. The extra cost to NR of borrowing money as a result of its quasi-non-governmental status is around £70m annually and will rise as borrowing increases. Moreover, the lack of accountability of NR means that ministers and civil servants have less control over its activity and that the overall level of funding being received by the railway is very difficult to work out, which means politicians are far less accountable than they were in the days of British Rail. The period of administration for Railtrack saw the beginning of the cost rise that was to dog the industry for years, as this increase in expenditure was not reversed once the company came out of administration. Indeed, quite the opposite.

The death of Railtrack and its replacement with what was effectively a publicly owned company meant that the position of the Strategic Rail Authority changed too, and ultimately became untenable. It was timely, therefore, that Richard Bowker, an inexperienced bright young thing of thirty-five who had impressed Byers in his previous role as co-chairman of Virgin Rail Group, took over Sir Alastair Morton's position at the head of the SRA in December 2001 soon after the demise of Railtrack. Morton could not resist a few choice and angry thoughts on his departure which showed that he realised more fundamental reforms of the industry were required and that the Railtrack situation had been allowed to drift:

> Most of our rail problems are structural and deep-seated. We have scarcely begun to reverse the legacy of decades of under-investment, and short-term remedies will achieve little ... I leave to Richard the tasks of reconciling structure to reality, resources to needs and, more immediately, of imparting direction and urgency to the restructuring and remanaging of Railtrack. Little of long-term structural significance has happened there in nearly two months since 7 October [the day of Railtrack's demise]. The industry is drifting. There are many good people in and near the railway industry working hard to deliver what people want and need, but they are as frustrated as I am by its structure and by short-term responses to its long-term needs. No strategy will succeed unless it first deals with those fundamentals.[11]

These were prescient words. Morton had failed at the SRA because his vision was not shared by government and because he alienated both civil servants and ministers. Bowker was to encounter similar problems, which eventually resulted in the abolition of the SRA. Given the demise of Railtrack and the abandonment of any pretence that the railway was to grow rapidly, Bowker inherited a very different situation from that faced by his predecessor.

There was, soon, a new minister, Alistair Darling, who had moved up the ranks of ministerial office without leaving any trace of his existence, to such an extent that in his previous post at Work and Pensions civil servants called him 'the invisible man'. Indeed, Darling was put into the Department for Transport in May 2002, after Byers had got himself into the headlines for the wrong reasons once too often, precisely to ensure that transport received the low profile that would hide New Labour's failings on the issue.

Bowker, who was given a private-sector-level salary of £250,000 plus up to £50,000 in bonuses per year, prioritised three areas: the refranchising process, and sorting out the two biggest investment projects, the West Coast Main Line and the power upgrade on the Southern, delays in which had resulted in millions of pounds worth of new rolling stock sitting embarrassingly in sidings, unable to operate because the various organisations responsible had not sorted out the necessary increase in electrical supply (see Chapter 15). In two of those tasks, Bowker was to be relatively successful. He managed to sort out the power upgrade on the Southern, and set a strategy for the West Coast modernisation which, at last, specified exactly what needed to be done. Incredibly this basic task had never been undertaken before and to everyone's relief, the estimated projected cost, which had risen to £13bn at one point, started falling, with the expectation it would eventually be around £8bn. On refranchising, the programme did restart, but the new deals all cost considerably more than their predecessors without offering many new services. In some cases there was new rolling stock but overall the SRA budget for franchising exceeded the £2bn mark, which did not please the Treasury, especially as there was precious little to show for this extra cash. Bowker, therefore, lost the battle for an improved rail network. The Treasury felt it had been bounced into these expensive franchise deals and, given the costs of Network Rail, which were also soaring, put the dampers on any thoughts of expansionary schemes for the railway, apart from those that were politically essential such as the high-speed trains on the Kent domestic services on the Channel Tunnel Rail Link.

In trying to tackle the West Coast problems, Bowker got embroiled in a turf war with Tom Winsor which was to prove damaging to both men. The two organisations they headed, the SRA and the Office of the Rail Regulator, had a history of mutual dislike since their respective roles occasionally overlapped and Morton and Winsor had already clashed fiercely.

When Bowker replaced Morton, the two organisations thrashed out a concordat that was supposed to set out the boundaries and ensure there were no more disputes. Bowker and Winsor had been old drinking partners and it seemed, at first, that the two would cooperate. However, the very fact that they had to negotiate a deal demonstrated the complexity of regulation and, inevitably, the agreement proved to be a temporary cease-fire rather than a permanent peace settlement. There were, for example, still blurred frontiers when it came to deciding what the output of the network should be – i.e. capacity, line speed, maintenance standards and so on – and this led to an almighty row. Bowker had argued that it should be the SRA that specified the requirements for the West Coast line, while Winsor said it was up to him to make these decisions. In particular, Winsor, in his interim review published in October 2003, decided that improvements at Rugby and on the Trent Valley section, the latter involving quadrupling much of the line, should be delayed, thus saving an estimated £640m. But Bowker at the SRA thought this was a ridiculous cutback which would result in delays for passengers and reduced capacity. The two organisations started lobbing press releases at each other, which, of course, delighted the media but brought the wrath of the politicians down on them. The SRA said that it had 'consistently resisted' the view that this work should be postponed while Winsor issued another release saying, 'I am aware that the SRA has consistently resisted rephasing of the outputs of the project. However, my decision has been made and is final.' It was all pantomime stuff between two official organisations and would have been funny had the future of the railway not been at stake.

The Commons Transport Committee was not amused, concluding 'We are deeply concerned by the nature of the decision-making process revealed by the recent events on the West Coast Main Line upgrade project. Even now there appears to be no agreement on the entirety of the project. Neither the SRA, the Rail Regulator or Network Rail seems to have power to make a final decision. The Government seems powerless to intervene. It is hard to think of a more telling example of the divided leadership of the railway and the powerlessness of the SRA.'[12]

As both Bowker and Winsor had spent much time lobbying Alistair Darling, it was hardly surprising that the eventual result was a score draw with work starting early in 2005, earlier than Winsor had wanted but later than Bowker had hoped. But the damage had been done. This type of turf war convinced government ministers that there were too many players in the rail industry and spelled the end of the SRA.

The issue ultimately proved to be: can a body separate from government be responsible for strategy in the industry? The SRA under Morton had spent much of the two years of its shadow existence mulling over its strategic plan. Originally, this was supposed to have been published within a few months of the fully fledged organisation's creation, but the timetable kept slipping, leaving only a feeble *Strategic Agenda* in the public domain.

Bowker published *The Strategic Plan* soon after taking office, but essentially it was Morton's document and a bit of a dog's breakfast. Like the *Strategic Agenda* before the *Plan*, it contained no real thinking about what the railways are for and how they could best be fitted into a twenty-first-century transport infrastructure. There was, in effect, no strategy. As Mark Casson, Professor of Economics at the University of Reading, put it to the Commons Transport Committee, 'When you look at the SRA's view of what the railway system will be in twenty years' time, there is no view at all. In other words it is very much authority now to sort out problems, but not much strategy in terms of long-term thinking',[13] a view the committee felt 'summarises the opinion of many who talked to us'. The Committee concluded that the SRA was incapable of undertaking any visionary thinking, a view held by ministers and which helped the SRA on its way to oblivion.

Bowker tried to update the Strategic Plan for 2004 in an effort to make it more robust. The draft plan[14] promised that the SRA would continue to look at 'long-term initiatives such as Crossrail, an East Coast Route Strategy and a possible North South High Speed Line' despite 'budget stringency' but that is not what ministers wanted the public to hear. They saw the draft as yet another demand for a blank cheque and blocked its publication.

The SRA's unpopularity among ministers and civil servants was exacerbated by the increase in its own spending as it turned into a huge bureaucracy. Staff numbers went up from 342 in October 2002 to 454 eighteen months later[15] – nearly twice as many as were employed in BR's head office, which ran a whole railway. While the SRA claimed that this was the result of a reduction in consultants, in fact the opposite was the case, with the number of 'contractors' doubling from 90 to 181 in a similar period.[16] The extent of work carried out by consultants for the SRA was quite extraordinary, ranging from minor technical advice to major contracts such as one with Lazards, on special purpose vehicles, worth £3m, a waste of money since SPVs never materialised.

Indeed, the SRA was never good at sorting out the wood from the trees. It used to put out ridiculous press releases like 'Rail authority publishes strategic options for Isle of Wight railways' or 'SRA provides £455,000 for Witham interchange', matters which seemed to take up as much time in the organisation as major franchise renegotiations, while Bowker was reported as telling one petitioner that it was as difficult getting his finance director to cough up £5,000 as £5m.[17] That is clearly not a way to run a large organisation.

One of the problems was that Bowker had, with youthful arrogance, insisted on being both chairman and chief executive of the SRA, even though this is contrary to accepted business practice. He needed to have an experienced rail operator as chief executive but instead the team around him was heavy on brains but light on practice. Nor did Bowker endear himself to his staff by announcing from the outset that people could either 'fit in or eff off'. The SRA, as one operator put it, 'was always big on processes and procedures, but did not have a clear grip on the reality of the railway. We have found it very difficult to work with them on a cooperative basis.'[18] While some antagonism between operators and the SRA was inevitable, it did seem that there was a very poor relationship in some cases, which came to a head in the Greater Anglia affair.

In the spring of 2003, FirstGroup was not shortlisted for the large new Greater Anglia franchise even though it included First's existing Great Eastern operation. This was a major shock since incumbents would normally be expected to get through this first hurdle at least which was largely intended to weed out no-hopers. Moreover, First Great Eastern had an excellent reputation and a good record on several criteria. Great Eastern had been the most punctual of the London commuter operator and was still operating under the original contract. The other operators, including, in the case of GB Rail, Anglia itself, competing for the new contract all had existing franchises under management contract after getting into financial difficulties – that is, the franchisee had become seeking more subsidy and no longer took the revenue risk . On safety, too, Great Eastern's record was good and the reputation of its management, under the experienced and highly regarded career railwayman Bob Breakwell, was excellent.

The only explanation forthcoming from the SRA for its treatment of First was that the way their bid had been submitted was deficient, an argument backed by off-the-record briefings that the forms had not been filled in properly. However, given First's record on the franchise, a quiet word in the ear of the bid team might have been a more sensible response if the forms had mistakes or the answers were not sufficiently detailed.

The SRA's excuses made even less sense in the light of the fact that First had been shortlisted almost at the same time for the Northern franchise, suggesting its managers were competent form-fillers. Industry insiders felt that it was a case of the SRA being vindictive because First had earlier launched a strategy for a high-speed line from London to Bristol without having cleared it with the SRA. First launched a legal action but eventually, to avoid biting the hand that fed it, withdrew; the company may have been mollified when it had a relatively easy ride in taking over the Thames franchise when the SRA decided that should be merged with the other operator out of Paddington, Great Western, already controlled by First. In its desperation to retain the Anglia franchise, the company then shelled out £44m to buy the incumbent, GB Rail, in order to get back into the bidding process. The money was to be largely wasted since in January 2004 National Express was awarded what became known as Greater Anglia.

The Greater Anglia episode highlighted another of the SRA's failings during the Bowker regime – its handling of the press. Bowker had appointed Ceri Evans, at various times a former press officer for both the Labour and Tory parties, on the basis that he would be the SRA's own Alastair Campbell. Well, Evans might have been to the same charm school as Blair's famous bruiser, but the hapless SRA man had none of the latter's ability and, in any case, the last thing that a government body like the SRA needed was that sort of spin doctoring. Evans' ability to come up with highly entertaining, though wholly inappropriate, quotes made him a source of delight among transport correspondents. During the Anglia franchise row, Evans infuriated the company's chief executive, Moir Lockhead, by saying, 'not only have First Group thrown their toys out of the pram but they have now got out of the pram and they are scrabbling around on the floor'.[19]

Evans's performance reached its apogee – or rather nadir – when he left a message on a journalist's voicemail calling Tony Lord Berkeley, the widely respected chairman of the Rail Freight Group, 'a fucking dilettante'. The recording soon went round Fleet Street, much to the enjoyment of the transport hacks. Evans the Spin, as he had become known to journalists, managed to anger Winsor, too, by calling him 'little more than a supermarket price-checker'. It is difficult to understand why Bowker kept his gaffe-prone mouthpiece in his job right to the end as Evans did lasting damage to the reputation of the SRA, especially as Bowker twice had to apologise in print for his spokesman's insults.

Given the doubts about the strategic role of the SRA, antipathy to Bowker among civil servants and ministers, and the ridiculous carry-ons by Evans, by the beginning of 2004 it was becoming evident to Whitehall insiders that the SRA's days were numbered. A major announcement about the future of the railways was in the offing and rumours were rife. In the run-up to the ministerial coup which pushed Railtrack into administration in October 2001, there had been dark rumours about such a move for some time. Now, again, there was a palpable feeling of instability in the air, with many rail industry executives running scared about their fate – or that of their bottom line.

There had been precious little progress in the two years since Railtrack had been so hurriedly dispatched. The industry was absorbing more and more taxpayers' money and there was little apparent progress. The subsidy to the industry had reached £3.8bn by 2003/4, more than three times the amount British Rail could have expected during a similar phase in the economic cycle, and yet the bloody trains were still not arriving on time. Nearly a quarter of services had been late in the crucial period running up to Christmas, despite a spate of initiatives from ministers and the Strategic Rail Authority to get the industry 'back on track' following the disastrous drop in performance after the Hatfield rail disaster.

The last straw was Tom Winsor's announcement in his interim review published in October 2003 to allow Network Rail to spend £22.7bn over the following five years, a 50 per cent increase on the previous period and far more than Railtrack had asked for when Byers moved in on it. Winsor made much play of the fact that he was an independent economic regulator and that the government could not force him to cut back on the budget, once it had specified what outputs, such as timetable and line speed, it wanted. There was a strong difference of opinion between Winsor and ministers as to precisely how much freedom he had to pick the Treasury's back pocket. For his part, Winsor said that the government could determine the outputs – the number of trains, the extent of the network, and so on – and if ministers wanted to specify cuts, they could do so. He repeatedly said he had asked for advice but got only 'radio silence'. It was an unseemly row, highlighted by the report of the Commons Transport Committee whose exasperation was all too evident:

> Our inquiry exposed an astonishing and fundamental disagreement between the Government and the Regulator about the extent of the latter's powers. According to the minister, the Government had a choice about whether to accept the Regulator's access charges settlement; but the Regulator considered that the Government had no option but to accept his decision. This is a prime example of the confusion which lies at the heart of the present structure of the railway and why it is essential that this structure must be streamlined.[20]

On the one hand, the politicians were appalled that they seemed to have no power to fetter Winsor's spending, and yet on the other they proclaimed that independent economic regulation was essential to protect the interests of private investors. That muddle had to be sorted out. Back in the summer of 2003, Alistair Darling had privately told Tony Blair that the railway was simply not working effectively and that something had to be done. Previously, such warnings had been poohpoohed by Bowker, who had Blair's ear for a time supposedly because they once had a sing song together, but on this occasion he would not be deflected by any personal pleading.

All the rumours and premonitions came to a head on 19 January 2004 with a Commons statement by the Secretary of State. In preparing for this Darling had to steer a careful course. An Old Labour minister would simply have got up and said, 'we are sick of all this mess and we're taking back the railways into state ownership'. That, of course, is not Blair's way, despite his promise in opposition of a 'publicly accountable, publicly owned railway'. So Darling simultaneously had to defend and attack privatisation, explaining that it was the botched sale of the railways that had got them into the current mess but stressing that renationalising was not the answer.

The solution, of course, was to hold British Rail responsible because of its years of 'substantial under investment', a claim that does not bear scrutiny (see Chapter 2). He blamed, too, with some justification, the consequences of the Hatfield accident for the current state of the industry, but then he tackled the interesting bit: 'There remains a further and very serious difficulty facing this industry – that is its structure and organisation. The way in which it was privatised has led to a frag-mentation, excessive complication and dysfunctionality that have compounded the problems caused by decades of under investment.'

The target of the review, however, was soon made clear: 'There are too many organisations, some with overlapping responsibilities. And it has become increasingly clear that this gets in the way of effective decision making and frequently leads to unnecessary wrangling and disputes. That is no way to run a railway ... The long-term inefficiencies and costs of the privatisation settlement have, as time has passed, become an even bigger barrier to the success of the railways.'

So while the railways now had to be run as a partnership between private and public sectors, major structural change was needed to 'make better spending decisions'. While Darling admitted that 'privatisation had some disastrous and far-reaching consequences for the railway', the privatisation had also brought in 'considerable increased investment and in many cases train companies have provided some innovation that was conspicuously lacking in the past. We want to build on that which is why the Government believes that renationalisation would not solve the problems the railway faces. But what's essential is to put in place a structure that works and can deliver not just cost control but a safe reliable railway that works efficiently.'

He ended with what he hoped would be a rousing finale but the cheers on his own benches were decidedly muted: 'Passengers are rightly impatient. Improvements have been made but more needs to be done. We are determined to bring to an end the problems caused by decades of under investment and compounded by an ill-thought-out privatisation. Rebuilding Britain's railways needs a long-term commitment and it's something we're determined to deliver.'

Once stripped of what passes for rhetoric in New Labour-speak, the upshot of Darling's statement was that there was to be a major review of the structure of the railways. It was a bold promise, never to be fulfilled. For a time during the review process, it seemed the government was genuinely interested in looking at the possible alternatives for a new structure and was even considering a complete overhaul of the shape of the industry leading, in particular, to the vertical integration – bringing track and services back together – that many experienced railway managers see as the only effective and efficient way of running a railway.

However, such a major change was quickly consigned to the 'too hard' box despite the fact that Graham Eccles, a leading Stagecoach rail executive, had gone on a road tour with ministers promoting the idea of vertical integration. Instead, the results of the review published in July 2004 were an all-too-familiar fudge with little real change. But there had to be a sacrificial victim given that the starting point was the supposed overlapping responsibilities of various organisations in the industry and inevitably that was to be the SRA, which many insiders had suggested had been the target in the government's sights all along.

The SRA was, therefore, consigned to history in a few curt and unconvincing sentences in the resulting White Paper, *The Future of Rail*, which became the basis of the Railways Act passed just before the 2005 election. There was an air of desperation about how to cover up this rapid change in policy given that the organisation had so recently been created by the Labour government itself: 'When the SRA was conceived and legislation first introduced into Parliament, the scale of the industry's problems was not yet apparent [only because they did not ask the right people!], and a leadership model based on influence and persuasion seemed appropriate.'[21] Things had changed, the Paper said, because of Hatfield and the replacement of Railtrack with Network Rail: 'As infrastructure costs have risen, the Rail Regulator has played a more pivotal role, and without more direct powers the SRA has found itself in an increasingly difficult position. It cannot act as industry leader because it is positioned outside the industry in the public sector ... and it could never have full responsibility for determining the Government's rail strategy, because that is a role for ministers answerable to Parliament and the electorate.' Therefore, it had to go.

If the SRA had been a strong organisation, with the private operators firmly behind it, then abolition would have been much more difficult for the government. As it was, so many people had been insulted by Evans or ground down by the SRA bureaucracy that there were few mourners when the organisation's demise was announced. Moreover, despite Bowker's undoubted achievements in sorting out both the West Coast and the Southern power upgrade, he had made too many enemies with a style that, at times, appeared arrogant and unresponsive to criticism.

While the SRA's numerous mistakes undoubtedly contributed to its abolition, the real reasons were naked politics and money. With the government having announced a review on the basis that there were too many players, clearly something had to go and the SRA's role was, indeed, problematic. Some of its work, too, was duplicated or second-guessed by Network Rail, the regulator and the Department for Transport. And as the Commons Transport Committee had highlighted in its *Future of Rail* report, the SRA's role was unclear and there had been a failure to take a strategic view. A previous attempt to bump off the regulator had, as we have seen, backfired. Network Rail, newly created, was inviolable. So ministers trained their guns on the easiest target. Indeed, with hindsight, it seems clear where the review was heading right from the beginning. The death of the SRA was foretold in a front-page article in *The Independent* in January 2004[22] which said that ministers were preparing to strip the SRA of its powers. It was the first of a series of leaks by the paper's veteran transport correspondent, Barrie Clement, which clearly were well sourced in the Department for Transport, whose senior civil servants had been gunning for Bowker and the SRA for some time – indeed, according to Bowker's farewell speech later that year, ever since he had joined the organisation three years previously.

Underlying all this was the issue of money and Tom Winsor's supposed access to the Treasury's back pocket. By taking over directly the powers of the SRA so that the Department would be able to specify the outputs of the industry, and by bringing in new legislation to ensure the Office of Rail Regulation would have to work within a budget set by ministers, the government felt that such a situation would never arise again. Ministers argued that it was a constitutional anomaly to allow the Regulator to have direct access to the Treasury's coffers. This was true, but that situation had been sanctioned by the Labour government who could have changed the arrangement but chose not to do so.

On the face of it, abolishing the SRA did not make sense given that ministers' ire had been largely directed towards the Regulator. However, right at the outset of the review, in a statement on 9 February, Darling promised to maintain 'independent regulation' of the industry because otherwise investors would be scared off: 'There is no question of weakening the effectiveness of economic regulation. The Government recognises that maintaining fully effective and independent economic regulation is critical for retaining investor confidence.'[23] Hence the review, initiated on the basis that Winsor had too much power, was supposed to keep its tanks off his lawn.

However, the Railways Act 2005 will give the government far more control over the process of establishing Network Rail's access charges and therefore regulation is not quite as 'independent' as promised. The new system involves a process (that is 'iterative', to use the jargon) whereby the government will set a budget and a series of outputs which will then be assessed by the Regulator who will estimate whether it is sufficient to meet the required outputs. If not, it will be up to the Regulator to suggest ways in which the railway can be cut back in order to meet the given budget. How this will work in practice remains uncertain because any suggestion of major reductions in services or closures of lines will result in a public outcry. However, it is apparent from the legislation that the government has not kept to its promise, extracted by Winsor, of continuing independent economic regulation. This arcane, though important, point hardly elicited much interest from the public and the media. Nor did the rest of the review contain much to excite or concern rail users, which was hardly surprising given that it was published less than a year before the expected date of a general election. Apart from the abolition of the SRA, outlined above, there was little of significance. Her Majesty's Railway Inspectorate, which had long sat unhappily in the overly risk-averse Health & Safety Executive, was to be transferred to the Office of Rail Regulation while the regional Rail Passengers Council committees were to be abolished, and replaced by a system of local representatives who would keep an eye on their patch.

Indeed *The Future of Rail* and the subsequent legislation merely tinkered around the problem of the structure of the railways. The document reiterated many of the points made by Darling when he first announced the review, such as 'the weakness with the current structure of the British rail industry is the complex and adversarial relationships between the different parts of the industry'.[24] Yet there was little of substance to address that weakness. There was no long-term strategy or any attempt to set out what the railway is for. The Paper stressed the importance of the role of the private sector, stating that the industry had to be run on the basis of 'a stable partnership between the public and private sectors, with the Government offering clear strategic direction, a single independent regulator ensuring high levels of safety and protecting the rights of investors, and the private sector supplying the innovation, customer focus and commercial discipline'.[25] The aim of the review was 'to simplify the relationships within the industry'.[26]

It admitted, however, that one part of this partnership had not worked: 'The attempt to create a commercial market relationship between the train and track companies failed.' The logic, therefore, seemed to be to merge these two entities, to recreate the vertically integrated railway that is the best way to run a railway. However, this was ruled out on the basis that there was a considerable amount of track-sharing which could cause 'conflicts of interest between the dominant company in a region and the other passenger and freight users'.[27] Moreover competition 'for the right to operate services can be advantageous in terms of delivering improved value for money' and having a vertically integrated railway would mean that no such competition was possible. Given the increase in franchise costs and the success of the one franchise in public hands, South Eastern, this was hardly a convincing argument (see Chapter 13).

The White Paper and the subsequent legislation also seem to prepare the way for cuts. The procedure for closures has been streamlined, in itself a sensible measure but one which raised fears of shutting down lines, especially as a 'closure officer' was appointed by the Department. So did the fact that the Passenger Transport Executives, which pour millions of pounds of funding into local lines within their areas, were given powers to replace local rail services with buses. While major cutbacks would appear to be difficult for a Labour government to make, a downturn in the economy could trigger them and the new legislation would make this much easier than hitherto.

The real intentions behind the review were given in the leaked 'summary' sent to me a month before its eventual publication. The document highlighted the fact that 'there are regional services which are – and are likely to remain – very lightly used. They deliver real benefit, particularly in remote rural areas, but at what [is] probably an unrealistic cost.' There is bound to be less money available in the future, the document warns, and therefore the huge deficit in the industry created by Railtrack's loss of control over costs would have to be met by a combination of fares increases and 'service thinning or cuts'.

The document accepts that the changes in the Railways Act may well not be the last in the industry and crucially leaves the door open towards vertical integration: 'The structure should also be amendable without new legislation. If the industry wishes to move to vertical integration, it can do so by establishing joint ventures between Network Rail regions and TOCs.'

Thus, the review, when published, was less radical and fell short of any optimistic expectations of major structural change. But clearly, even as the Department for Transport was drawing up the legislation for the Railways Act 2005, doubts remained as to whether the new structure was robust. The review itself was pretty much what the cynics and pessimists had predicted: a few modest measures that did little to address the fundamentally dysfunctional nature of the railway highlighted by Darling himself in his speech on 19 January 2004. However, the likelihood of further change remains strong. In particular, the issue of reintegrating the railway was dodged on spurious grounds and the new structure places far too much reliance on the idea that civil servants have the ability to control the railway. As the final chapter suggests, it is only by abandoning any pretence that the private sector can play a major role in determining the future of the railway that a sensible way forward can be found. For the moment, we have an extreme form of state control sold to the public as a private-public partnership.

The other issue that was supposed to be addressed in the review was the continued poor performance in terms of delays. The recovery from the collapse of the timetable after the Hatfield accident was proving to be slower than expected. There was no single reason for this but instead a variety of factors, mostly greater risk aversion by everyone working in the industry who routinely begun to take more conservative decisions on the myriad issues concerning safety that they faced every day. Drivers approached red lights more slowly through fear of going into the overlap, trackworkers imposed speed restrictions more readily on dodgy sections of tracks and trains would be taken out of service for the most minor defects. The prevailing culture on the railways had become one of fear.

The continued high level of delays demonstrated that the complicated performance regime created at privatisation had failed. This was supposed to incentivise the various companies involved to avoid delaying trains through the imposition of financial penalties. Delays are counted through a system called Trust, which has 5,000 monitoring points, and attributed to train operators or Network Rail. This is not a simple process, as there are frequently knock-on delays through the system that may originate far away and with a completely different company. There are even TOC (Train Operating Company) on TOC and FOC (Freight Operating Company) on TOC delays that have to be allocated. Huge amounts of money swill round this system. In 2003/4, for example, Network Rail shelled out nearly £400m to compensate the operators but the following year, thanks to a 16 per cent reduction in delay minutes, the company had to make no such payment, boosting its profitability.

There is, however, no direct relationship between the penalty payments imposed for a delay and the effect of that delay on passengers. The measurement used to assess performance, the public performance measure (PPM), only penalises companies whose trains are five (short journeys) or ten (long distance) minutes late, making no distinction between heavily delayed trains and those which just miss the target. The PPM, introduced by the Strategic Rail Authority in 2000, plunged catastrophically following the Hatfield crash to 64.3 per cent[28] in the third quarter of 2000/1, which meant that more than a third of trains were late. The problem was compounded by the fact that this was the leaf-fall season, always the worst time of the year for punctuality, but the figure for the equivalent quarter a year before was 81.5 per cent. The average for the first full year after Hatfield was 76.3 per cent, which meant that for a whole year nearly a quarter of all trains were significantly late.

And the recovery was proving slow. For the year to December 2003, just before the announcement of the review, the figure was still only 80.5 per cent – a fifth of trains were still being delayed despite a panoply of measures in the industry and a host of injunctions by government to improve the performance.

In the event very little in the White Paper addressed the underlying causes for these continuing delays. The most positive move was the establishment around the country of a series of integrated control centres, where the operators and Network Rail liaise to minimise the effects of disruption. These are definitely a step in the right direction, albeit a limited one. However, they could have been introduced without legislation and the other upheavals.

Ultimately the review process delivered a classic dog's breakfast.

Admittedly, formulating the right structure for the rail industry has never been easy but the government's timidity in the face of the industry's major problems together with its desire to have control but not responsibility raises serious questions about the long-term viability of the railways, as subsequent chapters show. The creation and subsequent assassination of the SRA cruelly exposed the utter failure of the Labour government to deal with the problem of the railways. Again, it is worth repeating what happened just to savour the way that the railways have, to coin a phrase, been buggered about for a decade: within five years of creating an organisation whose remit was to give strategic direction to the industry, the same government abolished it, arguing that the railways' problems had been underestimated and that the organisation could never do the job it had been created to perform. Even more strangely, the powers of the SRA were transferred to the Department of Transport, effectively creating, for the first time in this country, a railways ministry – while Darling and his fellow ministers argued that they were not renationalising the railway. It is a script straight out of *Bremner, Bird and Fortune* except that they try to do sketches that are credible.

The SRA may not have been perfect, but the idea of having an organisation separate from Whitehall to give the industry direction was a good one. Yet, because Darling was too embarrassed to create a new organisation immediately on abolishing the old one, the industry is now to be run by civil servants. In effect it will be under much greater government control than when the railways were in state hands, but operated by an independent body, British Rail. And yet, with not a hint of irony, ministers insist that the railways remain a privatised industry.

CHAPTER 12

The risk paradox

The series of four major accidents, from Southall in September 1997 to Potters Bar in May 2002, was to prove highly damaging to the railways and raised wider concerns about safety in the industry. However, there is a paradox: while these highly visible and heavily publicised accidents were, as has been shown, mostly caused by changes brought about by privatisation, the overall record of the industry undoubtedly improved during this period. In fact, it was the reaction to the accidents, particularly Hatfield, and the public perception of railway safety thanks to the blanket media coverage of these disasters that had the greatest long-term impact on the industry.

While the evidence presented in earlier chapters strongly suggests that rail privatisation has made the railways less safe, the main statistics do not support this thesis. In particular, analysis of the rate of minor incidents demonstrates that they are at an all-time low. The key indicator used in the industry is 'significant train incidents per million train miles', which includes a vast array of incidents ranging from major train collisions to broken windscreens on a locomotive. These have been in steady decline for decades and the rate at which such incidents are occuring has fallen faster since privatisation than in BR days. The statistics[2] from Her Majesty's Railway Inspectorate show that the rate of 0.43 in 1993/4, at the start of the sell-off process, declined to 0.16 in 2003/4, suggesting the railway was more than twice as safe after it had been privatised.

So what can explain this apparent paradox – a series of major accidents caused by the failings of privatisation and yet a reduction in the number of minor incidents which, superficially, creates the impression of a safer railway? First, other statistics showed a more mixed picture.

During the early years of privatisation, the number of broken rails (as we saw in Chapter 8) and signals passed at danger both increased. Following Hatfield, the number of broken rails began to fall sharply after the massive increases in track work arising from the disaster. The trend in SPADs was not so clear cut, with the number starting to go down after 1995 and rising briefly in the year before Ladbroke Grove. After that, more defensive driving and other measures taken by the industry reversed that trend. Worryingly, however, even after the disaster the number of *serious* SPADs[3] remained for a time stubbornly level at just over 200 per year, with the majority of the reduction in the overall total being accounted for by very short technical overruns, which are mostly caused by wheel slippage or minor misjudgements by the driver. Even after the introduction of the new Train Protection and Warning System (see below) serious SPADs were still running at just under 150 per year – three every week – in 2003/4.

Secondly, there is a widespread suspicion within the industry that the level of reporting of incidents has gone down. Given the fragmented and competitive nature of the railways, there is little incentive for workers to report incidents, especially as staff do not have the same public-sector ethos with which they were imbued at BR. According to the Ladbroke Grove inquiry seminar, 'Staff are frightened of reporting slight incidents of a non-serious nature, as they get pulled in by their supervisor, asked to fill out a form and sometimes get disciplined. There is also the reluctance to "shop" a colleague.'[4] Indeed, this may not have changed much despite the accidents. One result of the accidents was the establishment of the Confidential Incident Reporting and Analysis Service but at a training course to allow me access to the track held in June 2005, the instructor said that CIRAS was viewed as a 'nark's friend' and its reputation was very poor among track workers.

Thirdly, the reduction in minor incidents – some of which have serious consequences, such as people on platforms being hit by slam doors that are opened while the train is still moving – is part of a long-term trend that stretches back almost as far as the creation of the railways. The trend line therefore merely confirms that the railways have continued the long-term improvement in safety that was under way under BR. This is hardly surprising. Improved technology, a much more conservative approach to safety following the 1988 Clapham disaster, the scrapping of most slam-door trains, the replacement of level crossings with bridges or tunnels, and the fitting of central locking devices on InterCity trains[5] all contributed towards a safer environment. Incidents involving track workers also decreased, as they were now all provided with such basic safety aids as fluorescent jackets and better-organised lookouts. There were also fewer people on the track, as we have seen, therefore reducing the overall exposure to danger. It would, in fact, be shocking if this extremely long-term trend towards a reduction in minor incidents had been completely reversed by privatisation.

Professor Andrew Evans,[6] an expert in railway safety statistics, criticised the earlier version of this book for arguing that privatisation had made the railway less safe. However, it is irrefutable that some – I have argued all – of these major accidents were attributable to the consequences of the way the industry was broken up. Professor Evans argues, quite correctly, that it is impossible to know what accidents might have occurred had British Rail not been broken up. Moreover, using a statistical analysis of accidents since the Second World War, Professor Evans states that the trend line under which safety was improving under British Rail has been exceeded by the privatised railway. In other words, the industry has been getting safer at a faster rate than might have been expected had BR continued in existence. Again, this is the world of hypotheticals and there may be several reasons for that such as the reduction in passenger operated doors, as mentioned above.

There is, too, one key statistic that points the other way – to a less safe environment on the railways. As Professor Evans puts it: 'Only one indicator is adverse: the number of fatalities in train collisions and derailments is higher than expected, because of the severity of the accident at Ladbroke Grove in 1999.'[7] That is an important finding and it is not good enough to say that the statistics have been distorted by the seriousness of the accidents in this series of major disasters.

It may be that the way the industry was privatised added to the risk of a major catastrophe, rather than to the more minor incidents on which Professor Evans bases his analysis. This is because privatisation intro-duced a new form of risk, 'interface risk', which resulted from the fragmentation of the network. In order to mitigate this risk, a whole paraphernalia of regulation had to be established, the safety case regime outlined in Chapter 4. As a former Railtrack manager, who is still working in the industry and therefore must remain anonymous, put it, 'safety will always be more difficult to manage in the fragmented railway than under BR. It has to be controlled through cumbersome safety cases and group standards that are always open to interpretation whether they concern maintenance or driver training.'[8]

The evidence of the chapters devoted to the accidents is clear. In each case the way the industry was broken up contributed to the accident. At Southall, the key factors include the botched reorganisation of the maintenance depot, the lack of clarity about reporting faults to 'control' and the complete lack of interest in implementing the Automatic Train Protection pilot programme; at Ladbroke Grove the main issues were Railtrack's failure to address the SPAD problem (a point reinforced by the comments quoted above from the inquiry seminar about the difficulties of coordinating the different players in the industry) and driver training; at Hatfield, the main elements were the very structure of Railtrack, which meant it was far too weak on engineering, and the way it was forced to contract out maintenance through very badly drafted contracts; and at Potters Bar, the finger of suspicion must point towards a failure on the part of the private maintenance company, although this will probably now never be fully determined.

Another possible explanation for this confusing set of statistics is that the safety case regime may have taken some time to bed in and, in the interim, the resulting uncertainty may have contributed to the spate of accidents because insufficient attention was paid to coordinating the network as a whole.

At the time of writing, in summer 2005, the railway has gone over three years without a fatal crash apart from the Ufton Nervet crossing accident in November 2004 caused by a suicidal motorist. That may mean the regime has now borne fruit but the price of that series of accidents and the reaction to them, both by the industry and the politicians, has been very high in terms of the extra cost of running the railway and the deterioration in performance measured by delays and cancellations. Moreover, given the fantastic amount of money that has been spent on reducing the risk, it remains a matter of concern among some safety experts within the industry that the looming cutbacks resulting from the attempt to rein back the cost explosion in the railways could compromise safety again.

Whatever the explanation for this apparent paradox, one thing is certain: the public perception that privatisation made the industry less safe has been deeply damaging to the railways. The industry became much more risk-averse and, as a result, massive amounts of money have had to be spent to allay concern about risk. What started as an increase in risk (or at least in catastrophic risk) caused by the new phenomenon of interface risk has become a problem of cost and performance. While, ironically, the figures for safety are improving, the cost of bringing about that improvement is so disproportionate that it threatens the future of the railway, pushing people into cars which, of course, are far more dangerous than rail travel. Public perception has been changed by this series of accidents and by the fact that they followed so swiftly in the wake of the controversial privatisation.

The fact the perception that the railway is less safe is wrong is no consolation. The truth is that there will always be some rail crashes, particularly on a crowded network like Britain's, which is one of the most intensively used in the world. The accident at Great Heck in February 2001 demonstrated this universal fact – who could ever have predicted that a Land Rover slipping off a main road would result in Britain's fastest-ever rail collision and cause ten deaths? Under British Rail this type of occasional event was broadly accepted. There were accidents, invariably caused by human error or technical failures, which were the subject of an inquiry, held within weeks without the presence of any lawyers, that made recommendations aimed at ensuring that, once identified, errors were not repeated.

Now, however, public tolerance of catastrophic disasters has been greatly reduced. This had begun to happen before privatisation. Lawyers first became involved fully at the 1989 Clapham inquiry and have played an important role in all subsequent investigations into major crashes. Media coverage of railway accidents has always been extensive but the advent of satellite television with news channels that give blanket 24-hour coverage and tabloid newspapers with a sensationalist approach has heightened public interest. The fact that most major accidents have happened around London within easy reach of TV studios has been a further factor in the disproportionately extensive coverage of railway accidents, a phenomenon that could be described as catastrophe pornography.

And then add in privatisation. One of the first questions that reporters will always ask is whether there has been a conflict between profit and safety. The answer is, of course, that there is always a trade-off between the cost and safety, as some safety measures are clearly not worth paying for in terms of the number of lives it is estimated they might save. The public perception is, therefore, unfair – private companies do not like rail accidents as they are terrible PR and damage the bottom line.[9]

This trade-off between safety and cost is carried out through a process called cost-benefit analysis which aims to evaluate safety projects by dividing the cost of an improvement by the number of lives the change is expected to save. The government's guideline figure is around £1.15m per life saved (or, in the jargon, value per prevented fatality, VPF). In other words, if a scheme costs more than this, it is not implemented and vice versa. On the railways this is increased by a factor of 2.8 for investment that would prevent multiple fatality incidents like Southall, Ladbroke Grove, Hatfield and Potters Bar, giving a VPF of something like £3.2m. In contrast, because so little money is available for safety schemes on the highways, according to Professor Evans,[10] the equivalent figure for accident-prevention measures on the roads is around £100,000. In other words, it is thought worth spending over thirty times more to save one life on the railways than to save one on the roads, where more than 3,200 people are killed every year. Equivalent sums spent on road safety, or indeed kidney machines or even other types of railway safety schemes,[11] would save many more lives.

The railways have always, to some extent, suffered this burden of having to be safer than other industries. That in itself is no bad thing, but there is an irrationality that pervades discussion of this issue. Take, for example, the VPF measure. Most deaths on the railway are of trespassers, often children or teenagers, and suicides. A concerted campaign to reduce those casualties, with expenditure on the same scale as that devoted to the Train Protection and Warning System, would undoubtedly save more lives. But the issue is unexciting and, rather like road accidents, does not attract headlines and funding is therefore not forthcoming.

Privatisation has heightened all these contradictions. Because the industry is being run privately and the public is suspicious of the motives of the rail companies, the traditional cost-benefit approach has been thrown away, wrecking the finances of the railways and absorbing incredible amounts of public money for schemes of very marginal value. This was clearly set out in a press statement that accompanied the publication of the report in March 2001 by Professor Uff and Lord Cullen on train protection systems. The report recommends the installation of the European Train Control System that will prevent trains from going through red lights by the year 2010. While the aim is laudable, the installation of the cheaper Train Protection and Warning System which was mostly completed by the end of 2003 at a cost of £500m will prevent something like 70 per cent of accidents caused by SPADs and will reduce the speed of impact for the others. Therefore, using the report's figures, ETCS is predicted to save two or three lives per year[12] at a cost of some £2bn–3bn – which, assuming a life of thirty years for the system, means a VPF of something like £30m.

In a remarkable passage in the press statement, which demonstrates both the failure of privatisation and the way that it has distorted railway economics, the two authors effectively argue that spending on rail safety should not be tested against any normal criteria of value for money:

> At the time of privatisation, it was foreseen that the railway industry would itself promote and fund major safety improvements through the regulation system. It is now accepted that the bulk of the cost of the next generation of train protection systems will be met by public funding. Accordingly, the need to justify expenditure on the basis of cost benefit analysis has largely been overtaken by decisions made by government, in conjunction with the Health and Safety Commission. *We have not, therefore, been concerned with establishing the economic justification of the new train protection systems*, but rather with ensuring that the relevant issues have been addressed with adequate transparency and that, where alternative courses are open, the one which is in the wider public interest should be adopted.[13] [my italics]

In other words, bugger the cost, the taxpayer is coughing up and so it does not matter. In fact, the recommendation over the new European Train Control System showed that Uff and Cullen were living in cloud-cuckoo-land – or, at least, they had been completely misadvised. Forced into action, the rail industry drew up a report examining the state of this technology and found that installing ETCS (which became subsumed into a larger concept called ERTMS or European Rail Traffic Management System, involving both train control and automatic train protection) by 2010 was a complete pipedream. The report[14] argued that to try to meet the Cullen/Uff recommendations would greatly reduce track capacity and cause disruption on the railways, as well as costing £6bn at a conservative estimate. Instead it recommended a slower introduction, preceded by a longer development period. A pilot scheme is being introduced on the Cambrian coast railway, a little-used line in mid-Wales, between 2006 and 2008 but there is no prospect of having the scheme introduced on all Britain's main lines for at least a couple of decades and probably much longer. Indeed, as we shall see in Chapter 15, a similar system of train control was supposed to be introduced on the West Coast Main Line as a part of its refurbishment but, in fact, it soon became clear that the appropriate technology was a long way from being available for what was one of the busiest long-distance rail routes in the world.

Pressure on the railways to spend disproportionately on safety was exacerbated by the attitude of Cullen and Uff to the accident survivors and relatives. Indeed, many in the rail industry felt that they were being held to ransom by these groups, a feeling reinforced by a strange passage in the joint inquiry report where the two not-so-wise men say: 'The interests of the public are represented most closely by HMRI and the Regulatory bodies, and in this Joint Inquiry, *by the Passengers' Group*'[15] (my italics). This is quite simply nonsense. The Passengers' Group (formed by survivors and relatives of the victims of the accidents) is, by definition, a very narrow interest group encompassing a small number of people who have had a particularly awful experience of the railway. This does not make their views more valid in representing the public interest than, say, the Rail Passengers' Council, the Department for Transport or the House of Commons Transport Committee. Survivors and relatives are clearly always going to be demanding a totally safe railway, something that is an economic and practical nonsense. Indeed, this approach is, as Professor Evans put it, 'Alice in Wonderland'[16] economics which, at some point, will return to haunt ministers because priorities in railway investment will be completely determined by safety considerations. He points out that the careful cost-benefit analysis approach used for many years 'has not been produced by out-of-this-world economists, but are our best estimate of the preferences of the public, who actually pay for and benefit from the safety measures'.[17] However, since the taxpayer is footing the bill, the industry has little reason to resist the process being foisted upon it and, indeed, as Professor Evans points out, 'quite a lot to gain, notably a reduced risk of the adverse publicity that surrounds high-profile accidents'.[18]

In other words, the whole economics of the railway have been distorted by the hasty reaction to these accidents. The huge expenditure on safety has resulted in a reduction in casualties but it is very doubtful if this could conceivably be considered as value for money under any rational system of cost-benefit analysis. The industry has, at least, acted quite cannily by producing the report on ERTMS mentioned above, which argues that it is only worthwhile introducing this safety system if it can be used as a new way of controlling trains without the use of colour light signals. If that turns out to be the case, it will bring benefits of increased capacity and higher line speeds, but the use of such technology on very busy parts of the network remains a distant prospect. Yet there is continued pressure from the European authorities to push for such safety measures, given impetus by every accident, and the industry may eventually find itself forced to spend vast sums of money that cannot be justified on any rational basis. The way in which money can be easily wasted in panics resulting from rail accidents is demonstrated by the attempt to fit a device (called 'cup and cone') on old Mark 1 rolling stock to minimise damage in the event of accidents. These old slam-door trains, used on the Southern commuter routes, had a very strong chassis but a weak superstructure. At the Cowden and Clapham accidents this design had caused extra casualties as the chassis of one vehicle smashed into the seating of another, and the Health and Safety Executive had become very exercised about this. It decided to require the train operators still running these old trains to fit a cup and cone system designed to stop the chassis from riding up into the body of other coaches in the event of a collision. However, the old carriages were due to be scrapped anyway, as John Prescott had announced that they should be phased out by the end of 2004.[19] This left a brief hiatus of a couple of years during which some Mark 1 stock would still be running, and the HSE decided to require these trains to be fitted with the cup and cone device. In fact, the chance of one of the remaining couple of hundred Mark 1 trains being involved in a major collision was minuscule. The £1.5m spent on this fruitless attempt to make old rolling stock a tiny bit safer would have been better invested in virtually anything else on the railway.[20] But, again, the structure of the industry meant that there was no Fat Controller to lobby the politicians about such distorted priorities. The Strategic Rail Authority should have stood up to such excesses but failed to do so, constrained by its position as a creature of government. The idea was quietly dropped anyway.

The most extensive safety change following the accidents was the introduction of the Train Protection and Warning System, the scheme that was on Prescott's desk (see Chapter 7) at the time of the Ladbroke

Grove accident. The go-ahead for the installation of this system, designed to reduce the risk of a collision after a train goes through a red light, had been given just before the Ladbroke Grove disaster in 1999 and the target for completion was the beginning of 2004, brought forward following the accident to the start of 2003. TPWS works through a system of electrical loops installed ahead of a signal which monitor the speed of a train approaching the signal. If it is going too fast to be able to stop, then the brakes are automatically applied. TPWS is designed to stop any train travelling up to 75mph within the safety overlap – the distance between a signal and the junction it is protecting. However, its one flaw compared with the full automatic train protection is that trains travelling at more than 75mph may not stop within the overlap, although the brakes will still be applied, therefore reducing the speed of any potential collision. A more sophisticated version, TPWS+, which will stop trains travelling at 100mph within the safety overlap, is being fitted by Network Rail at 500 signals on high-speed parts of the network.

The cost, for what the industry called the most significant new safety benefit on the railway for forty years, eventually totalled £585m. That works out at an estimated £15.4m per life saved, far greater than many other potential life-saving measures in, say, the NHS, demonstrating the disproportionate sums spent on rail safety. Fitting TPWS had, however, become politically necessary for the government and mandatory for the beleaguered industry because the two disastrous 'SPAD' accidents, Southall and Ladbroke Grove, came in such quick succession and attracted so much coverage. It greatly reduced one of the main causes of preventable accidents, trains going through red lights.

Would BR have reacted in the same way? Given Southall and Ladbroke Grove, a nationalised or an integrated railway would probably have still fitted TPWS despite the poor VPF. However, it would have done so in a more realistic and cost-effective way. For example, TPWS equipment would not have been fitted at buffer stops, where the speeds have been set far too low resulting in trains crawling into terminuses, much to the frustration of passengers. Nor would the system have been fitted at little-used signals where the risks of a collision are minimal.

The fragmented railway prevents rational decisions being taken over safety. As a safety expert put it,

Decisions on safety are sub-optimal because of the way the industry is split up. Say if you needed to improve TPWS, you might need to fit equipment on the track or on the trains. Clearly the operators and the rolling-stock companies would want it on the track, so that it was no hassle for them, and Network Rail would rather see it go on the trains. That kind of dispute is almost impossible to sort out and you end up with an unsatisfactory compromise.[21]

The most serious long-term impact of the accidents, therefore, proved to be financial. The risk had, in the minds of the public, been privatised, and there was to be a heavy price to pay for the perception of that privatisation because the public did not trust the private sector to deliver safety in the way that the nationalised BR had done. Moreover, the politicians felt they had to be seen to do something in response to these accidents, even though they no longer had direct control of the railways. As we saw in Chapter 7, the Ladbroke Grove disaster sent the politicians into a rare panic and a bit of judicious spinning in a Sunday newspaper led to Railtrack's Safety and Standards Directorate (SSD) being hived off into a separate subsidiary, Railway Safety, even though the old Directorate operated completely independently from its parent company and was non-profit making. This was an interim solution while Cullen, and ministers, decided what the long-term structure of safety regulation should be.

The old SSD had been responsible for implementing the 250 railway group standards which govern every aspect of operating the railway in great detail, from specification of the maintenance of wheel sets and the lighting of railway premises to writing rule books governing trackworker safety and specifying how to deal with a level crossing when the barriers have failed. When this responsibility passed to the new organisation, Railway Safety, in 2000, for the first time the setting of standards was completely divorced from people working in the industry, which had always being largely self-regulating in terms of safety matters. As one safety expert put it, 'these processes have a tendency to be driven by technical experts rather than people with practical experience who are working in the industry and therefore economic checks and balances on what was affordable were weakened.'[22]

Moreover, Railway Safety seemed to take a harder line on the implementing of standards than its predecessor, or at least that was the perception within the industry. Creating a totally separate body, while attractive to the simplistic populism of the politicians, inevitably led to a loss of a shared purpose between those setting the standards and the industry they were policing. In effect, it outsourced both costs and risks for Railtrack (and later Network Rail) and meant that there was now no one in a position to make a rational choice between them. If safety is a product supplied free by someone else, then it is bound to be over-ordered. Ultimately the taxpayer was paying, so no one in the industry was too bothered.

This separation was a politically motivated move designed to appease the media and the victims' groups rather than to improve safety and it was to have a big impact on costs because it meant that setting the standards became separated from the real needs of the railway. According to one senior railwayman,

> it means you have a unit that is divorced from the railway and the common sense of the railway. You end up with creeping standard improvement with worthy engineers, sitting in ivory towers, writing the perfect standard for themselves, which makes the railway very expensive. So one arm of the government, the Department for Transport, has separated the cost process from the industry whilst another, the Treasury, complains that the railway is unaffordable. So we will have more people on the roads and kill more people. [23]

The creation of Railway Safety with its harder line on implementing technical standards also came at a bad time for the industry, given the aftermath of Hatfield and the taking into administration of Railtrack in October 2001. Railtrack's administrators proved to be very conservative on safety issues which meant they were unwilling to take risks. A culture of fear, with managers and even ordinary staff fearing retribution in the courts should they make a mistake, had also become prevalent. The result of this combination of circumstances was that costs of work on the railways rose, sometimes exponentially. Everything had to be done to a gold standard, with both belts and braces.

Chris Green, who was chief executive of Virgin Trains until the end of 2004, gives the example of signal siting on the Carlisle to Glasgow part of the West Coast line where line speeds are being increased by 15mph to 125mph:

> That's a slight increase, but they wanted us to renew every single signal on that whole section. According to the standards, the driver must have seven seconds' uninterrupted view of the signal but if it is 6½ seconds, then they say

we have to move the signal, whereas in the old days common sense would have been used and we would have talked to a representative group of drivers to agree what was OK. In fact, we did discuss it with our drivers who reckon that only three signals need moving. The cost is £250,000 for each signal and the trouble is that these standards are divorced from money, so that when people discuss these issues, they no longer say 'what will it cost?' but instead specify the safest engineering standard and argue that the safest railway must have this.[24]

Another ludicrous example was given to me by an engineer:

Two tampers [which lift up the rails allowing the ballast to be relaid], both working on the same worksite, departing at the same time from the same stabling point. Two route conductors needed, but only one available. Simple answer: couple them together. Problem solved? Not on your life! The safety case of each company does not permit coupling to another company's machine because of the imported risk. What if the tamper at the rear became derailed and damaged the leading one? Who would pay? This is the sort of nonsense that I have to contend with every day. The fact that the two tampers in question may have been designed to couple together, and would have run together quite happily on scores of occasions under BR doesn't enter into it. This has nothing at all to do with 'Safety' and everything to do with liability and compensation, another example of the 'Safety' argument that few people dare speak against.[25]

There are countless other examples but the best, and the one cited most often in the industry, is the story of the 400-mile footpath. Built as part of the refurbishment of the line, this runs from London to Glasgow alongside the line, supposedly to give trackworkers a safe route to walk beside the railway; the rules specify that any line upgraded to 100mph or more requires a safe footpath at least a couple of metres away from the line. The cost ran into millions and as one train operator wearily noted: 'It is bound to be completely grown over within a couple of years because no one is going to fork out the huge sums it will need for maintenance.'[26]

How did this come about? Anson Jack, the executive director of standards at the Railway Standards and Safety Board, says: 'There is a mechanism to say that there was excessive cost in relation to safety benefit, but no one asked for a derogation. So it never happened.'[27] Effectively, the attitude was that it was more hassle to try to get a derogation than to just do the work, since the bill was effectively being picked up by the taxpayer.

Jack is part of the new team at the Railway Safety and Standards Board which is determined to move the industry away from the unthinking obedience of standards. The RSSB took over from Railway Safety in April 2003 and the new organisation has attempted to reassure the industry that railway group standards are not set in stone and that there is room for negotiation on projects if unreasonable safety considerations were being imposed. In February 2005, the Board issued a document called 'How safe is safe enough', which was a welcome attempt to rein back on some of the safety excesses of the past few years that have proved highly costly to the industry and delivered little safety benefit. The document recognised that the endless pursuit of greater standards of safety could ultimately be counterproductive because of the cost involved. However, reining back on the culture of fear and blame in the industry will prove a long-term task and in the meantime millions of pounds have been wasted.

Thanks to the series of accidents, privatisation, the opportunism of the politicians and weak ministers, the UK has ended up with a situation in which rail, the safest form of transport,[28] has become the most regulated and the one required to spend the most money on reducing risks which were already minimal. The public's mistrust of rail safety is completely irrational but the railways' unique selling point on safety was put at risk by privatisation. Because of the lack of public trust in a privatised environment, stirred up, ironically, by a right-wing media that favours privatisation, the industry is going to be saddled with enormous costs for safety improvements whose benefit will be, at best, marginal.

The worst aspect of all this is that, as the aftermath of Hatfield showed, we now have a paranoid railway in which decisions over safety are likely to be so conservative that performance and capacity will be diminished in the pursuit of illusory safety objectives. The slightest potential risk will lead to train cancellations or delays, further reducing the attractiveness of the safest form of transport. While this process had started before privatisation, the fragmentation of the industry, together with the recent disasters, has speeded it up. Although the creation of Network Rail and the taking back in-house of maintenance will improve the situation somewhat, the railways will find it very difficult to return to pre-Hatfield levels of performance because of this risk-aversion. We may, therefore, end up with a railway that statistically looks safer but causes more risk to society as a whole because fewer people use it and choose, instead, more dangerous forms of travel.

The statements put out by politicians at the scenes of disasters, like that made by John Prescott at Ladbroke Grove in which he talked about no penny being scrimped in order to ensure absolute safety, are pure political guff. As one exasperated railwayman put it, 'no attempt was made by ministers to address safety a sensible way'.[29] There is always a trade-off between cost and safety and rightly so. Because of the spate of accidents and the changes within the industry, the balance swung far too much towards the latter. While this is partly a consequence of the fragmentation of the industry, it is also part of a wider societal move towards risk-aversion prompted by the compensation culture and disproportionate media interest in accidents.

The extra burden of safety was merely one of the triggers for the rising costs on the railway, the issue that threatened to lead to major cuts and which prompted the rail review and White Paper of 2004. As the following chapters show, costs on the railway soared out of control in the aftermath of the Hatfield accident although even before that there were signs that the proper checks and balances on spending had been fatally undermined by the fragmentation.

Before looking at the question of costs, however, there is one further issue that must be added to the lengthy list of damaging but unconsidered side-effects of privatisation; a factor which has a strong but (literally) incalculable impact on much of the analysis that follows: the culture of the railway. Much of the additional risk injected into the railway by fragmentation arose because of the neglect of an all-important but intangible change, the destruction of the traditional way that work was undertaken and the perception of the industry by those who worked in it.

The cultural change that occurred in the railways as a result of transforming them from a single entity in the public sector into myriad private and often competing companies with contractual relationships that are often, necessarily, antagonistic, cannot be underestimated, although it is a much-neglected subject with implications for other industries.

To regret the destruction of a common railway culture is not, it should be stressed, to indulge in pointless nostalgia. Just because things used to be done in a certain way does not mean the same methods should be used for evermore. What has been important is the loss of experience and skills that can never be replaced. The distinction can be a difficult one and supporters of change often fail to recognise that it even exists. Of course developing technology and new management techniques mean that change is a necessary component of any industry. However, the rail industry, 170 years old at privatisation, contained a body of knowledge and experience inside the brains of its workforce whose value was impossible to calculate but easy to underestimate.

Traditionally, railway workers had learnt on the job. This was good for employers in that training costs were low and experience was recognised as valuable by the workforce. However, it also meant that there was a tendency towards conservatism and a Buggins' Turn system of promotion. Privatisation, therefore, was seen as more than just breaking the strength of the unions. It would also transform the workforce, enabling the introduction of new work methods by challenging the perceived conservatism of railwaymen[30] and their culture. It would allow more flexible working patterns and release entrepreneurial spirit among managers. As Tim Strangleman has explained in his authoritative book on the subject, 'One of the main focuses of criticism regarding negative aspects of the past has been the issue of corporate culture, with older workers being singled out as being unwilling to change, and one of the key factors is the supposed failures of state control.'[31]

But there was a downside, one that according to the experience of many in the industry, including supporters of privatisation, has far outweighed any advantages: the loss of corporate memory and with it, many skills. As Strangleman puts it, 'the process of privatisation and the restructuring that led up to it damaged the skills base in the industry in a number of ways'.[32]

The most obvious was, of course, the reduction in numbers. As with every privatisation, there are far fewer people working in the industry, particularly on the track. According to evidence given to the Cullen inquiry on Ladbroke Grove by Professor Christopher Baldry, head of the department of management and organisation at Stirling University, the railway workforce had fallen from 159,000 in 1992/3 to 92,000 in 1996/7. The rate of decline is exaggerated because the newer figure only includes main contractors and not subcontractors, but these statistics are a clear indication of the trend. According to evidence provided by the RMT union to the Commons Transport Sub-Committee,[33] the number of permanently employed maintenance workers had fallen from '31,000 in 1994 to between 15,000 and 19,000' by the end of 2000.

Professor Baldry describes this process as 'work intensification', a smaller number of people coping with a larger volume of traffic in the network. As he told the inquiry, the view of the contractors was that 'The only way we can survive is by reducing our costs in line with Railtrack's reducing their contract prices so more and more mechanisation, and fewer and fewer people, is the name of the game.'[34]

There was, too, a deliberate attempt to drive out the collegiate ethos of the railway. According to an ASLEF spokesman interviewed by Strangleman: 'One of the political ideas behind privatisation was to break up the idea of drivers as being a British Rail driver ... They sought to smash that.'[35] But, ironically, the drivers profited, pushing up wages by going from one firm to another as, understandably, they no longer felt any loyalty to their company.

Trackworkers were particularly affected by these changes. Chris Leah, Railtrack's safety director, told the same Transport Sub-Committee hearing that of the 18,000 staff working for the British Rail Infrastructure Companies at privatisation, there were only 12,000 left three years later. He added that because some tasks were being done by other staff, the real decrease was around 3,500[36] but, of course, these new workers did not have the same body of skills as the people they replaced. They were described by a lot of the old hands as 'industrial gypsies' or 'fruit picking gangs'.[37]

Reducing numbers in itself would have not been so damaging had it not been for the total reorganisation in the way that work was carried out on the railway. The aim of the privatisation was, in effect, to sabotage the cooperative ways of running the industry which had been the basis of its ethos since its creation. People worked for the *railway*, even when there were dozens of competing companies in the pre-1923 grouping era, and certainly that was the dominant ethos in the fifty-year history of British Railways. The break-up of this culture was a deliberate way of undermining the conservatism of older workers which consequently involved destroying the notion that people worked for the railway. They were supposed to see themselves as being loyal to Stagecoach, FirstGroup, Balfour Beatty or Jarvis rather than the railway, but that could never work because these companies only held temporary franchises or contracts, and what was the point of having any allegiance to them if they might be gone tomorrow?

The fragmentation of the railway, as we have seen, was a deliberate strategy by the architects of privatisation aimed at stimulating as much

competition as possible, resulting in the creation of over 100 organisations, separated out both horizontally and vertically – in other words, as
Strangleman puts it, 'command and control [was] replaced by competition and contract'.[38] He continues: 'The presumption on the part of
the Government and their advisors was that these individual units would
inherit the core competencies and expert knowledge of the BR workforce
and there would therefore be no loss of skill.'

It was a fantasy. Not only did large swathes of experienced people,
often attracted by generous redundancy packages, leave the industry,
making the numbers on staff reductions look good to the accountants
and shareholders, but those who remained spent much of their time
bickering and acting in the narrow interests of their company rather than
for the overall good of the industry. Many of the best and most
experienced people left as, having served longer in the industry, they
could get more money. One of privatisation's chief architects, John
Edmonds, Railtrack's first chief executive, admitted in a rare moment of
self-doubt that the problem of the management of Railtrack's contractors
'arose directly from the privatisation process, which had assumed the
principle of the "competent contractor". In fact, many skilled staff had
moved on during the various regroupings ... and Railtrack had to step up
the arrangements for the supervision and monitoring of its contractors
and the registration of personnel competent to work safely on the
network.'[39] The few older hands who remained played a crucial part in
keeping the railway going and indeed in 2005, ten years after privatisation, many TOCs were still being run by old BR managers.

The whole culture of the way that the railways were run was changed
by the contracting out of work. There were no longer railwaymen who
knew every bit of their patch of track and saw themselves as part of the
industry, they had been replaced by a new generation of railway navvies,
touring round Britain from job to job with their sometimes faked PTS
(Personal Track Safety) cards. The RMT research found that there were
54,000 people, working for more than 2,000 companies, who were
qualified to work on the track. These casual workers felt no allegiance to
the railway or, indeed, their colleagues from other firms. This most
cooperative of industries, traditionally operated on military lines because
of the need for safety, routine and integration, was now maintained by a
ragbag of individuals, some excellent, some hopeless, but few with any
real understanding of their role in keeping the trains running.

An RMT union official, interviewed by Strangleman, explained how traditionally,

> a maintenance gang had a particular section to look after. They took a pride in that they thought of themselves as valued skilled or semi-skilled labour. They came to work and they were very conscious if there was a fault on their particular part of the line ... That has been destroyed – they can be deployed on any part of the line now, working alongside contractors all the time who are often poorly trained, don't have a safety culture and basically don't give a shit.[40]

There is an important safety consequence resulting from all this: the railway is dependent on the sharing of information about dangers and risks. A track worker, 'Bert', described the casualisation of the railway labour force to the union paper, *RMT News*,[41] soon after privatisation. Although he had worked for the railways for forty years, he was now entirely casual. Once a job is finished, he has to move on: '[The private companies] expect you to travel round the country like nomads.' Companies like Balfour Beatty that had taken over the contracts had closed workshops and sacked apprentices, he added.

Strangleman, who interviewed many trackworkers for his research, found that, to some extent, the new companies were insulated from the most damaging consequences of this loss of skills and expertise as many longer-term staff looked after the newcomers, both formally and informally, when working on the track. However, it is almost certain, if impossible to prove conclusively, that both the Hatfield and Potters Bar accidents resulted from this loss of expertise which resulted in errors by inexperienced trackworkers.

Professor Baldry described to the Cullen Inquiry how the culture of trust and cooperation turned into one of deliberately stimulated antagonism, which also had safety implications:

> We were given on several occasions evidence that if track workers from Scotland had been sent down to York, for example, to work on a bit of track that was unfamiliar to them, they find themselves working with other employees from a different contractor. Their instinct is to ask the local people about the nature of the track. The local people may have been told by their employer 'Don't talk to these persons because they are employed by the opposition.' In other words, there are actual obstacles put in the way of this pooling of both site knowledge and hazards knowledge.[42]

Attendees at a seminar held as part of the Cullen Inquiry heard how this change in culture had undermined cooperative working practices:

> Privatisation has created a big cultural change. There is now little inter-linking of culture from one company to another. There has been a loss of comradeship between drivers, signalmen, cleaners etc. There is no longer a sense of working together. Questions of delays and attribution of blame strengthen the divide. This has led to a lack of confidence in others. No one is encouraged to discuss someone else's problem, or volunteers, or shares information. There has been a loss of learning and this leads to poor com-munication.[43]

Professor Baldry, too, highlighted this aspect of the way that the rail community had been broken up, telling the Cullen Inquiry: 'But, more worryingly, it used to be the case that signallers would probably know the personnel that were appearing in the stretch of track under their jurisdiction and when track maintenance was done on a more geographical basis. Now they have people requesting possession of track and they have no real idea of what their competence is or what their track awareness is or what their knowledge of the track layout is.'[44] He added that staff trying to enforce safety regulations sometimes faced hostility: 'It has been reported to us that safety representatives can be threatened with physical violence if this is way out in a remote rural situation.'[45]

Managers have, obviously, been most affected by the new culture. The Cullen Inquiry seminar reported that: 'There has been a fairly wide-spread loss of confidence [by junior staff] in local and middle management. ... Local managers appear to be more concerned with budgetary requirements, and new management structures appear to have been created to cope with performance and financial penalties.'[46] Amazingly, staff are sometimes banned from talking to their colleagues on other companies on the same site and, instead, have to go through an off-site manager.

It is not only trackworkers and their managers who were subject to these changes; many simple skills essential to the efficient operating of trains were lost in a similar way. One former BR man who was on the board of a privatised operator, but who still acts as a consultant and therefore must remain anonymous, outlined how the basic knowledge required to run trains punctually had been lost: 'For example, some of the train operators introduced ridiculously short turnaround times for rolling stock which makes it impossible to operate. There are basic timetabling and operational principles which must be returned to.'[47]

One key set of skills – BR's engineering management – was almost entirely lost, partly as a result of this general process, but mainly because of a deliberate policy on the part of the early bosses of Railtrack who embarked on a 'scorched earth' strategy, purging the upper levels of the company of anyone with engineering experience. John Edmonds, who had always disliked engineers in his BR days, instigated the policy but, according to one of his team, 'he was persuaded that he had to have a small cadre of engineers to be an informed buyer and the government persuaded him that there should be a bit more technical knowledge because the City was concerned.'[48] But this thin layer of engineering management, the same source says, 'was insufficient in both quantity and quality and orders of magnitude too small to go across the whole company'. No other industry attempts to function by outsourcing so radically and it is no surprise that the policy failed, having to be completely reversed in 2003 when Network Rail decided to take all its maintenance back in-house.

BR had a very good cadre of managers. Its graduate recruits were sent round the country working for all kinds of different departments, which meant they obtained a thorough knowledge of the whole industry. Most of the people at the top in the industry are still those ex-BR managers and they will be exceedingly hard to replace when they reach retirement age over the next decade or so. No one is now training people to be railway generalists in that way. BR had an internal management training scheme that was leading edge, and according to one member of that team, 'it was thanks to our expertise and our skills that the railway was privatised so efficiently. It is a terrible irony.'[49] BR also had a world-class research operation that was broken up with nary a thought as to how it would affect the railway and, as we saw in Chapter 8, the result was disastrous.

Not surprisingly, this whole cycle of change resulted in much re inventing of the wheel. For example, Network Rail and the train operators began to create integrated control centres where managers would cooperate in the event of a disruption to ensure that the service was brought back in the most efficient way possible. Decisions about what trains to cancel or delay in order to minimise the effect on passengers are made by a single 'fat controller' working for Network Rail. As Ian Coucher, deputy chief executive of Network Rail, put it, 'There corporate amnesia. There are a lot of very good people and they often say "we used to do it like that" when we try to make a change. Or they say "it does not work" or "it was badly executed".'[50] Indeed, contrary to the notion put forward by privatisation's architects, railway workers were able to adapt and change, because the railways had constantly evolved over their history.

The taking back in-house of maintenance soon after the creation of Network Rail was partly motivated by a recognition of the damage caused by the loss of the old railway culture as well as an awareness of the disadvantages of having a contractual relationship to cover what was basically Network Rail's core task – ensuring that the infrastructure of the railway was in a good condition and 'fit for purpose', in that ghastly jargon which pervades the industry. The decision by NR showed that the arrangements created at privatisation had been simply unworkable, in that they created an artificial barrier where a seamless relationship was necessary. Many old railway sweats had tried to point that out at the time but they had been ignored by the politicians. The move by Network Rail was also a response to the escalation of costs, the biggest problem facing the railways, to which we now turn.

CHAPTER 13

Why is the railway so expensive?
(1) The mess of franchising

Of the many things that have gone wrong with the privatised railway, the soaring costs have been both the most unexpected and, in the long term, the most serious. Remember, reducing the financial burden of the railways on the Treasury was the core purpose of the whole privatisation exercise. The private sector was supposed to be more efficient than the public sector and the two main sets of contracts were drawn up on that basis: train operators were on a downward curve in terms of franchise payments and the maintenance companies also received less year on year in Railtrack's original contracts.

But all this was wishful thinking. The decline in franchise payments proved to be an unattainable target and, while Railtrack did initially bear down on costs, this was only achieved by allowing the state of the network to deteriorate. Then, after Hatfield, costs soared to an unprecedented level. The annual subsidy is now running at several times the highest amount that BR ever received. All aspects of running a railway have become far more expensive: operating the service, covered in this chapter; rolling stock, examined in the next chapter; and maintenance and renewal of the infrastructure, which is the subject of Chapter 15.

Why should this be? First, of course, privatisation itself was a costly exercise. At a conservative estimate, the total cost of the process including the amounts paid out by bidders, was reported to be at least £1bn.[1] For the taxpayer, the direct cost was at least £600m, which only covers the obvious spending such as fees for consultants and lawyers redundancies and administration and does not include the damaging effect on train performance, safety and efficiency. If all this money had been spent on reducing the cost of the industry to the taxpayer, it might have been a worthwhile investment. But the effect has, in fact, been th opposite to what was intended; so much so that the railway industry is in a permanent state of crisis.

In the early years of privatisation, there was much talk of 'sweating the assets' and 'increasing efficiency'. Privatisation came at a time when the rail industry had already been deprived of resources for a long while and the economies required to create 'profits' to attract investors put intense pressure on what was, contrary to conventional wisdom, an already lean industry. As 'Insider' in *Rail* magazine commented,[2] under privatisation, 'year on year, we have sought to win more mileage from less rolling stock, more paths from less infrastructure and more passengers with a lower ratio of staff. ... The availability of resources has been cut to the point where there are no more belts and braces available when rail operations are disrupted.' It was hardly surprising that this sweating of assets resulted in a financial crisis which had already shown signs of emerging before the Hatfield accident.

In order to smooth the passage of privatisation and ensure that there were enough bidders, the level of subsidy to the operators was nearly doubled from £1.1bn to £2.16bn when Railtrack was hived off at the beginning of the 1994/5 financial year. The precise figures for the period 1994–6 are difficult to determine because the government disguised the real costs of privatisation by throwing the capital receipts from asset sales into one year's accounts and because, at first, the extra subsidy merely went to create quasi-profits for Railtrack, the train operators and the rolling-stock companies, which, since they were all still state-owned, were simply returned to the Exchequer. However, when the franchises and Railtrack went into the private sector the annual subsidy to operators remained at nearly £2bn, much more than BR had ever received. The plan was that the subsidy would then decline, slowly at first, but rather faster in the middle and later years of the franchises, the majority of which were scheduled to end in 2003/4.

Yet the doubling of the headline figure for subsidy was not quite as generous as it looked. As a study[3] by the Railway Forum showed, notional interest on the proceeds of sales (i.e. the interest the government saved on money it would otherwise have had to borrow) reduced the headline figure by some £300m per year and tax paid by the railway companies amounted to another £100m annually. The Forum concluded that subsidy had really risen 25 per cent, rather than doubled. While there are a lot of complicating factors, too detailed to go into here, the

Forum's basic argument was that, far from benefiting from a Treasury bonanza, the railways hardly did better than when they were state-owned. And since it was planned that the subsidy would go down in subsequent years, the railways were not being treated as well as the headline figures suggested. After all, cutting subsidy had been one of the Treasury's principal aims, so it always seemed unlikely that privatisation was going to be generously funded. In fact, the Treasury merely made sure that the path to privatisation was smoothed with a one-off injection of extra money which was then expected to quickly decline.

For the first few years of privatisation the subsidy to the train companies did, indeed, decline. Labour, bound by its promise of keeping to Tory spending plans, failed to understand that privatisation had not even provided much extra funding to the railways and rashly allowed the cuts in subsidy to proceed, reducing support for the railways from £1.85bn to a predicted £1.2bn (in real terms) in the four years starting in 1997/8.

The subsidy reduction looked good on paper for the bean counters, but in practice it was unsustainable. The train companies had been fortunate in that the railways were enjoying an unprecedented boom, thanks largely to the buoyant economy. However, behind the bald statistics, several operators got into trouble quite early in the life of their franchises. In particular, the companies who ran a lot of lightly loaded trains in rural areas began to find that they could not cope with the sharply declining levels of subsidy and started going into the red. They had been caught up in the bidding war at the end of the franchising process in late 1996 and early 1997 when the City, which had initially been wary of rail privatisation, suddenly became keen to get in on the act. It was a minor railway bubble that was to prove costly, not so much to the companies themselves as to the taxpayer. For franchisees covering these areas, fares from passengers represent only a small proportion of their income, most of which is made up of subsidy from the government and the Passenger Transport Executives in the major conurbations such as West Yorkshire, Greater Manchester and Merseyside. These franchisees had gambled that they could reduce costs dramatically, but once in control, they discovered that BR had been run more efficiently than they imagined. In desperation they tried the obvious tactics of cutting back on station staff and even drivers, but to no avail. One company, First North Western, was even rebuked by the Office of

Passenger Rail Franchising for having cut back too many staff.

MTL, which had won the Merseyrail and Regional Railways North East (Northern Spirit) franchises, had to be bailed out in February 2000 with their franchises being handed over to yet another bus operator, Arriva. The rescue, of course, came at a price, and Arriva received £208m in subsidy for the year 2001/2 to run Northern Spirit, £55m more than MTL had been slated to receive. This set a pattern for the future, by which companies which got into difficulties were rewarded by the Strategic Rail Authority with extra cash. Yet, the additional support did not ensure a good service. Arriva, for example, found it had a shortage of drivers in the summer of 2001 and had to cut 100 daily services from its schedule.

Similarly, Prism, which had won four franchises, was forced to allow them to be taken over by National Express Group because of sharp losses on their two sets of rural lines, Wales & West and Cardiff Valleys. FirstGroup would have also handed in its Regional Railways North West franchise (First North Western), which was losing money, had it not been for the fact that it also ran two highly profitable ones, Great Western and Great Eastern, which the company would also have been forced to give up. Eventually, when the Strategic Rail Authority started redrawing the franchise map, FirstGroup managed to buy its way out of most of its losses for £37m.

As TAS, a business monitoring organisation that researches railway company finances, pointed out, 'It is clear that some bidders in the first round took too much risk and, as a result, heavy losses are being incurred.'[4] But it was largely the taxpayer who had to make up for the shortfall. The railway could not be allowed to stop and therefore these regional franchises had to be bailed out. According to TAS, extra subsidy paid to Arriva and NEG for rescuing these franchises amounted to '£650m by 2003/4 – just to secure existing levels of service'.[5]

This demonstrated a harsh truth for the Labour government: the train companies had taken a one-way bet. Some were highly profitable, like Stagecoach, whose South West Trains franchise, in the absence of a mechanism to reclaim the money, made a pre-tax profit of £40m in 1999/2000. Others that got into trouble had to be rescued, even though, theoretically, there was no extra funding available. In other words, the fat cats got fatter while the thin ones had to be fed at taxpayers' expense. No wonder John Prescott seethed in private and harrumphed loudly in public whenever the train companies were mentioned.

TAS found that all but nine of the twenty-five train operators had declining profits or increasing losses in the financial year 1999/2000, the year before the Hatfield crash, showing that the railway system was already in a parlous financial state before that disaster. Moreover, seven companies were making a loss, principally those working with poorly loaded trains and highly dependent on the (declining) subsidy. Anglia and Virgin CrossCountry were also loss-making, the latter because it had been dogged by performance problems as its whole fleet was reaching the end of its useful life, and was eventually replaced in 2002/3.

On top of this already parlous state of affairs came the Hatfield disaster and its aftermath, which sent the economics of the railway into free fall. The former InterCity operators were hit worst by the speed restrictions, which crippled the railway and sent swathes of passengers back on to the roads. They had achieved a 16.5 per cent increase in revenue, compared with 1999, in the four weeks prior to the Hatfield disaster but suddenly they found themselves losing a large proportion of their customers. In the month after the disaster, revenue went down by 37.5 per cent,[6] which, given that the operators had expected the growth to continue, meant that expected income had reduced by over a half. Stagecoach, which owns half of Virgin Trains, reported that instead of an expected £15m surplus from its rail operations for that year, it had now budgeted for a £25m loss. The internet selling operation thetrainline.com, owned jointly by Virgin and Stagecoach, also lost £10m.

Commuter networks did not fare so badly, broadly retaining the same number of passengers who are, mostly, a captive market. There was no shortage of anecdotal reports on the radio and TV about people simply giving up their jobs rather than face the nightmare of commuting by train; but since the economy was still booming, the south-east train operators were largely protected from the effects of the Hatfield aftermath. The regional operators lost vast numbers of passengers, but since their principal form of income is subsidy, this did not have such a large effect on their overall economic performance. Indeed, they may well have profited out of the affair because of the compensation arrangements, yet another unintended consequence of the privatised structure.

The compensation issue again highlighted the anomalies and weaknesses of the privatised structure, with some companies receiving nothing like the amount they had lost and others getting more. As a result of its contractual obligations to train operators, Railtrack was having to fork out vast sums of money – estimated at £400m – to compensate the train operators who, in turn, had to reimburse many users for part or all of their ticket price. For example, Silverlink, one of the worst-affected companies, announced in a letter to commuters on 22 March that its season ticket holders were entitled to seventy-one days of free travel and refunds because of post-Hatfield disruption. Other commuter networks which managed to get through with fewer cancellations actually did quite well because the compensation they received from Railtrack for delays and cancellations exceeded their payments to passengers. That was because Railtrack's payments to the train operators were assessed on a different basis from the compensation paid by operators to their passengers. Many of the regional operators running sparsely used lines received far more in compensation payments from Railtrack than they paid out to passengers. Other companies, particularly the former InterCity operators, lost out heavily because Railtrack's compensation payments were restricted,[7] and Virgin even prepared to sue Railtrack for loss of revenue, but in the event the threat of legal action was bought off with an extra £15m.[8] Overall, in monetary terms the operators lost £63m revenue (7 per cent) in the final three months of 2000 compared with the previous year, a financial disaster for businesses which were already in a precarious position because of the long-term loss of subsidy and which had been budgeting for a growth in income of around £140m.[9]

Most of the companies accepted the amount of compensation offered by Railtrack, or asked the Strategic Rail Authority to bail them out. However, GNER, the company owned by Sea Containers which runs the franchise for the east coast, played hardball and entered into a fantastically complicated row[10] involving Railtrack (and later Network Rail), the Rail Regulator and the SRA, which demonstrated the extent to which the contractual structure in the railway was a lawyers' paradise. GNER lost in the disputes procedure but won in front of the regulator and eventually struck a deal with Network Rail for £80m. However, train operators are indemnified against increases or reductions in track access charges as these are set by the regulator and considered to be an unacceptable business risk for a private company. The SRA, therefore, argued that it should be entitled to the money while GNER argued the money was not a reduction in track access charges but compensation for loss of projected revenue as a result of the post-Hatfield panic. In a way, it was a dispute about whether taxpayers' money, having gone from Network Rail to GNER, should then be returned to the public sector via the SRA. Eventually GNER coughed up £25m of the £80m, which suggests that the SRA, which had argued that GNER should not make a profit out of Hatfield, did have something of a case.

But it was not only Hatfield which had squeezed the finances of the train operators. Franchises are inherently strange constructs since there is no asset base on which a 'normal' rate of return can be calculated. Their success or failure is highly dependent on the ability of the bidder to predict what the revenue is likely to be in the latter part of the franchise period five or six years ahead, a calculation that is little more than educated guesswork. For the second round of franchises, the companies had a bit more information on their cost bases; but, while this information had to be made available to competing bidders, all bids were nevertheless something of a stab in the dark. On the whole companies took a more cautious approach in the second round, because of the number of operators who had previously got their fingers burnt as a result of the over-optimistic assumptions. Therefore, far from being able to cut long-term costs out of the system, the SRA found itself facing a sharp increase in the cost of the franchise programme.

Even as bids for the early franchises coming up for renewal were being sought, a series of further bail-outs were under way, including two National Express franchises, Central and Scotrail, and many operators were running under management contract arrangements – in other words the companies were given a fixed fee, with a small percentage for profit, which meant that all the risk was effectively with the SRA rather than the private companies. This, of course, meant that they had no incentive to collect revenue or boost income through promotions – they were simply subcontractors. Therefore, as the franchises came up for renewal, the Strategic Rail Authority found itself having to negotiate new deals with a very limited number of companies who were by now much more aware of the real costs of running the railway. There were a few new entrants to the bidding process, several of which were joint ventures involving European railways, but many dropped out relatively early on. The Swiss, for example, quickly pulled out when the concept of twenty-year franchises was abandoned because they thought that a shorter time-frame did not provide a basis for investment.

The trends in costs of franchising are difficult to analyse because the rules of the game kept on changing. In particular, changes to the track access charges regime in 2001 meant that the amounts being paid by the TOCs varied, with some paying more and others less, even though this had no bearing on the overall amount of subsidy from the taxpayer. There is a further change scheduled for 2006. This should have taken place in 2004 when the new revised track access charges were introduced, but, instead, the government decided that the increase agreed by the regulator would be paid direct to Network Rail for the first two years of the new regime. This means, effectively, that it is very difficult to hold the train operators to account or to analyse whether they are making efficiency gains or not. Claims by some that they now pay a premium whereas they previously required a subsidy have to be taken with a pinch of salt because of these changes. There is, to be fair, some evidence that productivity has increased in the industry. Figures produced by TAS[11] suggest that revenue per staff member had gone up from £68,000 in 1996/7 to £91,000 in 2002/3, a rise of 33 per cent, while wages had risen by half that percentage. However, much of this can be attributed to higher passenger loadings – extra passengers on the existing trains – and this rise in productivity has not been reflected in a reduction in subsidy, which means taxpayers have not benefited.

Quite the opposite. The most remarkable rises in subsidy payments have gone to Virgin for its two franchises, West Coast and CrossCountry, and Stagecoach on South West trains. Virgin is a special case. The company effectively had the SRA and the government over a barrel because it signed a deal – called Passenger Upgrade 2 (PUG2) – with Railtrack in 1997 to allow trains to travel on the section of the West Coast Main Line below Crewe at 140mph. The concept was based on having a completely new form of radio signalling called moving block that would allow trains to travel closer together as well as a total refurbishment of the track to enable trains to tilt. But – as discussed further in Chapter 15 – it was a pipedream. This type of signalling system was in development and years from being ready to be introduced on a major railway, let alone on one of the busiest in the world. Railtrack, apparently oblivious to the risks, had signed the deal.

When it became apparent that PUG2 was not deliverable and that even the lesser improvements under PUG1 to 125mph would be delayed, Virgin had the government, which by then had effectively taken over Railtrack and vested it in the hands of Network Rail, at its mercy. The company was supposed to go from receiving £200m in subsidy to provide trains on the West Coast Main Line in 1997/8 to paying £200m in premium by 2012/13 but given the failure of Railtrack/Network Rail to supply the infrastructure, Virgin could justifiably argue that its revenue was severely affected and that it therefore needed extra subsidy.

After the replacement of Railtrack by Network Rail, it was clearly up to the government through the aegis of the SRA to sort out the mess. After much negotiation, Virgin Rail Group (which is a Virgin/Stagecoach joint operation with Virgin the majority partner) accepted a deal which was couched in vague terms despite the huge sums of money involved, with the SRA's press release[12] failing to include any figures whatsoever. A Stagecoach director, Graham Eccles, a long-standing railwayman, issued a statement suggesting that Virgin would be getting between £231m and £465m of financial support during the two financial years 2002/4. In addition, the franchises were, thereafter, to be run as a management contract, which meant that the risk was with the SRA and that Virgin was paid a management fee to run them. The extra amount to be paid out was very substantial indeed since, under the original subsidy regime, the two franchises should have received around £50m for those two years. According to a calculation by Roger Ford,[13] the additional payment by the SRA over these two years was £388m – all because Virgin, a private company, had signed a contract with Railtrack, another private company. This episode exposes, yet again, the fact that the privatisation of the rail industry was nothing of the sort because the risk was never transferred to the private sector.

The personalities involved in the original contract, moreover, make the whole thing seem rather incestuous. At the time the deal was negotiated, Richard Bowker – later head of the SRA from the autumn of 2001 to September 2004 – was in charge of contract negotiations for Virgin using the legal services of Tom Winsor, who, as rail regulator between the summer of 1999 and July 2004, would have the job of policing the contract and, indeed, become involved in a fierce row with his erstwhile mate Bowker over what parts of the line upgrade should be postponed in order to save costs. Meanwhile, Jim Steer, whose consultancy Steer Davies Gleave had advised Virgin on passenger forecasts, was by then managing director (strategic planning) at the SRA.

In 2004, the SRA finally lost patience with Virgin over the CrossCountry franchise. It had only renewed this conditionally – unlike the West Coast which was to remain with Virgin – and in August the SRA issued a statement saying that the offer to run the contract to 2012 from Virgin, which was the sole initial bidder, was 'significantly too high to pass the value for money test that the SRA undertakes on behalf of taxpayers'. With the government eager to cut back on the amount of money it was putting into the railways and having announced that the SRA was being abolished, by the autumn of 2004 the CrossCountry franchise and several others appeared to be heading for a lengthy period of limbo, with two-year 'temporary' renewals becoming the norm.

Stagecoach was an odder case, and the deal it was given when its franchise was renewed seems unaccountably generous, a reflection of the SRA's inability to manage contracts and keep down costs. South West Trains was, as mentioned above, one of the most profitable franchises on the network, having been one of the early deals when OPRAF was desperate to get some contracts signed off. Therefore, it was something of a milch cow for Stagecoach despite the company's earlier cock-up over shortage of drivers. In 2000/1, for example, SWT made a very healthy pre-tax profit of £51m, a generous 11 per cent of turnover, and almost precisely what it received in subsidy from the government. This was the backdrop for the franchise renegotiations which began around that time and yet, by the time the deal was concluded a couple of years later, the subsidy to Stagecoach had increased enormously.

The story of why the deal turned out to be so generous to SWT is a convoluted one and shows the inherent difficulty of managing the franchise arrangements. SWT had been the first franchise to start operating in March 1996 and by March 2000 the SRA thought it would be a good idea to begin looking at the rebidding process. A competition was run but there was uncertainty over whether the Waterloo to Exeter line should be included. By then Alistair Morton was in charge at the SRA and hoping to let twenty-year franchises on the basis that the train operator would provide considerable investment through a mechanism called a Special Purpose Vehicle. This would be a joint venture to carry out the investment but the inherent problem with the idea was the lack of clarity about how the debt would be serviced and financed. The basic concept was that any enhancement on the line would be handed over to Railtrack – who would be a partner in the scheme, and then charge more in access charges. For their part, the operators would be compensated with additional subsidy from the SRA.

The outline deal between the SRA and Stagecoach for the twenty-year franchise was signed in March 2001, but it never got further than that. The contract involved improvement in performance, with the SRA demanding that the franchisee guarantee that only one train in fifteen would be significantly delayed, as well as a £1bn new rolling stock deal. The latter was necessary because the old trains had to be replaced for safety reasons as well as the fact they were time-expired. A further £1bn was to be spent on the infrastructure and there were to be a host of other improvements, such as station refurbishments, bus links and extra car park spaces. It was the kind of forward-looking plan for a modern railway that, if replicated across the board, would transform rail travel in Britain.

However, the fly in the ointment was that the Treasury had twigged that this type of contract was going to prove very expensive as it would have to fork out extra money for each improvement on the railway. While notionally it was a public-private contract, the bulk of the money would come from the public sector, one way or another. The private companies might borrow the cash but ultimately the extra costs would be borne, mostly, by the taxpayer and only to a very limited extent by passengers. The concept of twenty-year franchises was based on the notion of an expanding railway, in line with John Prescott's vision of an integrated transport system, with people transferring in droves from car to rail. The problem with the whole concept is that there is a fundamental law of railway economics to which there are very few exceptions: expansion, once it requires significant extra capital expenditure, can never pay for itself and therefore needs increased subsidy. As Dieter Helm, an expert on regulation, wrote, 'It was soon recognised that, in fixing the outputs, the Treasury was in effect committed to writing a blank cheque. There followed relatively quickly thereafter an attempt to quantify the consequential costs, producing the so-called 10-Year Plan for railway finance.'[14] And the 10-year plan had to be drawn up in a climate of ignorance – there was no asset register to allow an accurate assessment of the state of the infrastructure and, as we shall see, the costs of maintaining and renewing the railway were soaring. The Treasury does not do blank cheques.

The targets for growth set out in 2000 by the government in its ten-year transport plan, for a 50 per cent increase in passenger numbers and an 80 per cent rise in freight by the end of the decade, were quietly dropped. And with them went the notion of twenty-year franchises with lots of expensive enhancements. The SRA was floundering, not quite knowing what to do with the franchises which came up for renewal and got in the habit of giving short one- or two-year extensions to incumbents. And usually extra money was thrown in, since the SRA was in a weak negotiating position because the operator knew that there was no alternative. This is what happened with SWT. In July 2002, the SRA issued a press release, under the rather optimistic title '£29m benefits package secured for South West Trains passengers',[15] which outlined a pretty thin deal – a few extra rush-hour and Sunday services and driver training and maintenance depots for the 785 new Desiro coaches from Siemens, the leasing costs of which were in any case being met by the SRA. By that November, the SRA changed its mind again. This time, with the twenty-year deal consigned to the dustbin of history, the SRA said it was seeking a one-year extension to February 2004 but, in the event, it announced the following July that a three-year franchise had been signed. Major improvements such as remodelling Clapham Junction and Waterloo stations to allow for more passengers on the system were shelved, and some of the new trains were now to be used elsewhere on the network since there was not the capacity to run them.

The figures for extra financial support, though, were extraordinary. The annual subsidy of £48m was to be increased to £170m. While £55m of that was to pay the leasing costs of the new trains, the rest was for a vague set of 'performance-focused measures' and a maintenance depot. This seemed remarkably generous, an opinion that has been confirmed to the author in a private conversation with a senior Stagecoach manager. With amazing candour, he said: 'The SRA had two problems. First, the government did not know what it wanted and that meant the SRA could not be clear about its aims. Secondly, it had no good negotiators. They just did not know how to go about it. We got a very good deal and we are very pleased with it.' Indeed. One of the most profitable operators on the network, which the SRA and train operator managers knew had got a very generous deal as a result of being the first franchise, was getting extra money in various interim and short-term deals because the SRA was in a weak negotiating position and had been chopping and changing the specification. Its profits stayed very healthy, an expected £43m for 2004/5.

One twenty-year deal, Chiltern, was signed before Morton was pushed out of the SRA and replaced by Richard Bowker, who was made to

understand right from the start that ambitious plans for the expansion of
the railway were not on the agenda. Chiltern is a fairly simple service
using lines from Marylebone to Birmingham, and benefited from a
comprehensive renewal of the line, with new trains, by British Rail in the
late 1980s. However, demand had increased and the SRA was anxious to
cater for the increase. The deal was thrashed out in 2001 and became one
of the only twenty-year deals on the network. Again, there was a
considerable increase in subsidy. Under the old agreement, the support
payments were supposed to have gone down to a mere £3.5m by 2002/3.
However, the SRA had to bail out the franchise with an extra £7.5m for
the two years 2000–2 because, it argued, a number of improvements,
originally scheduled for the twenty-year franchise, had been brought
forward. Under the deal which eventually began in March 2002, M 40
Trains (which is part of the John Laing group) will receive £150m in
subsidy in the first eight years.

Many other franchises had got into financial difficulties. By the end of
2003 nine of the franchises had effectively failed and been allowed to
continue on some kind of cost-plus basis. As the House of Commons
Transport Committee put it succinctly, 'Nearly a third of the franchises
were no longer expected to function in the entrepreneurial, risk-taking
way that was one of the fundamental justifications for private sector
involvement in running train services but simply to function as fee-paid
agents of the SRA. This indicates the extent of the present malaise'.[16]

The poor negotiating skills of the SRA were compounded by the fact
that while all these franchise operators were coming to its offices begging
for more cash, the SRA never seems to have contemplated deploying the
ultimate weapon in its armoury: the idea of simply allowing a train
operator to go bust or simply hand the keys back, forfeiting the bond of
10 per cent of turnover that operators have to lodge on taking up their
franchise. In other words, the risk does not seem to have been transferred
to the private sector, one of the key benefits, it was claimed at the time of
privatisation, of the franchise system. Whether this was a deliberate
policy decision, borne of the fear that taking back a franchise would
cause upheaval, result in higher costs anyway, and make private
companies reluctant to bid for franchises, or whether it was simply
another feature of the lack of commercial nous at the SRA was unclear.
Either way, it meant that the costs of franchising soared.

The Commons Transport Committee in its *Future of the Railway*[17] report in April 2004 was particularly critical of the SRA's decision to shell out an extra £58m to Connex, which had clearly formed an over-optimistic view of revenue projections and possible cost reductions when it had won the franchise for South East Trains. The committee concluded: 'In our view, the essence of private sector involvement is that the private sector pays if it gets its sums wrong. It is outrageous that such astonishingly large sums of taxpayers' money have been used to prop up palpably failing businesses.'[18]

In fact, the SRA did finally act on Connex, which became the only franchise that it took back under direct control. Connex had always been a poor-performing franchise on a difficult railway built on the cheap by the London, Chatham and Dover and the South Eastern Railways but also badly run by Connex, which was intent on making as much money as possible out of it for the least investment. While the arrival of a highly competent manager, Olivier Brousse, had resulted in some improvements, the company had got into financial difficulty and was rescued in December 2002 by a controversial 'one-off' payment of £58m on top of its £55m annual subsidy in return for cutting back the end of the franchise from 2011 to 2006. The SRA's chief operating officer, Nick Newton, claimed 'this package has short and long term benefits for passengers'.[19] Well, clearly these benefits failed to materialise and the company came back for more a year later – reportedly £200m. This time the SRA, which was concerned about the basis of the figures it had been presented with, decided enough was enough.

In June 2003, Richard Bowker called in the Connex executives and told them that the game was up. He said that he was not satisfied that the company had adhered to the terms of the agreement when the £58m bail-out had been agreed. In particular, Connex had not delivered the required improvements which were a precondition for any future increase in subsidy – he was concerned about what he called the lack of 'provision of short-term financial stability'. Bowker also suggested that some of this money had leaked back to the parent company: 'We made it an absolutely explicit requirement that the money cannot be moved outside the operating company, that there can be no leakage of funds whatsoever'.[20] Connex was given six months' notice and the contract was actually terminated in November 2003, although, once again, financial details were not forthcoming.

South East Trains thus became the first franchise to be run directly by the Strategic Rail Authority – in effect it was renationalised and run by a management team installed through a specially created company. The demise of Connex, incidentally, rescued the SRA from another cock-up. It had originally attempted to specify the additional domestic Kent services that would be run on the new high-speed Channel Tunnel Rail Link without amending the existing Connex services, partly because this would have been contractually complicated. Now, it was able to relaunch the bidding process on the basis of an Integrated Kent Franchise for which, however, it had not specified a new timetable, something it should have done in the first place.

Despite pressure from backbench Labour MPs and the unions, the SRA refused to countenance a long-term in-house franchise. The logic seems strange. The government argues that it likes to apply the 'what works' principle but clearly the South East Trains franchise has worked effectively since, in September 2004, the SRA announced in its regular performance figures that there had been a 2 per cent reduction in delayed trains. However, ministers insisted it should not remain in the public sector, even though it would have provided a useful comparator for costs on other franchises.[21] Ministers were so embarrassed about the success of South East Trains that they prevented the SRA from publicising the good performance of the franchise. As *The Times* reported, 'The SRA is under pressure from the Government not to publicise its success in operating the franchise. Ministers fear that they would face demands to re-nationalise all train companies if it became widely known that SET was performing well in the public sector.'[22]

Given all this, far from being able to reduce subsidy, the SRA increased it at every negotiation, sometimes sharply, for benefits which were unclear. By 2003/4 the annual subsidy to the train operators had crept back up to the £2bn mark. This was the total at the time of privatisation after it had been doubled to smooth the passage into the private sector, and it was supposed to have declined gradually to £800m by the end of 2002/3. Clearly, franchising, as an effective mechanism for driving down costs and subsidy from taxpayers, had failed lamentably.

Yet, ironically, money was apparently the sole factor driving refranchising decisions. However well a company had performed it did not get any preferential treatment when the franchise term ended. Alistair Darling, in setting out the results of the rail review in July 2004, announced that this would change, with performance now being taken into account, but that raises another difficulty with the franchise process: would not an incumbent whose performance was ostensibly good by any reasonable criteria then be able to milk the system by bidding higher?

The awarding of the new franchises – an opaque process carried out in secret by the SRA on the basis that commercial confidentiality precludes an open publication of the bids – involved an incomprehensible game of musical chairs in which companies were removed from one franchise area only to be allocated another one. Thus Arriva lost Merseyrail but gained the new Welsh franchise; FirstGroup lost Anglia, but was awarded Thames and Scotrail; and Govia lost Thames but won SouthCentral.

The franchise system was originally presented as a cheap way of passing on responsibility for a bundle of services to a private company. But as the refranchising process unfolded, it became obvious that it was merely a subcontracting operation to buy specific services from the private companies and that any additional requirement would have to be paid for. Moreover, despite the promises made at privatisation, no one knows how much it costs to run a particular service. Therefore the SRA is pretty much guessing when it tries to assess the cost of these extra items. As a former BR man, and now a consultant to operators, put it, 'I know that bidding is supposed to ensure that the SRA pays the minimum, but what happens is that the bidder puts in an attractive preliminary offer, gets granted preferred bidder status and then really squeezes Whitehall [through the SRA] when it comes to extras it wants. So the operator might be running at a loss on the basic subsidy, but gets all the losses back on extras. Franchise people are in a strong position and that position would be much better balanced towards Whitehall by calculating bids on an individual line-by-line or service-by-service basis.'[23]

Although that would be a difficult enterprise, he thinks it is feasible and points out that under nationalisation, when Barbara Castle was transport minister in the late 1960s, 'each line was costed and Whitehall would have a simple choice: it could either buy that service at that price or not'. Such an arrangement would encourage franchisees to ensure that subsidy they received was minimal.

In fact, under the current structure, the situation is quite the opposite and the process is very opaque. Bids are not published and nor is a priced assessment of what each service costs. Therefore, when additional payments are made, as in the examples of Chiltern and SWT mentioned above, but also in many other instances too numerous to detail here, it is very unclear whether the SRA, and therefore the taxpayer, is obtaining value for money. Oddly enough, the Transport Act 1985, which concerns bus deregulation, requires the local authorities to publish information about the range of bids and an explanation if the lowest one is not accepted. Yet the whole process by which the SRA determines how best to spend £2bn of taxpayers' money remains completely hidden.

According to an analysis by the *Evening Standard* in early 2005,[24] the train operators were expected to make profits totalling £288m during that financial year, an increase of 20 per cent on the previous year. National Express, for example, the largest operator with eight franchises, announced the following month that its profits had increased by 76 per cent to £58.5m[25]. The improvement was attributed to a 5 per cent increase in passenger numbers and the replacement of the loss-making ScotRail franchise with the new, stupidly named One franchise which operates services out of Liverpool Street.

The entire franchising operation has proved to be vastly expensive and its workings have had to be altered several times in the light of circumstances; moreover, its purpose still remains unclear. The process creates great uncertainty and instability in an industry where long-term thinking is needed. Chris Garnett, the head of GNER, for example, complains that he has spent most of the length of the franchise having to work on bids for extensions or reletting. He has long pressed to have a ten-year franchise which would allow train operators to make some investments and his efforts finally bore fruit in March 2005 when GNER's parent company, Sea Containers, was finally awarded a new ten-year deal. In a governmental attempt to reverse the trend of ever more expensive franchise deals, GNER has committed itself to paying a staggering £1.3bn[26] in premium payments, including, in the final year of the franchise, 2014/15, nearly £400m. After the first four years, the risk is shared with the Department, which will take 80 per cent of any major shortfall in revenue, but also benefit from any excess profits. The deal is incredibly ambitious, based on GNER expecting passenger revenue to continue growing at 8.7 per cent, the rate achieved in recent years, although Garnett is confident that target can be met. This will undoubtedly require some steep rises in ticket prices but the company has not revealed what they might be. If this is the case, then the travelling public will be made to pay for the high cost of the railway. Far from attracting people onto the railway to get them off the roads, the government will be deterring them from using the trains by effectively taxing rail passengers.

The GNER deal marks yet another new departure in franchise policy but experience of the various different approaches and time frames adopted since the creation of the franchise system in 1996 suggests that there is no ideal solution. Allowing companies very long franchises might allow them to invest, but it could also result in inferior operators being allowed to run parts of the network for extended periods; on the other hand, short franchises create a feeling of uncertainty. Another factor is that, since franchise bids are based on estimates of future revenue, the longer the franchise, the greater the margin for error and, therefore, the higher potential operators are likely to bid as they seek to minimise their risk. In a sense, this has happened already. The universal increase in franchise payments in the second round suggests that operators have got canny and are simply putting in higher bids because they want to insulate themselves against any losses should revenue suddenly fall. Again, on the other hand, simply letting franchises without any transfer of revenue risk makes little sense as the operators will have no incentive to boost usage and income. In fact, the SRA has somewhat compromised on this issue by taking back part of the risk – in future all new franchises will incorporate an arrangement similar to the GNER one by which excess profits or losses will be evened out, with the SRA getting a cut if profits exceed expectations and providing partial compensation if there are losses.

Richard Bowker, the former head of the SRA, says a franchise is simply a contract between the state and the operator to provide a service. He admitted early on in his tenure in March 2002 that the system had been failing and later said: 'The franchising model created at privatisation has proved unable to withstand the exogenous market shocks experienced in the past few years. Many of the first round of passenger franchises were let on the basis of bids that have subsequently proved to be unsustainable.'[27] Yet, the welcome changes he introduced, such as tighter specifications and a profit sharing arrangement, failed to address the fundamental question on the purpose of franchises. Indeed, the experience of franchising so far suggests that it has brought few benefits, apart from a bit of private sector expertise, and cost an awful lot of money. The success of South East Trains certainly raises the issue of whether a wholly public sector solution, or at least a mixed economy of private and public, would be a better option, but the Labour government has set its face against that. The fundamental question – 'what is a franchise for?' – has never been answered.

CHAPTER 14

Why is the railway so expensive? (2) The cost of trains

When the railway was privatised, train operating companies were granted short-term franchises using rolling stock that had a much longer life, thus necessitating the creation of rolling-stock companies (roscos) which inherited all passenger trains from BR. As outlined in Chapter 3, the three roscos (Angel, Eversholt, later called HSBC, and Porterbrook), which owned all 11,260 coaches and locomotives, were sold off cheaply to the private sector then quickly resold, making huge windfall profits for the original purchasers rather than the public which originally owned the trains. All three have ended up belonging to major banks.

The roscos have spent over £4bn investing in new rolling stock in the first decade of privatisation, and this apparently high rate of investment has led the roscos to present themselves as the one untarnished success story of privatisation. However, while there are, indeed, plenty of new trains whizzing round the network, they have come at a high price for passengers, and ultimately taxpayers, which raises doubts about whether the system has been the fantastic achievement that the roscos would have us believe – doubts that have now reached the higher echelons of the Labour government.

Right from the beginning, the policy of creating roscos which leased out trains was recognised as more expensive than the old system whereby BR owned everything. To create the system in 1992, the government dropped its policy of allowing BR to lease only when this represented at least as good value for money as borrowing from the government[1] – a recognition that this would probably not be the case. The model adopted by the Tory government in the early stages of privatisation was intended to create an entirely free market for rolling stock, an expectation that has proved as fanciful as most of the other claims made for privatisation. This model has allowed the three roscos to make a very good rate of return on their investment and has made the leasing price of some older models of train very high, particularly given that their value was effectively written off under BR. It has contributed towards the creation of a complex, high-cost railway which, ironically, is far less flexible than the one it replaced.

The skewing of the valuations of the roscos in order to generate profits was demonstrated right from the beginning, when, pre-privatisation, the three companies, then still part of BR, made a profit of £332m on annual turnover of £707m. Given the roscos were sold for £1.8bn two years later, this was a very healthy rate of return on capital for a low-risk business – about 15 per cent.

There were two reasons for this high profit margin. First, the whole stock had originally been valued at £2bn[2] but this would not have given an adequate rate of return to the private companies and therefore the notional value on which the lease prices were determined was increased to £3.5bn (though the initial sale of the roscos netted half that amount). However, attracting the private sector in this way has had a lasting impact on the economics of the railway because the *annual* cost of rolling stock was increased by £400m as a result. Today, the roscos are paid over £1bn per year on which they make approximately £150m profit annually. This excessive cost of leasing trains has had to be met through higher payments to franchisees which in turn come from the pockets of passengers or taxpayers, distorting the economics of the railway and making rail travel more expensive relative to road transport.

Secondly, the pricing structure created at privatisation, called indifference pricing, deliberately set the cost of older trains at a high level in order to encourage investment in new stock. This system was designed to make older trains cost more than they would have had the leasing charges simply been based on their depreciated value. This financial structure generated enormous surpluses, as was the intention, but these were supposed to be reinvested in the railways. However, the government had not established a mechanism to ensure this money stayed in the railway industry. So although the leasing charges were set at a level that ensured that they generated sufficient cash for future investment, there was no requirement on the companies to use that money for new stock. Even Richard Bowker, the former head of the SRA and a stout defender of the leasing system, is critical of how expensive older trains are to rent. He wrote: 'Many would argue that since the taxpayer had purchased the trains made available to the roscos at privatisation, their cost was effectively a sunk cost. It was therefore wrong to inflate their theoretical value simply to generate a theoretical lease rental from the TOC.'[3]

Of course, before the sale of the roscos the high profits remained in the public sector but similar returns continued to be obtained in subsequent years after they were sold off. Indeed, once privatised, and resold, the roscos became tremendous generators of profit for their new owners. They provided virtually a licence to print money, especially as it was an almost risk-free business; in order to make the roscos saleable, the government had guaranteed 80 per cent of the income from the initial leases, which had between four and eight years to run at the time of the sale. Between 1996 and 2002 the roscos, while apparently taking minimal risks, amassed pre-tax profits of £1.8bn,[4] precisely the amount obtained from their sale at privatisation in 1996.

One simplistic, but not ridiculous, way of looking at the risk is to accept that trains have a thirty-year life. Therefore, 3 per cent of them become redundant every year. Unless the requirement for trains suddenly falls dramatically, an unlikely event, the rolling-stock companies, as a whole, face very little risk. Sure, there is some rigidity, in that not all the rolling stock is interchangeable, but the overall exposure for the companies is very slight and it was a fundamental mistake to have privatised that risk.

While the annual net profit margins on turnover are of the order of 15 per cent, on some stocks they are much greater. To take just one example, it is difficult to see any justification for HSBC charging £121,117 (plus VAT) annually for a sixty-seven-year-old two-car Tube train on the Isle of Wight. These trains, which first saw service in 1938, when Neville Chamberlain popped over to Munich, had long since been written off by London Transport and the charge, which HSBC claims is 'a good deal', does not even cover maintenance, which is carried out by the train operator. Thus, for the six sets of two-car coaches needed to run the Isle of Wight service, Stagecoach, the train operator, is shelling out £850,000. It is no wonder that each passenger on the short 8.5-mile railway is subsidised by more than £3. While, privately, Stagecoach executives reckon the charge is an outrage, there is nothing they can do about it because there is no alternative source of supply; and since the money comes from the government there is little incentive for Stagecoach to dispute it.

The Isle of Wight story is a neat illustration of the way in which the complex structure of the industry, which means that the payments to HSBC come from the taxpayer only indirectly, obfuscates a scandalous situation. Since the roscos are entirely unregulated there is nothing to stop the owners from taking enormous surpluses out of the industry or simply rewarding their shareholders with dizzyingly large dividends. The roscos argue that their rates of return on capital are much lower, but, while that is true, they are still high for an investment that carries little risk. The SRA was supposed to sanction such deals but clearly it proved to be toothless in the face of what is basically a form of extortion by a monopoly supplier.

The lack of regulation had been designed into this part of the system: unlike the rest of the privatised rail industry, the roscos were deliberately not subjected to any regulation, apart, of course, from standard competition law. As an analysis of the roscos put it, 'the government consciously sought to facilitate the sale of the roscos, by minimising regulatory burdens and transferring risk wherever possible to the principal recipients of public subsidy, the train operating companies or, where this was not possible, providing state guarantees and indemnities to the roscos directly'.[5] Soon after it was elected, Labour considered regulating the roscos and asked the regulator, John Swift, to examine the issue. In 1998 he reported back saying that regulation might reduce the amount of investment and would be unworkable, although he did accept that the roscos potentially had the ability to control the market: 'I entirely reject the proposition that the roscos do not have, and may not be expected to have, market power,'[6] he concluded. Instead a code of practice was drawn up, which, though voluntary, was the subject of keen interest by the regulator. It covered such matters as fairness, flexibility, pricing and ensuring that cascades – transfers of stock – could take place between customers. The intention was to prevent the roscos from abusing their market power but in practice this has proved difficult because of the lack of new entrants into the market and the lack of flexibility, given that there is very little spare rolling stock.

The problem is that the train operators are in a weak and vulnerable position when negotiating with the roscos. They need both the trains and the maintenance, and there is rarely an alternative. Here, for example, is what FirstGroup, which runs the trains between London and the West Country, had to say: 'This oligopoly is able to maintain high lease rentals on existing stock without taking any risk on improving passenger facilities, running and maintenance costs and performance. The SRA should either seek to bring the roscos into the rail regulatory framework, as with major asset owners in other utilities, or open up competition. This would bring down prices.'[7]

Because the operators are in such a disadvantaged position, they rarely dare to criticise the roscos. While, technically, the operators can complain to the regulator, the process is convoluted and expensive, and therefore unlikely to be worthwhile. Take the example of GNER and its refurbished trains. When the company took over the franchise in 1996, it got Angel Trains to spend £70,000 on each of the coaches on its High Speed Trains to bring them up to standard. The rosco insisted that it would have to recover the cost, through higher leasing charges, by the end of the franchise, 2003, in case another franchisee did not believe the refurbishment was required. Ignoring the fact that it would be impossible to return the coaches to their unimproved state, GNER agreed, but when the franchise was extended for a couple of years after 2003, it continued paying the same charge even though the improvements were effectively paid for by then. According to a GNER manager, 'we thought of having a big row and challenging them over it, but it did not seem worthwhile for just a couple of years, especially as it only involved ten trains. They have us over a barrel – there are not enough HSTs available elsewhere, so why drop the price.'[8]

While the aim of the pricing model was to encourage operators to buy new stock, the effect has been to make some trains appear very expensive in relation to their original cost. The roscos have been reluctant to release information about the cost of their leases, but since most of the money to pay for them is coming from the state and it is already a very limited and flawed market, there is no sound reason for hiding behind 'commercial confidentiality'. The SRA's acceptance of the need for confidentiality undermines not only the principle that taxpayers' money should be spent in a transparent fashion but also the attempt to create a market, since buyers and sellers need such information in order to operate an effective one. This is another of the nonsenses that result from the government trying to play at capitalism on the railways.

Some information can be gleaned from secondary sources or the occasional leak. For example, the Passenger Transport Executives in the north of England have complained that a two-coach Pacer costs £144,000 to rent every year. Of that, £48,000 is the capital cost and £96,000 is for the heavy maintenance, both of which seem very high. The operators have no choice because leasing other, newer trains, say Turbostar class 170s, would cost £180,000 per year, a figure which would be doubled with maintenance costs. The Department for Transport would never sanction such a deal. Moreover, there are no spare Pacers available from either of the two roscos, Angel and Porterbrook, which have diesel trains.[9]

Yet Pacers are ghastly little trains which have bus-type bodies on a cheap, bumpy freight bogie and are over twenty years old. They cost only £350,000 to build, a sum that would by now have been written down to nothing under BR. Yet, the roscos continue to make considerable profits out of them, making it far more expensive to run services on lesser-used lines where, in the interests of economy, it is best to use rolling stock that has little remaining value. This profiteering has more wide-reaching strategic implications: it could cause little-used feeder lines to be deemed too uneconomic to retain, when this might not have been the case were a fairer charge to be levied. According to the SRA's strategy document on branch lines, the average annual cost per vehicle on these lines is a staggering £100,000.[10]

These high prices make adding new coaches to expand capacity on busy lines completely uneconomic. A three-coach 158 Sprinter train, the workhorse of many regional lines, was quoted as costing £630,000 per year by the Government Office for the South West in its Bristol/Bath to South Coast Study in February 2004.[11] Yet the train only cost £1m (at 2004 prices) to build.[12]

As we saw in Chapter 3, the roscos were sold off cheaply partly because no one in the City really understood how the rail industry worked and therefore there were very few bidders in the original sale. Once the City noted just how much surplus cash the roscos were generating they were quickly resold. While the resale price was more expensive, it still allowed scope for the new owners to earn considerable profits. However, the process entrenched higher costs in the industry. The roscos resist any attempt to beat down prices, arguing that this would be unlawful interference by government in the affairs of private companies, which bought the companies on the basis that existing policies in relation to rolling stock charges would remain in place. As one senior manager in a rosco put it, 'The prices may look high in relation to the original cost of the vehicle, but we bought the company on the basis that those prices would continue.'[13]

Therefore, on the question of the Pacers, the roscos say they have no choice but to levy this charge because that was the expected income taken into account when the company was bought. The Pacers are likely to last until 2012 and the roscos expect the level of payment to remain the same throughout that period. Thereafter, if the Pacers remain in use for another four or five years after 2012, the annual capital lease would be cheaper, say £30,000,[14] because the roscos would have got their money back; though, of course, the maintenance is likely to go up given the age of the trains. The roscos also justify their high charges with the claim that there is a considerable risk: namely that an existing operator – or more likely a new one after a franchise change – will decide to replace its fleet before the existing one has become life-expired, leaving them with valuable trains for which they have no customers. For the most part, however, this will never happen. The existing train service is likely to remain, more or less, the same. Moreover, this risk is an entirely political one. The Strategic Rail Authority, or its successor, has the power to veto any leasing arrangement between an operator and a rosco, so an operator wanting to change its train fleet would need SRA permission.

The payments to the roscos consist of two parts: the charge on the capital value of the trains, which as we have seen was artificially raised, and the fee for the heavy maintenance – the regular major overhauls and refurbishment of stock – which is the responsibility of the rosco. (Light maintenance, the day-to-day servicing, is the responsibility of the train operators.) Here, too, there has been an opportunity for the roscos to make a considerable profit. In 2002/3, for example, Porterbrook, the only company that separates out the two charges in its accounts, received £112 million for heavy maintenance services, of which £32 million was profit.

There have, too, been questions about the quality of the maintenance which is all subcontracted out by the roscos, who have no heavy maintenance facilities of their own. This arrangement involves yet another interface and another opportunity for profit to be taken out of the industry. Go Ahead claim that the time between major overhauls on their stock on the SouthCentral franchise had been increased from 300,000 to 450,000 miles. The company's director of engineering, David Sawyer, told *File on 4*: 'Because the arrangements that were set up meant that TOCs were required to pay less and less each year as a heavy maintenance charge, the roscos had every pressure to reduce the costs whilst not having any requirement to make the vehicles perform. Inevitably roscos have reacted to that regime by continually reducing specifications and prices paid to overhaulers'.[15] A company statement to the same programme said: 'Handing over heavy maintenance to the roscos was a fundamental mistake. It has produced a culture of heavy maintenance that is minimum cost, minimum specification and minimum reliability.'

The profitability of the roscos is also boosted by the generous tax breaks which they are able to claim – one reason why all three roscos are now owned by banks. Investment in trains is subject to tax relief, provided there are profits elsewhere in the company against which they can be offset. These capital allowances, designed to encourage investment, allow the cost of capital assets to be set against taxable profits at 25 per cent per year on railway assets. Effectively, they mean that, over a twenty-year period, the company can recover the entire cost of the asset by offsetting it against tax.

Moreover, the lease payments themselves will be treated as a revenue expense allowable against the profits of the train operating company – so that also offsets corporation tax. The banks which own the rolling-stock companies can also use internal transfers between their various subsidiaries to make them look more or less profitable and ensure that tax payments are minimised. The most recent estimate of the profitability of roscos suggested that they have made an average of £163m in dividend payments annually since their creation.[16] According to the published accounts, HSBC Rail and Angel Trains both made £55m profit after tax on their train rentals in 2002/3. Porterbrook shows up as making only £700,000 profit in its 2002/3 accounts, but that does not include £85m paid to its parent company, Abbey National, in interest, on money borrowed at the very high rate of 10.8 per cent. Since this is nearly three times the prevailing cost of borrowing, it is in effect a hidden transfer of profit from one company to another. As an accountant Richard Murphy, told the *File on 4* programme, 'it's a reasonable interpretation that someone somewhere else in the Abbey National Group is making a lot of money which is being paid out of Porterbrook leasing'.[17]

The government's stated reason for privatising the roscos was that it would free up investment in rolling stock, which had been restricted by the usual limits on public sector spending. Initially, though, the privatisation caused a three-year gap between 1994 and 1996 during which no trains were ordered because of the uncertainties about the future of the industry. Therefore, once the privatisation was completed, there was a rush to order trains. The first order came soon after privatisation, when Chiltern signed up for what eventually became thirty vehicles for £25m. Other orders quickly followed in what proved to be a bonanza for the manufacturers. Not only did the backlog created by the hiatus have to be cleared, there were also some franchises that had been granted for more than the standard seven years on the basis that new trains would be obtained.

The roscos claim that there was an unprecedented level of investment. For example, John Prideaux, the first chairman of Angel Trains, reckoned that coaches were ordered in the first three years of privatisation at nearly double the rate of BR's purchases in its last days.[18] However, an analysis of the rates of new rolling-stock purchase before and after privatisation suggests that around 4,500 coaches have been bought in the first ten years since the railway started to be broken up for privatisation, taking into account the hiatus during which no trains were ordered. In the last decade of British Rail, the total was around 4,000 so there has been no significant rate of increase.[19] This is borne out by the age of the stock. At privatisation in 1996/7, the average age of the rolling stock was sixteen years, exactly the same at the beginning of 2005,[20] though in 2001/2 this had increased to twenty years as a result of the hiatus in orders in the mid-1990s. Therefore, contrary to the suggestions of ministers, privatisation did not bring about increased investment in rolling stock. Moreover, while in theory it did get the expenditure off the government's balance sheet, another of the stated aims, in practice much of that money popped up elsewhere in the accounts. The increased leasing charges resulting from the higher cost of money to the private sector and the passing on of risk to the roscos mean that operators require higher subsidies. And, of course, the tax breaks mentioned above also come out of the Treasury's coffers.

It did not require a full-scale privatisation to shift expenditure on new trains off the balance sheet, if that had been the government's only aim. Trains are a clear, discrete product that can easily be leased, as is commonplace with many other forms of transport, ranging from company cars to Boeing 747s. It is a simple matter to work out a rate of return and to show a clear investment case for the suppliers. In opposition even John Prescott had suggested that railway coaches could be leased from private companies. Indeed, London Underground, while remaining in the public sector, leased its new trains for the Northern Line from the manufacturers, Alstom, under a private-finance-initiative deal which meant that the company was responsible for ensuring that sufficient trains were available for every scheduled service.

The claims that rolling-stock orders increased as a result of privatisation are therefore spurious. The other advantage of rolling-stock privatisation emphasised by its supporters is that it has driven down the cost of new trains. Indeed, this appears to be true, with most estimates suggesting that trains are 30 per cent cheaper than they were before. However, some of this may be due to new technology or the advantages of big orders such as the Mark 1 replacement stock. In addition, the reduction in price may be a function not so much of privatisation as of the fact that there was for a time, once the hiatus had ended, a period of stable long-term demand.[21] In any case, it would seem, given the extra money paid to franchisees who ordered new trains, and the high profits of the rolling-stock companies, that those reductions were not necessarily passed on to the train operators, let alone passengers.

Because of the fragmentation and lack of coordination, one of the cardinal errors of the British Rail era continued into the privatised railway: far too many train types were ordered and little effort was made to ensure that they could be used widely across the network, thus reducing any hope of developing a genuine market in rolling stock across the industry. There were many new classes of train introduced onto the network and because of the increased safety requirements, notably the need to have a safety case for every type of train and even any modifications, it took a long time to put the trains into service. Despite the sudden wellspring of orders, literally hundreds of fully built trains were stuck in sidings for several months – even, in some cases, for years.

Most of these delays were caused by the failure of the manufacturers to get their new designs through Railtrack's extremely onerous safety-case procedures. Railtrack's principal fear was electrical interference. There was evidence after the introduction of the cross-Channel Eurostar train that rogue electrical currents emanating from them could affect the track circuits that indicate the location of a train to signallers. The main concern was that such currents could cause a red signal to go green, as had happened (because of a wiring error) in the 1988 Clapham disaster. Adding to the problem was Railtrack's lack of knowledge of what types of track circuits were operating on various parts of the network.

A second problem was Railtrack's lack of clarity about what standards the trains needed to comply with. When manufacturers asked Railtrack about the maximum possible dimensions of their trains, not only was the infrastructure company unable to provide that information, but it even asked to be paid for providing information about the precise size of its own tunnels and platforms. To play safe, manufacturers built trains that were slightly smaller – a fact that has not gone unnoticed by passengers who complain of the lack of room. Moreover, with space at such a premium, facilities for extra luggage and, in particular, bicycles, have disappeared.

Railtrack had no incentive to let the new trains onto the track, so it pursued a policy of simply saying 'prove your train is safe', which is virtually impossible. As a result, the new trains sat in sidings or in factory yards while the manufacturers scrabbled about trying to pass the safety-case procedure. Here again, much of the problem had its roots in the way the industry had been structured after privatisation. Although the issue of electromagnetic interference clearly had to be considered, there was an element of overreaction on the part of Railtrack, whose safety and standards directorate had taken over the setting of standards upon the demise of BR (as explained in Chapter 12). During this process, the tolerances were raised in the belief that there should be a gradual and continuous rise in safety standards on the railway.

However, as one rail engineer put it, 'This can lead to ridiculous situations. For example, if the railway has been built to ensure there is a 30mm gap between platforms and trains, then there is nothing to be gained by increasing that to 50mm. Yet that is what happened with electrical interference. They raised the tolerances even though there has never been an accident caused by this type of electrical interference'.[22] In fact, even if there were interference, it would be intermittent, with signals returning to red very quickly.

Nevertheless, this tiny perceived risk led to massive delays, sometimes of up to two years, in the introduction of the new rolling stock. For example, Connex South Eastern was supposed to start introducing new trains by April 1999 but did not manage to do so until two years later. The London, Tilbury and Southend services out of Fenchurch Street were being operated by thirty-five-year-old trains well into 2001 while the whole new fleet, which should have been introduced in 1999, was standing idle. The manufacturers were not totally blameless in this process. They should have taken more care to ensure that the safety case procedures had been addressed and, moreover, many of their new trains, such as those for Fenchurch Street and the 175s for First North Western, were so unreliable that operators had to send entire fleets back for design changes.

There was, as well, a deep irony about these delays. The trains that were to be replaced were far more dangerous than the new ones that were sitting in the sidings. Not only were they much less crashworthy, as was demonstrated in accidents like the Cowden head-on collision where five died in 1994 and the Cannon Street buffer crash which killed two in 1991, but they actually emitted much higher levels of electrical interference than the new trains. They were only allowed to remain in use because of 'grandfather rights', the dispensation given to older trains without which the whole railway system would have ground to a halt.

This was another case where the needs of the railway and its passengers were not considered in a coherent way, nor was risk assessed sensibly. It could again be described as the 'absence of a Fat Controller' syndrome. For railways to be successful it is axiomatic that their various interdependent components need to be closely integrated and that they need to have clear leadership from the top to resolve the differing interests of the various components that make up the network. In the days of BR this was provided by the chairman who, backed by the board, was able to make decisions that might have impacted adversely on some departments but, overall, would benefit the travelling public. In this instance, the chairman would have been able to assess the relevant risk and insist that the new trains be introduced, taking the responsibility onto himself, although nowadays that may be more difficult given the more onerous safety regime. The fragmented structure of the railway means that no one can now take such decisions; this inevitably leads to a far more cautious approach, whatever the objective assessment of the risks involved.

The delays over introducing new trains even prompted an inquiry by the National Audit Office, which pointed out that the industry's performance in bringing new trains into service was appalling: 'Of the fifteen train operating companies that had introduced new trains at the time of our survey in spring 2003, twelve had not brought their vehicles into service by the due dates set in the manufacturing contracts.'[23] Delays had ranged from one to thirty months, the average being seven. Moreover, the new trains, which are fitted with sophisticated computer equipment and other new technology, have often proved less reliable than the older ones they have replaced. Partly this was down to the complexity of the task of bringing new trains on to the track. The NAO found that 'there is a lack of strategic direction or design of the process by a single body with, at least, nine organisations and 60 key stages involved'.[24]

The NAO also highlighted the inherent weakness of the different contracts between the SRA, train operators, the manufacturers and the roscos. It pointed out that only on two occasions were the train operators required to pay compensation for the delays in bringing new trains into service, even though this had been a commitment in their original franchise agreements. The agreements are couched in vague terms such as ensuring the operators make 'reasonable' or 'best' endeavours to bring the new coaches into use which have no clear meaning in law.

This highlights a wider point. The architects of privatisation argue that having clear contractual relationships between the various parties in the rail industry ought to ensure that the right outputs are delivered. A constant refrain in speeches by the former rail regulator, Tom Winsor, was that if the right agreements were brokered and enforced between parties, then the privatised railway would function smoothly. However, it is clear from examples like this that these contracts are largely unenforceable, either because of the understandable reluctance of the parties to become embroiled in legal disputes with monopoly suppliers or because, despite Winsor's best efforts, the wording of the contracts remained open to different interpretations. The costs would be huge, only the lawyers would benefit and the lengthy court hearings would permanently damage relationships between the TOCs and the roscos on whom they depend.

The NAO, which always uses measured language as it is only allowed to criticise the effects of policy, rather than policies themselves, makes it clear that the structure of the industry is to blame for the delays and failure of coordination: 'There is a lack of organisational coherence within the railway industry; not all of the key public and private sector parties involved have common interests in, or have been sufficiently incentivised for, the smooth introduction of new trains'.[25] The roscos are yet another example of the damaging effects of the fragmentation of the industry which has created scores of fiefdoms, each with its own corporate objectives and self-interests that often conflict with what is best for the rail network as a whole and its passengers.

One example of this in relation to rolling stock is the difficulty of transferring trains from one region to another. BR used to have a policy of 'cascading' rolling stock around the network as it got older, so that the busiest lines tended to have the best rolling stock. Now it is simply too complicated to do this. The hidden cost of this rigidity became apparent when Virgin begun to introduce its new Pendolino trains, displacing a lot of locomotives and 150 Mark 3 carriages that were not life-expired and which are generally reckoned, within the industry, to be the best coaches ever produced by BR or subsequently.

There are plenty of potential alternative uses for the Mark 3s. They could be used on branch lines, though the cost of locomotive haulage might be prohibitive; they could certainly be used on secondary inter-city-type routes, such as King's Cross–Hull, the Midland mainline services out of St Pancras, TransPennine or Waterloo–Exeter, 'all of which', as Alan Williams pointed out in *Modern Railways*, 'are currently worked by often unsuitable, and even more often, overcrowded'[26] coaches. In turn these displaced trains could be used to replace the ghastly Pacers, the worst carriages on the network. However, as Williams also pointed out, 'a cascade on such a scale, involving so many parties and the agreements that bind them in today's franchised railway, would be an astonishing feat'[27] and, in truth, impossible under the current structure. Some of these Mark 3s will be found new homes, but because of the rigidities of the current structure 'a mass bonfire' of many of the best coaches on the system appears inevitable, while inferior stock is allowed to continue running. Keeping stock on standby for busy times or mothballing it is much more difficult these days because the roscos operate on long-term leases. As a result a couple of small companies have emerged offering spot hire of coaches – a contingency for which, oddly no provision had been made at privatisation – and they have occasionally leased short-term stock to train operating companies to fill gaps, as well as to charter firms.

A side effect of privatisation and fragmentation, caused by the hiatus in orders and the subsequent explosion in the demand for rolling stock was the destruction of the rolling-stock manufacturing industry. The

NAO report exposes the causes: 'The paucity of orders for new trains in the two to three years leading up to privatisation in 1996 contributed to a shortage of manufacturing and managerial expertise within the UK railway industry. When this was followed by a surge in orders following the first round of TOC franchises ... there was insufficient expertise to deliver the orders on time.'[28] By 2005, nearly all the main centres of production – York, Birmingham and Eastleigh – had closed down, leaving Bombardier's works in Derby as the only UK manufacturing plant, with a very uncertain future. While this is partly a result of a worldwide consolidation of manufacturing facilities, it was undoubtedly hastened by the bust-boom-bust ordering pattern in the industry after privatisation.

The roscos themselves cannot be blamed for much of this state of affairs. Their capitalistic behaviour, like that of the scorpion in the fable with the frog, is predetermined. The responsibility for the high cost of rolling stock lies squarely with the government. By privatising the rolling stock, it has made the railway industry a pawn in a wider game played by finance houses and other City institutions which seek to maximise their profits with no regard to what effect their activities may have on the railway. This has been done not because it is an ideal solution for the railway industry let alone its passengers, but principally to avoid having the rolling stock on the government's balance sheet and to maintain the pretence that a free market has been created when this is clearly not the case. It is a daft game which ultimately costs taxpayers a lot of money.

The attempt by governments, both Tory and Labour, to try to create a free market in a product as inflexible as trains has proved to be a laughable failure. Even the SRA admitted as much in its Rolling Stock Strategy published in December 2003. There is no real market in trains for several reasons: many stocks are line specific; fleets may be too large or small to transfer; investment is lumpy (in that it comes as occasional big orders rather than steady flows). The idea that there would be lots of new entrants to the rolling-stock market, creating a genuinely competitive situation, has proved optimistic. There has been no challenge to the power of the roscos. Virgin tried desperately to use a bank directly to fund its purchase of the Pendolino trains but Barclays withdrew at a late stage. The lack of new entrants has bemused some in the industry but is mainly the result of the fact it is a highly specialised market that is relatively small for big financial players such as banks.

There was a great reluctance by the City to take on the initial purchase of the roscos. Today there are still too many perceived risks in entering the market against the established suppliers – such as the reliability of new rolling stock and the uncertainties of the political situation – and now the post-privatisation rush has died down there is little scope for new orders.

The answer, as suggested by many respondents during the consultation process on the strategy document, would have been for the SRA to specify what trains were needed where and ask manufacturers to supply them against that specification. But no. The mesmeric quality of the free market did not allow such a common-sense solution and the SRA did not want to be seen to control the market too much because that suggested renationalisation. Instead, it wanted the private sector to come forward with ideas for new stock and designs. According to the strategy document, 'an SRA plan could unduly influence individual companies' decisions about future rolling stock allocation and investment. This could undermine competition between roscos and between manu-facturers ... and could stifle innovation'.[29]

But this is all nonsense. Yes, a plan would influence company decisions but since the money is coming from taxpayers, that *should* be the case. There is, as we have seen, little competition between roscos anyway and the manufacturing industry has been virtually wiped out, thanks to the vagaries of rolling-stock purchasing policy which has prevented the manufacturers getting the steady stream of orders they needed to stay in business.

In any case, all leasing agreements between operators and roscos had to be approved by the SRA (and now by the Department for Transport) because ultimately most of the cost is coming from the taxpayer. The SRA's strategy document said that many respondents had wanted the SRA to produce a long-term plan for future rolling stock development, but this would 'raise issues of market sensitivity and commercial confidentiality and could compromise the SRA's negotiating position and those of industry players'. The SRA seemed to be saying that if it made clear what it wanted, it would undermine its own negotiating position. Secondly, the document said, unless a plan were updated, it would become out of date – so? – and, thirdly, a plan 'could unduly influence individual companies' decisions about future rolling stock allocation and investment'. This is all fantasy land. It is about pretending that there is some real market for a service that is determined by government strategies and priorities. Ministers know this. The reason they are playing this game is that the Treasury insists on it to simply to keep the rolling stock off the books, but the cost is high, both in terms of extra cash from public sources and of the lack of coordination.

In fact, many rolling-stock agreements are already guaranteed by the state under a mechanism called Section 54 of the Railways Act 1993. This arrangement covers nearly 4,000 carriages,[30] well over a third of the stock, and guarantees that future franchisees will be required to take on the existing rolling stock to operate the train service. This removes the long-term residual risk from the roscos which means the risk has been renationalised and therefore the leases are cheaper for the operators, requiring less subsidy. Of course, the cheapest way of leasing rolling stock would be to dispense with the roscos entirely, with the state taking on the risk and borrowing the money, which it can do more cheaply than anyone else. Section 54 is a sort of halfway compromise. The roscos don't like the arrangement because it means that they are no longer able to price – and make profits from – the risk. On the other hand, it means that the state does not have to pay for offsetting risk and overall the cost of franchises is cheaper. There is no reason why it should not be used universally.

Instead, as one operator complained, the catch-22 system effectively guarantees that roscos can dictate the terms of deals. When a franchise comes up for renewal, the bidders will present different rolling-stock strategies, but they cannot finalise a deal until they have signed the franchise – and therefore it is impossible for the SRA (or its successor) to select between bids on the basis of leasing charges, even though that is what it claims it wants to do. Therefore, the winning bidder can only negotiate with the rosco *after* it has obtained the franchise, which puts them at the mercy of the rosco which will know its requirements and be able to hold out for the best deal. The market power, in other words, is all with the rosco.

Far from the original dream of a free market in which the state played no role, rolling-stock decisions are made by a combination of civil servants and private sector interests that has created the worst of both worlds. This is well demonstrated by the case of the seven new nine-car Meridians, a derivative of the Voyager. In 2002 Midland Main Line ordered the seven new trains, worth around £100m, from Bombardier, using HSBC as the rolling-stock company. They were to be used for linking St Pancras with Leeds via Sheffield, providing an alternative to the heavily used GNER line. The SRA's *Strategic Plan*, published in early 2002, promised an extension of London–Sheffield trains on the Midland Main Line, giving an 'hourly service to and from Leeds between 0700 and 1900 from May 2004'. At the same time, Midland Main Line's parent company National Express Group ordered a new fleet of twenty-three Meridian trains (127 carriages as the trains were of varying lengths), seven of which were to provide that extra service – the rest were required to replace Turbostars which had proved unsatisfactory for long-distance services.

By the time that the trains started coming into service, the world had changed. No longer was the SRA talking of expansion and new services; cutbacks and trimming were the order of the day. In March 2004, the SRA published its Route Utilisation Study for the Midland Main Line with no mention of the St Pancras–Leeds service. Instead the SRA favoured a Nottingham–Leeds service running via Barnsley but although new rolling stock would be required, this would not be a Midland Main Line service and, in any case, would require extra funding which was unlikely to be obtained. So the Bombardier trains, built in Wakefield and Bruges, were stacked up in sidings in Derby, their fate unclear.

Who precisely was responsible for paying for the trains while they sat in the sidings remains something of a mystery. The SRA says it did not underwrite the deal, but it clearly approved the scheme, as was made clear in the company's press release issued when the order for the trains was confirmed. It said: 'Commenting on the order, Ian Buchan, Chief Executive of the NEX Trains Division said: "We are delighted that *as part of our franchise agreement* we can now confirm that this new fleet of trains is in the pipeline."' [my italics] As this book went to press, the trains had entered service and a deal involving the transfer of older High Speed Trains to FirstGroup was in the offing. However, the relaxed attitude of National Express during this affair suggested that the company was confident that the SRA – in other words taxpayers – would ultimately have to foot the bill whatever the outcome.

Even the train operators accept that the cost of rolling stock is higher than it would be under a more rational system. As George Muir, the head of the Association of Train Operating Companies, told *File on 4*: 'With the higher cost of rosco money, however, comes advantages.' And these advantages, the SRA concluded, 'are worth having'.[31] But what exactly are these advantages? The roscos get paid extra by the SRA (effectively by the Department for Transport) to take a risk which is largely a political one and therefore in the hands of the self-same department.

There is a simple way out of all this. If the Department for Transport underwrote all the leases, it would save the taxpayer tens of millions of pounds annually. The stock could still be leased from the private sector, but as there would no longer be the need to pay for the risk that the trains might not be used after the franchises ended, the charges would be much cheaper, as even the roscos privately admit. But this is politically unacceptable to ministers, especially Gordon Brown, because he aims to restrict what is counted as government spending in his accounts in order to stick to his golden rule. So while the Treasury is furious at the record levels of subsidy in the rail industry, its own obsession with getting borrowing off the government's balance sheet means that taxpayers' money is being wasted, despite the fact that from a macroeconomic point of view there is absolutely no difference whether the money is borrowed by the state or the private sector. The main advantage of keeping the borrowing off the state's books was that it was supposed to result in an increase in investment, but as we have seen, the average age of the rolling stock remained the same ten years after privatisation.

There was an opportunity to renegotiate the Rosco leases when many came up for renewal during 2004/5. However, the SRA seemed to have made little effort to exert downward pressure on the high lease costs. A third of all leases were renewed in March 2004 and, according to the SRA,[32] 'the deals were done at parity with the original deals', some being more expensive, some less. The SRA reckoned that this was a good deal since inflation had been around 15 per cent since the original contracts were signed in 1997, and justified itself with the bizarre and self-contradictory statement: 'The SRA has no direct levers to pull. The SRA buys franchises not leases, and the TOCs do the negotiations for the leases which they then submit to us for approval.'

Given that this opportunity to examine the rosco arrangement was missed, it was strange that only a few months later, the government belatedly cottoned on to the fact that the roscos seemed to be a profitable and virtually risk-free zone. In the *Future of Rail* review published in July 2004, the roscos were shocked to find a sternly worded warning to them. Ministers had suddenly noticed that the roscos were receiving over £1bn per year for leasing out the trains and that the money largely came from the government's own coffers. Moreover, they realised that the roscos were coining it because projections of high risk, for which the government was largely responsible, had not materialised. The White Paper said:

> When the industry was privatised, it was envisaged that a competitive market for rolling stock would drive cost improvements. In addition, the returns earned from leasing existing rolling stock were based on an assumption that there was a high risk that the roscos would find themselves with rolling stock they could not let once new stock came into use. However, this is another instance where assumptions made at the time of privatisation have not generally come to pass.[33]

The roscos countered with the argument that the profitability should be calculated in relation to the worth of the assets today, over £5bn, not as a percentage of turnover, and it therefore represents a modest rate of return. But that ignores all the other advantages, such as the tax concessions, and the fact that they are being paid for a risk that has not materialised.

But what could ministers do about it? The review merely promised that the government will ensure that risks are allocated to the parties best placed to manage them and 'securing best value for the taxpayer'. The 'Government will develop a longer-term strategy for the rolling-stock market, which will help the industry to plan ahead more effectively'. Not a lot new there, then. Indeed, ministers confirmed their adherence to the rosco model by insisting that the order for new Hitachi trains, confirmed soon after the 2005 election, would go through a rosco.

Of course 'developing a long-term strategy' is what the SRA was supposed to have done but utterly failed to achieve with its 2003 document on the subject. While the government's rather guarded threat in the White Paper has not kept the directors of the roscos awake at night, it does suggest that the days of excessive profits may be numbered. There were signs, too, that the government had begun to recognise that it needed to be more prescriptive. In March 2005, Alistair Darling announced[34] that the replacement High Speed Trains would be specified by the Department and put out to tender on the basis of a standard design rather than allowing roscos or train operators to come up with suggestions, a sensible move. And the government's anger had intensified to the extent that Ernst & Young had been commissioned to undertake a study on the roscos' profitability. Those seventy-year-old trains on the Isle of Wight may yet become a bit cheaper; but there is still a long way to go on the journey to common sense.

CHAPTER 15

Why is the railway so expensive?
(3) The soaring cost of maintenance
and new projects

The one Big Promise of rail privatisation was that it would herald a new age of investment that would transform the railways into a system of transport fit for the twenty-first century. The architects of privatisation argued that government, faced with the competing demands of basic services such as health and education, would never provide enough for transport and, in particular, for the railways. The private sector, on the other hand, would be eager investors in this newly opened-up industry.

It was a juicy prospect. I remember an old BR press officer, transferred in both body and soul to Railtrack, trying to convince me, just after privatisation, that Railtrack's ten-year £10bn investment plan was an unprecedented bonanza which would never have happened under the straitjacket of British Rail. In fact, a billion per year was pretty modest by historic standards and grossly inadequate for anything other than patching up the railway. Under pressure, the old lag agreed that it was not that much money, but it was great because 'The Treasury would never have allowed us to plan in advance in that way.'

That was true. The traditional short-termism of the Treasury had been one of British Rail's undoings. As we shall see in this chapter, much of the investment programme for the infrastructure of the railway comes straight out of the government's coffers and yet, because it is supposedly being spent by a private company, the usual short time-frame imposed by the Treasury has been extended. As Bob Horton, Railtrack's first chairman, put it, 'I realise that Railtrack gets a high proportion of its income from the Treasury but it would have been unable to get that money if it had not been privatised. Privatisation means that you can sign up to long-term contracts rather than being subject to annualised Treasury accounting. Privatisation has broken the Treasury logjam, forcing the Treasury to guarantee long-term funding.'[1]

This was wonderfully convoluted logic: the railway was privatised because it was not getting enough public money and it can now get that money because it is in the private sector, even though the taxpayer is still footing the bill. After the collapse of Railtrack and the creation of Network Rail, whose status is quasi-private, the logic became even more unfathomable. Alistair Darling, the transport secretary from 2002, was wont to say that private investment of £70m per week was attracted into the rail industry. However, two-thirds of that is money being spent on the railways by Network Rail, whose loans are underwritten by the government so that it gets an AAA rating on the money market, saving millions annually in interest payments, and much of whose income comes from the state anyway. The world of post-privatisation railway economics is, indeed, a fantasy land.

The cornerstone of the argument for privatising the railways – that BR suffered from perennial underinvestment – is simplistic and, to a large extent, wrong. In fact, BR had an active investment programme, which, though always insufficient – 'twas ever thus – was comparable with the level of the early years of privatisation and, indeed, would have exceeded it had the money spent on the sell-off been diverted into railway hardware. For example, the BR Rail Plan for 1989,[2] which covered schemes for the following five years, listed thirty-three infrastructure projects for Network SouthEast, InterCity and Regional Railways which had already been authorised, worth nearly £1.1bn. Approval for another sixty, costing £650m, had been sought. These sums only covered infrastructure and the plans for rolling stock were even more impressive. Over the same five years, BR planned to buy 2,267 coaches; of course, these plans might not have all received Treasury approval and, in the event, they were disrupted by the preparations for privatisation which resulted in the hiatus in rolling-stock orders discussed in the previous chapter. Sure, there never was enough money and the trauma of the 1950s Modernisation Programme still dominated the Treasury's view of the railway, but, as we shall see, there is not enough money under privatisation either.

The key flaw in the old structure was the Treasury's obsession with controlling the requirement for cash on an annual basis, which makes no

sense in a long-term business like the railways whose income is highly
dependent on the performance of the economy. So when BR started
doing badly in the recession that began in 1989, passengers numbers fell
and property sales dried up while the investment rate could not be
slowed immediately; as a result the cash requirement shot up, allowing
the Treasury to argue that the whole organisation was incompetent and
needed privatising. As an old BR sweat put it, 'The fact that costs were
being controlled quite effectively counted for naught.'[3]

Nevertheless, the conventional wisdom was that BR had neglected the
railway and that privatisation would remedy the situation, a line that
became a mantra for Labour after the party came to power in 1997, just as
it had been for the Tories earlier. And when spending on the railways got
out of control after Hatfield, the large amounts being spent on the
industry were justified in innumerable statements such as the one made
by Tony Blair in the Commons in July 2003: 'After the Hatfield rail
disaster, it was recognised that the state of the rail infrastructure was
infinitely worse than we supposed. This was the result of years of
underinvestment in our rail infrastructure which we are now putting
right.'[4] Richard Bowker, the chairman of the SRA, put the blame squarely
on British Rail which 'did not spend anything on renewals and
investment for the best part of thirty to forty years'.[5]

But the numbers do not support that argument; quite the opposite.
Expenditure on both maintenance and renewals was maintained fairly
constantly at a healthy level throughout the last twenty years of British
Rail's existence, although it did vary widely from year to year according
to the whims of the Treasury and the financial performance of the
railway. According to figures compiled for the official business history of
the railway[6] and adjusted to 2003/4 prices, BR averaged £575m every
year on renewals during the 1980s. Generally this was money well spent,
as BR had a fairly efficient programme run by people who knew what
they were doing – something that cannot be said, as we shall see, of the
subsequent regime. Sure, the money had to be tailored to what the
Treasury allowed British Rail, but that was the whole point. The railway
rightly, took its place among the different calls on government cash. And
it was not a matter of just accepting a figure from the Treasury; the figure
was arrived at through an ongoing dynamic process (as management
speak would put it) that involved compromise on both sides. As Ivor
Warburton, whose final job at BR was to run the West Coast, explained:

I would call BR a sponge because the whole organisation was like a sponge which could absorb the stresses and strains. It had a certain amount of liquid in there – because we were all working towards a common goal. The single contract was with government and at every level of the organisation the stress and strain was absorbed. Each sector had its own budget and you still had scope to move it around between operations, civil engineering, S & T [signalling and telecommunications] engineering, so that it was all optimised to meet the single government requirement, which was the financial one – the only target we were given was to operate more or less that level of service which we had hitherto operated.

While there were annual changes, and the Treasury did at times pull a late fast one by cutting back the amount it allowed BR to borrow, this level of spending broadly was kept up in the 1990s, although the renewals were concentrated on improving routes to the Channel Tunnel which took resources away from elsewhere.

The constant refrain of politicians that British Rail greatly underspent and that this would be remedied by the private sector does not, therefore, hold water. In terms of maintenance, figures under BR hovered around the £1bn to £1.2bn level (in 2003/4 money) for most of the twenty-five-year period[7] leading up to privatisation but then dipped sharply just as the sell-off was looming. BR's chief executive, John Welsby, slashed maintenance in the last two years of BR to under £800m in an effort to make the books look better, although renewals spending was maintained. The separation of Railtrack from BR in April 1994 did not herald an increase in spending either; the maintenance spend that year was around the £900m mark, still historically slightly low.

Renewals, which averaged around an annual spend of £600m during the early 1990s, fell when Railtrack took over and then started to rise steeply in line with Railtrack's policy of spending more on renewal in order to save on maintenance. But, as Roger Ford points out, even as late as 2000/1 maintenance and renewal of the railway 'was still short of BR's average spend and £140m short of BR's 1991/2 total'.[8]

On paper, Railtrack's investment performance during its first years looked good. John Swift, the first rail regulator, had calculated that the company should have been able to spend some £4bn on renewals in 1996–2001 and in the event Railtrack exceeded that target by £1.5bn.[9] It was able to borrow money for this because of its high profits and share price. The overall headline figures on investment were also impressive.

Railtrack spent[10] over £2.5bn in 2000/1, compared with just £740m in 1995/6, the last year before privatisation. Of that £2.5bn, £500m was for the Channel Tunnel Rail Link, which is separate from the rest of the rail network. The balance was split between £700m worth of enhancements – principally the West Coast Main Line project – and £1.35bn of renewals.

Out of the three main categories of investment – track and signalling, rolling stock and stations – Railtrack initially made much play with the last. The company promised to spend a billion pounds on stations in its first five years and it publicised its station regeneration programme widely in the media, with little panels showing how many had been improved. Much of the work, though, was cosmetic and not done to a good standard. Moreover, stations were easy; working on them did not involve stopping the trains – and the improvements are immediately and obviously visible to the public. The bulk of the spending was on big projects at major stations where redevelopment offered, as the jargon put it, 'new rental opportunities'.

In fact, the emphasis on station regeneration was a mistake. It was a distortion of Railtrack's spending which reinforced public criticism that it was a property company rather than a transport infrastructure operator, a perception Railtrack was quite happy to foster, particularly in the City. The misguided policy concentrated resources on a facet of the railway that was ultimately least relevant to travellers. Of course, having a shiny station with a warm waiting room is pleasant and should be a fundamental part of the service, but really passengers want the trains to be running frequently, quickly and on time above any other considerations. And that requires lots of spending on behind-the-scenes schemes like track renewal and, in particular, signalling; such matters have much less public relations appeal and therefore Railtrack paid little attention to them. Essentially, throughout most of its short life, Railtrack neglected its duty to ensure that the permanent way was in a good condition.

Railtrack's level of investment in stations and the infrastructure did seem, on the face of it, impressive in comparison with the past but, as is inevitably the case with these big numbers, closer examination reveals a more mixed picture. The original figure of £10bn to be invested over ten years jumped each year as the Network Management Statement (NMS) – the company's annual document setting out its plans to maintain and improve the network – was published each spring. The sum went up from £10bn in 1997, to £17bn, £27bn and £52bn in subsequent years. The initial statements were thin affairs – 'a disgrace', according to Swift. There was no detail and no ambition, with statements like 'A number of third parties ... have made proposals for new stations.'[11] To confuse the issue further, each annual statement differed completely in format from its predecessor, making it very difficult to see precisely what Railtrack had achieved in the past year and how its aspirations and commitments were changing.

However, as the statements got thicker, the proportion of firm commitments to be paid for by Railtrack got smaller and the NMS became a wish list. For example, the 1998 NMS identified fifteen bottlenecks and yet by the time the company collapsed in October 2001, work on tackling only two of them had started – Leeds station, the only project to be finished, and the massive, unfinished West Coast Main Line, discussed below. The others, such as the East Coast Main Line and Coventry–Birmingham and London–Brighton, remain on the drawing board (or merely on a sketchpad somewhere in the Black Tower) with no firm date for committing any money. By the time the massive *NMS 2000/1* was published in the spring of 2000, listing £52bn worth of investment on the railways, Railtrack had become quite open about the fact that the funding would have to come from elsewhere. It had become apparent that the NMS merely set out aspirations for the railway that were increasingly dependent on government subsidy for their realisation. In any case, as we saw in the previous chapter, the aftermath of Hatfield led to a moratorium by Railtrack on starting work on any enhancements to the network and the plans of Network Rail, its successor, also envisaged very little new investment as opposed to maintenance and renewal.

Not surprisingly, Railtrack performance comfortably exceeded the very modest targets that had been set by the first regulator, John Swift. In the complex system of finances in the privatised network, the regulator decided what Railtrack should spend on the railway in the next five-year control period (as explained in Chapter 3). The regulator did this by setting the access charges and making assumptions about Railtrack's other income (e.g. freight and property sales and rentals) and its efficiency savings. He then determined what Railtrack ought to spend on investment. However, this method of regulating Railtrack only resulted in establishing targets for expenditure, rather than outputs (such as miles of track replaced or signals upgraded), which immediately raised the question as to the effectiveness of the way money was being spent.

Another major flaw in this system was that the regulator had no powers to make Railtrack invest. The thinness of the early Network Management Statements was no accident. Railtrack did not want to invest in the railway – it wanted to maximise profits. As one of the managers from those early days put it, 'We perceived our job was to manage Railtrack's assets in such a way that we maximised the profit. As harsh as that. That's what all the bosses at the time – Bob Horton [the first chairman], John Edmonds [the chief executive], Norman Broadhurst [the finance director] – thought. Looking back, it was mad.'[12]

Swift quickly realised that his calculations for the first control period – 1996–2001 – had been too generous to Railtrack. Moreover, as he put it, Railtrack had 'got greedy', by concentrating on its share price rather than on improving and expanding the network: 'Its investment programme was still largely determined by renewal rather than enhancement.'[13] In other words, the company was not trying to make improvements to the rail system because of fears that it would not receive a proper rate of return.[14] Profits were being put before improvements.

Swift responded by imposing a new licence condition on the company, requiring Railtrack to ensure that it maintained, renewed and enhanced the network in a 'timely, economic and efficient manner'. Since this was the whole *raison d'être* of the company, it seems incredible that this had not been written into its licence conditions at the outset. The reason for the omission, however, was obvious. To have imposed such obligations on Railtrack would have made the company less saleable, or even unsaleable. Swift was rather regretful about forcing through the change, having hoped that Railtrack would have behaved more responsibly anyway. Fat chance. The narrow-mindedness of its early directors ensured that Swift was forced into imposing the new condition. As he put it, 'Train operators told me that Railtrack was simply not responding to their plans for investment. They were getting fed up because Railtrack was only interested in its shareholders.'[15] Swift added that, had Railtrack behaved differently to its customers and developed innovative schemes in conjunction with the operators and the government, then the new condition would not have been necessary. In the event, Swift also used the new condition to impose requirements on Railtrack to improve its performance in terms of delays, and this eventually led to Railtrack being fined £10m by his successor, Tom Winsor.

From the passenger's point of view privatisation did not seem to be working either. The public perception of the railways was that they were certainly not getting better and maybe even deteriorating. While, overall, the industry's performance did improve in the immediate aftermath of privatisation, this progress had disappeared by the time of the Hatfield accident. Indeed, by then the performance was rapidly deteriorating, as was made clear by the terrible passenger's charter figures for the period immediately before Hatfield, which showed 'a clear downturn in performance on a network suffering from real capacity and reliability problems'.[16] Yet, as the investment figures quoted above show, there is no doubting that Railtrack was actually starting to pour more money into the system.

The answer to this paradox is that, as we have seen, Railtrack took time to start investing even at BR levels on the railways and when it did the company did not get value for money because of the convoluted way in which the industry had been broken up. Put simply, Railtrack had to spend a lot more than BR to get the same result. Railtrack's increased spending on renewals was partly a result of rising and uncontrolled costs. As we have seen, Railtrack was not only forced to contract out maintenance and renewals, but to separate the two in a way that had never been done on the railway before. This not only increased safety risks, but sent the cost of the work soaring (see below).

Secondly, the difficulties that Railtrack experienced when it came to spending its money efficiently were compounded by the lack of a register listing its assets and their condition. This might seem like a mere oversight on the part of the company but, in fact, the reason was yet another demonstration of the cynicism of those who planned and implemented the privatisation. Had an asset register – normally an absolutely basic requirement of any sale – been drawn up before privatisation, the government would never have been able to privatise the company. If 'due diligence' had been carried out on the state of the railway in the normal way, it would have revealed major questions about what had to be spent to bring the system up to standard. British Rail had invested enough to keep the railway in a reasonable condition, but any in-depth examination of the assets would have revealed the need for a major programme of work which would have greatly reduced the value of the company when it was put up for sale to shareholders.

Another reason why Railtrack's spending failed to make the expecte
impact on the network was that it became geared to the performanc
regime rather than the needs of passengers. Railtrack did very we
financially, receiving £250m from the performance regime in the firs
three years, half of which was passed on to contractors. Booz Alle
Hamilton, the consultants, found that Railtrack renewed 50 per cer
more rail than expected, but 20 per cent less ballast and fewer sleepers
adding 'It is possible that this reallocation of the renewals budge
between track assets has been driven by a desire to maximise financia
benefits under the performance regime.'[17] This, as the consultant
pointed out, was because rail replacement shows an immediate improve
ment in performance while ballast and sleepers have more impact ove
the long term. Yet the rail replacement rate was still at a historically lov
level, allowing the rise in rail breaks highlighted in Chapter 8. Th
consultants also found that, despite the extra money going into th
system, 'it appears that the physical programmes have, in aggregate
been below those which were envisaged ... It is likely that there has been
decline in the underlying quality of the network assets as a whole.'
Moreover, much of the spending simply went on managers an
bureaucracy, which perhaps explains the lack of effectiveness of all thi
extra spending: 'Project management overheads have proved to be ver
high, *physical works representing less than 50 per cent of project expenditur*
within the station backlog programme.'[19] [my italics] No wonde
passengers did not notice any improvement.

After Hatfield, the finances of Railtrack simply went haywire. Th
costs of maintaining the infrastructure were increasing far more rapidl
than anyone, including the regulator, had expected and appeared to b
completely out of control. The bald figures are quite astonishing and i
they were better known and understood by the public, then they woul
stimulate much more political debate and, indeed, pressure to cut bac
on the railways. The overall subsidy to Britain's railways has soared i
recent years, requiring more taxpayers' money than at any time in thei
history. Although the rise was particularly marked after the Hatfiel
train crash, the cost of the railways had already begun to increase befor
then.

Britain's railways received £3.8bn in subsidy in 2003/4, according t
figures produced by the SRA. Most of this consisted of payments t
franchisees for running trains and grants to Network Rail for th

infrastructure, but the figures also include a few one-off items such as financial support for the second stage of the Channel Tunnel Rail Link. The cost of running the SRA itself ran to the rather high figure of £210m, showing that the privatised railway is expensive to regulate and certainly has far more 'pen pushers' and bureaucrats than British Rail, whose supposed administrative profligacy was one of the arguments produced in support of its abolition.

According to Roger Ford,[20] support for British Rail, which also included similar one-off items, peaked in 1982 and 1983 when subsidy was just under £2bn (at 2005 prices). In 1989/90, at the peak of the subsequent Lawson boom, BR's subsidy went down to £900m, and this figure provides a more valid basis for comparing today's levels since subsidy for railways always falls when the economy is rising and we have had uninterrupted steady growth since Labour came to power in 1997. In BR's last year as the operator of an integrated rail system, the subsidy was £1.325bn. Thus, as Ford concludes, 'after seven years of sustained economic growth, today's privatised railway needs nearly twice the subsidy of BR in the depth of the early 1980s recession, just over four times the subsidy of BR at its most successful or 2.8 times as much as in the year immediately prior to privatisation'.[21] This is despite a constant rise, in real terms, of revenue, which since privatisation has gone up from £2.9bn in 1995/6 to £3.9bn in 2003/4, an increase of 34 per cent.[22] (This almost exactly mirrors the 33 per cent rise in passenger numbers during the same period, suggesting that the promise made at privatisation, to keep fares rises below inflation, has not materialised; in fact the policy was formally abandoned in 2004.)

And that is not all. The subsidy is still rising. As the expenditure of Network Rail permitted by the regulator peaks, the subsidy for the railway in 2004/5 was £4.8bn, due to rise in 2005/6 to a staggering £6.5bn.[23] The figures are made more complicated by the fact that NR is allowed to borrow money, adding to its considerable debt which by March 31 2005 was £15.6bn (see next chapter for a discussion of this issue).

Network Rail had initially proposed a business plan under which it was intending to spend £35.5bn over the five-year period from April 2004. After its own review and the regulatory process this was reduced to £22.7bn, still far more than the railway has ever needed before. Essentially, at each of the two regulatory reviews Railtrack or Network

Rail received a 50 per cent increase on the previous one: thus during the first five years, Railtrack received £10bn, and was then supposed to get £15bn for the second period which started in April 2001; however the Hatfield crash forced the interim review that granted its successor, Network Rail, another 50 per cent rise.

How has this come about? Day-to-day spending on the railway is divided into running services, which was covered in the earlier chapter on franchising, and OMR (Operations, Maintenance and Renewal), essentially the costs of ensuring the trains can run through the provision of stations, track and signalling. This OMR figure has risen from £1.8bn under BR in 1989/90 to £2.8bn under Railtrack a decade later and £5bn today (at constant 2003/4 prices).[24] Network Rail budgeted to spend £6.7bn in 2004/5, compared with Railtrack's £2.5bn in 2000/1, its last year before the post-Hatfield debacle.

Ford argues that much of the 56 per cent rise in the first ten years (to 99/00) can be explained by external factors such as more stringent health and safety legislation aimed at reducing the number of deaths and injuries of people working on the track. However, after 2000, the figures go out of control and the equivalent OMR figure for 2002/3 is 80 per cent up on 1999/2000 and 2.7 times the figure of ten years earlier. Railtrack lost control of costs in the post-Hatfield panic and there was no chance of reining them back in the subsequent year-long period of administration because the administrators had no expertise in judging whether expenditure was necessary and were terrified of causing another Hatfield-type accident.

Both maintenance and major projects, of which the most important is the West Coast Main Line, have suffered from this massive cost inflation. In terms of the routine work on the railway, there are a variety of factors which have led to the creation of this unsustainably expensive railway. Many are detailed 'micro' issues which may be insignificant in themselves but which collectively make a big difference. The key, however, is to view the situation in terms of the structural changes that have taken place in the railway and the dysfunctional nature of the system which has resulted from them. As a leading expert in the field, an ex-BR man who has worked with operators in an attempt to understand the rise in costs put it, 'If we had had a totally unified railways, we would not have had the cost explosion'.[25] He stresses that it was not the post-Hatfield debacle which created the cost escalation, saying, 'fundamentally the foundation of these fantastic rises in costs were laid at privatisation but it was not until 2000 that there was so much activity on the railway that it became obvious'. Until then, Railtrack was simply not doing enough work on the railway for the inadequacies of the system to be exposed. The root of the problem is the contractual relationships created between, first, the train operators and Railtrack and, secondly and more especially, Railtrack and the maintenance and renewal (the infrastructure) companies. This manifests itself in a number of ways.

First, there is the very nature of contracting. Contractors are in the business of maximising profits and will always get away with doing the least they possibly can. They must, of course, do enough to ensure they get repeat business, but as we saw in Chapter 4, Railtrack's contracts with the infrastructure companies were long term and so badly framed that it was virtually impossible to police them.

Railtrack's contracts with the maintenance companies were fixed price and what is called 'closed book' – in other words, they were for a set amount of money no matter how much work was actually carried out and Railtrack had no right to question how much was being spent or on what. Railtrack, therefore, had no clear idea of what the costs were or the contractors' margins. And there was no clear basis on which to make decisions on whether to improve maintenance on a piece of track or replace it. Indeed, as we saw in Chapter 4, there was an underlying incentive for the maintenance contractor to pass on jobs to renewals because the maintenance company received no more cash for doing more work, while the renewals contractor did. This led to delays, as well as preventing Railtrack from having control over its spending. As a frustrated Railtrack insider put it, 'You cannot manage maintenance and renewal as separate things. The maintenance contractors would do as little as possible because they were driven by profit. You have to manage the whole-life costs. The renewals in the first five years will, by definition, have been spent badly because we had no idea of the economics of maintenance.'[26]

The concept of a fixed-price contract for maintenance work was disastrous, especially as there were good profits at the beginning of the mostly five-year contracts – which tailed off towards the end, leading to even more cost-cutting. However, without the fixed-price system the companies could never have been privatised. If they had had an open-ended duty to maintain sections of the railway, it would not have been

possible to convince the private sector to buy them. The breakneck speed
at which the Tory government set about privatisation meant that these
companies were sold without a track record and therefore no one knew
how profitable the contracts would be.

Second, there was Railtrack's scorched-earth policy, promoted by its
first chief executive, John Edmonds, whose vision was to keep only a
skeleton staff at headquarters and outsource everything, even the
management of contracts, leaving the organisation with no engineering
skills of its own. While this was a mistake right from the beginning, the
disastrous nature of this policy really started to manifest itself post-
Hatfield when a lot of extra work was commissioned very quickly. The
organisation's loss of all its expertise was reflected in the lack of
monitoring of the work and this has left a terrible legacy. The ex-BR man
put it succinctly: 'The end result of the rail industry is a great
agglomeration of a fantastic number of inputs. Unless you've got in-
house managers, who can coordinate these effectively and efficiently, you
lose the synergy that comes from having everything together and which
means the sum is greater than the individual parts.'[27]

This led to a situation where contactors specified the work they did
and carried it out to a standard which *they* monitored. The contractors
were not incentivised to keep the track up to the highest possible
standard but only to ensure it was within the tolerances necessary for a
particular speed. Therefore, lots of detailed work was skimped. Under
British Rail, there were engineers responsible for a particular section of
track, who strove to meet quality standards at the upper end, not the
lower end, of the scale, so that they did not suffer the indignity of being
forced to impose a temporary speed restriction in the event of a sudden
deterioration or, more seriously, risk being held to account for a
derailment. That level of personal responsibility disappeared completely.

Crucially, the contractors also decided when track needed renewing
rather than merely maintaining. There was a perverse incentive for
contractors to renew track unnecessarily instead of maintaining it
which, according to one senior train operator, 'cost this country tens of
millions of pounds. That is because they make more money renewing
track, which costs, say, £2m per mile and the job can be done efficiently
and quickly. To maintain a track, you have hundreds of staff doing little
things such as fettling up the ballast and renewing the odd rail and they
do not make as much profit from that'.[28]

Railtrack appointed a series of infrastructure contract managers with no experience of the industry. They may have been good people managers or accountants, but they had no idea how the railway worked. Without that expertise, they proved hopeless at keeping the lid on costs.

Signalling suffered particularly badly from cost inflation. There are very few suppliers in the UK and, stupidly, Railtrack even outsourced the specification of schemes, a move that was later reversed by Network Rail. There had been a hiatus in commissioning new schemes during privatisation but there were a lot of schemes in advanced stages of preparation. However, when Railtrack finally began to realise that implementing the schemes was necessary, it revised all the estimates and in many cases doubled the cost. The explanation, according to one insider, was a different approach towards cost: 'BR looked at the costs of each activity based on the latest information. It did not put in any allowances for risk on the basis that if a particular part overspent then usually, on balance, there would be somewhere else in the scheme that would underspend. They worked costings in detail and then would put in a maximum contingency of 5 or 10 per cent.'[29]

Railtrack, the same source explained, approached the matter differently, using procedures from the oil and offshore gas industries: 'Their major projects man, Gil Howarth, had been in nuclear and petrochemicals and instituted a system through which they worked out the basic cost and then put in every conceivable risk, adding percentages according to the likelihood of those particular risks occurring. So if there is a 10 per cent risk of a £10m overspend, then an extra £1m is put in.'[30] This was wholly inappropriate to the rail industry where cost estimates under BR had been very good because there was a wealth of experience gleaned from previous similar work. As the ex-BR man put it, 'they lost the incentive to manage costs tightly'.

Indeed, this approach to risk is one of the core reasons why contracting out often proves more expensive, and it applies across the board. Ironically, one of the original reasons for outsourcing is to pass on the risk to contractors, but ministers never seem to understand that this always comes at a price: any risk passed to the private sector is priced and has to be paid for.

There are two other ways in which fragmentation has substantially increased the costs of working on the railway: the management of possessions – periods when the track is closed in order for work to be carried out – and the compensation regime associated with them. Under BR, neither was a problem. The management decided what work had to be done and when, and worked out when lines had to be closed either overnight or at weekends. However, as there were twenty-five train companies and various freight companies and even a couple of open access operators running services, each of which could be inconvenienced and lose money as a result of closures, then a compensation regime had to be devised. Moreover, extra payments would have to be made if a possession overran, which is quite often the case, particularly with weekend closures that run on into the early Monday train services, disrupting the rush hour.

Because of its unwillingness to carry out its own work, Railtrack from the outset delegated responsibility for the management of possessions. This was a fundamental mistake. The management created the most bizarre protocol under which the first company which applied for a possession obtained the status of lead agent. Possessions are often used by several contractors simultaneously and this system meant that any subsequent applicant was at the mercy of the first one, irrespective of the relative importance of the work or potential conflicts over timings. This extremely ill-considered idea created all sorts of anomalies which added to costs. For example, it might be more sensible if the works train of the second company – if it was installing drains, say – came along the line before that of the lead agent, but no such practical issues were taken into account. This wasted resources and valuable possession time. The problem was that, as a result of its contracting-out policy, Railtrack did not have sufficient technically qualified people to manage possessions. Network Rail has now reversed this policy and takes responsibility for possession management.

The situation with compensation is equally daft. Essentially, the train operators are compensated for disruption on the line when the work being carried out is designed to improve services for them and their passengers. This increases the cost of schemes enormously and is a long-term deterrent to improving the railway. Big projects, such as the complete renewal of the trackwork at Leeds station with the provision of four new platforms, can generate £100m in compensation payments while a similar but more limited scheme at Manchester cost Railtrack £50m in payments to operators. These are big numbers, principally paid out of public funds. But precisely because the money was fed through from the Treasury, Railtrack did little about trying to change this ridiculous situation.

Roger Ford has developed the concept of 'boiling frogs' to describe what has happened to costs on the railway. If you throw a frog into hot water it will attempt to escape. But if you place it in cold water which is then brought up to the boil the frog does not notice it warming up and quietly boils to death. Similarly, the powers that be would have been appalled had railway costs suddenly jumped from the 1995 figure to the 2005, but because the increase has been gradual the alert has never really been sounded.

Ford highlights the re-laying of a complicated junction at Ledburn on the West Coast Main Line as an example illustrating the current excesses of spending on the railways. The scheme required the installation of eight new crossovers and associated re-signalling, which under British Rail would have cost just over £6m in modern money. Ford accepts that more onerous health and safety legislation and compliance with new standards would double that to £13m. Looked at another way, the hardware costs for the crossovers and the signalling equipment were around £6.5m and, after allowing for paperwork and installation costs, a broad estimate of £13m would seem acceptable. Yet, when Railtrack first assessed the cost, it calculated the work at a staggering £136m. There was never any clear explanation as to how the costs had soared to that extent, and gradually the estimate was reduced in various stages to £50m. Eventually, the work was carried out for £40m but another £50m was paid out in compensation.

How could such increases be possible? Ford[31] highlights an interesting detail. The new points were installed before resignalling and they were 'clamped and scotched' – i.e. fixed so that they could not move – in the interim. This is standard practice in the industry but it was not enough for the zealots from the Health and Safety Executive, who insisted that the points be 'detected' – i.e. connected to the signalling system temporarily to ensure that if they moved the signal would turn to red. This was entirely unnecessary; as Ford suggests, if there were still concerns, the clamping screws could have been welded to ensure that the switch blades could not be moved. The decision led to significant extra cost because a whole bespoke system had to be devised to provide the extra protection for a period of under a year between the installation of the points and the signalling. Moreover, during that time trains had to slow to 50mph to go over the points, adding to the compensation for operators and delays to passengers. Ford adds that the line was closed for eighteen weekends to do the work, boosting the compensation bill, while work was only undertaken during nine of them.

A Network Rail manager explained how the Ledburn cost explosion was typical of what was happening throughout the network and why managers will come out satisfied that they are getting value for money when, in fact, they have massively overspent: 'Say a project is budgeted at £10m. When the work is carried out, it only costs £6m and the managers proudly report to the board that they have saved money. In fact, however, the estimate was completely disproportionate and the work should have cost £3m. This has been happening all around the network.'[32] He outlined how the administrative and regulatory structure of Railtrack institutionalised these increases. Network Rail's income granted by the regulator was supposed to represent a set percentage return based on its asset base, a notional calculation about the worth of its assets[33] known as the RAB (Regulatory Asset Base). Any investment was added to the 'regulatory asset base', but at the actual price of the work, not on what it should have cost. Therefore, there was little incentive to keep expenditure down since Railtrack was guaranteed a return on the cost of the work, regardless of whether it was justified or not.

All this would have been bad enough had the work being carried out on the railway all been necessary. But this was far from the case. In an effort to ascertain the reason for rising costs while preparing for his interim review that was eventually published in December 2003, the Rail Regulator, Tom Winsor, commissioned a series of investigations into work being carried out by Network Rail to assess whether it gave value for money. The consultants examined nearly 800 rail replacement projects and found that only two-thirds of the jobs were wholly justified. Indeed, in 11 per cent of the cases, the work was totally unjustified – in other words, did not need to be carried out at all.[34] There was a plethora of other examples: only 70 per cent of electrification and plant work was fully justified, while the figure for work on stations was a mere 43 per cent; even on signalling nearly a third of schemes were only partly justified, and there were examples of complete waste such as heavy repairs being carried out on a junction that was scheduled to be entirely replaced less than six months later.

There was much more: the consultants had found no 'meaningful evidence' that NR made effective assessments of whether it obtained value for money from contractors and reported that 'the review of maintenance activities was made difficult by the absence of detailed information within Network Rail on the condition and maintenance needs of much of the asset base'. In other words, nearly a decade after the creation of Railtrack as a separate entity, the organisation still had no idea of what it owned and what condition it was in. And then there were little details, like the fact that NR has one member of its human resources department for every sixty-seven staff, compared with precisely half that number in similarly sized non-rail companies.

It is therefore not surprising that the railway is suffering an unprecedented increase in costs and that the mandarins at the Treasury are jumping up and down in fury at the industry's profligacy, though of course they only have themselves and their predecessors to blame. From an analysis of various projects pre- and post-privatisation, Ford calculates that costs on the railway have increased by a factor of around three (he actually reckons it is *pi*) since BR days, partly as a result of enhanced safety requirements, but mostly because of the chaotic structural changes whose consequences have been outlined above. But there was one project which dwarfed all the others, and which contributed much to Railtrack's bankruptcy and, indeed, to the crisis of privatisation: the West Coast Main Line refurbishment.

The West Coast Main Line is the mother of all projects on the railway, and its story encapsulates all the above features with the added ingredient of sheer scale. It is expected to cost around £8bn – although at one time the projected expenditure was in the region of £13bn and heading north – in addition to the £2bn spent on new tilting rolling stock for Virgin which was designed to go at 140mph, a speed that may now never be achieved on the line, because the scope of the project has been scaled down and speeds will be limited to 125mph.

The runaway costs on the West Coast modernisation cannot simply be laid at the door of the normal cost overruns which frequently occur on major projects. The roots of the problem were the way that the project was structured at privatisation and the fact that it was predicated on the basis that a new signalling technology, 'moving block', could be used, which would have lowered costs significantly. Indeed, if it had not been assumed that moving block could be used, the scheme's projected costs would have been so high that they would have threatened to derail the whole privatisation of Railtrack and raised doubts about whether the company's sale was viable. It is therefore misleading to try to treat the West Coast as a separate issue, distinct from the disaster of privatisation, as politicians have been wont to do.

The West Coast is Britain's premier rail line, a network of routes linking London with Birmingham, Manchester, Liverpool and Glasgow. It was built as a patchwork of railways mostly in the 1830s and 1840s, and still suffers from that legacy, incorporating an excessive number of bends and, at times, taking roundabout routes. In 1966, the electrification of the London–Liverpool/Manchester section of the WCML was the high point of the post-war railway modernisation programme. Passenger numbers boomed above expectations and the term 'sparks effect' was coined to explain the public's reaction to the brand-new electrified service, later extended to Glasgow. The success should, of course, have led to an investment boom on the railways, as happened in several other European countries, but successive British governments, influenced by a transport ministry that was always in hock to the road lobby and a Treasury deeply sceptical of rail investment after the Modernisation Plan debacle, failed to follow up this initiative.

As the WCML began to show signs of age, BR made two attempts to improve the service. First, in the mid-1980s, the tilting Advanced Passenger Train was developed with the aim of a four-hour journey time between London and Glasgow. The train briefly entered service, but passengers reported that the tilt made them feel sick, earning the train the unfortunate moniker of the 'vomit comet', and the project was cancelled because of teething problems. Ironically, these problems were on the point of being solved, but the government lost confidence in the technology and, as a result, Britain missed its chance to take a world lead in tilting train development.

Then, at the end of the 1980s, BR tried again. This time the solution was a conventional high-speed train – InterCity 250 – combined with progressive infrastructure upgrades that would gradually enable its 155mph top speed to be exploited. An order for the new trains had actually been put out to tender when, in 1992, the recession persuaded the Treasury that the project was overambitious and it ordered cancellation. Instead, BR drew up a more modest scheme to replace the power supply, signalling and some track on the WCML, which was estimated to cost £800m.

But privatisation intervened and BR's scheme went into abeyance. When franchising started in 1995, the government could not afford to let the WCML modernisation drift on. The trains and the track were quite literally falling apart, with breakdowns and delays increasing. Privatisation had been sold on the basis of bringing in new investment to the railways and therefore it had to provide the answer to the long-deferred modernisation of the WCML. The newly created Railtrack commissioned a £5m study on the future of the WCML from a consortium of consultants which assessed a number of options ranging from 'patch and mend' to complete refurbishment to allow the use of much faster trains.

The best financial option was the Core Investment Programme (CIP). By introducing new signalling concepts based on computers and radio, lineside signalling equipment could be eliminated and it was thought this would make great savings. The key feature of the system was to be the 'moving block' signalling system, a revolutionary concept that had only ever previously been used on simpler railways such as metro systems and dedicated high-speed lines. Conventional signalling divides the track up into sections, or 'blocks', typically a kilometre long. Safety is ensured by not allowing a train into a section until the preceding one has left it. With moving block, each train has an 'envelope' in front and behind which protects it from collisions through radio signalling directly into the cab. There are no lineside signals, which saves enormous sums on maintenance, dispenses with many signallers (who had just been on strike in the run-up to privatisation), and allows far more trains to run.

In theory, therefore, moving block had everything going for it. There was one problem. Nowhere, anywhere in the world, was a major, heavily used railway using the system. Moreover, the technology for adopting moving block on a complex network of lines like the West Coast was simply unavailable at the time and a decade later this still remains the case: there is no such system in operation on an equivalent railway. Sure, the Docklands Light Railway driverless trains uses moving block, as does the most modern Paris Métro line but these are simple shuttle services, and the system is not fitted even on the newest Japanese or French high-speed trains.

There are only two possible explanations for why, in 1994/5, Railtrack's executives managed to persuade the government that the moving block system was not only feasible but would save a fortune: they either deceived themselves royally or, in their anxiety to get Railtrack into the private sector, they were deliberately dishonest.

Cock-up theories are generally more realistic than conspiracies, but in this case there does seem to have been deliberate obfuscation on the part of Railtrack to ensure that the project appeared feasible at the given price. For his brilliant and detailed exposé of the fiasco,[35] James Meek, of the *Guardian*, spoke to a former consultant with Booz Allen & Hamilton, the consultancy which was responsible for recommending the signalling system. Interestingly, Meek's contact, 'Arthur', told him that very little information was obtained from abroad. They contacted a few railways in what seemed a rather desultory exercise and found that the system was not used elsewhere. Arthur said: 'We asked the Japanese what they'd got [in terms of moving block] and they said "Well, nothing really", which amazed us.'[36]

Yet, crucially, Railtrack added a sentence which was not contained in the consultants' report to the public summary of that work. This said 'Most of the hardware for this train control system already exists, the technology required being relatively mature.' Asked about this in 2004 'Arthur' told Meek: 'I am amazed at that statement because I don't know where they had any proof of that.'[37] Indeed, the opposite seemed true. Railtrack ignored the fact that in January 1995 a group of nineteen European railways had decided that moving block was not ready to be used on their systems and that other, simpler, technology should be developed.

Railtrack was privatised in the spring of 1996, but it took some time before it dawned on the company that it had signed up to an impossible vision. Indeed, Railtrack compounded the situation by signing a contract with Virgin which it would never be able to deliver. Virgin had won the franchise to run trains on the West Coast in early 1997 and thrashed out an amazing deal with Railtrack. The company committed itself to providing the signalling and infrastructure for Virgin to run high-speed 125mph tilting trains by 2002. Three years later, they would be able to travel at 140mph, bringing the time between London and Manchester down to a mere 105 minutes, while Glasgow would be less than four hours from the capital. It was to be a brave new world, announced with much fanfare and the usual Branson promises. Moreover, if Railtrack failed to deliver the new railway by 2005, it would face crippling financial penalties. The initial cost of the resignalling was estimated to be £1.35

and under the Virgin deal there was to be a further £600m upgrade which would ensure twelve trains an hour could run in and out of Euston, with a 140mph top speed south of Crewe from 2005.

But the exciting prospect of turning the WCML into Britain's best rail line for such a comparatively small sum turned out to be pure fantasy. Even if the idea had been technically feasible, the policy of Railtrack's chief executive, John Edmonds, of dispensing with engineering expertise meant that such a sum was never going to be realistic since it was impossible for the company to keep control of the spending by the myriad contractors needed on such a massive project.

Then the complexities of seeing through such a major project on the privatised railway also came into play. As one insider put it, 'The railway has not been privatised in a way that facilitates or enables capacity enhancement.'[38] In fairness to Railtrack, modernising a lengthy, difficult and heavily used railway would have been a Herculean task under any circumstances. The trouble was that Railtrack had rushed off to do a deal with Virgin on the West Coast without giving any thought to what the other users wanted and before having any discussion with them, let alone figuring out the implications for the timetable. However, the agreement for the West Coast had to be approved by the regulator, who was concerned about capacity for other passenger operators and the rail freight companies. His acceptance of the scheme was conditional on Railtrack providing forty-two extra paths daily on the slow lines from 2005, an almost impossible requirement.

In addition to problems over the number of train paths and the signalling, there was an overall lack of commitment from Railtrack to the project. According to insiders, the scheme just seemed to be drifting along even though it was supposed to be completed, in two stages, by 2002 and 2005. Chris Green, who took over at the head of Virgin's two rail franchises in 1999, was surprised to see so little activity on the track and pushed hard to get Railtrack to take the project seriously. The main contract to overhaul and renew the overhead electrification had still not been signed after the initial bids had come in at twice Railtrack's expected figure of £400 million. There was uncertainty about the scale of track renewal and major capacity issues, such as four-tracking the bottlenecks, were unresolved. And the issue of the forty-two extra paths also remained hanging in the air, which soon engendered another crisis for Railtrack when the rail regulator issued an enforcement order to get the information by March 2000, together with costings for the extra infrastructure work and train timetables.

Inevitably, Railtrack soon learnt there were no off-the-shelf systems available for what was extremely complex, safety-critical signalling equipment, and that the consultants had been far too confident about the availability of the technology. Brian Mellitt, the engineer who had specified similar moving-block signalling for the Jubilee Line Extension, which also proved impossible to implement, had been taken on in a similar role by Railtrack and made the same mistake by pushing for the revolutionary system. It soon became apparent that this was unrealistic and that Mellitt was a serial over-optimist whose schemes cost both London Underground and Railtrack (and of course taxpayers) dear. There had been two bidders for the West Coast scheme and the contract had been awarded to Alstom, which was now warning that the signalling system would not be available until 2007/8, three years after the West Coast modernisation was supposed to be completed.

Railtrack was forced into a humiliating retreat. In November 1999 the company announced that the moving-block system was now considered too expensive. Instead, it would switch to a system using cab signalling. This involved the installation of sophisticated radio systems, but would still require much lineside equipment. As a result the maintenance savings predicated on having no lineside equipment, which underpinned the whole project, disappeared.

Worse, the existing signalling was becoming time-expired and would have to be patched up while a new signal system was installed, requiring further spending. The extra costs created by the privatised structure such as huge compensation payments to train operators and the need for every party involved to make a profit, also came into play. Overnight, the cost of the West Coast modernisation more than doubled, to £5.8bn. What had started out as an £800m upgrade for BR and become a £2.2bn Railtrack project had now transformed into a near-£6bn behemoth. Even worse was to come. When Railtrack was given its £1.5bn bail-out in April 2001 as a result of the crisis brought about by the Hatfield accident, the company also let slip the fact that costs on the project had gone up further £500m, and by the time of its demise in October the total was estimated to have risen to £8bn.

The apparently exponential increase in costs is not easy to explain. When the project was estimated at £6bn, analysis revealed that the were two main categories of work where costs had risen steeply: 'signalling and control', for which the original estimate of £485m for the moving block system had leapt to £1,900m for its less sophisticated replacement; and 'remodelling track layouts', which jumped from £640m to £1,800m. In contrast, electrification renewal merely doubled from £285m to £580m and 'track and structures renewal' rose from £570m to £780m. There was, also, the extra £1,000m cost of providing extra capacity and a few other minor increases. How could Railtrack have not realised that the costs were increasing in this way? The only explanation is that, as Railtrack insiders later admitted, the project had simply drifted, with no one taking responsibility.

But it got worse. Much worse. After the Hatfield accident, the project's costs simply ballooned out of control. Railtrack sought to establish a new baseline for the cost of the project which worked out the full upgrade to a 140mph railway at £13.5bn. Reducing the specification to 125mph reduced the estimated baseline cost to £9.8bn. However, that is for a much reduced specification. Most of the money being spent is now for renewals of track, signalling and electrification, rather than enhancements, which account for only £632m. In other words, passengers are getting a refurbished railway rather than the completely upgraded and renewed one that they were originally promised. As Ford put it, 'In effect the "route modernisation" is now "route renewal".'[39] Of course the line needed renewing, but it is worth noting that in April 1994 when the line was transferred from BR to Railtrack, there were no temporary speed restrictions, a clear indication of its good condition and something Railtrack hardly ever achieved in the subsequent seven years.

The comparison with the costs of the parallel East Coast Main Line, refurbished in the late 1980s under BR, is illuminating. Authorised in 1984 and completed in 1990, British Rail's East Coast Main Line electrification cost £306m at 1984 prices (roughly £650m in 2005) and was delivered on time and on budget. The East Coast investment covered around 350 miles of mainline electrification with installation of overhead cable, some resignalling with state-of-the-art electronic equipment and new fibre-optic communications. It was done rather on the cheap, as witnessed by the delays when wind brings down the cables, an all-too-frequent experience.

Nevertheless, in contrast, the electrification renewal alone – power supplies and new overhead cables – for the 400-mile WCML cost around the same as the complete East Coast project under BR a decade or so earlier. Admittedly, the ECML did not require track renewal and rather than track remodelling the layout was simplified, but the enormous cost difference is still difficult to explain.

Apart from compensation payments, mentioned above, there are the extra costs of having to do work in small overnight bites, rather than long possessions. New safety regulations mean that it can take an hour simply to switch off the electricity so that work can start. With an hour setting up and closing down, productivity from a four-hour night-time possession will be low, even with high-performance track-laying machinery. It was only when Network Rail began to take control of the project that it insisted that much of the major work should be done in 'blockades', when the line is closed for a whole weekend or even several weeks.

Privatisation has made this more difficult. Under BR it was possible to close lines and divert trains on to other tracks. For example, Manchester trains were run into Paddington during the original electrification of the West Coast. In 2003/4, for seventeen months, a special Manchester service was operated out of St Pancras by Midland Main Line, but this required extra subsidy from the SRA in addition to the compensation paid out to Virgin which, as we saw in Chapter 13, was also receiving massively increased franchise payments.

Then there are the regulatory issues. After Railtrack or now Network Rail has drawn up a scheme, it has to be sure that the needs of all the potential users – the various freight and passenger operators – have been met. In practice, this is almost impossible. There are so many players with competing demands that within the context of a growing railway it is impossible to satisfy them all, as the example of the WCML improvement shows. This imposes costs in several ways. Schemes have to be drawn up with options to satisfy different criteria; time is wasted as ideas are circulated around the various operators; the regulator may then intervene, forcing Network Rail to include certain features; and the ultimate scheme may therefore end up being a Rolls-Royce where a Mini was needed. All these delays and decision-making complexities result in extra costs. This is not Network Rail's fault but a feature of the fragmented system. There is no one in charge who can ensure that speedy decision is taken. The whole regulatory framework, which is necessary feature of a railway operated by dozens of passenger and freight companies, imposes a considerable cost burden on the industry.

Finally, there are the extra costs caused by having several companies involved, all of whom have to 'make a turn' on every project. This has slightly improved now that Network Rail has taken maintenance in-house for precisely that reason. However, on a project like the West Coast, the work is all contracted out. Moreover, Network Rail still has to behave commercially and, for example, it will add in management and supervisory costs for all work undertaken on the network.

The way that costs escalated on the West Coast was rooted in the new structure of the industry in which the ability to control costs had been lost. The East Coast electrification project in the 1980s is a good comparator. It only just slipped through the government's project assessment procedure and, as a result, there was much cheeseparing which affected the reliability of the service, and the balance between keeping cost down and improving the railway probably leaned too much towards the former. The trains, for example, had serious air-conditioning problems, the locomotives had high failure rates and, most important, the overhead catenary was too light and tended to collapse whenever there was a high wind. In contrast, parts of the current West Coast project will be gold-plated because of the lack of discipline over costs and the absence of accountability. Moreover, since it is politically and probably contractually impossible for the government to leave a private sector scheme half finished by pulling the financial plug, the risks to the public purse have greatly increased. As a former senior BR executive put it, 'Without the government being there in the way it was under BR, there is no control over such projects.'[40] He made the point that there was no one to check on whether value for money was being obtained from the extra investment.

The cost rise was deeply embarrassing not only for Railtrack but also for the Labour government, which was so wedded to the notion that the private sector was more efficient at managing its costs. Labour had, indeed, predicated its whole controversial Private Public Partnership scheme for the London Underground on this notion, and ministers frequently referred to the huge cost overruns on the Jubilee Line extension which were, in fact, much more modest than those on the WCML. The bill for the JLE had 'merely' doubled from £1.7bn in 1992 to £3.5bn on completion, partly because of the abandonment of the moving block signalling and also because the collapse of a tunnel being built for the Heathrow Express in October 1994 led to concerns over building methods which resulted in delays to the construction.[41]

The key point is that while the railway may be in private hands, with investors making a profit, *the risks to the taxpayer have not been eliminated*. This has been demonstrated several times since privatisation. We have already seen that the franchises which got into trouble because of the overoptimism of the bidders were rescued by the Strategic Rail Authority with extra money for the new franchisees. Railtrack's cost overruns on the West Coast Main Line have also resulted in extra costs for the taxpayer rather than the company. The West Coast project illustrates all the problems of investing in the railway under a privatised structure mentioned above: the difficult legacy from BR; escalating costs; conflicts between different operators; difficulty of managing contractors; enormous compensation claims for disruption; lack of coordination; and so on. It is hardly surprising that no other major project has even got off the ground in the first decade of privatisation, with plans for the upgrade of other major lines, such as the East Coast and Great Western, bogged down by delays and the absence of a clear vision. Indeed, many longstanding railway managers are worried that it will only be when these lines start deteriorating markedly that a decision to upgrade them will be taken.

Railtrack's second biggest project on the existing network, Thameslink 2000, has also suffered from cost escalation and delay. The scheme is intended to increase capacity on the heavily used north–south cross-London link opened up in the 1980s. At privatisation in 1996 Railtrack, after much lobbying of ministers, was effectively given £200m to fund the improvement, with the equivalent amount of debt being written off. The scheme was seen as an important flagship project for the company, which was keen to show the City that it could improve the rail network and therefore increase its income through access charges. Originally priced at £225m at the time of Railtrack's flotation, by February 2000 the cost had risen to £850m (at 1995 prices) and was soon soaring above £1bn. A planning inquiry further delayed matters and the financial crisis of the railways in the aftermath of the Hatfield crash meant that there was no prospect of the scheme starting in the first half of the new decade and little hope for it in the second. The £200m has, of course, long since disappeared into the accounts of Railtrack and Network Rail. Meanwhile, the box which would contain the new Thameslink station under King's Cross was completed in May 2005 but the estimated £70m required to fit it out has not been allocated, so when the new St Pancras Eurostar terminal opens in 2007 passengers will still have to make the long walk to the old cramped Thameslink station.

Yet Thameslink trains are among the most overcrowded on the network and it is conventional wisdom among transport planners that there is a lack of rail capacity in London, especially as the population is expected to increase by 10 per cent in the first fifteen years of the twenty-first century. The need for extra capacity on south-east commuter lines was well illustrated by the decision of the SRA in late 2004 to push for the abandonment of the dedicated Gatwick Express trains so that more commuter services could be accommodated. If privatisation had really harnessed market forces, then it is clear London would have got a massive increase in rail capacity. In fact decisions about the strategy for the industry have remained in public hands because such capacity increases inevitably require major public support; but since the extra costs created by privatisation became clear no money has been available for such enhancements.

Another serious debacle resulting from the fragmentation of the privatised railway was the Southern power upgrade. By 1998, the three Southern commuter operators knew they would need more than 2000 new carriages to replace the old slam-door rolling stock that were being phased out, with a target date of the end of 2002, because of age and extra safety requirements. There was confusion over who would buy the trains and just in case the operators did not get their act together, the SRA started its own procurement exercise in parallel. Either way, it was clear the new trains would use considerably more electricity than the old slam-door stock because of faster acceleration, higher line speed, greater weight, air conditioning and all the other electrical apparatus that is now considered standard on new coaches. But no one quite got round to sorting out how that would affect the power supply on the third-rail system used throughout the old Southern Region. Without the upgrade, the power of the trains would cause the sub-stations to overheat and bring services to a standstill.

The new Electrostar trains for South Eastern and SouthCentral had started being introduced in the spring of 2001 and the order by South West Trains for Siemens Desiros was placed around the same time. Railtrack was aware of the need for extra power but did not know exactly how much would be required and was therefore unable to start work on a project to upgrade the system. While Railtrack had information about the Electrostars, the Desiros were a bit of a mystery and the infrastructure company had not been given any details of their specification.

The problem was that this issue needed coordination between the four parties involved – Railtrack (later Network Rail), the train operators, the rolling-stock companies and the Strategic Rail Authority. Ensuring the new trains could operate on the network and assessing their precise requirements in terms of power was a tricky business which required an overall guiding mind: precisely what the railways did not have. The matter was further complicated by the fact that the SRA was trying to stitch up a twenty-year deal with Go Ahead for SouthCentral, which involved large investment on the track, but which was killed off by the collapse of Railtrack. All the parties blamed each other and, as Network Rail later told the House of Commons Transport Committee which investigated the fiasco, 'The current legacy reflects a past industry arrangement where the relationship between Railtrack and the Train Operating Companies was less than ideal.'[42] An understatement indeed.

It was only when Richard Bowker took over from Sir Alastair Morton at the helm of the SRA that any sense of urgency was injected into the issue. The problems had been highlighted by an article in *Modern Railways*[43] in January 2002 and were becoming a major public embarrassment for the railways and ministers. Bowker called a meeting of all the parties involved – there were twenty-five in the room – and read them the riot act, refusing to allow them to leave until a way forward was clear. He created a team to sort out the issue and managed to badger the Treasury into coughing up extra money, which it was forced to do given that it was simply politically unpalatable not to put the trains into service. As it was, hundreds of new coaches at places like Brighton remained in sidings in full view of passengers travelling in the old decrepit rolling stock, a sad monument to the dysfunctional structure created by people who did not understand the need for coordination and integration in the railways. By early 2004, some 300 coaches were sitting in sidings, which was a considerable drain on the public purse as leasing charges had to be paid on these trains, wasting, according to the National Audit Office, an estimated £7m.[44]

At first Railtrack estimated the bill would be well over £1bn, but this was brought down to around £700m when the scheme was completed in

2004, thanks to the SRA's belated but necessary focus on the issue. However, there was a downside to this saving as the specification had to be reduced. According to Roger Ford, 'there is only enough power to supply 1500 amperes per train when they need between 2000 and 2350'.[45] The system may be upgraded, but with no money available for enhancements in the near future it is unlikely. That has affected the timetable, particularly on routes out of Waterloo, which in December 2004 were retimed to allow longer stops at stations, because it takes longer for people to get in and out of the new coaches as they have fewer entrances and exits than the old slam-door stock. Had the trains been able to use their full power to accelerate, that time would have been made up between stops.

Network Rail told the Commons committee that there would be no repeat of such a fiasco because new arrangements had been established: 'Network Rail believe it is essential that as the network operator, we are involved in the process of specifying and designing new trains as early as possible to ensure the smooth introduction of new rolling stock.'[46] Of course Network Rail is effectively a government-run company and can take responsibility for these matters. How that would work in practice, however, is difficult to imagine because it represents a major extension of Network Rail's remit (see final chapter for discussion of these issues). As a private concern, Railtrack would have found it much more difficult to coordinate the work. Moreover, responsibility for paying to sort out the problem would have been a subject of dispute over whether shareholders or the government would have picked up the bill and could have been another blow to its share price.

The absence of any prospective enhancement schemes on the rail network is highlighted in the *Rail Industry Monitor 2004*[47] which recalled that Railtrack had listed 324 projects in its 2000 Network Management Statement. This was whittled down to 100 in the SRA's 2003 annual report, which stated that, of these, eighteen had been implemented without the need for infrastructure works', ten had been withdrawn following a value for money review and six had been given the highest priority, with work being carried out on four. Of the remaining sixty-six, Network Rail reported in its 2004 Business Plan that five schemes were currently being implemented and a further nine were being developed to the stage of being ready to proceed in 2005/6, *if funding were made available*. Work on all other projects has ceased, which means that barely

10 per cent of those listed by Railtrack have much chance of being completed in this decade. So the record levels of spending on the railway are not being used to improve it but merely keep the existing infrastructure going.

Thus virtually all the major schemes to improve the railway have been killed off or kicked into the long grass by the cost escalation. For example, the steady stream of station reopenings, often promoted by local groups, which had run from the mid-1970s to the mid-1990s has almost dried up because of the extra costs imposed by privatisation. In the days of British Rail, there was less need to show all ancillary costs against a particular project as they were subsumed into the general accounts. Nowadays, the functions of design, construction and project management are divided amongst a number of private companies, each of which needs to be run profitably.

There are reasons other than privatisation which caused some of the cost escalation on the railways. Enhanced safety requirements during the construction phase add to the cost, as do new directives for the provision of access for wheelchair users and other facilities for the disabled, required by the Disability Discrimination Act 1995. Higher expectations of quality for the built environment mean that cheap, concrete structures and rolled hardcore for car parks can no longer be contemplated.

BR also used to have the advantage of an annual Parliamentary Bill to allow developments, whereas Network Rail has to go through the lengthy Transport and Works Act process which, inevitably, is expensive. However, while not all the extra costs can be attributed to privatisation and fragmentation, it is clear that under the current system it is much harder to get value for money and to make such schemes appear worthwhile to the bean counters. The Strategic Rail Authority admits as much in a pamphlet[48] aimed at helping local groups reopen stations, which states that even a most basic station with little requirement for track or signalling work would cost in the region of £2m–4m, whereas a list of 300 new and reopened stations in a book[49] by the Railway Development Society (now Railfuture) lists dozens of projects in the 1980s where costs averaged around the £100,000 mark and many cost less than that. According to one former BR director, 'The Passenger Transport Executives in regional conurbations such as Manchester and Leeds used to get all their schemes done by BR and they suddenly found that they were costing three and a half times more. Railtrack was putting up the price to make a profit, and then there is the cost of all the interfaces between customers, contractors, and subcontractors which all add overhead.'[50]

Nor did the advent of Network Rail in 2002 appear to solve this problem, as the PTEs still reported prohibitively high quotes for any improvements they sought. During the 1980s and early 1990s, West Yorkshire PTE had opened a series of new stations and improved services on much of its network. Now, costs and the involvement of so many organisations (such as the SRA, Network Rail, the rail regulator, the HSE and above all, their expensive lawyers) make this much more difficult to achieve. New stations are becoming prohibitively expensive. Whereas in 1999 Brighouse was built by the PTE at a cost of £900,000, Network Rail charged £2.3m for Glasshoughton, opened in 2004, which included £90,000 for insurance against a mega catastrophe required by Network Rail, a completely unnecessary expense. Even a simple platform extension of a few yards to cater for the slightly longer trains now used in the area costs £72,000 – a staggering £144,000 per station. Putting up a bus-type shelter on a station will cost £20,000 compared with just £3,000–4,000 if it were at a bus stop.

Remarkably, there is even the threat that some stations will no longer be able to have a service because of the cost of adapting them to modern trains and the intransigency of the safety authorities. Portchester, near Portsmouth, is a busy little station used by many local residents for commuting and consequently it is served by fifteen trains per day. When the new Desiros were introduced, they were found to be 4.5m longer than the platform and the Health and Safety Executive refused to sanction a system of allowing only some of the doors to be opened in case the person controlling them made a mistake, even though the procedure has been used widely on the rail network including for decades at Portchester without incident. The simple expedient of lengthening the platforms was reckoned to be a major undertaking by Network Rail as it quoted a fantastical £750,000 for the work and Stagecoach, the franchisee for South West Trains, was unwilling to stump up that level of cash. Eventually, because this little fiasco attracted widespread publicity,[51] the work was carried out for a fraction of the cost.

The chief irony of these stories is that they show how the privatised structure, far from freeing the railway from the constraints of the state as promised, created a much more rigid and inflexible railway. It became harder to open stations, or even increase or reduce services quickly to respond to changes in the market.

These last three chapters have shown that for a whole variety of reasons, some totally unexpected, privatisation has created a complex and expensive structure that threatens the future of the network. The final chapter suggests a way forward, even though it is difficult to be optimistic in the face of this chequered history.

CHAPTER 16

How ideology and incompetence wrecked Britain's railways

This book is the detailed story of a scandal. The privatisation of the railways is not often described in those terms, but there is no doubt that it represented one of the great political and economic crimes of the twentieth century, and that its victims were not only the railways but ourselves, the taxpayers and passengers who support them. Ideology was a crucial factor in the havoc that ensued. Quite apart from the privatisation itself, the way in which the industry was fragmented was incredibly damaging. The notion that a relatively efficient industry like British Rail could be broken up into 100 parts, all of which had to be profitable, could only have been dreamt up by rabid ideologues, more concerned with theory than practice. Certainly none of the ministers and civil servants who invented the structure of privatisation had ever got near running a railway or, with rare exceptions, anything else.

They were, quite simply, dangerous, the sort of people who had dreamt up the poll tax. As we have seen, the chaos for which taxpayers and passengers are paying was created by a coterie of ministers, surprised to find themselves in power for another five years and therefore prepared to do the unthinkable, aided and abetted by politically motivated civil servants in the Treasury and the Department of Transport.

To say the privatisation was 'botched', as politicians are wont to do, does not do justice to the facts. The privatisation was a deliberate decision to break up the railways with little regard to the consequences. It was not an absent-minded bit of poor government, but a malicious attack on an industry which the Tories disliked, with calamitous results. The tragedy is that none of those responsible have ever really been called to account, except, to some extent and anonymously, in the theatre in David Hare's wonderful bit of reportage, *The Permanent Way*. Certainly, the guilty should be in the dock over the way they separated out the railway without a thought as to the safety consequences. While the safety problems have been partly addressed, with Network Rail not being profit-oriented and maintenance having been taken back in-house, the legacy of excessive structural costs remains; a delicious irony given that the enterprise was Treasury-inspired. Now, however, that same high temple of the mandarins seeks to cut back service levels to reduce the spiralling costs for which the department is responsible.

This is where incompetence merges with ideology. The Hatfield accident is the most obvious example of this; the succession of mistakes that led to the disaster, followed by another catalogue of errors that compounded its effect, amount to incompetence on a monumental scale. But the cast of ministers and Treasury officials who created the system that caused Hatfield were also incompetent. They did not listen to anyone who knew how to run the railway and they deliberately continued with a structure designed to foster on-rail competition when they knew already that it was not possible. The comment by the then Permanent Secretary, Patrick Brown, quoted in Chapter 4, to the effect that he knew open access was not possible but could not say so is painfully revealing about the failings of our system of governance.

That this record of ideology and incompetence, in equal measure, was perpetuated by the Labour ministers who took over in 1997 is the most unpalatable part of this dreadful story. There is, perhaps, a third feature of the behaviour of the politicians that deserves equal billing, and that is dishonesty. How else can one describe Tony Blair's assertion in opposition that he wanted to see 'a publicly accountable, publicly owned' railway? Was he simply lying? Or did he change his mind? Or did he simply not understand what he was talking about, as seems to have been the case with the Iraqi weapons of mass destruction which could allegedly be launched within forty-five minutes?

This was not the only instance of deceit. The whole story is full of attempts by politicians to pull the wool over the eyes of the public. I have already mentioned the fiasco over open access perpetrated by the Tories but Labour have presided over a privatised railway for far longer and have many more episodes of deceit to their name. Take, for example, the constantly repeated mantra that the private sector is investing £70m weekly in the railway. In effect, two-thirds of this comes from Network Rail and a third from the rolling-stock companies. But Network Rail i not really a private company, since most of its money comes from the Treasury, either directly or indirectly. And the roscos have an income stream from the operators that is also backed by subsidy from government. As for investment from the operators, there was a revealing statement in the Commons Transport Committee's report on the railways: 'We tried, but failed, to identify private sector investment which is neither rolling stock, nor infrastructure funded by Network Rail. The Department for Transport has told us that such investment has been made in "plant and machinery" but that details are not available for reasons of "commercial confidentiality".'[1] Oh, so the electorate is not allowed to know that private companies are spending their money for the benefit of the great British public.

There was a particularly nasty demonstration of this type of dishonesty at the Labour Party conference in September 2004. The unions had tabled a motion calling for the franchises to be allowed to come back into the public sector, given the apparent success of South Eastern which had been taken back in-house by the SRA following the poor performance of Connex. The motion had been cannily phrased so as to demand not full renationalisation but only the taking back of the franchises as they ran out. There is a debate to be had here. It may be that Labour ministers think there are good reasons why the services should continue to be franchised out to the private sector. It would have been interesting, at least, to hear them. But instead the conference audience was treated to a series of speeches by hapless delegates from obscure constituencies who simply repeated by rote the line they had been fed by the party apparatchiks: that it would cost £20bn to renationalise the railways, a mantra that Alistair Darling repeated in his summing up. Where does this figure of £20bn come from? Presumably it is made up of the estimated cost of buying the rolling stock and paying off Network Rail's debt but no one was suggesting that.

It would be simple to cite many further instances of dishonesty, but let's turn now to Labour's record on ideology and incompetence. John Prescott's promise, after the Ladbroke Grove accident, that money would be no object in ensuring safety on the railway was sheer incompetence. And when, in order to save his skin, Alastair Campbell, Blair's rottweiler, briefed journalists that Railtrack's perfectly competent and separate Safety and Standards Directorate would be hived off from the company, causing all kinds of complexities and cost rises, that too was incompetence.

Again, there are countless other examples. Any government is allowed a few mistakes. However, combine them with a slavish adherence to an ideology that had already been discredited when Labour took office, and the mix becomes all too potent. Labour's attraction to private-sector involvement in public services, which its frontbenchers denounced when in opposition, has been the most surprising aspect of its policy in government. Tony Blair had been fiercely critical of what the Tories were doing. In a 1995 speech he said that the Tories wanted to 'replace a comprehensive coordinated railway network with a hotchpotch of private companies linked together by a gigantic bureaucratic paperchase of contracts – overseen, of course, by a clutch of quangos'[2]. Yet, after he won the election, all Blair did was to ensure that this failed system survived for as long as possible. Indeed, in government, Labour became even more wedded to the idea of private finance initiatives and private-public partnerships than its predecessors. The railway, ministers said, had to be a partnership between the private and public sectors.

But this is based on a false premise, that it is possible to get capital from the private sector without paying for it. Since the railways are loss-making, any investment from private companies will ultimately have to be serviced either by taxpayers or by passengers. There is the golden rule of railway economics: as more people are attracted on to the railway, more subsidy will be needed because very few lines are able to service the capital investment required. The recent need for more railway investment has been stimulated by the fact that the number of passengers grew by 30 per cent in the five years prior to the Hatfield crash and has now started growing steadily again. Whilst it was possible to accommodate much of this growth on existing assets, there is a limit as to how many people can be crammed into a particular train or how many services can be run on a particular line. Once that point has been reached – which it clearly has on many routes – and every last drop of sweat has been extracted from the assets, this golden rule of the railways comes into play. Whether it is more rolling stock, extra train paths, better signalling to increase throughput, faster trains, longer trains, more stations, extended platforms or whatever, the investment required will never earn a commercial rate of return.

This need for investment, together with the Chancellor's strictures on keeping government spending down, led Labour to seek alternative sources of capital and to endorse the notion that the railway has to be a 'public-private partnership'. But given the fact that the railway will always need subsidy, and that the need for government support rises as passenger numbers increase, the state will pay for the railway one way or the other. The private sector, therefore, is merely lending money that it will earn back for its services and on which it will expect a commercial rate of return. As the Catalyst think tank has pointed out,[3] the PFI and PPP schemes are not supposed to be a device for finding new money for investment in public services but, instead, are supposed to offer a more efficient or innovative way of providing services. That is because governments can always borrow more cheaply through low-interest gilt and bond issues. But, as Catalyst put it, 'no one believes that the private sector offers good value for money when it comes to running the railway system. It is now recognised that the limitations of British Rail were primarily due to low levels of government funding and investment – in fact it delivered the most efficient railway system in Europe in return for the lowest public subsidy'.[4]

Viewed as an industry, the railways are a medium-sized business, with passenger revenues of £4bn and subsidy of £4bn–6bn. While there is some scope for considerable growth in the off peaks, and a small amount during peak times, there is no hope of, say, doubling the size of the business within a decade. Therefore, income is unlikely to increase much and any profit that is taken out of the business will have come from this limited source – or else from taxpayers. Looked at on this macro scale, the proclaimed benefits of the privatisation project are exposed as a ridiculous conceit. In effect, the railways are almost a zero-sum game. You can only increase the profit by reducing what is available for investment or raising the amount that you need to extract from tax-payers. There is some scope for efficiency gains, but few can be obtained under the current disaggregated structure.

As we saw in the last chapter, the bald economic facts of the railway are quite startling. At the time of privatisation in 1993/4, British Rail was given £1.35bn of subsidy annually at today's prices (before the figure was doubled when the operations were separated out in preparation for privatisation), some of which went on enhancements to the network. In 2005/6, the railways will cost the taxpayer around five times that figure, £6.5bn.

Maintaining the infrastructure cost BR around £650m and renewals amounted to about the same in 1993/4. These figures had remained fairly constant over the years. In 2005/6, Network Rail[5] is slated to spend £5.3bn on maintaining and renewing the infrastructure,[6] in addition to the rather small figure of £428m on enhancement. Neither this figure nor the one for subsidy mentioned above takes into account the £1.4bn due to be spent that year on building the Channel Tunnel Rail Link, whereas the BR figure includes spending on improvements to the routes to the Channel Tunnel, which was running at several tens of millions per year.[7] Sure, there are excuses, such as the chaos in the aftermath of Hatfield, Railtrack's suicidal policies of dispensing with engineers and much of its expertise and contracting out maintenance work, and a much more intrusive safety regime, but most of that can be put down to the way the industry was privatised.

Indeed, the rise in safety costs is intrinsically linked to the privatised structure. Consultants A.D. Little were commissioned by the Department for Transport to look at the issue of risk aversion and how that had contributed to the way costs had risen. Their findings,[8] unsurprisingly given no publicity by the Department, showed that there was very widespread risk aversion in the British rail industry compared with its counterparts in Europe and that this phenomenon was compounded by 'The fragmented structure of the industry – managing the contract has become more important; confusion over roles within the industry and a lack of clear leadership – no single vision for the railway and the safety objectives it should achieve; poor communications both between and within organisations leading "to urban myths"'. The researchers found several examples of 'infrastructure and rolling stock enhancements proposed by TOCs, where Network Rail has no incentive to support the proposals or to minimise the TOC's implementation costs'.

Of course, not everything can be blamed on privatisation – and in one sense the railways have been enormously successful in the past decade, with numbers passing the billion passengers per year mark in 2003 and rising again in 2004.[9] However, that success has largely been a result of the economic conditions and the growing congestion on the roads. Patronage on the London Underground, for example, grew just as fast during the late 1990s, and that had remained as a wholly state-owned and -run enterprise. Moreover, the growth has been largely confined to commuter lines, since InterCity services have not done that well. As John Prideaux, the former head of InterCity at BR and a man who made £15m through his involvement with one of the roscos, Angel Trains, said

The general impression is that the railway industry has not done particularly well. I find it depressing that despite a large reduction in fare levels, InterCity patronage is down by 2.4 per cent in 2002/3 from the previous peak in 1989/90. Moreover, that instead of being profitable, InterCity requires very substantial taxpayer funding (£265m direct to TOCs and a fair proportion of the £1bn grant going direct to Network Rail), that trains are generally slower and that trains are less punctual ... None of this is in line with what people hoped for from privatisation.[10]

Even the Tories who invented the system have started to recant. David Willetts, a former Tory minister and in 2005 shadow work and pensions minister, in an interview in the *Daily Telegraph*[11] made the remarkable admission that rail privatisation had been a big mistake for which the Tories are sorry. Willetts said that, in particular, the separation between the track and the operations was 'ideologically driven and wrong'. Willetts confirmed that it was the Treasury who were the guilty party: 'Rail privatisation was a classic example of taking a model that had worked for one industry and wrongly applying it to different circumstances. The Treasury applied that model to the railways and it was the wrong model.' While the Tories have not worked out what to do, Willetts makes clear that he thinks the management of the track should be reintegrated with the running of the trains: 'Historically, the way the railways had worked was by what the economists call vertical integration' which, he argued, was the way to provide a good service.

As the evidence in this book shows time and again, it is not possible to run an efficient railway with the disaggregated fragmented structure that was created at privatisation and which the railway review has failed to remedy. Even Gerald Corbett who was in charge of Railtrack for three years is now a convert to the idea that a vertically separated railway will necessarily be dysfunctional.

But here is a tale from Japan to prove it. In the autumn of 2003, the Shinagawa station in south-west Tokyo opened to allow people in that part of the city easy access to the high-speed Shinkansen services. Simultaneously, the operating speed of the whole line was increased to 70kph, shortening the standard travel time between Tokyo and Osaka from three hours to two and a half. In a speech given before the opening,[12] Yoshiyuki Kasai, the president of the Central Japan Rail Company, stressed that these improvements would not have been possible had the

Japanese railway been broken up in a different way on privatisation. It was split into six regionally based companies, each vertically integrated, which meant that the services and infrastructure were under the same control. Kasai argued that the improvements had come about because of a sustained long-term investment programme. Had management responsibility been split between a track company and an operator, 'it would have never been possible for them to make comprehensive and integrated investment, and continue it over the long term'.

There would have been practical problems, too, under a different structure. Introducing the new fast Nozomi trains over time meant that other services had to be changed or curtailed. Had these been run by different operators, a not dissimilar situation to the one that led to rows over train paths on the West Coast Main Line, then it would have been difficult, if not impossible, to create a reasonable timetable. Kasai concluded: 'In order to modernise and improve railway services, investment in ground facilities and rolling stock, which have different time scales, and train operations planning should be managed in a comprehensive manner ... railways require a form of vertical integration, that is integrated management and unified operations, to improve efficiency and have good results. It is not an accident that railways traditionally have preserved an integrated management and operation structure. British railways' disaster resulted directly from failure in recognising this fact'.

A Swiss researcher, Carlo Pfund, examined the way that the railways had been separated between operations and infrastructure across Europe.[13] Although none have gone for the extreme form of separation and privatisation adopted in the UK, nevertheless the restructuring has caused problems in all the seven countries Pfund examined. He found myriad problems, many of them similar to those in the UK. Separation did not improve the economics of the railway and prevented, rather than stimulated, transparency. There was friction and lack of coordination between the various organisations and costs increased. Indeed, his conclusion is unequivocal: 'Separation has no benefits. The implementation of the separation philosophy of the EU is a fundamental error.'

Then there are the thousand stories on the ground. I have talked to countless people who work at the coalface of the railway and almost everyone can give an example of why the vertically separated structure will simply never deliver an efficient railway because of the lack of coordination and the need for all too stringent safety rules. Here is one instance:

> I work as a manager at a London station and we desperately want to improve it. However, it is near impossible to get basic things done like routine repairs, full station repaints and the removal of graffiti. We can't repair the leaking roof because no one will go up there without a scaffold underneath (the costs of the scaffold exceed that of the work, so Network Rail refuse to do it). Meanwhile the water pours in, onto the slippery surface below, which is a major hazard and a danger to our passengers. In the railway's eyes though the 'real' hazard and danger is the minute risk that under possession and/or current isolation I could be hit by a passing train, so I am unable to go onto the track to paint out the graffiti which is blighting the station and distressing the people who use it. Even station re-paints, a vital part of maintaining the asset, are not properly finished because we can't get the possessions to finish off the canopy edge closest to the track. The railway today has inconsistent and frankly bizarre priorities – on the one hand safety rules over us in all that we do, but on the other hand basic maintenance can't get done because of these safety procedures. All the while the station asset is degraded and ultimately will put not just passengers' safety and security at risk, but will also turn them away from travelling altogether.

The triple whammy of incompetence, ideology and dishonesty that came together in a malevolent mix ensured the railway review of 2004 never had a chance of bringing about a lasting solution. What has exacerbated the difficulty of sorting out the railways is the dishonesty of Labour in failing to address the real issue underlying the dysfunctional nature of the industry: its fragmentation and the unrealistic expectation placed on what the private sector will and can do. Whenever Labour ministers are forced into any discussion of the structure, they immediately rule out renationalisation, almost in the same breath as recognising that the industry is dysfunctional and needs radical change.

What is obvious from all the arguments in this book is that the railways need one big organisation that is able to balance the required outputs with the available inputs. That sounds boringly technical but it is the heart of the matter. Essentially, the railways are a single network whose various components interact so intimately that separating them out inevitably leads to what, in management speak, are called 'non-optimal outcomes'. The railways will always operate within tight financial constraints set by government (though at times under privatisation they seemed to have gone out of control). There will always be a need to strike difficult balances: between engineering maintenance and enhancements (Do we repair this bridge now or impose a speed restriction and wait till next year? Will this set of points survive another winter?); between short- and long-term operational considerations (Can we close the line for a weekend to fix it or should we do it at night when it is more expensive? Should we double the track between Coventry and Birmingham because there is so much demand?). There will always have to be compromises: over the timetable (Do we need to run more trains because there is so much overcrowding on this route and, if so, should we cancel some other services?); over safety (Should we continue operating with these old trains which are less safe than newer ones or should we now replace them even though that means we cannot afford to buy additional trains for another line?); and over fares (If we increase fares, how much demand will be lost? Can we try to attract motorists onto the railways through special deals?). The logic of the rail industry is that such decisions have to be made in the best interests of the railway as a whole, which leads to the inevitable conclusion that only a large British Rail-type organisation can manage the railways.

Only if there is a single body which takes overall responsibility for the railways will it be possible to regain control over costs and run the industry efficiently. As the consultants Robson Rhodes put it, 'There is no industry wide model of the kind available to Network SouthEast ten years ago, for example, which enabled the trade offs between fares financing, investment and service quality to be made.'[14] That is the key and fundamental point about any future structure. It has to enable these trade-offs. Reunification is the only structure that will allow these decisions to be made.

A classic example of why a single railway organisation is the only solution is given by Ivor Warburton, who was the last manager to run the West Coast Main Line under British Rail. He tells of how British Rail's budget limits informed the whole organisation:

> In the course of setting the budget for the next year, I concluded that to meet the target, the budget had to be reduced and I knocked out of the year's work programme the immediate rebuilding of a culvert somewhere on the slow line somewhere between Nuneaton and Rugby. I asked the district-level civil engineer, Derek Smart, what were the chances of it requiring attention during the year. He was an old-style engineer who knew his patch, and used to chew

on the end of his pipe. He said, 'Might last, might not – about 40 per cent.' I said right, I take the risk – 'mutter, mutter' and much sucking on his pipe was his only response. In the course of the year, the culvert collapsed and Derek just muttered and sucked on his pipe and did not say things like 'I told you.' That is one example; the single negotiation with government over the budget feeds through the whole organisation and someone makes a rational judgement that has a risk associated with it, with a possible operating inconvenience that has to be contained within the overall target.

Even though the culvert collapsed, Warburton remains convinced that he made the right decision at the time, given the constraints he was working under.

Under the current system, no one would be able to make such a reasoned risk assessment. The work would be carried out to minimise the chances of a breakdown, even though in most cases it could wait a year or more. That, in essence, is at the root of much of the cost escalation and it is only through having a single organisation responsible for the whole railway that it can be reined back. Now, when the crisis brought about by the massive increase in subsidy is finally addressed by government, the response will not be sensible cheeseparing of the odd culvert or section of slightly worn track as in the days of Warburton; instead whole services or chunks of the railway will face closure. The financial mechanisms under privatisation and fragmentation simply do not lend themselves to the type of measured response which enabled the railway to function efficiently in the past. The fragmented railway can never operate at anything like the optimal cost. Until the politicians accept that, we will have an expensive railway struggling to find any funds for investment. It is the saddest irony of all that privatisation and fragmentation was embarked upon because it was thought that they would deliver an efficient railway that would attract investors.

It should be stressed, finally, that the very notion of having a regulator determining the expenditure of the infrastructure company as much as seven or eight years ahead in five-yearly reviews, from an office in Holborn, is a pretty ludicrous way of running a railway. Running a railway requires a multitude of small decisions that make up a massive investment programme, and while a regulator can set broad parameters, the idea that he or she can determine the precise expenditure down to the nearest million pounds is just plain daft, as demonstrated when Network Rail underspent by around £1bn in the first year of the current five-year control period.

The structure of the railways is now inherently unstable and there remains a big question mark over whether Network Rail is ultimately viable. The notion that NR will ever repay any of its debt is fanciful. It could only do so if the access charges were increased massively, and that would simply mean the subsidy was being poured in via the train operators rather than directly to Network Rail. The railway is living on the never-never. An analysis by a firm of accountants[15] suggested that twenty-five years from now the railways would build up a debt of £400bn. This would not be sustainable under the current arrangements. Servicing such a debt would require, say, £30bn–40bn,[16] and given that it would be much cheaper for government to undertake the borrowing directly, at some point NR's structure will change. Of course, a radical cut in costs would improve the long-term finances, but it is difficult to see how that can be achieved under the present structure, and taking the railway back to BR levels of subsidy is certainly not on the horizon. It is certain, therefore, that the present arrangements will need to be reviewed again, probably sooner rather than later, as NR's debt continues to rise.

The solution for the railways, therefore, is simple. Any new structure must have at its heart an integrated railway. Decisions over all aspects of the railway must be made by a team of managers sitting at the same table. Second, the role of the private sector can only be a limited one. Its contribution can be investment in certain well-defined areas, but purely as a contractor, not to determine how resources should be allocated.

The trend is towards vertical integration anyway. As we have seen there are now control centres where train operators and Network Rail work together and agree recovery plans after incidents, with the latter taking the lead role if there are disputes. Some managers in the industry believe that a vertically integrated railway will emerge automatically over the next few years, though accounting separation will have to remain because of European rules. That is not good enough. When the government is forced again to look at the structure because of the soaring costs, ministers must finally bite the bullet and admit that the model of fragmented railway is fundamentally discredited, as it was in the early days of the railways, which quickly became integrated for precisely the reason that any other method is impractical and wasteful of resources. will be a bitter pill to swallow, but there is no alternative. It is interesting that ministers no longer refer to the suggestion that a vertically integrated railway would not be allowed by Europe and that the possibility of a future integrated railway was set out in the leaked version of the review mentioned in Chapter 12. There is evidence that even very cautious ministers like Alistair Darling would have liked to have seen a more integrated structure emerge from the review but that they were scared off by Winsor and the likelihood of upheavals in the pre-election period.

All that remains, therefore, is a series of practical questions relating to how to do it. Should Network Rail take over the operators, or vice versa? Should the structure be regional or consist of one central organisation? And how would the government be represented within the structure? At the risk of sounding very retro, the most sensible option is undoubtedly a re-creation of some type of British Rail structure. Network Rail is clearly the most important railway company and it could be allowed to gradually take over responsibility for operations. Sure, there could be some independent operators like Hull Trains who would pay track charges, but only if they did not get in the way of other people's services. Freight could stay in the private sector, as an open access service, protected by a regulator with a light touch, but essentially there would be one large railway organisation at the heart of the network. It could then be divided into regions (as during most of BR's history) if that were deemed to be the best form of organisation (or alternatively market-based sections like InterCity), but how powerful these would be is open to debate. And the government, as paymaster, would have a clear role in setting the strategy and the outputs, as is right given the amount of taxpayers' money going into the industry.

To those who argue that the creation of one central body – one could even call it British Rail – is a retrograde step, I would simply respond with this fact: the railways are costing five times what they did under British Rail with no discernible improvement in quality above and beyond what would probably have happened anyway. What could have been achieved BR, which was always under tight financial control, had been given the sort of money currently being spent on the railways? It is up to those who argue that BR was a flawed model to come up with a better idea, something they have patently failed to do in the past decade. Until then, the overarching idea should be to bring the railway back together again.

Integration is essential for another reason. Under the structure created by the review, Network Rail has a major role in determining the outputs on, for example, track standards and speed limits. And yet it is not a customer-facing organisation; it will inevitably act in its own narrow interests, with little regard for the needs of the train operators, let alone the passengers. So currently, we have half a nationalised British Rail, the engineering side. But there is no forum in which the needs of the other side, the operators, are properly considered. It is as if British Rail's engineering division ran the railway. Since, therefore, we have half of BR, we may as well have the rest.

Again, an example from abroad is useful. In the US, there have been enormous productivity gains at the wheel-rail interface. One example was the recent introduction of a lighter bogie which required a lot of cooperation between people responsible for the track and those ordering the rolling stock – who, of course, work for the same company. The new bogie required some extra maintenance costs on the track, but overall it made the operation more efficient and cheaper. In Britain such co-operation would be almost impossible, which explains one of the problems of introducing new stock onto the tracks.

And should the new organisation be private or public? The logic ultimately, is unavoidable: the case for a publicly owned railway incontestable. Since the railways need massive subsidy, an entirely private solution is a nonsense, as the past ten years' attempt to create one has shown. A private company which knows that, in the last resort, the government will have no option but to bail it out with further injection of government cash and which, already, effectively pays its shareholder with taxpayers' money is never a good idea. The parts of the railway that unequivocally need to be in state hands – the infrastructure, the maintenance, the planning, the timetabling, specification of safety standards and so on – are already there (ignoring, for the moment the spurious argument that Network Rail is a private company). Indeed the railways have been half-renationalised and their structure is very different from what it was when the Tories left office. The trouble is that these various functions are split up between various organisation. Moreover, the train services are in private hands and that means they are separate from the infrastructure. The solution is simply to allow the franchises to run their course and take them back in house. The old arguments about the failings of BR are about the quality of the management and the workforce, not about the structure. And, in fact, much of BR was better managed than the current privatised railway.

As for rolling stock, it could remain in private hands but with much tighter control. If future requirements were made clear, and guarantees provided that certain stock would remain in its present use on a particular line until it was life expired or 'cascaded' (transferred to another route), huge sums of money would be saved. A senior manager in a rolling-stock company admitted to me, privately, that this arrangement would be cheaper because it would take out of the equation the political risk – that the government might suddenly decide that a train service is no longer required. Guaranteeing that the stock would be paid for and used over its life would make leasing much cheaper, and is hardly an onerous commitment given that passenger numbers on the railways are expected to grow.

The other objection to so much central control is that there would be no room for open-access operators. But they have very limited scope anyway, with only Hull Trains managing to run a successful organisation. Even under the current system, open-access operations have been very difficult to establish. In 2004, the regulator turned down a request for a mere four trains per day service between Manchester and Newcastle, on the grounds that it would abstract revenue from existing operators rather than providing a genuine new service for passengers. However, there is no reason why a limited number of open-access trains in addition to freight services could not run on a mostly integrated railway, provided their activities were subject to regulation.

The only substantial objection to this structure, then, is the fact that governments are not very good at running industries. That is true, but British Rail was at arms' length to the government and its chairman had considerable independence; far more, indeed, than many of the private companies have now. Of course the government should not run the railways directly. But, ironically, that is precisely what is happening under the hybrid system created by the rail review, under which civil servants in the Department for Transport will have a far more hands-on role in the industry than they ever had previously. This is, in a way, the greatest deceit. Ministers are obsessed with telling us that the railway cannot be renationalised and yet through the creation of Network Rail, the taking in-house of maintenance, and now the work of the SRA being transferred to the Department, the government has obtained control of the industry while retaining the fig leaf of the private sector to take the blame when the trains don't run on time. Ten years of privatisation has left us with the worst of both worlds and wrecked the railways by making them unaffordable. One thing is certain: further upheavals lie ahead and in a decade's time, the structure will not be the same as the one created by the 2005 Act. Only if the government grasps the nettle of vertical integration will stability return to the benighted industry, wrecked by a decade of ideology and incompetence.

Privatisation has left another gap – there is no vision for the railways. There are no plans to increase capacity, either through improving existing lines or building a new high-speed network, something that is being done in every other major European country. And the present cost structure makes it virtually impossible to conceive that this could be done.

The privatisation of British Rail was a terrible calumny inflicted on the British people, an act of sheer, wanton violence by ideologically driven but ill-informed politicians. It has cost, quite literally, billions of pounds of taxpayers' money and put at risk the most efficient mode of transport – all at a time when concerns about energy conservation, global warming, pollution and road congestion call for a much greater role for the railways. Instead, the privatisation has hindered the growth of the industry, made it inflexible to changing demands and resulted in a lower standard of performance. Moreover, the current turmoil in the industry could lead to major management problems as it discourages young people from choosing the railways as a career. What will happen when the current cohort of BR-trained managers is lost is a question that worries many people in the industry. And the error of the Tory politicians has been compounded by the failure of their Labour successors to consider any viable alternative to their free market, privatised and outsourced model.

The importance of this goes far beyond railways and transport. The privatisation of BR can be likened to other serious governmental policy failures such as the poll tax and the war in Iraq. In each case, the politicians refused to listen to the advice of experts and proceeded with a policy on the basis of instincts and whim. By focusing in detail on particular case history, this book reveals much about the failure of our political system in preventing such disasters. Hopefully, it will help people stop the bastards next time.

Notes

INTRODUCTION (pp. 1–4)

1 Speaking on *Witness to History: Privatising the Railways*, BBC4, 23 October 2003.

CHAPTER 1: GOVERNMENT AND THE RAILWAYS (pp. 5–25)

1 B.R. Mitchell, *Abstract of British Historical Statistics*, Cambridge University Press 1962, p. 225.
2 R.W. Kostal, *Law and English Railway Capitalism, 1825–1875*, Oxford University Press 1994, p. 115.
3 Adrian Vaughan, *Railways, Politics and Money*, John Murray 1997, p. 123.
4 Ibid.
5 Nick Faith, *The World the Railways Made*, Bodley Head 1990, gives many further examples.
6 By 1859 ninety-six railway company directors sat in the House of Commons, and forty-four in the House of Lords.
7 It was actually the third Railway Regulation Act and was passed in 1844.
8 Michael Freeman, *Railways and the Victorian Imagination*, Yale University Press 1999, p. 4.
9 T.R. Gourvish, *British Railways 1948–1973: a Business History*, Cambridge University Press 1986, p. 13.
10 E.T. MacDermot, *History of the Great Western Railway*, David & Charles 1964, p. 436.
11 Interestingly, the state did prevent the growth of steam-powered road transport through the 1831 Locomotives on the Highway Act, which prevented steam buses from running fast; had it not done so, many branch lines might not have been built as the buses would have been a more economic proposition.
12 T.B. Macaulay, *Speeches, 1854*, quoted in Jack Simmons and Gordon Biddle, eds, *The Oxford Companion to British Railway History*, Oxford University Press 1997.
13 P.J. Cain, 'Railways 1870–1914' in M.J. Freeman and D.H. Aldcroft, eds, *The Atlas of British Railway History*, David & Charles 1985.
14 W.M. Ackworth, *The Railways of England*, 1900.
15 Michael Freeman, *Railways and the Victorian Imagination*, Yale University Press 1999, p. 107.
16 See, for example, *Danger Signals* and *Danger on the Line*, both Ian Allan.
17 Jack Simmons and Gordon Biddle, eds, *The Oxford Companion to British Railway History*, Oxford University Press 1997, p. 3.
18 Andrew Dow in *Steel Wheels*, *Britain's Railways 1825–2000*, Emap Active, 2000.
19 *The Economist*, 9 August 1919.
20 Jon Shaw, Clive Charlton and Richard Gibb, 'The competitive spirit reawakens the ghost of railway monopoly', *Transport Policy* 5, 1998.
21 A comprehensive list of legislation which governed railways' business practices and often restricted their profits can be found in E.A. Gibbins, *Blueprints for Bankruptcy*, Leisure Products 1995.
22 Jack Simmons and Gordon Biddle, eds, *The Oxford Companion to British Railway History*, Oxford University Press 1997, p. 289.
23 Andrew Dow in *Steel Wheels*, *Britain's Railways 1825–2000*, Emap Active, 2000.
24 David Wragg, *Signal Failure, Politics and Britain's Railways*, Sutton Publishing 2004, p. 87.

25 T.R. Gourvish, *British Railways 1948–1973: a Business History*, Cambridge University Press 1986, p. 2.

26 In 1947 the chief inspector of the railways, Sir Alan Mount, commented in his annual report that five serious accidents in which sixty-one people died would probably not have occurred had there been no maintenance backlog and had the installation of colour light signalling proceeded.

27 T.R. Gourvish, *British Railways 1948–1973: a Business History*, Cambridge University Press 1986, p. 14.

28 David Henshaw, *The Great Railway Conspiracy*, Leading Edge 1991, p. 37.

29 From a staff memo quoted in T.R. Gourvish, *British Railways 1948–1973: a Business History*, Cambridge University Press 1986, p. 67.

30 T.R. Gourvish, *British Railways 1948–1973: a Business History*, Cambridge University Press 1986, p. 27.

31 The Great Western directors managed to retain their free first-class travel passes!

32 Sir Norman Chester, *Nationalisation of British Industry, 1945–1951*, HMSO 1975.

33 In Nigel G. Harris and Ernest Godward, *The Privatisation of British Rail*, The Railway Consultancy Press 1997, p. 139, and adjusted for 2005 prices.

CHAPTER 2: WAS BR AS BAD AS ITS SANDWICHES? (pp. 26–47)

1 See C. Wolmar, *Down the Tube*, Aurum 2002, Chapter 3 for details of the BTC's disastrous stewardship of the London Underground.

2 See E.A. Gibbins, *Blueprints for Bankruptcy*, Leisure Products, for a very detailed explanation of the statutory disadvantages faced by the newly created British Railways.

3 David Henshaw, *The Great Railway Conspiracy*, Leading Edge 1991, p. 45.

4 T.R. Gourvish, *British Railways 1948–1973: a Business History*, Cambridge University Press 1986, p. 67.

5 David Henshaw, *The Great Railway Conspiracy*, Leading Edge 1991, p. 44.

6 Quoted in T.R. Gourvish, *British Railways 1948–1973: a Business History*, Cambridge University Press 1986, p. 68.

7 David Henshaw, *The Great Railway Conspiracy*, Leading Edge 1991, p. 55.

8 Quoted in T.R. Gourvish, *British Railways 1948–1973: a Business History*, Cambridge University Press 1986, p. 270.

9 Though it would cost far more than that today – see later chapters on cost.

10 T.R. Gourvish, *British Railways 1948–1973: a Business History*, Cambridge University Press 1986, p. 289.

11 Gerald Fiennes, *I Tried to Run a Railway*, Ian Allan 1967.

12 British Railways Board, *The Reshaping of Britain's Railways*, HMSO 1963.

13 David Henshaw, *The Great Railway Conspiracy*, Leading Edge 1991, p. 147.

14 Ibid., p. 177.

15 British Railways Board, *The Development of the Major Railway Trunk Routes*, BRB 1965.

16 David Henshaw, *The Great Railway Conspiracy*, Leading Edge 1991, p. 234.

17 Direct trains have been restored and the schedule recently improved by Chiltern Trains.

18 David Henshaw, *The Great Railway Conspiracy*, Leading Edge 1991, p. 233.

19 Actually, that was probably wrong because, as we shall see, InterCity consistently achieved profitability in the late 1980s and early 1990s and even Network SouthEast did so briefly.

20 T.R. Gourvish, *British Railways 1948–1973: a Business History*, Cambridge University Press 1986, p. 39.

21 David Henshaw, *The Great Railway Conspiracy*, Leading Edge 1991, p. 198.

22 See Wolmar column in *Rail* 513, 11–24 May 2005, p. 32.

23 Nigel G. Harris and Ernest Godward, *The Privatisation of British Rail*, The Railway Consultancy Press 1997, p. 52.

24 John Welsby and Alan Nichols, 'The Privatisation of Britain's Railways', *Journal of Transport Economics & Policy*, Vol. 33, Part 1, 1999.

25 Jack Simmons and Gordon Biddle, *The Oxford Companion to British Railway History*, Oxford University Press 1997, p. 57.

26 Interview with author.

27 Nigel G. Harris and Ernest Godward, *The Privatisation of British Rail*, The Railway Consultancy Press 1997, p. 55.

28 Reliable source.

29 T.R. Gourvish, *British Railways 1948–1973: a Business History*, Cambridge University Press 1986, p. 30.

CHAPTER 3: THE POLL TAX ON WHEELS (pp. 48–78)

1 Conservative Research Department, *Report of the policy group on nationalised industries*, 1968.
2 Jon Shaw, *Competition, Regulation and the Privatisation of British Rail*, Ashgate 2000.
3 Ibid.
4 *Hansard*, 1990, col. 606.
5 Interview with author.
6 As we have seen, this was a misreading of data. While the proportion of journeys undertaken by rail has declined as car use has risen enormously, the number of rail trips has remained largely static since the Second World War, ebbing and flowing according to economic growth but demonstrating remarkable long-term stability.
7 Interview with author.
8 Interview with author.
9 Detailed in Christian Wolmar, *Down the Tube*, Aurum 2002.
10 Reliable source.
11 Yoshiyuki Kasai, *Japanese National Railways, Its Break-up and Privatization*, Global Oriental 2003, pp. 184–205.
12 *Financial Times*, 1 May 2001.
13 In fact, by creating twenty-five different train companies, all requiring drivers, the hand of the drivers' union, ASLEF, was greatly strengthened and drivers' wages soared as the union managed to strike lucrative deals for its members. This was an example of the law of unintended consequences that dogged the whole privatisation process.
14 Interview with author.
15 13 April 2001.
16 Christopher Knill and Dirk Lehmkuhl, *An alternative route of legal integration: the community's railway policy*, European integration online papers, Vol. 2 (1998) No. 3; http://eiop.or.at/eiop/texte/1998-003a.htm
17 Interview with author.
18 Interview with author.
19 *Witness to History: Privatising the Railways*, BBC4, 23 October 2002, and quoted in the *Independent*, 13 October 2002.
20 Interview with author.
21 *Independent*, 18 November 1992.
22 Interview with author.
23 Interview with author, quoted in Freeman and Shaw, eds, *All Change: British Railway Privatisation*, McGraw Hill 2000.
24 *Independent*, 20 January 1993.
25 Roger Freeman and Jon Shaw, eds, *All Change: British Railway Privatisation*, McGraw Hill 2000.
26 *Witness to History: Privatising the Railways*, BBC4, 23 October 2003.
27 *Hansard*, cols 156–255, 2 February 1993.
28 *Hansard*, col. 719, 18 January 1995.
29 Margaret Thatcher's downfall in 1990 was widely attributed to her disastrous decision to replace local rates, based, like the present council tax, on property values, with a flat rate community charge or 'poll tax'.
30 Interview with author, quoted in Freeman and Shaw, eds, *All Change: British Railway Privatisation*, McGraw Hill 2000.
31 *Evening Standard*, 29 November 1992.
32 Interview with author.
33 *Hansard*, 15 November 1996.
34 *Guardian*, 24 October 1995.
35 *Independent*, 20 November 1995.
36 Christian Wolmar, *Stagecoach*, Orion Business Books 1999, p. 151.
37 Interview with author.
38 *Independent*, 1 November 1995.
39 See Christian Wolmar, *Stagecoach*, Orion Business Books 1999, for a full account of this story.
40 Although a deal announced in March 2005 for the new East Coast franchise involves the predicted

payment of similar massive premiums, worth a total of nearly £2bn over ten years, again an optimistic target that is highly unlikely ever to be met. target that is highly unlikely ever to be met.
41 Christian Wolmar, *Stagecoach*, Orion Business Books 1999, p. 136.

CHAPTER 4: COMPOUNDING THE CATASTROPHE (pp.79–98)

1 Interview with author.
2 John Edmonds in Roger Freeman and Jon Shaw, eds, *All Change: British Rail Privatisation*, McGraw Hill 2000, p. 59.
3 Interview with author.
4 Interview with author.
5 Interview with author.
6 Interview with author.
7 Interview with author.
8 Shoji Sumita, *Success Story*, Profile Books 2000, p. xvi.
9 Interview with author.
10 John Edmonds in Roger Freeman and Jon Shaw, eds, *All Change: British Rail Privatisation*, McGraw Hill 2000, p. 75.
11 Interview with author.
12 Interview with author.
13 Interview with author.
14 Interview with author.
15 National Audit Office, *The Flotation of Railtrack*, December 1998, The Stationery Office, HC25 1998/9.
16 Ibid, p. 36.
17 Ibid, p. 4.
18 Ibid, p. 53.
19 Quoted in Christian Wolmar, 'What track is the Labour Party travelling on?', *Independent*, 5 February 1996.
20 *Independent*, 16 April 1996.
21 *Independent on Sunday*, 1 October 1995.
22 *Independent*, 26 September 1995.
23 *Independent*, 9 March 1996.
24 In Roger Freeman and Jon Shaw, eds, *All Change: British Rail Privatisation*, McGraw Hill 2000, p. 225
25 Interview with author.
26 Railtrack, *Network Management Statement, 1996/7*, May 1996.
27 Railtrack annual report and accounts, 1999/2000, p. 9.
28 Interview with author.
29 *Observer*, 2 April 2001.
30 In Roger Freeman and Jon Shaw, eds, *All Change: British Rail Privatisation*, McGraw Hill 2000, p. 64.
31 Interview with author.
32 The structure was changed again following the publication of the second part of Lord Cullen inquiry in September 2001, as described in Chapter 10.
33 *Maintaining a safe railway infrastructure*, HSE, March 1996.

CHAPTER 5: SOUTHALL (pp. 99–118)

1 *Maintaining a safe railway infrastructure*, HSE, March 1996.
2 *Railway Safety*, Annual report of HMRI, 1996/7, HSE 1997.
3 The two accidents caused by vehicles on the line are not covered in any detail in this book because neither resulted directly from failings on the part of the railway industry and the wider implications that they raise about safety on the roads are outside its scope. They did, however, demonstrate that the media will initially attempt to blame any such accident on the railway, and they also highlight the different approaches taken to risk by the railways and the highway authorities.

4 Professor John Uff, *The Southall Rail Accident Report*, HSE Books 2000, p. 64.

5 Ibid., p. 173.

6 Ibid., p. 168.

7 Ibid., p. 145.

8 Ibid., p. 143.

9 Ibid., p. 140.

10 Ibid., p. 87.

11 The case is different for aeroplanes, where two pilots will clearly always be required in case of sudden illness; on trains there is a foot pedal which has to be released and depressed every minute and this modern version of the dead man's handle ensures that the train will stop if the driver is incapacitated.

12 Professor John Uff, *The Southall Rail Accident Report*, HSE Books 2000, p. 60.

13 In fact, estimates now suggest that the cost of network-wide implementation on 100mph lines will be in the order of £2bn–3bn.

14 Such cost-benefit analyses of safety schemes are standard practice, although people outside the industry – notably TV interviewers – often find it shocking that such a relatively low figure can be put on a life saved. However, these calculations are essential. Of course, the value of the life of a spouse, sibling or child is infinite, but these calculations are based on the notion of the potential death of an anonymous person at some future date.

15 Reproduced in Annex 26B in Professor John Uff, *The Southall Rail Accident Report*, HSE Books 2000.

16 Ibid.

17 Interview with author.

18 Professor John Uff, *The Southall Rail Accident Report*, HSE Books 2000, p. 154.

19 Southall inquiry hearings, day 27.

20 Southall inquiry hearings, day 27.

21 Professor John Uff, *The Southall Rail Accident Report*, HSE Books 2000, p. 164.

22 Ibid, p. 207.

23 Southall inquiry hearings, day 25.

24 Professor John Uff, *The Southall Rail Accident Report*, HSE Books 2000, p. 207.

25 Sir David Davies, *Automatic Train Protection for the Railway Network in Britain: a study*, Royal Academy of Engineering 2000, p. 18.

26 Interview with author.

27 Professor John Uff, *The Southall Rail Accident Report*, HSE Books 2000, p. 166.

28 Ibid., p. 43.

29 Ibid., p. 87.

CHAPTER 6: LABOUR FAILS TO GRASP THE NETTLE (pp. 119–136)

1 *On the Record*, BBC1, 2 May 1998.

2 The legislation was eventually passed in 2000 but at the time of writing the only major scheme is in London; Edinburgh rejected the idea in a February 2005 referendum, so it is unlikely to be a major source of revenue even in the medium term.

3 See Wolmar, *Down the Tube*, Aurum 2002, for a comprehensive account of the PPP saga.

4 *Guardian*, 6 June 1997.

5 *Evening Standard*, 5 June 1997.

6 *Rail Professional*, February 2001.

7 *Daily Mail*, 21 July 1998.

8 *Modern Railways*, January 1999.

9 *Daily Mail*, 'War on the motorist'; *Daily Express*, 'Blair's war on drivers', both front-page headlines, 18 November 1999.

10 The Tories kept up this onslaught, featuring a promise to 'end Labour's war on the motorist' in their 2005 manifesto.

11 Although the real cost of motoring has remained unchanged or even has gone down slightly over the past thirty years as improved technology has nullified the effect of the rise in fuel prices, there was a widespread perception that motorists were being 'ripped off'.

12 According to a letter from Blair's private office, his last significant mention of public transport before the 4 June election was in a speech on New Year's Day 2001.

13 Interview with author.

14 Jon Shaw and William Walton, quoted in *The Times*, 4 January 2001.

15 Interview with author.

16 Memo reproduced on the Railtrack Private Shareholders Action Group website www.rpsag.org.uk. See also *Modern Railways*, June 2005, p. 19.

17 An engineer told me that several schemes for new stations in West Yorkshire were blocked even though there was private-sector money available from developers, because of opposition from operators who were unwilling to add to their journey times by stopping at them.

18 Reliable source.

19 Interview with author.

20 Press release, 15 February 2001.

21 Morton died in September 2004.

CHAPTER 7: LADBROKE GROVE (pp. 137–154)

1 The speed of impact in the Great Heck disaster in February 2001, a head-on crash caused by a Land Rover on the tracks, is thought to have been even faster, at over 140mph, than the Ladbroke Grove crash.

2 Lord Cullen, *The Ladbroke Grove Rail Inquiry, Part 1 report*, HSE 2001.

3 Ibid., p. 109.

4 Ibid., p. 258.

5 Ibid., p. 3.

6 Oddly, one of my contacts, John Fowler, a former railwayman, was on a train stuck as a result of the safety procedures following that SPAD. He spotted the flaw in the track layout and regrets not having done anything about it at the time: 'My former signalling bosses at Waterloo would have gone ballistic had they been presented with the design for the interlocking at Paddington,' he says.

7 Ending bi-directional working would have posed major problems for Railtrack, as it would have reduced the capacity of the station and led to reductions in the number of train services and thus revenue for the company. Indeed, Railtrack HQ made clear that such a scheme was not viable.

8 Lord Cullen, *The Ladbroke Grove Rail Inquiry, Part 1 report*, HSE 2001, p. 129.

9 Ibid., p. 131.

10 Ibid., p. 113.

11 Ibid., p. 113.

12 Ibid., p. 113.

13 Ibid., p. 114.

14 As an aside, Lord Cullen and, indeed, everyone else who has investigated the accident is at a loss understand why the gantry was sited there, instead of in front of the bridge where it would have afforded much better visibility. The stated reason was to accommodate fast freight trains which have longer braking distances, but this was a passenger line and therefore this reason does not make sense.

15 Lord Cullen, *The Ladbroke Grove Rail Inquiry, Part 1 report*, HSE 2001, p. 259.

16 Evidence to the inquiry, p.m., 12 June 2000.

17 Ibid.

18 Lord Cullen, *The Ladbroke Grove Rail Inquiry, Part 1 report*, HSE 2001, p. 108.

19 The Great Western was on a different radio system and the Slough signallers would have had contact Swindon control to communicate with the driver of the HST and that would have taken much too long to prevent the accident. Railtrack had cancelled a plan to install a national system for all trains without explanation in 1999.

20 Lord Cullen, *The Ladbroke Grove Rail Inquiry, Part 1 report*, HSE 2001, p. 99.

21 Ibid.

22 There had been none under British Rail but the organisation had long experience of training drivers to the right standard.

23 Lord Cullen, *The Ladbroke Grove Rail Inquiry, Part 1 report*, HSE 2001, p. 58.

24 Ibid., p. 61.
25 Ibid., p. 61.
26 Net Present Value: that is, a notional sum which involves rolling up future years' spending and discounting it back to get a sum expressed in today's money.
27 Professor John Uff, *The Southall Rail Accident Report*, Annex 26D, HSE Books 2000.
28 *The management of safety in Railtrack*, a review by the Health and Safety Executive, HSE 2000.
29 These recommendations were eventually carried out with the creation of the Railways Safety and Standards Board, as a stand-alone organisation rather than as part of Railtrack, and a separate Rail Accident Investigation Branch.

CHAPTER 8: HATFIELD (pp. 155–188)

1 A short summary of the report is available on the Railway Safety and Standards Board website, at http://www.rssb.co.uk/hatfield.asp, but the full report has never been published.
2 They are not being 'soft'. The force and wind effects generated by the trains are awesome, as anyone who has stood at a station while a High Speed Train thunders past will know.
3 Kevin Sawley and Richard Reiff, *Rail failure assessment for the Office of the Rail Regulator*, Transportation Technology Center Inc., October 2000, p. 42.
4 Shown to the author.
5 *Financial Times*, 22 February 2001.
6 *Guardian*, 16 January 2001.
7 Ibid.
8 Interview with John Ware, not broadcast.
9 Demonstrating, incidentally, the amazing improvement in rolling stock over the subsequent thirty-three years given the very high survival rates at both Hatfield and four months later at Great Heck, where a derailed GNER train smashed head-on into a freight train at a combined speed of around 140mph and only ten out of the one hundred people on board were killed.
10 *Maintaining a safe railway infrastructure*, HSE, March 1996.
11 Ibid., p. 19.
12 Interview with author.
13 *Railway accident at Bexley*, HSE, March 1999.
14 Ibid., p. 18.
15 Ibid., p. 17.
16 Ibid., p. 21.
17 Ibid., p. 21.
18 Ibid., p. 21.
19 Health & Safety Executive, *The collapse of NATM tunnels at Heathrow Airport*, July 2000.
20 BBC Online, 22 March 1999.
21 *Financial Times*, 7 May 2001.
22 Press release accompanying *Railway Safety Statistics Bulletin, 1998–99*, HSE, December 1999.
23 *Railway Safety Statistics Bulletin, 1998–99*, HSE 1999.
24 Chris Bolt, who was acting rail regulator after John Swift's departure.
25 *Financial Times*, 22 February 2001; amazingly, still by the summer of 2005, Network Rail still did not have a complete fully accessible asset register though most of the information had at least been compiled.
26 Kevin Sawley and Richard Reiff, *Rail failure assessment for the Office of the Rail Regulator*, Transportation Technology Center Inc., October 2000, p. 11.
27 Quoted in Ian Jack, *The Crash That Stopped Britain*, Granta 2001.
28 Kevin Sawley and Richard Reiff, *Rail failure assessment for the Office of the Rail Regulator*, Transportation Technology Center Inc., October 2000, p. 31.
29 Ibid., p. 51
30 Information on grinding provided to author by Railtrack.
31 Stuart Grassie, 'Preventive Grinding Controls RCF Defects', *International Railway Journal*, January 2001.
32 Interview with author.

33 According to the Association of Train Operating Companies, there were 17,426 trains on a normal weekday in the summer of 1996 and 18,664 four years later.
34 Information supplied by Rail Freight Group.
35 Roger Freeman and Jon Shaw, eds, *All Change: British Railway Privatisation*, McGraw Hill 2000, p. 87.
36 Kevin Sawley and Richard Reiff, *Rail failure assessment for the Office of the Rail Regulator*, Transportation Technology Center Inc., October 2000, p. 40.
37 Interview with author.
38 Kevin Sawley and Richard Reiff, *Rail failure assessment for the Office of the Rail Regulator*, Transportation Technology Center Inc., October 2000, p. 27.
39 House of Commons Transport Select Committee, Fourth report 1994/5 *Railway Finances Volume 2, minutes of evidence*, House of Commons, July 1995, Q 141, p. 97.
40 *Network Management Statement 1995/6*, Railtrack 1996, p. 20.
41 Network Rail has now (2005) managed to reduce this total by half to 300 per year through proper management, better detection and early replacement of defective rails, greater use of modern testing technology and a return to rail grinding.
42 Interview with author.
43 Interview with author.
44 Interview with author.
45 Interview in *Rail* 406, 4–17 April 2001.
46 House of Commons, Environment, Transport and Regional Affairs Committee, *Recent Events on the Railway*, December 2000, p. 7, Q 57.
47 Ibid., pp. 7–8, Q 57/59.
48 Interview with author.
49 *Rail* 398, 13–26 December 2000.
50 Interview with author.
51 Railtrack press statement, 27 November 2000.
52 Speech reported in Strategic Rail Authority press release, 27 November 2000.
53 *Daily Mail*, 12 March 2005.
54 *Financial Times*, 12 May 2001.
55 *Sunday Telegraph*, 29 October 2000.
56 Defined as arriving within ten minutes of schedule for long-distance (formerly InterCity) trains and five minutes for London commuter and other operators.
57 Strategic Rail Authority, *National Rail Trends*, 2000–1, March 2001.
58 Interview with author.
59 At a speech to the Institution of Electrical Engineers, 12 June 2001.

CHAPTER 9: RAILTRACK: SUICIDE OR LYNCHING?

(pp. 189–200)

1 Legally, the right term is administration, which is a somewhat different process, but Railtrack documents and the company's executives kept on referring to 'receivership'.
2 Press statement by Railtrack, 15 October 2001.
3 Available on their website: http://www.rpsag.org.uk/Writ.pdf
4 This would have been done by securitising the future payments from the government – in other words, selling them on the money markets in return for a capital sum, which was estimated to be £445m. The money was eventually paid on 16 November but that was too late.
5 *Mail on Sunday*, 14 October 2000.
6 Of course, this is a very optimistic view, since the liabilities on the West Coast were unclear and Railtrack had never carried out an asset register.
7 See his evidence to the House of Commons Transport Select Sub-Committee, 7 November 2001 and his speech to the Incorporated Council of Law Reporting, 5 April 2004, available on the ORR website for a full account of this episode.
8 *Hansard*, 13 November 2001.
9 Evidence to the House of Commons Transport Select Sub-Committee, 7 November 2001.

10 Interview with author.
11 Reliable source.
12 See Tom Bower, *Gordon Brown*, HarperCollins 2004, pp. 355–61 for an account of Brown's role.
13 Albeit paid through the track access charges from the operators.
14 *Rail*, 30 Oct–13 Nov 2001.

CHAPTER 10: POTTERS BAR (pp. 201–211)

1 Health & Safety Executive, *Train derailment at Potters Bar 10 May 2002*, interim report, June 2002.
2 Nigel Harris, 'Comment', *Rail* 440, 24 July–6 August 2002.
3 BBC News online, 19 May 2002.
4 Rails have to be stressed when fitted so that they do not buckle in the heat or shrink excessively in the cold.
5 BBC News online, 10 October 2003.
6 Allyson Pollock and David Price, 'We are left footing the PFI bill', *Guardian*, 27 July 2004.
7 Quoted in the *Evening Standard*, 8 July 2004.
8 Interview with author.
9 Health & Safety Executive, *Train derailment at Potters Bar 10 May 2002*, third progress report, May 2003.
10 Ibid., p. 6.
11 Available at http://www.rssb.co.uk/pdf/reports/Potters%20Bar%20derailment%20%20report%20 and%20recommendations.pdf
12 Interview with Nigel Harris, *Rail* 475, 26 November–9 December 2003, pp. 29–35.
13 As above.
14 House of Commons debates, *Hansard*, 28 October 2003, col. 162.
15 *The Observer*, business section, 26 October 2003.

CHAPTER 11: REBUILDING THE RAILWAY (SORT OF)
(pp. 212–233)

1 Tony Grayling, *Getting Back on Track: reforming the ownership and regulation of Britain's railways*, Institute of Public Policy, 2001.
2 IPPR press release, 7 October 2001.
3 Ibid.
4 Its German name is Westdeutsche Landesbank.
5 Statement by Stephen Byers on the Network Rail bid, 25 March 2002.
6 National Audit Office, *Network Rail – Making a Fresh Start*, HC 532, 14 May 2004.
7 House of Commons Transport Committee, *The Future of the Railway*, HC 145-1, 1 April 2004, par. 59.
8 Public Sector Classification Committee, *Classification of Network Rail*, 27 June 2002.
9 Joint statement from National Audit Office and Office of National Statistics, 24 October 2002.
10 Not surprisingly, this formulation did not survive into the final version.
11 SRA press release, 28 November 2001.
12 House of Commons Transport Committee, *The future of the railway*, seventh report, 2003/4, 1 April 2004, par. 160.
13 Ibid., par. 179.
14 A leaked copy was sent to the author.
15 *Hansard*, 17 June 2004, Col 1049W.
16 *Hansard*, 21 June 2004, Col 1246W.
17 Reliable source.
18 Interview with author.
19 Wolmar column, *Rail* 459, 16 April 2003.
20 House of Commons Transport Committee, *The future of the railway*, seventh report, 2003/4, 1 April 2004, par. 48.

21 Department for Transport, *The Future for Rail*, July 2004, p. 48.

22 *Independent*, 5 January 2004.

23 Written answers, *Hansard*, 9 February 2004, Col 1238W.

24 Department for Transport, *The Future of Rail*, July 2004, p. 62.

25 Ibid., p. 7.

26 Ibid., p. 7.

27 Ibid., p. 61.

28 All these performance statistics taken from the quarterly bulletin, *National Rail Trends*, produced by the SRA.

CHAPTER 12: THE RISK PARADOX (pp. 234–256)

1 I have largely ignored the two accidents caused by vehicles on the line that resulted in deaths of rail passengers – Great Heck in February 2001 and Ufton Nervet in November 2004 – because they have little relevance to rail safety issues.

2 Unless otherwise mentioned, the statistics in this analysis of safety are all taken from Railway Safety reports published annually by Her Majesty's Rail Inspectorate. This used to be a glossy and very detailed report but in 2002/3 was degraded into a tatty photocopied bulletin, with fewer statistics and less analysis, but with the compensation that it is all available on the internet.

3 These are Category 3 (overrun greater than 200 yards with no damage) to Category 8 (fatalities to passengers or staff). The definition of Category 3 was changed slightly in May 2000 to include overruns of less than 200 yards where the train went into the overlap and figures readjusted afterwards.

4 Ladbroke Grove Inquiry, seminar on employee perspectives on safety, 18 October 2000.

5 The high number of deaths of passengers falling from InterCity trains – around twenty per year – was a scandal in the 1980s and early 1990s which was finally addressed only after a lengthy press campaign, notably in *The Observer*, by the simple and cost-effective fitting of central locking devices on all InterCity trains.

6 Andrew W. Evans, 'Rail safety and rail privatisation in Britain', Imperial College London, June 2004, available at http://www.cts.cv.ic.ac.uk/documents/publications/iccts00410.pdf

7 Ibid.

8 Interview with author.

9 It is noticeable that the safety record of the civil airline industry, now mostly in private hands, has been improving virtually since its creation nearly a century ago for precisely the same reason – there is nothing like an accident to reduce numbers travelling – though at times it has taken outside regulation to force the airlines to get their act together. There can be few US airline executives who do not wish that there had been tighter security at American airports prior to 9/11, though they lobbied against it strenuously at the time.

10 For an excellent analysis of road-traffic safety schemes, see Andrew Evans, *Economic Evaluation of Road Traffic Safety Measures*, Economic Research Centre, 2001.

11 Roger Ford in *Modern Railways*, May 2001, points out that in 1994 BR compiled a list of 250 safety projects by order of Value per Prevented Fatality and there were many in the region of £1m–2m several of which may well not have been implemented.

12 Professor Evans in fact estimates that it is probable that, on average, only one life per year will be saved.

13 Press statement 29 March 2001, accompanying publication of Professor John Uff and Lord Cullen, *The Joint Inquiry into Train Protection Systems*, HSE Books 2001.

14 Strategic Rail Authority, *ERTMS: towards a better safer rail system*, 2002, summary at http://www.sra.gov.uk/publications/index_page/index_page_ERTMS_Summary_Report/other2002_04_25ertms_web.pdf

15 Professor John Uff and Lord Cullen, *The Joint Inquiry into Train Protection Systems*, HSE Books 2001, p. 39.

16 Email to the author.

17 Email to the author.

18 Email to the author.

19 In fact, getting rid of Mark 1 coaches should have been a requirement during the first franchise round but

the opportunity was missed through the feebleness of the Health and Safety Executive which ducked the issue rather than pressing for it. In the event, the 2004 deadline could not quite be met and the Health & Safety Executive agreed a derogation for the few remaining vehicles until the end of November 2005.

20 Interestingly, the HSE ignored the fact that Pacers, the terrible carriages based on a bus design, reacted similarly in an accident, and hundreds of these coaches continue to operate on many northern routes.

21 Interview with author.

22 Interview with author.

23 Interview with author.

24 Interview with author.

25 Email to author.

26 Interview with author.

27 Interview with author.

28 The statistics from the Railway Standards and Safety Board suggest that rail is eight times safer than car travel and twice as safe as aviation. However, the statistics for the railways include people who have fallen down stairs at stations and even those who are killed 'surfing' on the top of trains (as happened in 1998/9), provided they have a ticket or were expected to buy one; this contrasts with figures for air safety which do not include people killed or injured at airports. Using alternative methodologies suggests that taking the train could be 20 or even more times safer than motoring.

29 Interview with author.

30 The vast majority of workers were – and remain – men, especially in the various engineering disciplines and on the track.

31 Tim Strangleman, *Work Identity at the End of the Line? Privatisation and culture change in the UK rail industry*, Palgrave Macmillan 2004, p. 123.

32 Ibid., p. 153.

33 House of Commons, Environment, Transport and Regional Affairs Committee, *Recent Events on the Railway*, December 2000.

34 Ladbroke Grove Inquiry hearings, 8 December 2000.

35 Tim Strangleman, *Work identity at the end of the line? Privatisation and culture change in the UK rail industry*, Palgrave Macmillan 2004, p. 156.

36 Ibid.

37 Ken Loach's film *The Navigators* focuses on this process with great accuracy.

38 Tim Strangleman, *Work Identity at the End of the Line? Privatisation and culture change in the UK rail industry*, Palgrave Macmillan 2004, p. 153.

39 John Edmonds, 'Creating Railtrack' in Roger Freeman and Jon Shaw (eds), *All Change: British Railway Privatisation*, McGraw-Hill 2000, pp. 67–8.

40 Tim Strangleman, *Work Identity at the End of the Line? Privatisation and culture change in the UK rail industry*, Palgrave Macmillan 2004, p. 151.

41 *RMT News*, March 1998, p. 11.

42 Ladbroke Grove Inquiry hearings, 8 December 2000.

43 Ladbroke Grove Inquiry, seminar on employee perspectives on safety, 18 October 2000.

44 Ibid.

45 Ibid.

46 Ibid.

47 Interview with author.

48 Interview with author.

49 Interview with author.

50 Interview with author.

CHAPTER 13: WHY IS THE RAILWAY SO EXPENSIVE? (1)

(pp. 256–274)

1 National Audit Office, *The Award of the First Three Passenger Franchises*, Stationery Office 1996.

2 *Rail* 398, 13–26 December 2000.

3 Railway Forum, *Financial Support to the Rail Industry Before and After Privatisation*, April 1998.

4 *Railway Finance Monitor*, TAS Publications and Events Ltd, April 2001.

5 Ibid.

6 Association of Train Operating Companies, press release, 12 April 2001.

7 Under the Byzantine contractual arrangements between Railtrack and the train operators, compensation payments were restricted to the amount of access charges Railtrack received from each company. For example, GNER paid £2.6m per month in access charges but revenue from passengers was around £7m per month before Hatfield. Therefore, since the company lost over half its revenue because of Railtrack's failings, even free access was insufficient compensation to make up the losses. On the other hand, the regional operators, for whom access charges were a huge proportion of their costs, found that the compensation paid by Railtrack more than made up the loss of income from passengers not travelling.

8 *Financial Times*, 18 April 2001.

9 'Insider', *Rail*, 4–17 April 2001.

10 Sea Containers chairman James Sherwood reckoned it was the most complicated deal he had ever been involved in during his long business career.

11 *Railway Finance Monitor*, TAS Publications and Events Ltd, April 2004.

12 Interim agreement between SRA and the Virgin Rail Group, SRA press release, 22 July 2002.

13 *Modern Railways*, August 2003, p. 19.

14 Dieter Helm, 'What to do about the Railways', submission to the rail review, New College, Oxford, 17 March 2004, available at www.dieterhelm.co.uk

15 SRA press release, 1 July 2002.

16 House of Commons Select Committee on Transport, *The Future of the Railway*, March 2004, par. 123, available at http://www.parliament.the-stationery-office.co.uk/pa/cm200304/cmselect/cmtran/145/14502.htm

17 Ibid.

18 Ibid., par. 122.

19 BBC News website, 11 December 2002.

20 Quoted on the unofficial Connex South East website at www.csnews.net/connexthrownout.html

21 See Wolmar column in *Rail* 498, 13–26 October 2004.

22 Ben Webster, 'Most punctual commuter trains are those run by the state', *The Times*, 18 November 2004.

23 Interview with author.

24 Robert Lea, 'Fury at 20 per cent rise in train firms profits', *Evening Standard*, 27 January 2005.

25 *Independent*, 25 February 2005.

26 In new present value, in other words rolled up into a lump sum discounted for future inflation at a rate of 3.5 per cent per year.

27 SRA, *Annual Report 2002/03*, p. 13.

CHAPTER 14: WHY IS THE RAILWAY SO EXPENSIVE? (2)

(pp. 275–295)

1 Department of Transport, *Railway Privatisation: Passenger Rolling Stock*, January 1993.

2 That was the book value, representing the depreciated historic cost.

3 Richard Bowker, 'Who pays for the railways', *Rail* 515, 8–21 June 2005.

4 *Renaissance Delayed: New Labour and the railways*, Catalyst 2004, p. 40.

5 Christopher Irwin, 'Roscos: success or excess?', unpublished paper prepared for Rail Passenger Council.

6 Office of the Rail Regulator, *Review of the rolling stock market, report to the Deputy Prime Minister*, May 1998, p. 9.

7 Statement to *File on 4* on train leasing companies, BBC Radio 4, 27 January 2004.

8 Interview with author.

9 The third rosco, HSBC, is all electric.

10 Strategic Rail Authority, *Community Rail Development Strategy*, November 2004.

11 Christopher Irwin, 'Roscos: success or excess?', unpublished paper prepared for Rail Passenger Council.

12 This may have been somewhat of an overestimate, as according to another source a three-coach 158 cost £460,800 per year, about half of which was for maintenance. This figure is still very high, though.

13 Interview with author.

14 According to a briefing given to the author by a rosco.

15 *File on 4* on train leasing companies, BBC Radio 4, 27 January 2004.

16 Research by Jean Shaoul for Catalyst, *Railways in a third term*, March 2005.

17 *File on 4* on train leasing companies, BBC Radio 4, 27 January 2004.

18 John Prideaux, 'Trains: the rolling-stock companies' in Roger Freeman and Jon Shaw, eds, *All Change: British Railway Privatisation*, McGraw Hill 2000, p. 107. His calculations show that there were 1,043 BR coaches delivered in 1993–7 at a price of £890m compared with 1,952 vehicles at a cost of £2001m ordered in 1996–9 by the privatised rolling-stock companies. The higher cost reflects the fact that some maintenance is now usually included as part of the deal.

19 Carried out by Roger Ford for *File on 4* on train leasing companies, BBC Radio 4, 27 January 2004.

20 Terry Gourvish, *British Rail 1974–97: from integration to privatisation*, Oxford University Press 2002; 'Britain's trains are younger', *Rail*, 5–18 January 2005, p. 11.

21 See Roger Ford, *Modern Railways*, April 2003, pp. 16–17.

22 Interview with author.

23 National Audit Office, *Improving passenger services through new trains*, HC 263, 2003/4, p. 2.

24 Ibid.

25 Ibid., p. 4.

26 Alan Williams, *Modern Railways*, July 2004, p. 78.

27 Ibid.

28 National Audit Office, *Improving passenger services through new trains*, HC 263, 2003/4, p. 3.

29 SRA, *Rolling Stock Strategy*, December 2003.

30 Information supplied to the author by the SRA.

31 *File on 4* on train leasing companies, BBC Radio 4, 27 January 2004.

32 Information supplied to the author by the SRA.

33 Department for Transport, *The Future of Rail*, Cm 6233, July 2004, p. 70.

34 In a speech to the *Rail* conference, 9 March 2005.

CHAPTER 15: WHY IS THE RAILWAY SO EXPENSIVE? (3)

(pp. 296–328)

1 Interview with author.

2 Analysed in *Modern Railways*, October 1997.

3 Interview with author.

4 *Hansard*, 2 July 2003, col. 375.

5 Speech to Railway Forum, 30 June 2003.

6 Terry Gourvish, *British Rail 1974–1997: from integration to privatisation*, Appendix B, pp. 460ff. See also the analysis by Roger Ford in *Modern Railways*, August 2003, pp. 16–18.

7 Roger Ford, 'BR Infrastructure maintenance spend shock', *Modern Railways*, August 2003.

8 Ibid.

9 In this paragraph, all figures are outturn.

10 The definition of 'investment' is not straightforward. Broadly, anything that Railtrack spends could be called investment, and often was by its spin doctors. In fact, merely replacing existing equipment – maintenance – or even renewing it without any enhancement should, arguably, not be called investment.

11 Railtrack, *Network Management Statement*, 1995/6.

12 Interview with author.

13 John Swift, 'The role of the rail regulator', in Roger Freeman and Jon Shaw, eds, *All Change: British railway privatisation*, McGraw Hill 2000, p. 225.

14 Actually, Railtrack was, in a sense, right. There are no commercially viable investments on the

network which can pay for themselves without subsidy. That was a harsh truth which those who privatised the railway failed to understand.

15 Interview with author.
16 *On Track*, the bulletin of the Strategic Rail Authority, No. 2, covering the period 1 April 2000 to 14 October 2000.
17 Booz Allen Hamilton, *Railtrack's Performance in the Control Period 1995–2001*, p. 13, Office of the Rail Regulator, March 1999.
18 Ibid., p. 22.
19 Ibid., p. 22.
20 Roger Ford, *The Rising Cost of Britain's Railways*, Transport 2000, November 2003. All figures in this paragraph are at 2003/4 prices.
21 Ibid, p. 3.
22 All at 2003/4 prices.
23 Figures compiled by Roger Ford in *Modern Railways*, April 2005. They do not include funding of the Channel Tunnel Rail Link, which brings the 2005/6 figure up to £7.8bn.
24 Roger Ford, *The Rising Cost of Britain's Railways*, Transport 2000, November 2003, p. 5.
25 Interview with author.
26 Interview with author.
27 Interview with author.
28 Interview with author.
29 Interview with author.
30 Interview with author.
31 Roger Ford, 'Poikilothermia at Ledburn', *Modern Railways*, February 2003, p. 19.
32 Interview with author.
33 In practice, this was a guess determined more by how much the regulator estimated Railtrack needed to maintain the railway, rather than any genuine attempt to ascertain the worth of its assets which, in any case, was probably very low or even negative.
34 *Interim Review of Track Charges Draft Conclusions*, Office of the Rail Regulator, October 2003, p. 37. The original consultancy report went by the bizarre name *Bottom-up Review of Network Rail's Business Plan 2003/4–2005/6*, produced by Halcrow, TTCI and LEK.
35 James Meek, 'The £10bn rail crash', *Guardian*, 1 April 2004.
36 Ibid.
37 Ibid.
38 Interview with author.
39 Roger Ford, *The Rising Cost of Britain's Railways*, Transport 2000, November 2003, p. 11.
40 Interview with author.
41 See Chapter 6 of my book *Down the Tube*, Aurum 2002, for more details about the Jubilee line cost overrun.
42 House of Commons Transport Committee, Southern Region Power Supply Upgrade, memorandum by Network Rail, PSU 08, 2003–4 session, ordered to be printed 7 July 2004.
43 Roger Ford, 'Power supplies compound Mk 1 crisis', *Modern Railways*, January 2002.
44 National Audit Office, *Improving Passenger Rail Services Through New Trains*, HC 263, 2003/4, p. 36.
45 Interview with author.
46 As above.
47 *Rail Industry Monitor 2004* Volume 3, TAS Publications & Events Limited 2004, p. 13.
48 Strategic Rail Authority, *New stations: a guide for promoters*, 2004.
49 Alan Bevan, *A–Z of Rail Reopenings*, Railway Development Society 1998.
50 Interview with author.
51 For the best account of the issue see Paul Clifton, 'Question: how do you make the railways risk-free? Answer: You cancel all the trains', *Rail Professional*, June 2004.

CHAPTER 16: HOW IDEOLOGY AND INCOMPETENCE WRECKED BRITAIN'S RAILWAYS (pp. 329–34)

1 Commons Transport Committee, *The Future of the Railway*, 2003/4, par. 167.
2 In a speech given on 23 March 1995, quoted in the *Guardian*, 1 November 2003.
3 Catalyst, *The Railways in a Third Term*, March 2005.
4 Ibid.
5 Figures provided by the Department for Transport. A full analysis by Roger Ford of the figures for 2005/6 to 2008/9 can be found in *Modern Railways*, April 2005.
6 This also includes operations, which is impossible to separate out in NR's accounts.
7 It is more difficult to disentangle given that some of the improvement to the network for the Channel Tunnel trains might have taken place anyway.
8 A.D. Little, *Risk Aversion in the British Railway Industry*, Department for Transport 2004.
9 Though unlike comparable BR statistics, there is some double counting when people change trains on a journey and travel with two different operators.
10 Paper given to Institute of Transport and Logistics and the Institute of Rail Operators, Leeds, 11 November 2003.
11 12 December 2003.
12 Yoshiyuki Kasai, 'Vertical or horizontal integration? – let's not make the wrong choice', Nihon Keizai Shimbun lecture on economics, 5 September 2002, Central Japan Railway Company.
13 Carlo Pfund, *Separation Philosophy of the European Union – blessing or curse*, LITRA, Service d'information pour les transports publics, Berne.
14 'Network Rail: is it financeable?', Robson Rhodes.
15 Ibid.
16 Assuming average historic rates of interest over the past thirty years rather than the current low ones.

Index